HENRY CLEPPER, Chairman of the Editorial Committee for the Natural Resources Council of America, is a graduate of the Pennsylvania State Forest Academy at Mont Alto, and for fifteen years was a forester in the Pennsylvania Department of Forests and Waters. From 1937 to 1966 he was executive secretary of the Society of American Foresters and managing editor of the *Journal of Forestry*. In 1969, under the sponsorship of the Forest History Society, Inc., he completed writing a history of forestry in America. He is a consulting editor for *Forestry Handbook*, a contributing editor of *America's Natural Resources*, and editor of *Careers in Conservation* and *Origins of American Conservation*, published by The Ronald Press Company.

LEADERS

OF

AMERICAN

CONSERVATION

Edited by

HENRY CLEPPER

Chairman of the Editorial Committee
Natural Resources Council of America

**Sponsored by the
Natural Resources Council of America**

THE RONALD PRESS COMPANY • NEW YORK

Library of Congress Catalog Card Number: 75–155206
PRINTED IN THE UNITED STATES OF AMERICA

Dedicated to
JOSEPH WELLER PENFOLD
Whose High Ideals and Selfless Devotion to
the Defense of America's Natural Resources
Have Earned Him the Affection and Esteem
of His Colleagues in Conservation

The subjects of these biographies were chosen by the member organizations of the Natural Resources Council of America. Criteria for making the nominations were set forth by the Council's Editorial Committee as follows:

Each biographee should be, or should have been, a person whose personal activities and career contributed in a distinctive way to the preservation or wise use of one or more resources. All varieties of service may be considered (administration, research, education, writing, and editing) provided the contribution is of national or at least regional significance; and provided also that the individual making the contribution is recognized, by those competent to judge, as having rendered outstanding leadership or guidance in the advancement of resource knowledge and its application.

A basic requirement is that the contribution shall have been meritorious; that is, above and beyond the rendering of long and faithful service, or appointment to a high position in state or federal government, or election to a political office. An essential qualification for listing is the individual's performance of those acts that accomplished socially desirable results.

Under these criteria may be nominated many worthy individuals who once had decisive or influential roles in resource conservation but whose participation is now almost forgotten. Special effort should be made to identify such individuals, for this book is to be a history of dedicated involvement in American conservation.

Keep these further considerations in mind:

A person's interest in conservation, however sincere or dedicated, is not alone a qualification.

The part-time enthusiast—the week-end or summer-vacation conservationist—is not the person who should be included among "leaders."

The political figure, however friendly he may be to conservationists and however favorable his voting record on conservative issues, should be passed over. As a rule, the only politicians nominated should be those whose political careers were noteworthy for important legislation. Remember, this book seeks to memorialize the authentic conservationist, not the professional politician. Thus the conservationist who inspired great legislation or the person who drafted it should be singled out, not necessarily the politician who introduced it.

A nomination should not be made because of the nominee's popularity. Nor should a nomination be used to accord honor to an otherwise obscure individual.

Preface

The men and women whose biographies are presented in *Leaders of American Conservation* were nominated by one or more member organizations of the Natural Resources Council of America. Criteria for making the nominations appear on page iv. Formed in 1947, the Council is a nonprofit, nonpolitical body of 40 constituent associations and societies. Its objective is to advance the attainment of sound management of natural resources in the public interest. Its role is that of a service agency to its member organizations.

For the purpose of this book, the term "American conservation" is equated with conservation activities carried on principally inside the United States. Hence, most of the biographees are citizens or residents of the United States. But foreign nationals have been included provided their careers or contributions have been intimately associated with education, management, or research in natural resources in the United States.

To be sure, the editors realize that many eminent conservationists in other nations have been students in United States institutions or have had keen scientific and professional interest in the development of natural resources in the United States. But to have included all such individuals would have inordinately lengthened the book. Thus, the editors perforce had to limit its geographic scope to conform to the practical exigencies of the project—in short, to what they were able to accomplish.

In the expanding annals of America, the lives and careers of most conservationists included are unlikely to be accorded permanent recognition by history. Yet what they did for their nation is too valuable to be forgotten. That is why this book was written. No comparable compilation has been made. Its reception will prove whether it was justified. Its aim is to provide a succinct and factual account of the career of each leader. The biographies are short to keep the volume a reasonable length. The length of a subject's sketch is not to be taken as a measure of his importance. In the case of some biographies, more extensive than others, it may simply mean that these persons either had longer or more varied careers, or that more information was available about them.

If *Leaders of American Conservation* is found useful as a reference work for workers and students concerned with this rapidly-growing field, a more comprehensive, world-wide biographical directory would be in order. Its compilation might be undertaken by a qualified international organization; for example, the International Union for the Conservation of Nature and Natural Resources. For obvious reasons, the Natural Resources Council of America is ill-equipped to assay such a global project.

The contributors and editors undertook this book in the hope that it would be useful to the student, the research worker, the writer about resources, and the practicing conservationist. In no case is a biography intended to tell all that is known or may be found out about the subject. At the end of most sketches is at least one reference where additional or corroborative information may be obtained.

Serving with me on the Editorial Committee were my friends and conservation colleagues, James B. Craig, editor of *American Forests* magazine, and Daniel A. Poole, president of the Wildlife Management Institute. I thank them for their generous cooperation and encouragement. As a Committee, we are grateful to the contributors of the sketches whose efforts made the work possible.

Some readers may fail to find biographical sketches of certain individuals who they think should have been included. Such omissions are unintentional oversights, inevitable in a seminal undertaking of this kind. Nor can we hope to have avoided, in the first edition of this book, some errors. Every effort was made to keep them out; we hope to have kept them to a minimum. We urge reviewers and readers to call errors to the attention of the Editorial Committee. I make this appeal with the same sincerity as did Izaak Walton when he asked the reader's forbearance in his introduction to *The Compleat Angler:*

> I might say more, but it is not fit for this place; but if this Discourse which follows shall come to a second impression, which is possible, for slight books have been in this Age observed to have that fortune; I shall then for thy sake be glad to correct what is

defective; but for this time I have neither a willingness nor leisure to say more, than to wish thee a *rainy evening* to read this book in, and *that the east wind may never blow when thou goest a fishing.* Farewell.

HENRY CLEPPER
Chairman of the Editorial Committee

Arlington, Virginia

Contents

Introduction

Within the memory of living men, the number and extent of now-threatened natural resources were legendary. During the second half of the nineteenth century, a few persons began to realize that America's resources were in reality limited, however abundant they appeared to be, and that man had to learn to manage those resources together with his environment. This book is a biographical recapitulation of the conservation movement in the United States, and of the development of professional resources management in the public interest. The chronicle began more than a century ago.

Shortly after the close of the Civil War, a few scientifically minded Americans started to express concern about the destruction of the nation's forest, soil, and water resources. That their concern was based on solid evidence was proved by the publication in 1864 of the monumental treatise *Man and Nature* by George Perkins Marsh. It was the first book by an American that dealt at length and in detail with the alteration of the earth's surface by man's actions. It explained how the removal of woods and other vegetative cover resulted in floods, the washing away of soil, and fluctuations in stream flow.

Thinking citizens began sounding alarms about the extirpation of natural resources. Action to halt the depletion of the fishery resource started in 1870 with the formation of the American Fisheries Society, an association of scientists and others interested in fish culture. It was the first native biological society organized to foster research and management of a natural resource. In 1871, creation of the United States Fish and Fisheries Commission was authorized by Congress with Spencer F. Baird of the Smithsonian Institution as commissioner. He was directed to investigate the conservation of food species of the coasts and lakes of the nation.

The most conspicuous example of resource loss in the United States was the widespread devastation of timber by logging and fire. In 1873 the American Association for the Advancement of Science appointed a committee, with Franklin B. Hough as chairman, to memorialize the Congress about the worsening forest conditions. The result was the appointment in 1876 of Hough as an agent in the Division (now the Department) of Agriculture to make an investigation of the forest situation. From this modest beginning grew the present Forest Service.

Meanwhile, in 1875, John Aston Warder of Ohio had called together a group of citizens to create an organization for forest conservation. They formed The American Forestry Association. Thus were set in motion two forces by action of government and private citizens that marked the beginning of the forest conservation movement in the United States.

Yet, the immediate influence of these developments on the officialdom of the government was negligible. Neither in the executive branch nor in the Congress was there much, if any, concern about the timber resource. It was the era of timber abundance; the prevailing belief was that the forests were inexhaustible. During the period from 1877 to 1881, Carl Schurz, then Secretary of the Interior, was almost the only high official in the federal government advocating legislation to stop forest destruction and the adoption of a policy for forest renewal. He was little heeded.

Ravage of the forest resource—by settlers, by land speculators, by the government itself—continued for a few more decades. This episode would be a notable scandal in American history were it not for the fact that the course of despoliation was gradually brought to a halt. Demands for a halt emanated not from legislators and the upper hierarchy of government, but from plain citizens—that is to say, from conservationists—organized for that purpose.

During the last quarter of the nineteenth century, a growing number of thinking citizens began sounding alarms about the extirpation of other natural resources. Probably because forest depletion was the most noticeable example of resource loss, it was the one that received the most attention. But soon after the national forest conservation movement was launched, action to aid wildlife resources was also started.

In 1883 the American Ornithologists' Union, another citizens' organization, was formed and immediately began promoting the protection both of game and nongame birds. A pioneer in this cause was George Bird Grinnell, who led the movement that resulted in the establishment in 1886 of the Division of Economic Ornithology and Mammalogy in the United States Department of Agriculture, the forerunner of the Bureau of Biological Survey and the present Bureau of Sport Fisheries and Wildlife in the Department of the Interior. The first director of the Division was C. Hart Merriam who was an ornithologist concerned about bird protection but who was also active in the protection of all wildlife. In 1905 William Dutcher, for several years chairman of a national committee of state Audubon Societies, incorporated the National Association of Audubon Societies, now the National Audubon Society, one of the nation's largest and most influential associations dedicated to conservation.

When another movement to preserve the country's scenic resources was started by a group of early conservationists, their motivation was wholly esthetic rather than economic. John Muir, an epic personality, was the leading advocate for safeguarding undisturbed nature, a cause that subsequently waxed into a program for national and state parks and for wilderness preservation. Although the Sierra Club, which he founded in 1892, was originally interested primarily in the protection of California's Sierra Nevada and its resources, the Club's growth into a national organization dedicated to interpreting and defending all scenic resources followed logically from its beginnings.

These early conservation organizations were pitifully weak in membership and finances, but their determination was strong. Because of their vigilance and tenacity, they were able to influence events. Indeed, the association as a means of conservation reform is possibly the strongest ever devised. The indignation of the citizen-conservationist against the wasters and despoilers did not stop with vocal dissent. It was a colossal force that helped bring about a peaceful revolution: the adoption of improvements in policies, by governmental agencies as well as by private corporations, for the management of the resources in their custody.

During the first decade of the present century, the movement for the conservation of renewable natural resources, and of the soil and water that support them, gathered momentum. The attention of the whole nation was drawn to the Governors' Conference on natural resources, held in the White House in May 1908 at the invitation of President Theodore Roosevelt. One result of this conference was the formation of the National Conservation Commission under the chairmanship of Gifford Pinchot and the first inventory of the nation's natural resources presented at the National Conservation Conference in Washington, D. C. in December 1908. The conservation crusade, so tentatively and obscurely begun in the 1870s, was now fairly launched.

From the start, this enterprise attracted men and women who symbolized the social conscience of America. A few were national figures—Carl Schurz, Theodore Roosevelt, Gifford Pinchot, for example. But, by and large, the pioneer conservationists, like those who followed them, were scarcely known to the general public. Even to our present generation they are almost wholly unknown. Yet they were the founders of a movement that has been one of the most glorious and most productive manifestations of our democratic republic.

The history of conservation is essentially the record of the struggles and successes of a few thousand men and women who, aware that certain conditions needed to be corrected or improved, devoted their time and talents to getting the job done. A small number only were persons of prominence or influence. Many rose out of the relative obscurity of a business or a profession; few attained high office or public renown.

To be sure, Theodore Roosevelt is rightly esteemed as one of our pioneer statesmen in resource conservation. Gifford Pinchot is remembered as a national leader. When we think of soil conservation we immediately think of Hugh Bennett, another national figure, and Aldo Leopold's name brings to mind not only wildlife management but wilderness preservation as well. Likewise, John Muir has left his imprint on the annals of park and wilderness preservation.

Certain other figures, of less historical prominence than those mentioned, are still well remembered by the present generation of conservationists. From the recent past we recall Ovid Butler, influential editor of the magazine *American Forests*; Rachel Carson of *Silent Spring* fame; R. W. Eschmeyer, exponent of fisheries management; Edward H. Graham, soil conservationist and biologist; Henry S. Graves and William B. Greeley, spokesmen for forestry; Robert Marshall, wilderness enthusiast; Stephen T. Mather of the national parks; Olaus Murie, respected wildlife observer and writer; Fairfield Osborn, zoologist and foundation executive; Ernest F. Swift, expounder of resource philosophy; and Howard Zahniser, father of the wilderness system.

When we go back beyond a few decades, the imprint of those who helped start the conservation crusade and kept it a vital force in American affairs is much fainter. The debt we owe the pioneers who founded and nurtured the movement is no less real because we may have forgotten the precise character of their contributions. Of many names we may pick at random, contemporary conservationists may have difficulty identifying them as to their professions, spheres of action, and specific services. For example, it is no longer easy to identify Edward A. Bowers, William H. Brewer, Austin Cary, Bernhard E. Fernow, Henry Gannett, Frederick V. Coville, W J McGee, T. Gilbert Pearson, John Wesley Powell, and Robert Sterling Yard. Yet these men, each in a significant way, made essential and enduring contributions to conservation.

In contrast to the homage rendered many conservationists is the vilification they received when their efforts to safeguard a resource interfered with profit seekers. Few conservationists became authentic leaders without exposure to the contempt and derision of the exploiters of resources and their political allies. In our own time, the gentle and respected Rachel Carson was castigated and ridiculed by representatives of the chemical industry when she documented the losses of birds and other wildlife following the spraying of vegetation with certain persistent pesticides, and then ventured to propose that greater care with the application of such chemicals be enforced, and that increased research be undertaken to seek alternate methods of control less dangerous to the natural environment.

Senator Boise Penrose of Pennsylvania, whose own career was not redolent of the rose, used to refer to Gifford Pinchot as "that damned tree doctor." Senator Henry M. Teller of Colorado, a former Secretary of the Interior, declared in 1909, "I do not believe there is either a moral or any other claim upon me to postpone the use of what nature has given me, so that the next generation or generations may have an opportunity to get what I myself ought to get." These sorry examples could be continued; their purpose is to show that conservationists did not rise to positions of leadership without suffering the hostility of opponents and even defamation by them. It is not a pleasant matter, and we need not dwell on it.

Since the conservation movement began, the exploiters of resources have resented interference with their plans because such interference can be bad for business, which is doubtless true. And many continue to believe that exploitation without interference is still possible, which is certainly false. The history of this movement is replete with instances of exploiters whose main desire was to wrest riches from the resource; many had no more moral purpose than looters. To be sure, it would be unfair to include all commercial fishermen, all lumbermen, all livestock operators, all mining interests, and all water users in this category. But selfish waste and destruction of resources had to be stopped.

When reading about the lives of conservation leaders one notes an attribute common to all. They were activated—one might say obsessed—by a concept of duty to society, to the nation. Most put their obligation to the cause above personal advantage. This is not to say that they lacked ambition or were indifferent to approbation. As in any group of spirited Americans, there have been conservationists with a thirst for glory, or at least for public recognition. But in general they reached out for opportunities to preserve or improve their native land rather than for applause or emolument.

The reader will observe that many of the conservationists listed in the pages that follow have been accorded honors of various sorts —honorary academic degrees, medals, and similar awards; election to office in scientific societies and citizens' associations; and having buildings, parks, and landmarks named for them. Considering their manifest services to their country, one realizes that these testimonies constitute modest recognition indeed.

No one who has studied the conservation movement in the United States can have failed to observe that certain individuals from time to time have dominated the action in its various sectors. It is revealing to note how often we find academicians among the activists, a fact that explains why some of the most profound influences on the course of conservation have flowed from the classroom, the laboratory, the museum, and the scientific society.

Of the thousands of men and women who contributed to the advancement of knowledge about resources and to their management in the public interest, a few hundred stand out. They stand out because of the particular nature of their contribution to a specific resource, or because of the significance of their influence on the attainment of a national goal or policy, or because their achievements and activities were or are noteworthy. These are the leaders of American conservation. This book has been compiled to grant them the recognition they deserve.

ADAMS, ANSEL (1902–   )

Born February 20, 1902 in San Francisco, California. His formal education was erratic and primarily obtained through private instruction at home and through self-education in music and photography. Received an honorary Doctor of Fine Arts degree from the University of California in 1961, and an honorary Doctor of Humanities degree from Occidental College in 1967. Visiting Yosemite National Park every summer during his youth to photograph and explore, he developed into an ardent conservationist of the Sierra Club, serving four years as custodian of the Le Conte Memorial, the Sierra Club headquarters in Yosemite, and from 1934 onward as a continual board member and club representative. His first portfolio of original photographs, "Parmelian Prints of the High Sierra," issued in 1927, launched his career as a foremost American photographer. In 1936 he represented the Sierra Club in Washington and New York. In 1938, he published *Sierra Nevada: The John Muir Trail*, acclaimed for its pictorial beauty and effectiveness in the Kings Canyon campaign. In 1941 he was appointed photomuralist to the Department of the Interior, and in 1946 founded the first department of photography at the California School of Fine Arts; also that year he received a Guggenheim Fellowship, renewed in 1948 and 1959, enabling him to photograph the national parks and monuments during their peaks of seasonal beauty. In 1955 in conjunction with Nancy Newhall, he produced the famous exhibition and later book, *This is the American Earth*, for the Sierra Club. During 1956–57, he was president of the Trustees for Conservation, and in 1963 received the Sierra Club's John Muir Award for his services to conservation. In 1966 he was elected a Fellow of the American Academy of Arts and Sciences. Author and photographer of numerous books, articles, technical manuals (including his famous five-volume *Basic Photo Series*) and four portfolios, his pictorial books include *Illustrated Guide to Yosemite Valley*, (rev.

1963); *My Camera in Yosemite Valley,* 1949; *My Camera in the National Parks,* 1950; and *These We Inherit; The Parklands of America,* 1962.

HOLT BODINSON

"Ansel Adams, Interpreter of Nature." *The Picture History of Photography.* New York: Abrams, 1958.
NEWHALL, BEAUMONT, and NEWHALL, NANCY. *Masters of Photography.* New York: George Braziller, 1958.
NEWHALL, NANCY. *The Eloquent Light.* Sierra Club, 1963.
Who's Who in America, 1968–69.

ADAMS, CHARLES CHRISTOPHER (1873–1955)

Born July 23, 1873 in Clinton, Illinois. Illinois Wesleyan University, B. S. (biology) 1895, Sc. D. (honorary) 1920; Harvard University, M.S. 1889; University of Chicago, Ph.D. (zoology) 1908. He was a strong leader in ecology, especially during the early years of development of this field in North America, emphasizing the relation of human ecology to land use and urging a broad ecological approach to the problems of interrelationships of human ecology and public policies. He was assistant biologist at Illinois Wesleyan University, 1895–96; assistant entomologist, Illinois State Laboratory of Natural History, 1896–98; curator, University Museum, Michigan, 1903–6; director, Cincinnati Society of Natural History, 1906–7; and associate professor of animal ecology at the University of Illinois State Laboratory of Natural History, 1908–14. He became assistant professor of forest zoology, New York State College of Forestry, Syracuse, in 1914, and was professor during 1916–26 while at the same time serving as director of the Roosevelt Wildlife Forest Experiment Station. In 1926 he moved to the New York State Museum, Albany, from which he retired as director in 1943. He was president of the Ecological Society of America in 1923, and vice president of the Association of Geographers in 1927. Although his bibliography includes more than 150 titles, mainly journal papers, his book *Guide to the Study of Animal Ecology* (1913) ranks among the important pioneer ecological treatises written in North America. Died May 22, 1955.

GEORGE SPRUGEL, JR.

American Men of Science, 1955.
Bulletin of the Ecological Society of America, vol. 37, no. 4, 1956.

ADAMS, SHERMAN (1899–   )

Born January 8, 1899 in East Dover, Vermont. Dartmouth College, A.B. 1920, M.A. 1940, LL.D. 1953. Also awarded D.C.L. New England College, 1951; LL.D. University of New Hampshire, 1950; Bates College, 1954; Bryant College, St. Lawrence University, 1954; Center College, Kentucky, 1955; University of Maine, Middlebury College, 1957. Began his career in forestry as treasurer, Black River Lumber Company, Vermont, 1921–22; manager, timberland and lumber operations, the Parker-Young Company, Lincoln, New Hampshire, 1928–45. After the disastrous New England hurricane of 1938, he served on the State Timber Salvage Committee. Member of the New Hampshire House of Representatives, 1941–44, serving as chairman of the Committee on Labor, 1941–42, and Speaker of the House, 1943–44. He helped frame and enact a New Hampshire timber tax law, aided in formation of a Northeast Forest Fire Compact, and improved forest policy in New Hampshire. He also helped improve working conditions of woodsmen. Elected to the Seventy-Ninth Congress in 1945, he was author of a law to create state forestry advisory boards. Governor of New Hampshire, 1949–53; chairman, New England Governors' Conference, 1951–52. As assistant to the President of the United States, 1953–58, he furthered the cause of forest conservation at every opportunity, specifically the Fourth American Forest Congress, 1953, the Southern Forest Fire Prevention Conference, 1956, and the annual forest fire prevention campaigns. He is a life director of the New England Lumber Manufacturers, and president of the Loon Mountain Recreation

Corporation. The esteem in which he is held by foresters is attested by his election to the Society of American Foresters although he is not a professional forester. He was formerly a director of the American Forestry Association. He is the author of *First Hand Report* and articles for *Life* and other magazines.

KENNETH B. POMEROY

American Forests, August, 1958.
Who's Who in America, 1968–69.

AHERN, GEORGE PATRICK (1859–1942)

Born December 29, 1859 in New York City. Graduated from United States Military Academy, 1882; law degree from Yale University, 1895. Served with United States Infantry in Dakota Territory, Minnesota, and Montana, 1882–98. Became interested in forestry about 1885. In 1894, advised Edward Bowers of the General Land Office regarding creation of forest reserves in Montana; in 1896, guided Gifford Pinchot and Henry S. Graves through Montana and Idaho in search of potential forest reserves; in 1897 introduced and taught forestry courses at Montana Agricultural College, and obtained reservation of the Gallatin Forest Reserve as a demonstration forest. Served in Cuba and the Philippines in the Spanish American War. In the Philippines, organized the Philippine Bureau of Forestry in 1900 and headed it until 1914. He succeeded in establishing the Philippine School of Forestry. In 1914 he was instrumental in assisting Ngan Han to set up the Chinese Forest Service, and assisted in establishing a school of forestry at Nanking University. During the 1920s he was active in the work of the Tropical Plant Research Foundation. He was elected a Fellow of the Society of American Foresters in 1929. He wrote many articles, particularly on tropical forestry. He was active in the controversy over public regulation of private cutting, and published two major books, *Deforested America* and *Forest Bankruptcy in America*, in support

of such regulation. He was a major figure in the development of
forestry both at home and abroad. Died May 13, 1942.

LAWRENCE RAKESTRAW

American Forests, February, 1935.
Assembly, United States Military Academy, January 1943.
"Forestry Missionary," *Montana: The Magazine of Western History*, October, 1959.
"George Patrick Ahern and the Philippine Bureau of Forestry, 1900–1914," *Pacific Northwest Quarterly*, July, 1967.
Journal of Forestry. Obituary, July 1942.

ALBRIGHT, HORACE MARDEN (1890–   )

Born January 6, 1890 in Bishop, California. University of California,
B.L. 1912; Georgetown University Law School, LL.B. 1914; University of Montana, LL.D. 1956; University of California, LL.D. 1961;
University of New Mexico, LL.D. 1962. In 1913 he entered public
service as a confidential clerk to the Secretary of the Interior and
advanced to assistant attorney, assigned to National Park affairs,
in 1916. From 1916 to 1933 he was to remain in the newly formed
National Park Service, making significant contributions to early
policy formulation, planning, development, and management of
the emerging national park system. In 1917 he became assistant
director of the National Park Service, and in 1919 moved to the
field as superintendent of Yellowstone National Park, his position
for the next ten years. While superintendent of Yellowstone, he
also served as field assistant to the director, 1920–26, and as assistant
director (field), 1926–29. In 1929 he became director of the
National Park Service and served in that capacity until 1933 when
he retired from the federal service to enter private business. The
awards and recognition he has received for his contributions to
conservation and park management are numerous and unique. In
1963 the National Park Service established the Horace M. Albright
Training Center at Grand Canyon National Park. In 1961 the University of California initiated the Horace M. Albright Conservation
Lecture Series, an annual lecture given by a leading conservation

specialist; and in his honor, the American Scenic and Historic Preservation Society established the Horace M. Albright Scenic Preservation Award. His other awards include the Distinguished Service Award of the American Forestry Association; the Frances K. Hutchinson Medal of the Garden Clubs of America; the Gold Medal of the Camp Fire Club of America; the Theodore Roosevelt Medal for the Conservation of Natural Resources from the Theodore Roosevelt Association; and the Pugsley Gold Medal of the American Scenic and Historic Preservation Society. He has served as honorary vice president of the American Forestry Association and of the Sierra Club, and is an honorary member of the American Society of Landscape Architects. Following retirement from government, he has served as a director and trustee on the boards of numerous national conservation organizations and has held the following offices: president (1952) and chairman (1952–61) of Resources for the Future; vice-president of the Boone and Crockett Club; and chairman of the Southern California Chapter of the Nature Conservancy (1964–65). Author of numerous articles on resources and management, he is co-author of the book, *Oh, Ranger!* with F. J. Taylor.

HOLT BODINSON

Who's Who in America, 1968–69.

ALLEN, ARTHUR AUGUSTUS (1885–1964)

Born December 28, 1885 in Buffalo, New York. Cornell University, A.B. (zoology) 1907, M.A. 1908, Ph.D. 1911. He began teaching at Cornell in 1910, and in 1926 became the first full professor of ornithology in the United States. His entire academic career was spent at Cornell where he founded the first ornithological laboratory in the country to achieve formal status as a university department (1954). He retired from active teaching in 1953. Instrumental in placing ornithology in colleges and universities, he also awakened wide public enthusiasm and interest in preserving vanishing species of birds through his lectures, teaching, and written works. He pioneered in color photography of birds and in recording the songs and calls of North American birds. He was chairman of Cornell's Commission on Wildlife Conservation, president of the Eastern Bird Banding Association, a founder of the American Society of Mammalogists and of the Wildlife Society, and a trustee of the American Wildlife Institute. Awarded the *Outdoor Life* gold medal in 1924, and the Burr award from the National Geographic Society in 1948. The author of many articles, he also wrote nine books, the most important being his two volumes of *American Bird Biographies*, 1934, *The Book of Bird Life*, 1930 and 1961, and *Stalking Birds with a Color Camera*, 1951. Acknowledged as one of the leading ornithological scientists of his generation, he has left an invaluable legacy in the vast store of knowledge he passed on to his students, many presently holding important positions in conservation throughout the country. Died January 17, 1964.

EVE HERBST

New York Times. Obituary, January 18, 1964.
Who Was Who in America, 1961–68.

ALLEN, DURWARD LEON   (1910–   )

Born October 11, 1910 in Uniondale, Indiana. University of Michigan, A.B. 1932; Michigan State University, Ph.D. (zoology) 1937. Joined the Michigan Department of Conservation in 1937; he was biologist in charge of the Swan Creek Wildlife Experiment Station for two years; transferred to the Rose Lake Wildlife Experiment Station in 1939. During World War II, he served in the Medical Corps of the United States Army. In 1946 he joined the United States Fish and Wildlife Service in Maryland and began wildlife investigations on agricultural lands; he was assistant chief of the Branch of Wildlife Research in the Washington, D. C. office, 1951–54. Appointed associate professor of wildlife management in the Department of Forestry and Conservation at Purdue University in 1954, he has been professor since 1957. He was assistant secretary general for the Inter-American Conference on Renewable Natural

Resources in 1948. He was recipient of the medal of honor of the Anglers Club of New York in 1956. During 1956–57, he was president of the Wildlife Society; in 1969 he received the Society's Aldo Leopold Memorial Medal. Previously, he had received two awards from this society for outstanding publications: one for territorial wildlife in 1945 and the other for conservation education in 1955. He is a Fellow of the American Association for the Advancement of Science. Author of *Michigan Fox Squirrel Management*, 1943; *Pheasants Afield*, 1953; *Our Wildlife Legacy*, 1954; *The Life of Prairies and Plains*, 1967; he was also editor of *Pheasants in North America*, 1956.

HENRY CLEPPER

American Men of Science (The Physical and Biological Sciences), 11th ed., 1965.
World Who's Who in Science, 1968.

ALLEN, EDWARD TYSON (1875–1942)

Born in 1875 at New Haven, Connecticut. Tutored by his father, an ex-Yale professor. Entered the United States Division of Forestry in 1898 as ranger, one of the first forest rangers in the Pacific Northwest. State forester of California, 1905 and 1906. During 1908–10, district inspector in the United States Forest Service and first district forester of the Pacific Northwest Region. Helped organize the Western Forestry and Conservation Association and served as its forester and manager for over thirty years. Also organized western timberland owners for forest protection and created the machinery for cooperation between federal, state, and private agencies in the five western states and British Columbia. In his 44 years of service to forest conservation he was called upon for advice and counsel in numerous capacities by the Federal Trade Commission, the Council of National Defense, the National Lumber Manufacturers Association, and the American Forestry Association. In each instance, his vast knowledge of the art of forestry, of economics, and of the forest industries marked him with the stature of a statesman. Leadership in promoting harmonious working relations between lumbermen and professional foresters was his primary contribution to conservation. He was a charter member (1900) of the Society of American Foresters, and a Fellow since 1939. Author of a forward looking book, *Practical Forestry in the Pacific Northwest,* 1911. Died May 27, 1942.

SOCIETY OF AMERICAN FORESTERS

Journal of Forestry. Obituary, 40:574–75, 1942; ALLEN, SHIRLEY W., "We Present E. T. Allen," *Journal of Forestry,* 43:222–23, 1945.

ALLEN, ROBERT PORTER (1905–63)

Born April 24, 1905 in South Williamsport, Pennsylvania. Lafayette College, 1923–25; Cornell University, 1925. He served the National Audubon Society for thirty years, as research associate and sanctuary director, and from 1955 to 1960 as research director. His life was dedicated to the protection of vanishing species of rare birds. Instrumental in preventing the extinction of the whooping crane by discovering the nesting grounds of the remnant wild flock in 1955 near Great Slave Lake, almost at the Arctic Circle, he was a leader in having whooping crane habitats in Texas and Canada proclaimed as refuges. He helped establish a working protective plan for flamingos and recommended methods of saving the small surviving colonies of roseate spoonbills, thus helping to perpetuate the species. His monographs on the whooping crane, the roseate spoonbill, and the American flamingo are the standard authoritative works on these species. His most noted book, *On the Trail of Vanishing Birds,* 1957, won him the 1958 John Burroughs award for the outstanding nature book of the year. He was also awarded the Brewster medal by the American Ornithologists' Union in 1957 and the Nash Conservation Award in 1955. His important popular literary works include *The Flame Birds,* 1947, *Our Vanishing Wildlife,* 1957, and *Birds of the Caribbean,* 1961. His projected 16-volume series on *Birds of North America* was interrupted by his death on June 28, 1963. He left a priceless legacy in his research, in the interest generated by his writings, and above all in the rare species he helped save from extermination.

EVE HERBST

Audubon Magazine, September–October 1963.
New York Times. Obituary, June 29, 1963.
Who Was Who in America, 1961–68.

ALLEN, SHIRLEY WALTER (1883–1968)

Born October 14, 1883 in Sherman, New York. Iowa State College, B.S. (agriculture) 1909, M.F. 1929. Entering the United States Forest Service in 1909 as a forest assistant in California, he advanced to deputy supervisor of the Lassen National Forest in 1912. Professor of forestry extension at the New York State College of Forestry at Syracuse during 1914–18, he was then for a year with the Forest Products Laboratory at Madison, Wisconsin. Returning in 1919 to the Forest Service in California, he was promoted a year later to supervisor of the Angeles National Forest. During 1922–23, he was in the lumber business in southern California and was briefly with the Chamber of Commerce in Los Angeles. In 1924 he began four years as forester for the American Forestry Association in Washington, D. C. In 1928 he joined the faculty of the School of Forestry and Conservation at the University of Michigan where he remained for three decades, retiring as professor emeritus of forestry in 1958. Throughout his career he was active in the Society of American Foresters, as associate editor of the *Journal of Forestry*, 1927–28, as a member of the Council, 1940–41, as vice president, 1942–45, and as president, 1946–47; he was then elected a Fellow in 1948. In addition, he held numerous advisory and consulting assignments; for example, he was on the official United States delegation to the Second World Forestry Congress in Budapest in 1936. During 1935–38, he was a consultant to the National Parks Service, and subsequently to the National Research Council. He was a member of the secretariat of the Inter-American Conference on Natural Resources in 1948; and was a member of the Michigan Conservation Commission (chairman the last year) during 1953–58. He was a Fellow of the American Association for the Advancement of Science. The author of many articles on forestry, parks, wilderness, and general conservation, he was widely known for his books *An Introduction to American Forestry*, first published in 1938 and periodically revised since, and *Conserving Natural Resources* (3rd edition, 1966). Died in September 1968.

HENRY CLEPPER

American Men of Science (The Physical and Biological Sciences), 11th ed., 1965.
Journal of Forestry. Obituary, 66(12):947, December 1968.

ANDREWS, CHRISTOPHER COLUMBUS (1829–1922)

Born October 27, 1829 in Hillsboro, New Hampshire. After Harvard Law School he was admitted to the bar in 1850 and began legal practice in Massachusetts. He moved to Minnesota in 1857 and practiced law; was elected to the Minnesota State Senate in 1859, and was founder and co-editor of *St. Cloud Union* in 1861. He rose to the rank of brevet major-general during the Civil War, returned to Minnesota in 1865, and was minister to Norway and Sweden from 1869 to 1877. His ministerial reports included information on Swedish forest culture. He was census supervisor in Minnesota in 1880, and consul-general to Brazil from 1882 to 1885. He was an early advocate of applying European (especially Swedish) forestry principles to American forests. After the tragic Hinckley, Minnesota forest fire in 1894, he gave his support and influence in the Minnesota Legislature to establish the office of chief fire warden in 1895. He was chief fire warden (later forestry commissioner) from 1895 to 1911. His plan for the reforestation of Minnesota included the concept of multiple use. He campaigned successfully to get Congress to establish the Minnesota National Forest in 1908 (now the Chippewa National Forest). He influenced the General Land Office to withdraw from entry lands which became the nucleus of the Superior National Forest in 1909. He is considered the father of the Quetico-Superior Wilderness Area because as early as 1905 he advocated the creation of an international park on the Ontario-Minnesota border. He was secretary of the Minnesota State Forestry Board, 1911–22. His *Recollections* were published in 1928. Died September 21, 1922.

ELWOOD R. MAUNDER

Dictionary of American Biography, 1928.
Who Was Who in America, 1897–1942.
WIDNER, RALPH R., ed., *Forests and Forestry in the American States*. The National Association of State Foresters, 1968. Chapters 6 and 32.

ANDREWS, HORACE JUSTIN (1892–1951)

Born October 31, 1892 at Sidnaw, Michigan. A forestry graduate of the University of Michigan in 1916; instructor in forestry at the university for three years following graduation with time out for service in the Aviation Corps of the United States Army in 1918. Also taught forestry at Iowa State College. In 1924, became director of the Land Economic Survey for the Michigan Department of Conservation, serving in that capacity until 1927 when he was appointed assistant state forester. Pioneering the Land Economic Survey marked him as a leader of a movement in which economic surveys of forest resources were applied in all important forest regions of the United States. In 1930 he joined the United States Forest Service as director of the forest survey of Washington and Oregon, Pacific Northwest Forest Experiment Station, Portland, Oregon. Remained there until 1938 when he returned to Michigan as a research professor in wild-land utilization. In 1939 he went back to the Forest Service at Portland, Oregon as assistant regional forester in charge of the Division of State and Private Forestry of the Pacific Northwest region; appointed regional forester in 1943. Member, Society of American Foresters, 1924. Died March 23, 1951.

SOCIETY OF AMERICAN FORESTERS

Journal of Forestry. Obituary, 49:388, 1951.

ARNOLD, RICHARD KEITH (1913–   )

Born November 17, 1913 in Long Beach, California. University of California, B.S. (forestry) 1937; Yale University, M.F. 1938; University of Michigan, Ph.D. 1950. During 1951–53, he was fire research officer for the California (now the Pacific Southwest) Forest and Range Experiment Station at Berkeley, then was on the forestry faculty of the University of California, 1954–55. In this assignment he was manager of "Operation Firestop," a cooperative project with the United States Forest Service, the Civil Defense Administration, the Universities of California and Southern California, the California Division of Forestry, and the forest industries to develop new techniques in fire control. In 1955 he returned to the Pacific Southwest Forest and Range Experiment Station as chief of the Division of Fire Research, and was appointed director of the Station in 1957. Transferred to the Washington, D. C. office of the Forest Service in 1963; was director of the Division of Forest Protection Research until 1966 when he went to the University of Michigan as dean of the School of Natural Resources. Returned in 1969 to the Forest Service in Washington, D. C. as deputy chief in charge of research; he directs a national research program that includes eight regional forest experiment stations, the Forest Products Laboratory of Madison, Wisconsin, and the Institute of Tropical Forestry in Puerto Rico. He was an associate editor of the *Journal of Forestry* during 1956–58; was a member of the Council of the Society of American Foresters during 1964–69; was chairman of the Forest Fire Working Group for the North American Forestry Commission, Food and Agriculture Organization of the United Nations, 1965–66; and was vice president in 1959 of the Association of State College and University Research Organizations. He is the author of many papers published in scientific journals and has served on numerous national and international committees dealing with natural resources research.

HENRY CLEPPER

ASHE, WILLIAM WILLARD (1872–1932)

Born June 4, 1872 in Raleigh, North Carolina. University of North Carolina, B. Litt. 1891; Cornell University, M.S. 1892. He was forester of the North Carolina Geological Survey from 1892 to 1905, then worked for the United States Forest Service from 1905 until his death in 1932. Secretary of the National Forest Reservation Commission and editor of its reports from 1918 to 1924. Vice president of the Society of American Foresters in 1919. He was appointed a member of the Forest Service Tree Name Committee and served as chairman, 1930–32. An authority on forest types and vegetation, he discovered 100 new species in the Southeast, including several kinds of trees. Determined much of acquisition policy of Forest Service for many years after the Weeks Law (1911) went into effect. Did significant work on comparative costs of operating large and small timber. His experiments in getting gum out of trees with cups and gutters influenced the development of the system now used by the naval stores industry. He solved the problem of successfully transplanting longleaf pine. A prolific writer, his scientific writings number 166 and include such subjects as botany, logging costs, forest economics, erosion, forest influences and forest types, land acquisition, and forest management. His monograph, *Loblolly Pine*, is regarded as a model in its field. Died March 18, 1932.

SOCIETY OF AMERICAN FORESTERS

Journal of Forestry. Obituary, 30:652–53, May 1932.
DAYTON, WILLIAM A., "William Willard Ashe," *Journal of Forestry*, 44:213–14, March 1946.

AUDUBON, JOHN JAMES (1785–1851)

Born April 26, 1785 in Santo Domingo (now Haiti). Reared in France, he developed an interest in natural history and a gift for drawing. In 1803 he came to the United States to enter business, and lived near Norristown, Pennsylvania, at Mill Grove, a farm his father had purchased. During the next seventeen years, he embarked on a number of business ventures, but the study of birds and his drawings of bird species became his main interest. He disposed of his capital to free himself from the obligation to pursue trade and, in 1819, turned entirely to the drawing of American birds with the hope of eventual publication. In 1824 with a nearly completed portfolio of watercolor paintings, he visited the Philadelphia Academy of Sciences, where he was advised to publish his work in England because the engraving facilities there were better and he would then escape the resentment of George Ord, an influential but rival American ornithologist. *The Birds of America* in four volumes was published in England from 1827 to 1838, and its text, *Ornithological Biography* in five volumes, from 1831 to 1839. During the 1830s he became the world's pre-eminent ornithologist, and is still the world's best known. During the 1840s, he began a work on American mammals, which was completed by his sons. His lifespan ended before conservation became a pressing need and a cause, but his work, which was the first cultural and scientific achievement by an American to receive full European recognition as the greatest in its field, made a lasting impression on Americans and paved the way for the conservationists who were to follow. In addition to the aforementioned books, he was the author of *A Synopsis of the Birds of North America*, 1839; and *The Viviparous Quadrupeds of North America* (completed by his son), 1845–48. Died January 27, 1851.

NATIONAL AUDUBON SOCIETY

Concise Dictionary of American Biography. 1964.
Encyclopaedia Brittanica,
HERRICK, FRANCIS HOBART, *Audubon the Naturalist*, 2 vols., New York: Dover Publications, 1968.
Who's Who in American History (Historical Volume), 1607–1896.

AVERY, CARLOS (1868–1930)

Born January 25, 1868 in Minooka, Illinois. A newspaperman, he was owner and editor of *The Leader*, acquired in 1897 and published in Hutchinson, Minnesota. In 1905 he was appointed to the

Minnesota Game and Fish Commission, which he headed for 14 years. Becoming vice president of the American Game Protective Association in New York City in 1924, he was advanced to the presidency in 1928. In addition, he served as editor of the Association's bimonthly journal, *American Game*. During his career he held numerous offices, both elective and advisory, in conservation affairs. He was active in the International Association of Game, Fish and Conservation Commissioners, which organization he served as secretary–treasurer for two decades. The Secretary of Agriculture appointed him a member of the Federal Advisory Committee under the Migratory Bird Treaty Act. President of the American Fisheries Society during 1919–20, he was the Society's secretary from 1924 until his death, at which time he was also chairman of the National Committee on Wildlife Legislation. He was one of the pioneers in securing state laws for hunting licenses as a means of financing the work of state game commissions and the establishment of game refuges. Died October 5, 1930.

HENRY CLEPPER

American Game. Obituary, vol. 19, no. 6, November–December. 1930.
New York Times. Obituary, October 6, 1930.

AYLWARD, DAVID ARCHER (1882–1970)

Born November 15, 1882 in Salem, Massachusetts. Educated at Harvard University. Beginning in 1921, he was active in the reorganization of the Massachusetts Division of Fisheries and Game and in the recodification of the state's game and fish laws. In 1929 he became executive secretary of the Massachusetts Fish and Game Association. He was instrumental in the establishment of the Parker River National Wildlife Refuge in 1942, a sanctuary for waterfowl along the Massachusetts coast. When the National Wildlife Federation was formed in 1936 he was elected its first vice president and succeeded to the presidency in 1937, an office he held for 13 years during which he successfully guided the federation through this critical period in its development. He cooperated with other conservation leaders in the attainment of numerous progressive goals, including the Federal Aid in Wildlife Restoration Act of 1937, the earlier Fish and Wildlife Coordination Act of 1934, and other significant laws that formed the basis for modern wildlife management practices. Died March 21, 1970.

E. WARNER SHEDD, JR.

BAIRD, SPENCER FULLERTON (1823–1887)

Born February 3, 1823 in Reading, Pennsylvania. Dickinson College, A.B. 1840, Sc.D. (honorary) 1856; Columbia University, LL.D. 1887; Harvard University, LL.D. 1887. In 1845 he was appointed professor of natural history at Dickinson College, and in 1848 received a grant from the Smithsonian Institution to explore the bone caves of Pennsylvania, the first grant made by the Institution for scientific exploration and field research. In July 1850 he was appointed assistant secretary of the Smithsonian, then, starting with his own personal collection which he gave to the Institution, he developed the United States National Museum, and was in charge of explorations and collections made by the government in the expanding West. He became secretary of the Smithsonian in 1878. Meanwhile, when the new United States Commission of Fish and Fisheries was created in 1871 he was appointed its first commissioner, to serve without additional salary, which he did until his death. He established the first marine laboratory in the United States, at Woods Hole, Massachusetts, and started a federal fisheries program to rehabilitate the nation's fisheries resources. A prolific editor and writer, he was head of the science department of *Harper's Magazine* and was editor of *The Annual Record of Science and Industry*. His list of titles exceeds one thousand, covering such diverse fields as mammals, birds, reptiles, fish, geology, and travel. Two of his scientific works are still classics: *Mammals of North America* and *Birds of North America*. In 1850 he became permanent secretary of the American Association for the Advancement of Science, and in 1863 he helped organize the National Academy of

Sciences. He held honorary memberships in 15 foreign academies and scientific societies, and received decorations from Norway, Australia, France, and Germany. Died August 19, 1887.

HERBERT W. GRAHAM

BILLINGS, J. S. *Memoir of Spencer Fullerton Baird 1823–87.* Biographical Memoirs, vol. 3. National Academy of Sciences, 1915.
DALL, W. H. *Spencer Fullerton Baird, a Biography.* Philadelphia: Lippincott, 1915.
Dictionary of American Biography, 1928.
RIDGEWAY, R. et al. *Biographical Memoirs of Spencer Fullerton Baird.* Annual Report of the Smithsonian Institution, 1888.
World Who's Who in Science, 1968.

BAKER, HUGH POTTER (1878–1950)

Born January 20, 1878 in St. Croix Falls, Wisconsin. Michigan State College, B.S. 1901; Yale University, M.F. (forestry) 1904; University of Munich, Doctor of Economics 1910; Syracuse University, LL.D. 1933; Rhode Island State College, LL.D. 1945; Boston University, D.Sc. 1945; Amherst College, LL.D. 1947; University of Massachusetts, LL.D. 1947. Entering the Division of Forestry, United States Department of Agriculture, in 1901, he spent several years on part-time duty in the West making examinations of public domain lands for forest reserves. In 1904 he joined the faculty of forestry at Iowa State College, leaving in 1907 to set up the Department of Forestry at Pennsylvania State College. From 1912 to 1920, he was dean of the New York State College of Forestry at Syracuse, and established the New York State Ranger School as a unit of the College. He left in 1920 to become executive secretary of the American Paper and Pulp Association, and in 1928 was named manager of the trade association department of the Chamber of Commerce of the United States. He returned to the New York State College of Forestry again as dean in 1930, then left in 1933 to become president of Massachusetts State College (renamed the University of Massachusetts), retiring as president in 1947. During his incumbency, professional curriculums in forestry and wildlife management were established. He was a Fellow of the American Associa-

tion for the Advancement of Science and of the Society of American
Foresters. He wrote extensively on forestry and educational subjects. Died May 24, 1950.

HENRY CLEPPER

Journal of Forestry. Obituary, 48(7):516, July 1950.
National Cyclopaedia of American Biography, 1954.
Who Was Who in America, 1951–60.

BAKER, JOHN HOPKINSON (1894–   )

Born June 30, 1894, in Cambridge, Massachusetts. Harvard University, A.B. 1915. Began bird studies as a boyhood hobby; became
a youthful member of the famed Nuttall Ornithological Club at
Cambridge. Later, as a businessman in New York City, he served
as president of the Linnaean Society and a director of the National
Audubon Society, becoming chairman of the Audubon Board in
1933. In 1934 he abandoned a successful brokerage business on
Wall Street to assume full-time duties as chief executive officer of
the National Audubon Society, first with the title of executive
director and after 1944 as president. He retired as president emeritus in 1959. An innovative leader, he started the Audubon Camps,
summer workshops for teachers and other adults with courses in
natural history and ecology, the first being the Audubon Camp of
Maine which opened in 1936. He also initiated nature study centers
for children, the first being the Audubon Center of Southern California in Los Angeles County (1939), and the Society's annual,
nationwide lecture series known as Audubon Screen Tours (1944).
Instrumental in securing government action to establish Everglades
National Park, he was influential in other national conservation
policies for a quarter of a century. Under his direction the National
Audubon Society established its own research program with
emphasis on endangered species and produced or sponsored scientific monographs on the ivory-billed woodpecker, California condor,
roseate spoonbill, whooping crane, and West Indian flamingo.
Chairman of the Fish and Wildlife Advisory Committee to the

Secretary of the Interior from 1948 to 1953; continued as a member, 1957–60. He served also on the Board of Trustees of the National Parks Association, and on the Executive Committee of the Natural Resources Council of America. In 1969 the National Audubon Society established the John H. Baker Scholarship Fund for Conservation Education in his honor.

CHARLES H. CALLISON

Audubon Magazine, vol. 71:6, pp. 81–85.
National Audubon Society, Staff biographies.
Who's Who in America, 1963.

BARNES, WILL CROFT (1858–1936)

Born June 21, 1858 in California. Following public school education, he served in the Army (1879–82), and was awarded the Congressional Medal of Honor "for bravery in action with hostile Apache Indians." He engaged in open range cattle business in Arizona and New Mexico, served in the territorial legislatures of both states, then in 1907 entered the United States Forest Service as a grazing inspector. He gained an intimate knowledge of western range conditions and the livestock business, and a wide acquaintance with stockmen. He had a leading role in formulating range management policy and developing range administration of the national forests. From 1915 to 1928 he was in charge of the Branch of Grazing, Forest Service. For two years thereafter he was secretary of the United States Geographic Board, then resigned from government service to devote his time to writing. His published works are numerous and include many magazine articles descriptive of the West's range lands and related resources. His books include *Western Grazing Grounds and Forest Ranges*, 1913; *Tales from an X-Bar Horse Camp*, 1920; *The Story of the Range*; and *Cattle*, 1930, of which he was co-author. He was a persuasive exponent of range conservation and sound range administration. Although his accomplishments were practical rather than scientific, he was an outstanding figure in introducing stability and efficiency to the chaotic national-forest range conditions of the early 1900s. Died December 18, 1936.

HENRY CLEPPER

Who Was Who in America, 1897–1942.

BATES, CARLOS GLAZIER (1885–1949)

Born October 14, 1885 in Topeka, Kansas. University of Nebraska B.S. (forestry) 1907. Joined the United States Forest Service in 1907, advancing from forest assistant to principal silviculturist at the time of his death. In charge of one of the first forest experiment stations, the Fremont Station, in Colorado from 1909 to 1927; at the Forest Products Laboratory, Madison, Wisconsin in 1927; and at the Lake States Forest Experiment Station, St. Paul, Minnesota from 1928 on. His research contributions, many of them pioneering, concerned prairie tree planting, forest and watershed influences, tree seed, physiological requirements of trees, shelterbelt influences, and genetics of forest trees. He was in charge of research that guided the Prairie States Forestry Project in the Great Plains from 1933 to 1942. He devised instruments for measuring evaporation and stream sediments. The forest watershed influence study at Wagon Wheel Gap, Colorado which he supervised in cooperation with the United States Weather Bureau (1909–26) gained international recognition. A Fellow (1940) in the Society of American Foresters, he served that organization as vice president in 1920, as chairman of the Rocky Mountain Section in 1919, and as chairman of the Minnesota Section in 1930. From 1925 through 1932 he was associate editor of the *Journal of Forestry* for dendrology, silvics, and silviculture. Author of some 60 scientific papers and monographs. Died July 2, 1949.

PAUL O. RUDOLF

American Men of Science, 8th ed., 1949.
Journal of Forestry. Obituary, vol. 47, 1949; 54, 1956.

BEAR, FIRMAN EDWARD   (1884–1968)

Born May 21, 1884 near Germantown, Ohio. Ohio State University, B.Sc. 1908, M.Sc. 1910; University of Wisconsin, Ph.D. 1917; University of Chile, D.Sc. (honorary); Rutgers University, D.Sc. (honorary). During his 50 years of professional activity, he won national recognition as a teacher, scientist, author, administrator, and conservationist. He taught at three universities: Ohio State, 1912–14 and 1916–26; West Virginia, 1914–16; and Rutgers, 1940–54. He also served as chairman of the soils departments at West Virginia and Rutgers. A prolific writer, he was author or co-author of 78 scientific papers and several hundred semi-technical or popular articles. His first book, *Soils and Fertilizers*, 1924, served as a text for over forty years. He wrote *Theory and Practices in the Use of Fertilizers*, 1928; edited a monograph *Chemistry of the Soil*, 1955; wrote *Earth, the Stuff of Life*, 1961; and *Soils in Relation to Crop Growth*, 1965. He was science editor of *Country Home Magazine*, 1938–40, and editor-in-chief of *Soil Science*, 1940–66. Director of agricultural research for American Cyanamid Company, 1929–38, he traveled widely in this country, Central America, and Europe. He served as president of the Soil Science Society of America in 1943, of the American Society of Agronomy in 1949, and of the Soil Conservation Society of America in 1950. He spent twelve years on the Secretary of Agriculture's Soil and Water Conservation Advisory Committee, six years on the New Jersey State Soil Conservation Committee, was an active board member of the Conservation Foundation, and served as a special consultant of world food problems for the State Department. He was a Fellow of the American Association for the Advancement of Science, of the American Society of Agronomy and of the Soil Conservation Society, and was an honorary member of the International Society of Soil Science. Died April 6, 1968.

GRANT F. WALTON

American Men of Science (The Physical and Biological Sciences), 11th ed., 1965.
Soil Science. Obituary, vol. 105, no. 5, May 1968.
Who's Who in America, vol. 35, 1968–69.

BELDING, DAVID LAWRENCE (1884–1970)

Born July 24, 1884 in Dover Plains, New York. Williams College, A.B. 1905; Harvard Medical School, M.D. 1914; Harvard University, M.A. 1915. Biologist for the Massachusetts Fish and Game Commission (full-time and part-time) from 1905 to 1917. Captain in the United States Army Medical Corps, 1917–19. He held the following positions: part-time biologist for the Massachusetts Fish and Game Commission, 1919–22; research associate, Evans Memorial Hospital, 1919–46; director of laboratories at Massachusetts Memorial Hospitals, 1924–44; assistant professor of bacteriology at Boston University School of Medicine, 1920–24; professor of pathology and bacteriology, 1924–28, and professor of bacteriology and experimental pathology, 1928–49; associate scientist at Woods Hole Oceanographic Institution, 1950–54; collaborator for the United States Fish and Wildlife Service Branch of Fishery Biology, 1950–57; member, Province of Quebec Salmon Commission, 1936–40. In addition to books and papers on medical subjects he wrote *A Report upon the Mollusk Fisheries of Massachusetts*, 1909; *A Report upon the Quahaug and Oyster Fisheries of Massachusetts*, 1919; *The Soft-shelled Clam Fishery of Massachusetts*, 1930; *The Quahaug Fishery of Massachusetts*, 1931; *The Scallop Fishery of Massachusetts*, 1931; *A Report upon the Alewife Fisheries of Massachusetts*, 1921; and numerous papers in *Transactions of the American Fisheries Society* and elsewhere. A life member of the American Fisheries Society, he was president 1929–30, and was elected an honorary member in 1967. Died December 5, 1970.

ROBERT F. HUTTON

American Men of Science (The Physical and Biological Sciences), 11th ed., 1965.

BENNETT, HUGH HAMMOND (1881–1960)

Born April 15, 1881 near Wadesboro, North Carolina. University of North Carolina, B.S. 1903, LL.D. (honorary) 1936; Clemson Agricultural College, D.Sc. 1937; Columbia University, D.Sc. 1952. In 1903 he joined the Bureau of Soils, United States Department of Agriculture, and in 1909 was appointed soil survey inspector of the southern and eastern divisions. In 1904 and 1905, during soil surveys in Virginia, he became aware of accelerated soil erosion and decided that soil erosion was the most serious agricultural problem. In November 1928, he gave a statement on the problem and of his plans for study and action to a subcommittee of the House of Representatives. As a result an appropriation of $160,000 was made available to the Department of Agriculture for investigations of soil and water conservation; he was put in charge of the work for the Bureau of Chemistry and Soils. In September 1933 when the Soil Erosion Service was set up as an emergency public works agency in the Department of the Interior, he was appointed director of it. In April 1935 when the Soil Conservation Service was created in the Department of Agriculture he was named as its first chief, and he continued in this position until his mandatory retirement at the age of 70, in April 1951. His term was extended one year so he could serve as a special assistant to the Secretary of Agriculture. He was the author of many technical articles and of five books: *The Soils and Agriculture of the Southern States*, 1921; *The Soils of Cuba* (with R. V. Allison), 1928; *Soil Conservation*, 1939; *Elements of Soil Conservation*, 1947; and *This Land We Defend* (with William C. Pryor), 1942. A Fellow of the American Society of Agronomy and of the American Association for the Advancement of Science, he was founder, Fellow, and past president of the Soil Conservation Society of America. He was chairman of the Pan American Soil Conservation Commission. His awards included the Frances K. Hutchinson Medal by the Garden Club of America, 1944; Medal of Merit, National Agricultural and Industrial Society of Cuba, 1947; Audubon Medal, National Audubon Society, 1947; Distinguished Service Medal, U. S. Department of Agriculture, 1947; Cullum Medal, American Geographical Society, 1948; Silver Medal, Federated Garden Clubs of New York State, 1949; and the John Deere Gold Medal of the American Society of Agricultural Engineers, 1949. Died July 7, 1960.

F. Glennon Loyd

Brink, Wellington, *Big Hugh: The Father of Conservation*. New York: Macmillan, 1951.
Who Was Who in America, 1961–68.

BENNETT, LOGAN J. (1907–57)

Born August 29, 1907 in Festus, Missouri. Central College, Missouri, B.S. (biology) 1930; Iowa State College, M.S. 1932, Ph.D. (zoology) 1937. His doctoral degree was awarded after he had served as game technician for the Iowa State Conservation Commission in 1934, junior refuge manager of the Trempealeau National Wildlife Refuge in Wisconsin in 1935, and leader of the newly organized Iowa Cooperative Wildlife Research Unit. In the latter two positions he was an employee of the Bureau of Biological Survey in which agency and its successor agency, the Fish and Wildlife Service of the United States Department of the Interior, he was to serve with distinction; next as organizer and leader of the Pennsylvania Cooperative Wildlife Research Unit; as biologist in charge of the nationwide Cooperative Unit Program; and from 1948 until his retirement from the Department in 1953 as chief of the Branch of Wildlife Research. Then for nearly four years he was executive director of the Pennsylvania Game Commission. A charter member of The Wildlife Society, he served as Secretary in 1942, 1943, and 1946 and was president in 1947. He was also a member of the American Ornithologists' Union, the American Society of Mammalogists, and the Outdoor Writers Association. He received the Winchester Award for Outdoorsman of the Year for 1956. Among his many technical writings, one of his best known publications is *The Blue-Winged Teal—Its Ecology and Management*, 1938. Bird-dog fanciers will remember him for his book, *Training Grouse and Woodcock Dogs*. Died September 12, 1957.

DANIEL L. LEEDY

Journal of Wildlife Management. Obituary, vol. 22, January 1958.

BENSON, ARTHUR RAGNAR (1896–)

Born October 16, 1896 in East Berlin, Connecticut. Middletown, Connecticut High School, 1915. As president of the Associated Fishing Tackle Manufacturers from 1936 to 1953, he assumed the leadership in obtaining membership support for the important Federal Aid in Fish Restoration Act in 1950 (popularly known as the Dingell-Johnson Act), financed by a ten percent excise tax on fishing tackle manufactured by them. He helped convince the fishing tackle industry of its responsibility in the conservation and proper utilization of sport fishery resources, and as a result, the Sport Fishing Institute was founded in 1949. This institute, the only national fish conservation agency, was a revolutionary development in that the industry recognized an obligation to advance responsible husbandry of fishery resources by reinvesting in fish conservation part of its income from the sale of manufactured products used by anglers. Under his leadership, the tackle manufacturers organized the Institute as a non-profit, tax-exempt organization, professionally staffed, to carry out its now well-established program of research in fishery biology, education in fish conservation problems and principles, and technical service to official agencies and key citizen groups. He served as its first president from 1949 to 1959, and is currently a vice president and a member of its executive committee. He was also the first president of Sport Fishery Research Foundation from 1962 to 1967, and continues on its board of trustees. He has been a trustee of the North American Wildlife Foundation since 1946 and presently serves on its executive committee. In February 1968, he was elected to the Sporting Goods Hall of Fame by the National Sporting Goods Association for "his work behind-the-scenes in the field of conservation," the only man ever so honored for any reason other than the development of a manufactured product. He is a life member of both the American Fisheries Society and the Izaak Walton League of America.

R. H. STROUD

BESLEY, FRED WILSON (1872–1960)

Born February 16, 1871 in Vienna, Virginia. University of Maryland, A.B. 1892, Sc.D. 1912; Yale University School of Forestry, M.F. 1904. Public school teacher 1892–1900; student assistant in the Bureau of Forestry, United States Department of Agriculture, 1901–02; returned to the Bureau of Forestry, 1904. Appointed state forester of Maryland, 1906; also professor of forest management, University of West Virginia, 1943–45. On his retirement as state forester in 1942 he held the national record for continuous service, having served for 36 years. During this period he maintained the political independence of the Department. He also established high standards of service for the employees under his direction. Associate professor of forestry, University of Maryland, 1923–42. A member of the Society of American Foresters for 52 years; elected Fellow in 1940. Served as treasurer of the Society, 1922–24; chairman of the Allegheny Section, 1927; and a member of the Council for three terms, 1934–37. President of the Yale Forestry School Alumni Association, 1925–26; president of the Association of State Foresters, 1925–26; a director of The American Forestry Association; and a member of numerous state and federal boards and committees. After retirement as state forester, he acquired timber holdings in Maryland, managing them through Besley and Rogers Forest Land Company. Died November 8, 1960.

SOCIETY OF AMERICAN FORESTERS

American Men of Science, 8 ed., 1949.
Journal of Forestry. Obituary, vol. 59:55, 1961.

BIRGE, EDWARD ASAHEL (1861–1950)

Born September 7, 1861 in Troy, New York. Williams College, A.B. 1873, A.M. 1875; Harvard University, Ph.D. 1878; University of Pittsburgh, Sc.D. 1897; Rensselaer Polytechnic Institute, Ph.D. 1924; University of Wisconsin, LL.D. 1905; University of Missouri, Ph.D. 1919. During 50 years at the University of Wisconsin—from instructor in 1875 to retirement as president in 1925, and for an additional 15 years as president emeritus—Birge, together with Chancey Juday, laid much of the foundation of limnology. His were the first detailed accounts (in Lake Mendota) of the summer stratification of temperature and oxygen; the first description of wind-induced water movements in stratified lakes (introducing the term "thermocline"); the first systematic measurements of penetration of solar radiation; and the concept of heat budgets. Pioneering studies with Juday on the chemical composition of plankton, dissolved gases, and on regional differences in water chemistry laid the basis for understanding and conservation of lake environments. He was commissioner of fisheries in Wisconsin, 1895–1915; member of the Wisconsin Conservation Commission, 1908–15; commissioner of forestry, 1907–15; director, Wisconsin Geological and Natural History Survey, 1897–1919; president, American Microscopical Society, 1902; president, American Fisheries Society, 1906–07. His bibliography lists 68 titles, which include 38 papers under single authorship and 21 in co-authorship with Juday. Died June 9, 1950.

CLIFFORD H. MORTIMER

MORTIMER, C. H., *An Explorer of Lakes.* University of Wisconsin Press, 1956.
SELLERY, G. C., *A. E. Birge, A Memoir.*

BOWERS, EDWARD AUGUSTUS (1857–1924)

Born August 2, 1857 in Hartford, Connecticut. Yale University, A.B. 1879, LL.B. 1881. Lawyer and judge in Dakota Territory 1882–86; then served for three years as an inspector of public lands for the United States Department of the Interior; assistant commissioner of the General Land Office, 1893–95. He practiced law in New Haven from 1898 onward, and from 1901 to 1917 he lectured on forest law at the Yale University Forest School. One of America's pioneer forest conservationists, he was a director and twice secretary of The American Forestry Association. As early as 1887 he prepared a detailed plan for the reservation from sale and exploitation of the nation's vast acreage of public timberlands. His report on "The Present Condition of the Public Lands," at a joint meeting of The American Forestry Association and the American

Economic Association in December 1890, brought about demands for reform in their protection from theft and trespass. He is credited with drafting the act of March 3, 1891 that provided for creation of forest reserves (now the national forests), the act named by Gifford Pinchot as "the most important legislation in the history of forestry." In addition, he was influential in initiating the events leading up to the act of June 4, 1897 which provided for the administration of the forest reserves and made it possible for the practice of forestry on them. The author of numerous papers and speeches on resource conservation, he was an effective critic of the government's neglect of the public lands and timber, and an exponent of action leading to their eventual management in the public interest. Died December 8, 1924.

HENRY CLEPPER

Who Was Who in America, vol. 4, 1961–68.

BRADLEY, HAROLD CORNELIUS (1878–)

Born November 25, 1878 in Oakland, California. University of California, A.B. 1900; Yale University, Ph.D. (chemistry) 1905. In 1905 he taught chemistry at Yale University Medical School. Beginning in 1906 he taught physiological chemistry at the University of Wisconsin until his retirement in 1949. During part of his career, he was a director of research at the Woods Hole Marine Laboratory in Massachusetts. From 1908 to 1914 he was a volunteer aid to John Muir in the attempt to prevent flooding of the Hetch-Hetchy Valley of California. In 1912 he wrote the first article on ecological changes involving soil erosion from overuse in the Sierra Club *Bulletin*, and contributed articles to other journals and conservation magazines. In 1952 he began the first of several trips on the Colorado River and its tributaries; his findings were used in the Sierra Club campaign in opposition to the construction of dams in Dinosaur National Monument. In 1955 he started a campaign for the clean-up of litter in national parks, forests, and desert areas; his efforts resulted in an educational program whereby many visitors now carry out their litter. He served as a member of the Board of Directors of the Sierra Club, 1951–61; was president, 1957–59; and has been honorary vice president since 1961. He received the John Muir Award for Conservation from the Sierra Club in 1966, and was appointed to the Hall of Fame for Skiiers in 1968 for pioneering mountain and cross-country skiing in the Sierra Nevada and midwest areas.

LUELLA K. SAWYER

American Men of Science (The Physical and Biological Sciences), 10th ed., 1960.
Sierra Club Handbook, 1967.
Who's Who in America, 1950–51.

BRADLEY, PRESTON (1888–   )

Born August 8, 1888 in Linden, Michigan. Hamilton College of Law, D.C.L.; Lake Forest College, LL.D.; Yankton College, LL.D.; Meadville Theological School, University of Chicago, D.D.; Lincoln Memorial University, L.H.D. He was one of the "54 Founders" of the Izaak Walton League of America in Chicago in 1922 and gave his national organization its name. He has served three terms as president of the League, was elected honorary president in 1968, and was elected to its Hall of Fame in 1960. Founder of the Peoples Church of Chicago in 1912, he has been its pastor since that time. He has conducted 46 years of continuous broadcasting on Chicago radio stations as well as numerous television appearances; his sermons and broadcasts have dealt much with natural resource conservation. He was honored in 1967 by proclamation of the Governor of Illinois and Mayor of Chicago designating October 20 as Preston Bradley Day. He is a life member of the Chicago Art Institute, the Adventurer's Club, and the Chicago Historical Society, and has served for 46 years as a member of the Board of Chicago Public Library. He has been publisher of *The Liberalist*, a church magazine, for 47 years, and is the author of ten books and numerous special articles, many dealing with environmental problems.

ROBERT L. HERBST

BRANDBORG, STEWART MONROE (1925–   )

Born February 2, 1925 in Lewiston, Idaho. University of Montana, B.A. (wildlife technology) 1949; University of Idaho (wildlife management) 1951. He was then employed by the Idaho Cooperative Wildlife Unit, University of Idaho, through 1953. One of his studies was published in 1954 as the *Life History and Management of the Mountain Goat in Idaho* by the Idaho Department of Fish and Game. As assistant conservation director of the National Wildlife Federation, 1954–60, he prepared and edited its *Conservation Report*. Elected to the Council of The Wilderness Society in 1956, he joined its staff as director of special projects in 1960, and became executive director in 1964. He was associated with the development of the Wilderness Act of 1964 from its introduction as a bill in 1956. He has lectured and presented numerous papers on the subject of wilderness preservation later published in *The Living Wilderness* and other publications. He conducted a seminar on conservation classics for the Audubon Naturalist Society of the Central Atlantic States, and has participated in state and regional conferences and workshops in conservation. He is a Fellow of the American Association for the Advancement of Science, and a director of Defenders of Wildlife and of the Gifford Pinchot Institute for Conservation Studies. He was a member of the National Conservation Committee of the Junior Chamber of Commerce, 1958–59, and has been a member of the Executive Committee of the Natural Resources Council of America. His affiliations include other national conservation organizations. His career has been notable for assistance to forestry and range management, wildlife research, public education in general natural resources conservation, and for effective communication with citizens organizations and resources agencies, both federal and state.

MICHAEL NADEL

BREWER, GEORGE EMERSON, JR. (1899–1968)

Born November 13, 1899 in New York City. Yale College, B.A. 1922. He taught English at Yale University, 1922–25, at the University of Buffalo, 1926–27, and at Columbia University in 1928. During the 1930s he lived in Massachusetts, and was associated with the Federal Theater, 1936–38. During World War II, he was a lieutenant colonel in the Army Air Force. In 1948 he participated in the establishment of the Conservation Foundation in New York City (now with headquarters in Washington, D. C.), and as vice president was active in formulating its educational program. He was vice president until 1965 when he retired, and a trustee thereafter. He served as governor of the Pinchot Institute for Conservation Studies and was a director of the National Parks Association. He helped organize and later held the position of director of the Student Conservation Association. He was a member of the Advisory Committee of the Hudson Valley Conservation Commission and was trustee of the Association for Protection of the Adirondacks. He was author of many articles on conservation topics, and co-author and producer of the "Yours Is the Land" and "Living Earth" series of educational films distributed for the Conservation Foundation by the Encyclopaedia Britannica films. Died February 20, 1968.

THE CONSERVATION FOUNDATION

BREWER, WILLIAM HENRY (1828–1910)

Born September 14, 1828 in Poughkeepsie, New York. Yale University, Ph.B. 1852, A.M. 1859, LL.D. 1903; Washington and Jefferson College, Ph.D. 1880. After teaching chemistry and geology at Washington College, Pennsylvania, from 1858 to 1860, he assisted in the geological survey of California, 1860–64. He returned to the Yale Sheffield Scientific School as professor of agriculture in 1864, and retired in 1903 in emeritus status. He was one of a small group of scientists concerned about the destruction of the nation's timber. For the ninth census of 1870 he prepared a special report "The

Woodlands and Forest Systems of the United States," published in the *Statistical Atlas* of 1874; it contained most of the knowledge about forests available at that time. As early as 1873 he gave lectures on forests and forestry at Yale, probably the first such instruction ever offered in an American university. During the 1870s and 1880s, he helped bring to the attention of the government the need for forest conservation. He was a member of the committee of the American Association for the Advancement of Science that memorialized the government in 1874, resulting in the appointment of the first forestry agent in the Department of Agriculture and the beginning of forestry as a function of the federal government. He was a member of the Forest Commission of 1896, appointed by the National Academy of Sciences at the request of the Secretary of the Interior, to make recommendations for a federal forest policy. He was active in The American Forestry Association, and was one of the early associate members of the Society of American Foresters. He was the author of more than 100 papers on agricultural, geological, and related subjects, and edited *Botany of California* in 1876, one of the first botanical treatises of that state. Died November 2, 1910.

HENRY CLEPPER

National Cyclopaedia of American Biography, 1906.
Who Was Who in America, 1897–1942.

BREWSTER, WILLIAM   (1851–1919)

Born July 5, 1851 in Wakefield, Massachusetts. Amherst College, A.M. (honorary) 1880; Harvard University, A.M. (honorary) 1899. He left his career in banking in 1880 to assist in developing the collection of birds and mammals at the Boston Society of Natural History. In 1885 he was head of the Department of Mammals and Birds at the Cambridge Massachusetts Museum of Comparative Zoology, and after 1900 was curator of the Department of Birds. A founder of the Nuttall Ornithological Club in Cambridge in 1873, he was president for many years. One of the three organizers of the American Ornithologists' Union in 1883, he was president from 1895 to 1898. He was organizer also of one of the first Audubon Societies, was later a director of the National Association of Audubon Societies, and was long the president of the Massachusetts Audubon Society. For years he was a director of the Massachusetts Fish and Game Department, and was a founder of the American Game Protective and Propagation Association in 1911. He maintained a private museum of ornithology at Cambridge and a wildlife sanctuary near Concord where he studied the ecology of birds and small mammals. He wrote more than 300 papers, scientific and literary, as well as books and bulletins but is best remembered for his book *Bird Migration*, 1886. His writings comprise important additions to the literature of American ornithology, whose development he notably influenced. He was a Fellow of the American Association for the Advancement of Science and of the American Academy of Arts and Sciences. The William Brewster memorial (gold) medal was created by the American Ornithologists' Union in 1919 in his honor, to be awarded periodically to authors of works on birds of the Western Hemisphere. Died July 11, 1919.

NATIONAL AUDUBON SOCIETY

Dictionary of American Biography, 1929.
National Cyclopaedia of American Biography, 1932.
Who Was Who in America, 1897–1942.
"William Brewster, 1851–1919," *Bird Lore*, 21(5):277–86, September–October, 1919.

BROMFIELD, LOUIS (1896–1956)

Born December 27, 1896 in Mansfield, Ohio. Student at Cornell University College of Agriculture and Columbia University School of Journalism; Marshall College, Litt.D. (honorary). During World War I, he served both in the French Army and with the American Expeditionary Forces. Internationally known author, soil conservationist, and scientific farmer, he lived abroad until 1938 collecting material for his many books and extensive writings, and a year later purchased Malabar Farm in Pleasant Valley, Ohio. Here he developed his philosophy of agriculture and conservation, summed up in several of his books, notably *Pleasant Valley*, 1945; *Malabar Farm*, 1948; *Out of the Earth*, 1950; and *From My Experience*, 1955. In addition to his conservation writings, he gave thousands of talks on radio and television, and before live audiences throughout the world. He was an active promoter and vice president of the organization Friends of the Land. Besides awards and honors, including the Pulitzer Prize conferred on him for his literary attainments, he received wide recognition for his conservation work, including the Audubon Medal of the National Audubon Society and the medal of the Garden Clubs of America. Died March 18, 1956.

H. T. MARSHALL

ANDERSON, DAVID, *Louis Bromfield*. New York: Twayne Publishers, Inc., 1964.
Oxford Companion of American Literature, 4th ed., 1965.
Who Was Who in America, 1951–60.

BROOME, HARVEY (1902–68)

Born July 15, 1902 in Knoxville, Tennessee. University of Tennessee, A.B. 1923; Harvard Law School, LL.B. 1926. He entered private law practice in 1926 and made the legal profession his career, but his avocation was conservation. One of the eight original organizers of the Wilderness Society in 1935, he was a member of the governing council from its inception, was vice president in 1948, and was president from 1957 until 1968. He became a Trustee of the Robert Marshall Wilderness Fund in 1948. In 1959 he was appointed a member of the Advisory Council of the Outdoor Recreation Resources Review Commission. He was president of the Smoky Mountains Hiking Club in 1932, a director of the Great Smoky Mountains Conservation Association from 1932 to 1935, and president of the East Tennessee Historical Society from 1945 to 1947. He was a member of the Board of Directors of the Student Conservation Association. He contributed to the educational process which led to the establishment of the National Wilderness Preservation System in 1964. He traveled this country's wildernesses from coast to coast, on foot, by horse, and by canoe, but his knowledge of the Smokies was especially profound. A skilled essayist, his published writings include articles in *The Living Wilderness, National Parks Magazine, Nature Magazine,* and elsewhere. An unpublished book, tentatively called *Out Under the Skies of the Great Smoky Mountains,* was distilled from a series of his journals. He was a member of numerous conservation organizations, including an honorary membership in the Tennessee Outdoor Writers Association. Died March 8, 1968.

MICHAEL NADEL

The Living Wilderness, Winter 1967–68, vol. 31, no. 99.
Who's Who in America, 1964–65.

BROWER, DAVID ROSS (1912–   )

Born July 1, 1912 in Berkeley, California. University of California, 1930–31; Hobart College and William Smith College, Geneva, New York, Sc.D. (honorary) 1967. From 1941 to 1952 he was editor for the University of California Press. Elected a director of the Sierra Club, 1941–43 and 1946–53; appointed executive director in 1952, a position he held until 1969. He was narrator and script writer for three influential motion pictures on endangered wilderness areas: "Wilderness River Trail," 1954; "The Two Yosemites," 1955; and "Wilderness Alps of Stehekin," 1958. Among the related organizations in which he has been active as an officer are the Natural Resources Council of America (chairman, 1955–57); North Cascades Conservation Council of which he has been a director since 1957; Trustees for Conservation (secretary, 1960–61 and 1964–65); California Conservation Council (vice president, 1959); president of Friends of the Earth; and executive director of the John Muir Institute. Editor of *Manual of Ski Mountaineering,* 1942 revised 1961; *Going Light,* 1951; *The Meaning of Wilderness to Science,* 1960; *This Is The American Earth,* 1960; *Wilderness, America's Living Heritage,* 1961; *These We Inherit, The Parklands of America,* 1962; *The Place No One Knew: Glen Canyon on the Colorado,* 1963; *Time and the River Flowing: Grand Canyon on the*

Colorado, 1963; *Gentle Wilderness; The Sierra Nevada,* 1964; *Wildlands in Our Civilization,* 1964; *Sierra Club Wilderness Handbook,* 1964; *Not Man Apart,* 1965; *The Wild Cascades: Forgotten Parkland,* 1965; *Everest: The West Ridge,* 1965; *Summer Island: Penobscot Country,* 1966; *Glacier Bay: The Land and the Silence,* 1967; *Central Park Country: A Tune Within Us,* 1968; Sierra Club *Bulletin,* 1946–53. He was a leader in movements to keep dams out of Dinosaur National Monument and the Grand Canyon, and was involved also in a battle for a North Cascades National Park. Recipient of merit award from the California Conservation Council in 1953; certificate of merit, Nash Conservation Award in 1953; Paul Bartsch Award of the Audubon Naturalist Society of Central Atlantic States in 1967; Cary Thomas Award in 1964 for originating Format Books to bring public attention to endangered places.

LUELLA K. SAWYER

Sierra Club Handbook, 1967.
Who's Who in America, 1968–69.
Who's Who in the West, 1968.

BROWN, CARL BARRIER (1910–63)

Born November 12, 1910, in Salisbury, North Carolina. University of North Carolina, B.S. 1929; University of Cincinnati, M.A. (geology) 1931. He was assistant geologist with Virginia Geological Survey, 1931–32; then surveyor in the Bureau of Chemistry and Soils, United States Department of Agriculture, 1932–33; and junior geologist with the United States Geological Survey, Department of the Interior, 1934. Joining the Soil Conservation Service of the United States Department of Agriculture in 1934, he was successively junior engineer, assistant engineer, associate geologist, geologist, senior soil conservationist, and research specialist (sedimentation). From 1950 until his death, he served as assistant chief of operations, director of the Planning Division, and assistant to the assistant administrator for watersheds. One of the principal architects of the legislation that gave life to the small watershed idea, he was for several years in charge of the agency's sedimentation research. After passage of the Flood Control Act of 1936, he concentrated on watershed protection problems, and was instrumental in the development of small watershed conservation techniques. He was consultant to the Secretary of Agriculture, the Bureau of the Budget, and Congressional committees during the planning and drafting of the legislation that became the Small Watershed Protection and Flood Prevention Act of 1954; after its enactment he was one of its leading implementers. In recognition of his work in 1959, he received the Superior Service Award of the United States Department of Agriculture. Author of *The Control of Reservoir Silting*, a Department of Agriculture publication, he wrote 75 other papers on sedimentation, watershed protection, soil conservation, water supply, flood prevention, and geology. He was a member of the World Bank Agricultural Mission to Japan in 1954, and a member of the American Society of Civil Engineers, the American Geophysical Union, and the Soil Conservation Society of America. Died May 5, 1963.

F. GLENNON LOYD

Who's Who in Engineering, 8th ed., 1959.

BROWN, CLAUDEUS JETHRO DANIELS (1904–   )

Born August 15, 1904 at Farr West, Utah. Brigham Young University, M.S. (zoology); University of Michigan, Ph.D. (limnology) 1933. He conducted fisheries surveys in Utah, Washington, and Oregon in 1934–35 for the United States Bureau of Fisheries; served as instructor in zoology, Montana State University, 1935–37; and was assistant director of the Institute for Fisheries Research, Michigan Department of Conservation, 1937–44, his principal responsibilities being the day-to-day operation of the Institute and the supervision of lake and stream surveys. During 1944–45, he served as chief of the Technical Section of the Washington State Pollution Commission; and was in charge of reservoir investigations

in the Portland, Oregon office of the United States Fish and Wildlife Service, 1945–47. Since 1947 while on the zoology faculty at
Montana State University, he organized the curriculum in fish and
wildlife management, conducted in-service training courses for fish
and game personnel in Montana and Wyoming, and advised candidates for M.S. and Ph.D. degrees. On leave from Montana State, he
served with the FAO in Paraguay, 1956–57, and with the Ford
Foundation in Egypt, 1963–64 and 1966. He has served as executive secretary, editor, and president of the American Microscopical
Society, as president-elect of the American Fisheries Society, and
on the Editorial Board of the American Society of Limnology and
Oceanography. He is a charter member of the Wildlife Society, a
fellow of the American Institute of Fishery Research Biologists, a
member of the Fisheries Society of the British Isles, and of numerous other professional societies. He is the author of over 50 papers
in fisheries and limnology. His broad experience in research, the
academic field, and with state and federal fisheries agencies have
made him especially effective in the training of fishery biologists.

JOHN L. FUNK

American Men of Science (The Physical and Biological Sciences), 11th ed., 1965.

BROWNING, BRYCE COGSIL (1894–   )

Born June 19, 1894 in Adamsville, Ohio. Educated at Muskingum
College, LL.D. His career in conservation began in 1927 with his
appointment as manager of the Zanesville, Ohio Chamber of Commerce, which, under his leadership, undertook a campaign to establish the Muskingum Watershed Conservancy District. The conservancy proposal went beyond conventional flood control projects;
it incorporated concepts of total watershed protection, multiple uses
of reservoirs with emphasis on soil conservation, forestry, and public recreation. When the Conservancy District was established near
New Philadelphia, Ohio, June 3, 1933, he was appointed its secretary–treasurer. During his incumbency, the cooperative federal–
state–local undertaking involved 60,000 acres in 18 counties and

had attained international recognition. Prior to his retirement in 1965 he had been active in other national and regional conservation bodies. He is a former director and honorary life member of the American Forestry Association, a past president of the Ohio Forestry Association, and an honorary life member of the Soil Conservation Society of America. He served as a member of the Ohio Natural Resources Commission, 1949–58, then held a four-year membership on the Ohio Water Commission. In 1949 he received the American Forestry Association's award for public service in conservation; in 1956 Friends of the Land awarded him the Hugh Bennett gold medal for conservation service; and in 1958 he received the Ohio Farm Bureau agricultural service award as well as an award of recognition by the Ohio Forestry Association. On December 14, 1968 he became the first living person to be installed as a member of the Ohio Conservation Hall of Fame.

JOSEPH W. PENFOLD

BROWNING, GEORGE MONROE (1908–   )

Born December 4, 1908 in Verona, Missouri. University of Missouri, B.S. (agriculture) 1932; University of West Virginia, M.S. (agriculture) 1934; Ph.D. (soils) 1938. He was soil scientist in West Virginia for the United States Department of Interior Soil Erosion Service from 1934 to 1935. In 1935 he became soil conservationist for the United States Department of Agriculture Soil Conservation Service, in charge of soil and water conservation research, serving first in West Virginia then shifting to Iowa in 1941. He joined the Iowa State University staff in 1947 as research professor of soils and was advanced to assistant director of the Agricultural Experiment Station in 1949 and to associate director in 1951. In 1967 he was appointed regional director of the Association of North Central Agricultural Experiment Stations. He is the author of over 50 technical articles and bulletins dealing with soil structure, tillage, soil and water loss measurements, and other phases of soil and water conservation. He is recognized for his leadership in the development of soil erosion factors used universally for estimating run off and erosion. In 1958 he represented the state agricultural experiment stations in a study of national soil and water conservation research needs. In 1965 he was co-chairman of a joint United States Department of Agriculture–State Agricultural Experiment Station task force which prepared a report evaluating and projecting agricultural research needs for the decade ahead. The report was submitted to and approved by Congress. He is a charter member and Fellow of the Soil Conservation Society of America of which he was president, 1963–64; a Fellow of the American Society of Agronomy; and a member of the Soil Science Society of America.

FRANK W. SCHALLER

American Men of Science (The Physical and Biological Sciences), 11th ed., 1965. Who's Who in America, 1968–69.

BRUCE, DONALD (1884–1966)

Born on July 23, 1884, in Newtonville, Massachusetts. Yale University, M.F. 1910. He served five years with United States Forest Service in Montana starting as forest assistant and advancing to forest supervisor. He spent six years as assistant and associate professor of forestry at University of California. After serving in France as captain on the staff of 10th Engineers during World War I, he spent seven years as part-time consultant with the Forest Service in Washington, D. C., in charge of forest measurements for purpose of improving methods of forest mensurational research and in training promising research foresters. From 1923 to date of death he was a partner in the consulting firm which started as Mason & Stevens and is now known as Mason, Bruce & Girard. During the time that the firm was known as Mason & Stevens, he was in charge of a branch office in Washington, D. C. An important contribution to conservation was his sound advice and assistance to industrial forest owners in the pine regions of the western United States in combining selective cutting practices with profitable utilization methods. The author of numerous Forest Service bulletins and articles in periodicals, his best known work, *Forest Mensuration*, written in collaboration with F. X. Schumacher, has been a standard college textbook since 1935. With James W. Girard he wrote *Board Foot Volume Tables for 16-Foot Logs, Board Foot Volume Tables for 32-Foot Logs*, and *Board Foot Volume Tables Based on Total Height*, standard references known to all professional foresters. In 1961 he published *Prism Cruising in Western United States and Use Thereof*. Died October 16, 1966.

CARL A. NEWPORT

American Men of Science (The Physical and Biological Sciences), 10th ed., 1955.

BUCHHEISTER, CARL WILLIAM (1901–   )

Born January 20, 1901 in Baltimore, Maryland. Johns Hopkins University, B.A. 1923; Pace College, LL.D.; Bowdoin College, L.H.D. Beginning in 1925, he taught in private schools in Baltimore and Long Island, New York, and was also for eight years founder–director of a camp for boys in New Hampshire. From 1936 to 1939, he was executive director of the Massachusetts Audubon Society, and beginning in 1936 was for two decades director of the Audubon Camp of Maine, a summer workshop for teachers and adult leaders. In 1940 he was appointed assistant director of the National Audubon Society, New York City; was advanced to senior vice president in 1959; and retired in 1966 as president emeritus. Active in other ornithological and conservation organizations, he has been on the Board of Directors of the Audubon Society of Canada; was honorary vice president of the American Forestry Association in 1963; was a member of the Citizens Committee for the Outdoor Recreation Resources Review Commission; was chairman of the Natural Resources Council of America, 1964–1966; and is on the Board of Trustees of the National Parks Association. A life-long field naturalist, he has written extensively for *Audubon Magazine* and other conservation publications, and is a popular lecturer on nature subjects. His career has been notable for his ardent defense of wildlife and its environment, and for his effective exposition through public education of the value of natural resources to the nation.

Henry Clepper

Who's Who in America, 1968–69.

BURNHAM, JOHN BIRD (1869–1939)

Born March 16, 1869 in Newcastle, Delaware. Trinity College, Connecticut, B.A. 1891, D.Sc. (honorary) 1939. From 1891 to 1897 he was business manager of *Forest and Stream Magazine* in New York City, resigning his position to join the first Klondike Gold Rush. In 1898 he purchased a farm in Willsboro, New York, which he operated as the Highlands Game Preserve. Early in 1905 he was appointed chief game protector of the State of New York and three years later was named deputy commissioner of fish and game; in 1911 he became acting commissioner. In that year he was selected by the founders of the American Game Protective and Propagation Association to become its first president. In 1915 he was a member of a three-man committee selected to codify New York's fish and game law. One of the first objectives of the American Game Protection and Propagation Association was to secure the enactment of a strong federal law for the protection of migratory birds. He became the organizer of the public support for such a law, which became reality with the enactment of the Weeks-McLean Law on March 4, 1913. He was named chairman of the Advisory Committee to the Department of Agriculture on the Migratory Bird Law established by the new law. When the constitutionality of the Weeks-McLean Law was challenged, he again led the campaign to obtain the ratification of the Migratory Bird Treaty with Great Britain for Canada. He also served as chairman of a United States Forest Service Committee on Game in the National Forests and was a member of the Committee on Game and Fur-bearing Animals of the National Conference on Outdoor Recreation of 1924. In 1921 he led an expedition to Siberia to collect specimens of the unclassified

Marco Polo sheep for American museums. His book, *The Rim of Mystery*, is an account of the expedition. In 1926 he was awarded the gold medal of the Camp Fire Club of America. Died September 24, 1939.

JAMES B. TREFETHEN

"John Bird Burnham, 1869–1939," *American Wildlife*, 28(6):244–46, November–December, 1939.
Who Was Who in America, 1897–1942.

BURROUGHS, JOHN (1837–1921)

Born April 3, 1837 near Roxbury, New York. Attended Ashland Collegiate Institute and Cooperstown Seminary; Yale University, Litt.D. (honorary) 1910; Colgate University, L.H.D. 1911; University of Georgia, honorary doctorate, 1915. After teaching school for eight years, he was a clerk in the Treasury Department, Washington, D. C. from 1863 to 1873. In 1874 he bought a farm at Esopus, New York, but continued as a national bank examiner until 1884. He wrote many books as well as nature essays, published in the nation's foremost literary journals. Through his writings he aroused wide public interest in the natural world and ornithology in particular. Although not a biologist in the technical sense, he was an accurate observer and contributed to scientific as well as popular information about the flora and fauna of the Hudson River Valley and the Catskill Mountains. He had the rare ability to express his love of nature in clear, poetic language which met with enthusiastic response in thousands of readers. He wrote twenty-seven books, among them: *Wake Robin*, 1871; *Winter Sunshine*, 1875; *Birds and Poets*, 1877; *Locusts and Wild Honey*, 1879; *Fresh Fields*, 1884; *Signs and Seasons*, 1886; *Indoor Studies*, 1889; *Walt Whitman: A Study*, 1896; *The Light of Day*, 1900; *John James Audubon*, 1902; *Literary Values*, 1904; *Ways of Nature*, 1905; *Camping and Tramping with Roosevelt*, 1907; *Leaf and Tendril*, 1908; *The Summit of the Years*, 1913. He was elected a member of the American Academy of Arts and Letters. In 1926 the John Burroughs medal was created in his honor to be awarded periodically by the American Museum of Natural History. Died March 29, 1921.

EVE HERBST

CHAPMAN, FRANK M. "John Burroughs." *Bird Lore*, vol. 23, no. 3.
Concise Dictionary of American Biography, 1964.
Dictionary of American Biography, 1929.
FISHER, CLYDE. "With John Burroughs at Slabsides." *Natural History*, vol. 31, no. 5.
National Cyclopaedia of American Biography, 1:247–48, 1898.
Who Was Who in America, 1897–1942.
WILEY, FARIDA, ed. *John Burroughs' America: Selections from the Writings of the Hudson River Naturalist.*

BUTLER, OVID McQUOT (1880–1960)

Born July 14, 1880 in Indianapolis, Indiana. Butler University, A.B. 1902, D.Sc. (honorary) 1956; Yale Forest School, M.F. 1907. Entered United States Forest Service in 1907, assigned to the Boise National Forest in Idaho and later to Ogden, Utah, district office where he was assistant chief and chief of the Division of Forest Management. At the outbreak of World War I he made investigations of lumber distribution with reports published by the Forest Service; and in 1922 was named assistant director of the Forest Products Laboratory at Madison, Wisconsin. In that same year he was appointed forester by the American Forestry Association; was executive secretary and editor, 1923–45; and executive director emeritus from 1948 until his death. As editor of *American Forests* he was one of the nation's most influential exponents of forestry and resource conservation; the Association was in the forefront of every national movement for improved resource management and for the development of parks and recreation. He was a Fellow and president (1928) of the Society of American Foresters; United States delegate to the 1936 World Forestry Congress in Budapest; member of the advisory board of the National Arboretum; member-at-large of the National Council, Boy Scouts of America. Named in 1950 as "one of the ten most influential men in American forestry"; recipient in 1952 of the American Forestry Association's Distinguished Service Award. Author of hundreds of articles and editorials on forestry and conservation, and author–editor of the books, *American Conservation, Rangers of the Shield,* and *Youth Rebuilds,* all published in 1935. Died February 20, 1960.

FRED. E. HORNADAY

New York Times. Obituary, February 21, 1960.

CAHALANE, VICTOR HARRISON (1901–   )

Born October 17, 1901 at Charlestown, New Hampshire. Massachusetts Agricultural College, B.S. (biology), 1924; Yale University, M.F. (forestry) 1927. During further graduate studies at the University of Michigan, he also served as an instructor in the School of Forestry and Conservation followed by employment as a deer investigator by the Michigan Department of Conservation in 1929–30. From 1931 to 1934 he was director of the Cranbrook Institute of Science. In 1934 he began his career in the National Park Service as a wildlife technician, and became chief of the Wildlife Division in 1939. When wildlife studies in the national parks were transferred to the Fish and Wildlife Service in 1940, he was put in charge of the section on national park wildlife. In 1944 he returned to the National Park Service as chief of the Biology Branch, which position he held until 1955. During his national park career he was a leader in pioneering and developing the modern philosophy of habitat protection and management through ungulate population controls. At the same time he maintained an interest in and contributed substantially to world-wide wildlife conservation through his active participation in the International Union for the Conservation of Nature, as well as writing his most important book, *Mammals of North America.* He participated in preparing *Fading Trails,* and conducted a study and wrote *A Biological Survey of Katmai National Monument.* In 1955 he became assistant director of the New York State Museum, and there continued his prolific writings on a variety of natural history subjects, retiring from this position in January, 1967. As extra-career contributions, he served as the first secretary of the Wildlife Society and became its president in

1940. He served as an advisor to the National Parks Board of Trustees of the Union of South Africa in 1950–51, and as president of the Society of Mammalogists in 1959. Currently he is president of the Defenders of Wildlife.

C. GORDON FREDINE

American Men of Science (The Physical and Biological Sciences), 11th ed., 1965.

CAIN, STANLEY ADAIR (1902–)

Born June 19, 1902 in Jefferson County, Indiana. Butler University, B.S. 1924; University of Chicago, M.S. 1927, Ph.D. (plant ecology) 1930; University of Montreal, Sc.D. (honorary) 1959. From instructor in botany at Butler University he advanced to associate professor; he was then an assistant professor at Indiana University, and a Waterman instructor from 1933 to 1935. At the University of Tennessee he rose from assistant professor to professor. In 1940 he was chosen a Guggenheim Fellow. In 1945 he was the chief of the science section at the United States Army University in France, and from 1946 to 1950 he was botanist at the Cranbrook Institute of Science. Currently, he holds the position of professor of conservation at the University of Michigan, and is chairman of the Department of Conservation. From 1966 to 1969 he served as assistant secretary of the Department of the Interior in charge of wildlife and national parks. In 1938 he held the office of treasurer of the Ecological Society of America; later he became vice president and president. He has served as a member of the advisory board of the Conservation Foundation, and was an ecological expert on the Technical Assistance Mission to Brazil for UNESCO in 1955. In 1956 he was chairman of a panel on environmental biology for the National Science Foundation. Three years later he was vice president of the International Botany Congress held in Canada, and in 1959 received a distinguished achievement award from Michigan. He is a member of the Michigan Conservancy, and has served as its chairman. He is a member, and has been chairman, of the advisory board of National Parks, Historical Sites, Buildings, and

Monuments; a member of the advisory board of the United States Department of the Interior; and chairman of the ad hoc committee of the International Biological Program of the National Academy of Science, 1963–64. He has served as secretary and vice president of the American Association for the Advancement of Science. The Botanical Society of America presented him a certificate of merit in 1956. He is the author of many books and papers including a *Manual of Vegetation Analysis* and *Plant Geography*.

THE CONSERVATION FOUNDATION

American Men of Science (The Physical and Biological Sciences), 11th ed., 1965.

CALLISON, CHARLES HUGH (1913–)

Born November 6, 1913 in Alberta, Canada. University of Missouri School of Journalism, B.J. 1937. Started employment in 1937 as a newspaperman in Kansas and Missouri; joined the staff of the Missouri Conservation Commission in 1941 as education and information specialist. After helping to establish the Commission's magazine, *Missouri Conservationist*, he became its editor. Resigned in 1946; was named executive secretary of the Conservation Federation of Missouri, a league of sportsmen's and conservation organizations, and edited the quarterly *Missouri Wildlife*. In 1951 he was appointed to the staff of the National Wildlife Federation in Washington, D. C., serving from 1953 onward as secretary and director of conservation. While with the Federation he gained recognition as an authority on federal and state laws and policies affecting natural resources. He was editor of the information bulletin *Legislative News Service*, issued to the 40 member organizations by the Natural Resources Council of America, and from 1957 to 1959, he was chairman of the Council. In 1960 he was appointed assistant to the president of the National Audubon Society in New York City, and in 1966 was elected as the Society's executive vice president. He contributes the department National Outlook, a current report on national and state conservation matters, to *Audubon* magazine, the Society's bimonthly organ, and serves on its Editorial Board.

His official appointments to conservation bodies have included the President's Advisory Committee on Youth Fitness; the Advisory Committee on Fish and Wildlife of the Department of the Interior; the chairmanship of the Legislative Committee of the International Association of Game, Fish and Conservation Commissioners; the Federal Water Pollution Control Advisory Board; and President Nixon's Task Force on Natural Resources and the Environment, 1968–69. He has written widely on conservation subjects, including the book *Man and Wildlife in Missouri*, a history of Missouri's Conservation Commission, and is the editor of *America's Natural Resources*, revised printing 1967, sponsored by the Natural Resources Council of America.

HENRY CLEPPER

National Audubon Society, personnel files.
Who's Who in America, 1968–69.

CARHART, ARTHUR HAWTHORNE (1892–   )

Born September 28, 1892 in Mapleton, Iowa. Iowa State College, B.S. (landscape engineering) 1916. Following service in the United States Army during World War I, he was employed as recreation engineer by the United States Forest Service in 1919 and was assigned to the Rocky Mountain District with headquarters in Denver. He made land-use studies and management plans for recreational development in the national forests of Colorado, Minnesota, and elsewhere. Leaving the Forest Service in 1922 for private practice in landscape architecture and city planning, he returned to government employment in 1938 as the first director of the "federal aid to wildlife restoration program" in the Colorado Game and Fish Department. During World War II, he was information specialist for the Office of Price Administration in Denver. A prolific writer, he is the author of hundreds of published articles and 25 books, including *Water or Your Life, Timber in Your Life, The National Forests, Planning for Wild Land Management, Fresh Water Fishing*, and *Hunting North American Deer*. His writings have earned him an award from the Authors League, the Founders Award of the Izaak Walton League of America in 1956, the Jade of Chiefs Award of the Outdoor Writers Association of America, and the Distinguished Service Award of American Forest Products Industries, Inc. in 1964. He conceived and promoted the establishment of the Conservation Library Center of the Denver Public Library and has been its consultant since its creation in 1960.

JOSEPH W. PENFOLD

Who's Who in America, 1968–69.

CARLANDER, KENNETH DIXON (1915–)

Born May 25, 1915 in Gary, Indiana. University of Minnesota, B.A. 1936, M.S. 1938, Ph.D. 1943. He joined the Minnesota Department of Conservation as aquatic biologist in 1938; resigned in 1946 (after two years' leave of absence for military service) to become assistant professor of zoology and leader of the cooperative fishery research unit at Iowa State University. In the years since, he has achieved distinction at Iowa State by guiding upwards of 100 graduates (28 with doctorates) in fishery science, many of whom hold important positions in government, industry, and education. Under auspices of the Ford Foundation, he spent a year (1965–66) helping to organize the proposed Institute of Aquatic Resources associated with the University of Alexandria, United Arab Republic. Active in the affairs of his profession, he is a member of more than 20 scientific and educational organizations, and holds (or has held) offices in many of them. Editorially, he assists seven scientific periodicals dealing with research in fishery biology. He has served the American Fisheries Society in numerous capacities for over 25 years, becoming the president in 1961. He received the Certificate of Merit, Nash Conservation Awards, 1953. Author or co-author of over 100 technical and semipopular articles in fields of ornithology, herpetology, and fisheries, he compiled the *Handbook of Freshwater Fishery Biology and First Supplement*, 1950, 1953, a useful source document for information on the biology of North American freshwater fishes. One of our leading conservation educators.

JOSEPH H. KUTKUHN

American Men of Science (The Physical and Biological Sciences), 11th ed., 1965.
World Who's Who in Science, 1968.

CARR, WILLIAM HENRY (1902–   )

Born April 11, 1902 in Astoria, New York. He left high school in 1919 to study museum techniques at the American Museum of Natural History in New York City, becoming assistant and later curator in the Department of Public Education, 1926–44. He was joint builder and director of the New York State Bear Mountain Park trailside museums, nature trails, and zoo, and also served as park naturalist for the Palisades Interstate Park Commission of New York and New Jersey, 1936–44. In 1938 he was recipient of the medal of the American Scenic and Historic Preservation Society. In 1946 he was technical editor for the United States Forest Service's Southwest Forest and Range Experiment Station, Tucson, Arizona, and was president of the Arizona Wildlife Federation from 1947 to 1950. As co-founder and director (now director emeritus) of the Arizona–Sonora Desert Museum in 1952, he originated the underground tunnel exhibit and the watershed exhibit "Water Street, U. S. A." From 1957 to 1959, he was co-founder and director (now director emeritus) of the Ghost Ranch Museum at Abiquiu, New Mexico. In 1959 he became director for outdoor education of the American Nature Association, was made a member-at-large of the National Council, Boy Scouts of America, received the conservation award and honorary life membership in the American Forestry Association, and was elected vice president of the Charles Lathrop Pack Forestry Association; in 1960 he was made an honorary life member of the American Museum of Natural History. He is the author of *Stir of Nature*, 1930; *African Shadows*, 1933; *Desert Parade*, 1947; and of 15 bulletins, together with numerous magazine articles, on the building and operation of living (outdoor) museums, a field of public education in which he has been a pioneer.

JAMES B. CRAIG

CARSON, RACHEL LOUISE (1907–64)

Born May 27, 1907 in Springdale, Pennsylvania. Pennsylvania College for Women, A.B. 1929, D. Litt. (honorary) 1952; Johns Hopkins University, A.M. 1932; Oberlin College, D.Sc. (honorary) 1952; Drexel Institute of Technology, D. Litt. (honorary) 1952; Smith College, D. Litt. (honorary) 1953. In 1931 she was engaged as a staff biologist at the University of Maryland, and in 1936 was appointed an aquatic biologist in the Bureau of Fisheries, Department of the Interior. This Bureau was merged with the Biological Survey of the Department of Agriculture to become the Department of the Interior's Fish and Wildlife Service, for which she was designated editor-in-chief in 1949 and from which she resigned in 1952 to devote her remaining career to writing. In addition to her widely read contributions on biological, ecological, and conservation subjects to periodical publications, she was the author of *Under the Sea Wind*, 1941; *The Sea Around Us*, 1951; *The Edge of the Sea*, 1956; and her enormously popular *Silent Spring*, 1962. One of the leading authors on natural history of the present century, she probably had as much influence as any contemporary conservationist on the developing concern by thinking Americans about their environment. Her books have been published throughout the world in many languages. In *Silent Spring*, her best known and most controversial work, she documented the massive injury to the ecology caused by unwise use of pesticides, but urged not that pest control be abandoned, but that more research be undertaken to enable pesticides to be used safely and to find alternate techniques for pest control. This book finally alerted Americans to the threats to their environment. For it, together with her previous writings, she was accorded many honors. In 1950 the American Association for the Advancement of Science conferred on her its science writing award. In 1952 she received the John Burroughs medal from the John Burroughs Memorial Association, the Frances Hutchinson medal of the Garden Club of America, the Distinguished Service Award of the Department of the Interior, and the Henry G. Bryant gold medal of the Geographical Society of Philadelphia. In addition, she received the Audubon Medal of the National Audubon Society, the gold medal of the New York Zoological Society, in 1963 the "conservationist of the year" award of the National Wildlife Federation, and other honors and citations, both literary and scientific. In 1969 the Coastal Maine Refuge was named the Rachel Carson National Wildlife Refuge by the Department of the Interior. Died April 14, 1964.

NATIONAL AUDUBON SOCIETY

National Cyclopaedia of American Biography, 1960.
Who Was Who in America, 1961–68.
Who's Who of American Women, 1964–65.

CARY, AUSTIN F.   (1865–1936)

Born July 31, 1865 at East Machias, Maine. Bowdoin College, A.B. 1887, M.A. 1890, D.Sc. 1922; studied entomology and biology at Johns Hopkins and Princeton Universities from 1888 to 1891. He taught at Bowdoin, 1887–88, then worked as a land cruiser and topographical surveyor and made entomological studies in Maine and New Hampshire. Some of his reports were published by the State of Maine and by *Paper Trade Journal*. He made several trips abroad, especially to Germany, to study forestry practices. In 1898 he was employed by Berlin Mills Company in New Hampshire, the first company forester in America, but was only partially successful in converting the company to conservative cutting practices. He left to teach at the Yale Forest School, 1904–5 and then at Harvard, 1905–9. In the latter year he became superintendent of forests in New York State. In 1910 he began his long employment with the United States Forest Service; it lasted until his retirement in 1935, and from 1917 onward he worked wholly in the South. His official title was logging engineer, but he functioned as a roving extension forester. A believer in individual enterprise, he spent most of his time with private landowners inducing them to manage their holdings with the intention of producing continuous crops of timber. In allying forestry practice with business, he was so successful that he was known as the Father of Forestry in the South, and he is remembered as one of the most influential proponents of industrial forestry in this century. The present well-managed condition of many New England and southern woodlands is the result of his teaching the possibilities of good forest practices in on-the-ground demonstrations as well as in articles, speeches, and letters. The author of numerous papers in trade journals and forestry magazines, he wrote the long-used *Manual for Northern Woodsman*, 1909. Died April 28, 1936.

DAVID C. SMITH

HEYWARD, FRANK. "Austin Cary, Yankee Peddler in Forestry." *American Forests,* June 1955.
SMITH, DAVID CLAYTON. "A History of Maine Lumbering, 1860–1930." Doctoral Thesis, Cornell University, 1965.
WHITE, ROY RING. "Austin Cary, the Father of Southern Forestry." *Forest History,* vol. 5, no. 1 (Spring), 1961.
———. "Austin Cary and Forestry in the South." Doctoral Thesis, University of Florida, 1961.
Who Was Who in America, 1897–1942.

CHAPLINE, WILLIAM RIDGELEY (1891–   )

Born January 10, 1891, in Lincoln, Nebraska. University of Nebraska, B.S. (forestry) 1913. On graduation joined the Forest Service, United States Department of Agriculture; made studies of range problems in mountains of central Utah. Transferred to Washington, D. C. office in 1915; in charge of Office of Grazing Studies, 1920–28, with responsibility for range investigations. With passage of the McSweeney-McNary Act in 1928, his office was changed to Division of Range Research, and included supervision of 30 full-time scientists stationed throughout the United States.

Duties included responsibility for planning, developing, directing, and coordinating range research of the Federal Government. By 1946 wildlife considerations were growing in importance and soon thereafter it was set up as the Division of Range and Wildlife Habitat Research. Cooperative investigations were expanded with Fish and Wildlife Service, United States Department of the Interior, and state fish and game departments and universities. Thus he was a pioneer in range and wildlife habitat research and the first person to direct these activities under the research and experiment station program of the Forest Service. During 1951–52, executive secretary, Organizing Committee, United States Department of State, for the Sixth International Grassland Congress. On retirement from the Forest Service in 1952, he became chief of section of the Forest Policy and Conservation Branch, Food and Agriculture Organization, Rome, Italy. This two-year assignment involved global contacts and technical guidance in grazing, watershed management, and shifting cultivation. During 1955, he served as professor in Second International Graduate Course on pasture management in Argentina, Chile, and Peru; during 1956–57, he was consultant to government of Spain in range management. He has continued to serve as consultant at the national and international levels and during 1968–69 traveled 18 months on range management investigations and consulting under auspices of the United States Department of Agriculture and other agencies. He is the author of numerous articles and technical papers, primarily in the field of range research.

LLOYD W. SWIFT

American Men of Science (The Physical and Biological Sciences), 11th ed., 1965.

CHAPMAN, FRANK MICHLER (1864–1945)

Born June 12, 1864 in Englewood, New Jersey. Attended Englewood Academy; Brown University, Sc.D. (honorary) 1913. Self-educated in ornithology while employed in a bank for six years, he left this work to devote himself entirely to collecting and catalog-

ing bird skins. In 1888, he was appointed assistant to the curator of
ornithology and mammalogy of the America Museum of Natural
History in New York City, beginning 54 years of active service at
the Museum during which he advanced to associate curator in
1901, to curator of birds in 1908, and to chairman of the Bird
Department from 1920 until his retirement in 1942. One of the
founders of the National Audubon Society in 1905, he served continuously on its Board of Directors for 32 years. In 1899 he founded
the magazine *Bird Lore* which he edited and published for 36
years, giving it to the National Audubon Society in 1935 to be
published subsequently, as it is today, as *Audubon*. He started the
traditional Christmas bird count, an annual survey of winter bird
life still sponsored by the Audubon Society. He is credited also
with persuading President Theodore Roosevelt to issue the proclamation in 1903 that set aside Pelican Island in Florida as the first
federal bird reservation, thus starting the national wildlife refuge
system. Active in the American Ornithologists' Union, he was president in 1911, and was elected a Fellow. For his literary and scientific contributions to ornithology, he was elected to the National
Academy of Sciences, and was the recipient of the Academy's
Elliot medal in 1918. In addition, he received the first award of the
Linnaean medal by the Linnaean Society of New York in 1912;
the medal of the Theodore Roosevelt Memorial Association in 1928;
and the John Burroughs medal of the American Museum of Natural
History in 1929. Author of 225 articles in periodicals, he also wrote
17 books, among the most important of which were *Handbook of
Birds of Eastern North America*, 1895 and subsequent editions;
The Distribution of Bird Life in Columbia, 1917; *The Distribution
of Bird Life in Ecuador*, 1926; and *Autobiography of a Bird Lover*,
1933. Died November 15, 1945.

CHARLES H. CALLISON

National Academy of Sciences Biographical Memoirs, 25:111–45, 1948.
National Cyclopaedia of American Biography, 1950.
The Auk, 67:307–15, July 1950.
Twentieth Century Authors. New York: H. W. Wilson Company, 1942 (and 1st
    supplement, 1955).
Who Was Who in America, 1943–50.

CHAPMAN, HERMAN HAUPT (1874–1963)

Born October 8, 1874 in Cambridge, Massachusetts. University of Minnesota B.S. 1896, B.Agr. 1899, D.Sc. 1947; Yale University M.F. 1904. While superintendent of Minnesota Agricultural Experiment Station at Grand Rapids (1898–1903) he helped obtain passage of the Morris Act of 1902 which started a system of national forests in Minnesota. After two years (1904–5) as forest assistant in the Forest Service, he was appointed instructor in Yale School of Forestry; in 1911 he was named Harriman professor of forestry, the position he filled with distinction for three decades. From 1917 to 1919 he was on leave of absence with the Southwestern Region of the Forest Service; and in 1927–28 he conducted field studies in the Lake States for the Forest Taxation Inquiry. For many years he was a director of the American Forestry Association. In 1922 he was elected a Fellow of the Society of American Foresters, served as president 1934–37, and was awarded the Sir William Schlich memorial medal for outstanding service to forestry in 1948. He was the first chairman of the Society's Committee on Accrediting Schools of Forestry which in 1937 established bases for the accreditation of professional forestry education. Later he was chairman of the Society's Committee on Ethics which drew up the canons of professional ethics adopted in 1948. A prolific writer, he was the author of textbooks on forest finance, management, mensuration, and valuation. In addition he wrote numerous bulletins and hundreds of periodical articles on forestry. On his retirement from his Yale professorship he was a consultant in forest management and policy, and continued working for the advancement of forestry. For a half-century he was one of the most influential foresters in America. Died July 13, 1963.

HENRY CLEPPER

American Men of Science (The Physical and Biological Sciences), 10th ed., 1960.
"Chapman Retires," *Journal of Forestry*, September, 1943.
"Herman Haupt Chapman Retires," *Yale Forest School News*, July, 1943.

CHEPIL, WILLIAM STEPHAN (1904–63)

Born January 1, 1904 at Gimli, Manitoba, Canada. University of Saskatchewan, B.S.A. 1930, M.S. 1932; University of Minnesota, Ph.D. 1940. He was officer in charge, Dominion Substation, Regina, Saskatchewan, from 1931 to 1936. In 1936 he was appointed agricultural scientist at the Dominion Soil Research Laboratory at Swift Current, Saskatchewan, where he studied the mechanics of wind erosion and developed methods and equipment, including laboratory and portable wind tunnels and rotary sieves, for studying wind erosion and soils. In 1946 he began an assignment as soil reclamation specialist with the United Nations Relief and Rehabilitation Administration Mission to China for which he received a meritorious service citation from the Chinese government. In 1948 he became professor of soils at Kansas State College and soil scientist, Agricultural Research Service, United States Department of Agriculture, on a soil erosion project. In 1953 he was made officer in charge of soil erosion research at Manhattan, Kansas, and in 1961 he was appointed research investigations leader for soil erosion in the Southern Plains Branch of the Soil and Water Conservation Research Division of the Agricultural Research Service. Regarded as a world authority on wind erosion and its control, his research has been reported in more than 100 scientific publications. He and his associates developed a universal wind erosion equation to determine erodibility of fields and conversely the requirements for reducing erosion. He also developed a wind erosion climatic factor for the United States and a method of predicting duststorms and wind erosion potential. He was elected Fellow of the American Society of Agronomy in 1962. Died September 6, 1963.

ORVILLE W. BIDWELL

American Men of Science (The Physical and Biological Sciences), 10th ed., 1960.

CLAPP, EARLE HART (1877–1970)

Born October 15, 1877 in North Rush, New York. Attended Cornell University, 1902–3; University of Michigan, B.A. (forestry) 1905, Sc.D. (honorary) 1928. Joined the United States Forest Service as a forest assistant in 1905; in charge of forest management, 1907–8; associate district forester, Southwestern District, 1908–11; forest inspector (silviculture), 1911–15; assistant chief in charge of research, 1915–35; associate chief, 1935–39; acting chief, 1940–42; retired in 1945 after four decades of service. Appointed Forest Service representative to the Agricultural War Board in 1941. Elected Fellow of the Society of American Foresters in 1930; awarded the Gifford Pinchot Medal for distinguished service to forestry by the Council of the Society in 1960. Author of many governmental and scientific publications, particularly the report *A National Program of Forest Research*, published by the American Tree Association in 1926; it provided the basis for the McSweeney-McNary Act of 1928 which broadened the scope of forestry research in America. He was the editorial director of the monumental Copeland report, *A National Plan for American Forestry*, issued by the Senate in 1933. During his career, he was an advocate of the acquisition of private forest lands by public agencies and of the regulation of private forest management by the federal and state governments. He was the principal architect of the Forest Service's nation-wide system of forest experiment stations and of its forestry research policy. Died July 1, 1970.

HENRY CLEPPER

American Men of Science, 11th ed., 1965.

CLAPPER, LOUIS SHIRLEY (1916–   )

Born November 10, 1916 in St. Louis, Missouri. University of Missouri School of Journalism, B.J. 1938. His professional career began in 1938 with employment on the sport staff of the Kansas City *Journal* and writing a weekly hunting and fishing column. After Navy service during World War II he and a partner edited and published the Donelson (Tennessee) *Diary*, a suburban weekly newspaper. When the Tennessee Game and Fish Commission was set up under a new "model law" in 1949, he became its first public relations officer; subsequently he developed the agency's information–education program, became assistant director and, for two extended periods, served as its acting director. During that period, he was co-editor of *Tennessee Conservationist* magazine and wrote news releases, including a column, "Outdoors in Tennessee." He served as secretary–treasurer of the forerunner of the American Association for Conservation Information from 1952 to 1954 and is an honorary life member of that organization. He also was secretary–treasurer of the National Water Safety Congress, 1956–58, and served in a similar capacity for the Tennessee Outdoor Writers Association for several years. In April 1958, he joined the Washington, D.C., staff of the National Wildlife Federation and served as editor of *Conservation News* from 1958 to 1962, and from 1964 to 1965. Since 1960 he has been editor of *Conservation Report*, and since 1962 has been Washington editor of *National Wildlife* magazine and contributes a "Washington Report" page in each issue. He has edited the "Legislative News Service" for the Natural Resources Council of America since 1960 and began as a contributing editor to the organization's "Executive News Service" in 1959. He currently serves as director of conservation for the National Wildlife Federation. He is a member of the President's Water Pollution Control Advisory Board.

THOMAS L. KIMBALL

CLARK, WILSON FARNSWORTH (1921–   )

Born February 25, 1921, in Schenectady, New York. Middlebury College, B.A. 1942; Cornell University, Ph.D. (conservation education) 1949. He was a research chemist on the Manhattan (A-bomb) project, 1945–47. He was then on the staff of the Conservation Department, Extension Service of Cornell University, until 1954, when he joined the faculty of Eastern Montana College where he now is the chairman of the Division of Science and Mathematics. He is a past president and, since 1955, a director of the Montana Conservation Council; member of the Education Committee of the Soil Conservation Society; member of the Education Committee of the National Association of Soil and Water Conservation Districts; member of a panel of the Commission on Education in Agriculture and Natural Resources of the National Academy of Sciences; and belongs to several other organizations. He was also a member of the Board of Governors of the Pinchot Institute for Conservation Studies. For the Conservation Education Association he has served since 1954 as editor, director, secretary–treasurer, vice president, and since 1966 as president. Author of Extension 4-H bulletins while at Cornell; has had several articles in such publications as the *Journal of Soil and Water Conservation*, the *Montana Business Quarterly*, the *Journal of Forestry*, and has written articles for the Newsletters of the Montana Conservation Council and the Conservation Education Association. Has published a beginning college science book, *Summaries and Problems in General Physical Science*, and has collaborated with colleagues at Eastern Montana College on the Chem-i-Guide series of student aids.

GEORGE H. GLOEGE

American Men of Science (The Physical and Biological Sciences), 11th ed., 1965.

CLAWSON, MARION (1905–)

Born August 10, 1905 in Elko, Nevada. University of Nevada, B.S. (agriculture) 1926, M.S. 1929; Harvard University, Ph.D. (economics) 1943. For nearly 24 years he was in the service of the United States government, first in the Bureau of Agricultural Economics, Department of Agriculture, from 1929 to 1946, directing extensive studies of agricultural development on major irrigation projects. Appointed regional administrator in the Bureau of Land Management, Department of the Interior, in 1947; named director a year later and held the directorship for five years, 1948–53. From 1953 to 1955 he was economic consultant in Israel, and has been on assignments to Chile, India, the Middle East, Pakistan, and Venezuela. Since 1955 he has been director of the Land Use and Management Program for Resources For the Future, Inc., Washington, D. C., a nonprofit private research and educational institution financed by the Ford Foundation. He has studied intensely the effect of urban expansion on the rural countryside. He was a consultant to the Ford Foundation in 1960 and 1962, and to the Natural Resources Agency in California during 1964–65. He was vice president of the American Agricultural Economic Association in 1947; is a charter member of the Society of Range Management; and was executive secretary of the Society for International Development, 1959–62 and vice president, 1963–66. He is author, co-author, or editor of 15 books; among them *Western Range Livestock Industry*, 1950; *Uncle Sam's Acres*, 1951; *The Federal Lands* (with Burnell Held), 1965; *Soil Conservation in Perspective* (with Burnell Held), 1965; *Economics of Outdoor Recreation* (with Jack L. Knetsch), 1966; and *Policy Directions for U.S. Agriculture*, 1967.

HENRY CLEPPER

American Men of Science (The Social and Behavioral Sciences), 11th ed., 1965. *Who's Who in America*, 1968–69.

CLEMENT, ROLAND CHARLES (1912–   )

Born November 22, 1912 in Fall River, Massachusetts. Studied wildlife management and forestry at Stockbridge School of Agriculture, University of Massachusetts; Brown University, A.B. 1949; Cornell University, M.S. (wildlife conservation) 1950. While serving with United States Air Force Weather Service during World War II, he conducted investigations in ornithology and subarctic ecology in Labrador. Executive secretary of the Audubon Society of Rhode Island from 1950 to 1958, he joined the staff of the National Audubon Society, New York City, in 1958 to serve successively as membership director to 1962, as staff biologist to 1967, and as vice president since 1967. He has supervised the Audubon Society's long campaign for revision of pest control policies and pesticide technology, and is in demand as a lecturer on the ethics and economics of natural resource conservation. Author of numerous articles for scientific and popular journals, he was editor of *A Gathering of Shorebirds*, 1960; and was a contributor to *Life*

Histories of North American Birds, U.S. National Museum, and to
W. E. Clyde Todd's *Birds of the Labrador Peninsula.*

CHARLES H. CALLISON

American Men of Science (The Physical and Biological Sciences), 11th ed., 1965.
National Audubon Society, Staff biographies.

CLEMENTS, FREDERIC EDWARD   (1874–1945)

Born September 16, 1874 in Lincoln, Nebraska. Educated in biological sciences at University of Nebraska, Ph.D. 1898, LL.D. 1940.
During and following his graduate studies he held appointments at
University of Nebraska, starting as an assistant in botany and
advancing to full professor of plant physiology. For ten years, starting in 1907, he was head of the Department of Botany, University
of Minnesota. Thereafter he was with the Carnegie Institution until
retirement in 1941. During this period he directed research in
origin of plant species by means of physical factors in their environment, primarily from field stations at Pikes Peak in Colorado and
Santa Barbara in California. After leaving Carnegie Institution his
studies were continued from Santa Barbara with private funds. He
was a consultant and collaborator to several federal agencies and
a member of and active in the Botanical Society of America, American Association for Advancement of Science (Fellow), and many
other professional societies. His writings were mainly in botany and
ecology. His book *Plant Succession,* 1916, a basic work in ecology,
has served as a guide for foresters, soil scientists, and others in
natural resources conservation. He was co-author of *Plant Ecology,*
1929, with J. E. Weaver and *Bio-ecology,* 1939, with Victor E. Shel-
ford. Mrs. Clements, as illustrator and assistant, helped to make an
effective scientific team, both in investigations and publications. As
a noted botanist and ecologist, he was regarded as a national and
international authority in these fields. Died July 26, 1945.

LLOYD W. SWIFT

National Cyclopaedia of American Biography, 1948.

CLEPPER, HENRY EDWARD (1901–   )

Born March 21, 1901 in Columbia, Pennsylvania. Pennsylvania State Forest Academy, Mont Alto (subsequently a unit of Pennsylvania State University), B.F. 1921. He entered the Pennsylvania Department of Forests and Waters, in which he was employed for 15 years, first as field forester and later as assistant chief of the Bureau of Research and Education; then followed a year as information specialist in the Washington, D. C. office of the United States Forest Service. In 1937 he was appointed executive secretary of the Society of American Foresters; except for a two-year leave of absence with the War Production Board during World War II, he served in this position and as managing editor of the *Journal of Forestry* for 28 years. He helped establish the Society's quarterly journal *Forest Science* in 1955 and the research series *Forest Sciences Monographs* in 1959. Since his retirement in March 1966 he has written a chronicle of American forestry under the sponsorship of the Forest History Society, Inc. Author of more than 100 articles and bulletins on forestry and related resources, many historical in nature. Editor and co-author of *Forestry Education in Pennsylvania*, 1957; co-editor and co-author of *America's Natural Resources*, 1967; *American Forestry—Six Decades of Growth*, 1960; editor and co-author of *Careers in Conservation*, 1963, and of *Origins of American Conservation*, 1966; co-author of *The World of the Forest*, 1965; editor of *Leaders in American Conservation*, 1971; and author of *Forestry in America*, in press. From 1957 to 1965, he was an adviser to the Forestry Committee of the Food and Agriculture Organization of the United Nations at the FAO Council's biennial conferences in Rome. He is a Fellow of the Society of American Foresters and in 1957 was recipient of its Gifford Pinchot Medal. In 1965 he received the award of American Forest Products Industries, Inc. for distinguished service to forestry.

ARTHUR B. MEYER

Who's Who in America, 1968–69.

CLIFF, EDWARD PARLEY (1909–   )

Born September 3, 1909 at Heber City, Utah. Utah State University, B.S. (forestry) 1931, D.Sc. (honorary) 1965. A career forester with the United States Forest Service beginning in 1931, he was assistant ranger, Wenatchee National Forest, Washington; in charge of wildlife management, Pacific Northwest Region, Portland, Oregon from 1935; supervisor, Siskiyou and Fremont National Forests in Oregon, 1939–44; assistant chief, Division of Range Management, Washington, D. C., 1944–46; assistant regional forester, Intermountain Region, Ogden, Utah, 1946–50; regional forester, Rocky Mountain Region, Denver, 1950–52; assistant chief, Forest Service, 1952–62; and chief since March 1962. He is a charter member of the American Society of Range Management, a Fellow of the Society of American Foresters, and a member of the American Forestry Association, the Wilderness Society and the National Council, Boy Scouts of America. Chairman, 1963–65 of the North American Forestry Commission of the Food and Agriculture Organization of the United Nations; head of the United States delegation to the Sixth World Forestry Congress in Madrid, 1966, and vice president of the Congress. Recipient of distinguished service awards from Utah State University in 1958 and from the United States Department of Agriculture in 1962; in 1968 received similar award from National Civil Service League.

WILLIAM E. TOWELL

Who's Who in America, 1968–69.

COFFMAN, JOHN DANIEL (1882–   )

Born May 10, 1882 in Allentown, Pennsylvania. Yale University M.F. 1909. Entered United States Forest Service in California in July 1909 as forest assistant on Inyo and Shasta National Forests; promoted to deputy supervisor of the Trinity National Forest in 1911; advanced to supervisor of the California (now Mendocino) National Forest in 1916. In 1928 he transferred to the National

Park Service as fire control expert at Berkeley, California, and in 1933 was assigned to the Washington, D. C. headquarters where he was named chief forester of the newly created Branch of Forestry. This position he filled until his retirement in 1952, when he received the Distinguished Service gold medal honor award of the Department of the Interior. He then returned to California as a consulting forester in forest protection and recreational forestry. Elected a Fellow of the Society of American Foresters in 1936, he served on the Society's Council, 1946–47.

HENRY CLEPPER

American Men of Science (The Physical and Biological Sciences), 10th ed., 1960.

COLBY, WILLIAM EDWARD (1875–1964)

Born May 28, 1875 in Benicia, California. Hastings College of Law, LL.B. 1898; University of California, LL.D. 1937; Mills College, LL.D. 1937. He specialized in mining and forest law, was lecturer on mines at Stanford University, and on mines and waters at the University of California. He was associated with John Muir in the battle to save Yosemite and the Hetch Hetchy Valley. He initiated the Sierra Club high trips in 1901, led them until 1929, taking people into the wilderness to learn for themselves the values they contained. He contributed substantially to saving the Sierra redwoods, the enlargement of Sequoia National Park, and the establishment of Kings Canyon and Olympic National Parks. First chairman of the California State Park Commission, 1927–37; during his tenure $12 million was expended in the purchase of more than fifty new parks for the California State Park System, including the Point Lobos Reserve, Calaveras Big Trees, Bull Creek Flat, and other outstanding redwood areas. He drafted a forest fire law for California. The 185-mile John Muir Trail, which runs the crest of the Sierra Nevada to the summit of Mount Whitney, was his idea. He was author of articles on the law of mines and mining. He wrote for the Sierra Club *Bulletin* and was editor of *John Muir's Studies in the Sierra*. After retiring from 49 years on the Sierra

Club Board he was made honorary president. The Colby Award, established in his name, is presented annually to a Sierra Club member who has done outstanding conservation work for the Club. Colby was himself the first recipient of the Muir Award, set up in 1961 by the Sierra Club. He was also a member of the American Alpine Club, the Boone and Crockett Club, and Save-the-Redwoods League. Died November 9, 1964.

MICHAEL McCLOSKEY

Sierra Club Handbook, 1967.
Who Was Who in America, 1961–68.

COLLINGWOOD, GEORGE HARRIS (1890–1958)

Born May 27, 1890 in Fayetteville, Arkansas. Michigan State College, B.S.F. 1911; University of Michigan, M.A. 1917. He was a ranger for United States Forest Service in Arizona, 1911–12. Appointed assistant extension professor of forestry in Cornell University College of Agriculture, 1916; resigned in 1923 to be extension forester for United States Department of Agriculture, and helped develop the federal farm forestry extension program cooperatively with the state colleges of agriculture. In 1928 he was appointed forester for the American Forestry Association; for the next 12 years he directed the Association's educational program cooperatively with federal and state agencies, forest industries, and private woodland owners. An eloquent speaker and a persuasive writer, he carried the conservation message throughout America. In many appearances before Congressional and state legislative committees he was recognized as an informed spokesman for the public's interest in resources. In 1940 he became chief forester for the National Lumber Manufacturers Association, and helped establish an industry-wide conservation program. He was a forest products specialist for national housing agencies, 1946–47, a research consultant to the Hoover Commission in 1948, and a research consultant to the Chamber of Commerce of the United States, 1949. In that year he was appointed to the Library of Congress Legislative

Reference Bureau as a specialist in forestry and natural resources. Throughout his career he was one of the best known foresters in America; his knowledge of forestry policy and legislation was encyclopedic. Among his numerous writings, including bulletins and magazine articles, is the popular book *Knowing Your Trees*, 1937. He was a Fellow of the American Association for the Advancement of Science and of the Society of American Foresters. Died April 2, 1958.

HENRY CLEPPER

CONDRA, GEORGE EVERT (1869–1958)

Born February 2, 1869 near Seymour, Iowa. University of Nebraska, B.S. 1896, M.A. and Ph.D. 1902. He was a crusader in the field of scientific investigation of natural resources and their utilization. He participated in the Joint Conservation Congress held in Washington, D. C. in December 1908 as chairman of the Nebraska Conservation Commission. This congress gave marked impetus to the developing conservation movement. An organizer of the Conservation and Survey Division of the University of Nebraska, he was its director, and also state geologist, from 1918 to 1954. He was a member of the Nebraska State Soil Conservation Committee, serving as the chairman and assisting in the organization of Nebraska's Soil and Water Conservation Districts. In cooperation with the United States Geological Survey, he instituted a program of ground water investigation that is one of the longest continuous, cooperative programs in any State. His membership in scientific and professional organizations included the Geological Society of America, American Association of State Geologists, American Paleontological Association, American Soil Survey Association, Nebraska Academy of Science, Nebraska Reclamation and Nebraska Irrigation Associations, and Permian Section International Geological Congress. He received the Kiwanis Award for Distinguished Service in 1945. He was the author of more than 40 scientific publications and of the text books *Geography of*

Nebraska and *Geography and Agriculture of Nebraska.* He was an
early contributor to the Conservation movement. Died August 7,
1958.

D. E. HUTCHINSON
ROBERT W. EIKLEBERRY

CONNAUGHTON, CHARLES ARTHUR (1908–   )

Born May 25, 1908, in Placerville, Idaho. University of Idaho, B.S.
(forestry) 1928, Ph.D. (honorary) 1965; Yale University, M.F. 1934.
Held increasingly responsible positions with the United States
Forest Service in administration, then silviculture and watershed
management research, and became director of the Rocky Mountain
Forest and Range Experiment Station in 1936. He then served as
director of the Southern Forest Experiment Station, and in 1951
became regional forester of the Southern Region with responsibilities for national forest management and state and private forestry
programs. Held similar positions for the California Region and,
since 1967, in the Pacific Northwest Region. He is the author of
numerous articles and pamphlets on silviculture, watershed management, and multiple-use forestry, and has been a frequent
speaker at conferences and at university commencements. He
represented the Society of American Foresters as visiting scientist
lecturer in 1967–68, and has long been active in the Society, giving
leadership in sections, committees, and as a Council member; president in 1960–61. He was elected a Fellow in 1959, and was
awarded the highest professional honor bestowed by the Society,
the Sir William Schlich Memorial Medal Award in 1968. He has
been a director of the American Forestry Association since 1956,
and became president in 1971. He has contributed much to the
advancement of conservation and forestry programs in technical
and administrative fields. Of even greater long-term consequence
has been his leadership in harmonizing and reconciling competitive
uses of forested lands, and his ability to develop understanding
among competing user interests. Improved ability of resource pro-

grams on millions of forested acres in the nation has been his greatest achievement.

SOCIETY OF AMERICAN FORESTERS

Who's Who in America, 1968–69.

COOLIDGE, HAROLD JEFFERSON (1904–)

Born January 15, 1904 in Boston, Massachusetts. Harvard University, B.S. 1927; Cambridge University, 1927–28; George Washington University, Sc.D. (honorary) 1959; Seoul National University, Sc.D. (honorary) 1965. In 1926 he was assistant zoologist for the Harvard African expedition to Liberia and the Belgian Congo. Two years later he was assistant mammalogist and head of the Indo-China division of Kelley-Roosevelt's Field Museum expedition. In 1929 he became assistant curator of mammals, and in 1946 associate mammalogist, at the Museum of Comparative Zoology at Harvard University. He has served both as secretary and as chairman of the American Committee for International Wildlife Protection. In 1937 he was organizer and executive of the Asiatic Primate expedition to Siam and Borneo. As executive director of the Pacific Science Board of the National Academy of Sciences–National Resource Council since 1946, he has helped to plan and organize the various Pacific Science Congresses, and was secretary-general of the Tenth Congress in 1961. He was secretary of the National Parks Association for thirteen years, collaborator with the United States National Park Service, and director of the World Wildlife Fund. In 1953 he began consulting for the Bernice P. Bishop Museum in Honolulu, Hawaii. Active in the International Union for Conservation of Nature and Natural Resources, he has served it as chairman of the Survival Service Commission, the International Committee on National Parks, and during 1967–69 as president. In 1960 he was presented the 75th Anniversary Medal of Merit by the University of Arizona. He served as member of the organizing committee of the Sixteenth International Zoological

Congress. In 1962 he served as chairman for the First World Conference on National Parks in Seattle. The Garden Club of America presented him the Frances K. Hutchinson medal in 1963, and the New England Society in 1964 honored him with the Reginald Townsend Award. He received the 1966 Conservation Award of the African Safari Club of Washington. He has served on the advisory council of the Conservation Foundation, and is a Fellow of the New York Zoological Society. Author of *A Revision of the Genus Gorilla, Three Kingdoms of Indo-China, The Indo-China Forest Ox or Kouprey*; he has written also many scientific and conservation papers.

THE CONSERVATION FOUNDATION

American Men of Science (The Physical and Biological Sciences), 11th ed., 1965.
Who's Who in America, 1968–69.

COOPER, WILLIAM SKINNER (1884–   )

Born August 25, 1884, in Detroit, Michigan. Alma College, B.S. (botany and ecology) 1906, D.Sc. (honorary) 1930; Johns Hopkins University, 1970; University of Chicago, Ph.D. 1911; University of Colorado, D.Sc. (honorary) 1961. Concurrent with his biological studies he developed an intense interest and expertise in geomorphology which later contributed greatly to his recognition of geology–vegetation relationships. Lecturer in ecology at Stanford University, 1914–15; became instructor of botany at the University of Minnesota in 1915 and advanced to professor. He retired in 1951 as emeritus professor of botany, but has continued active research on dunes and their associated vegetation. A member of numerous scientific expeditions to southern Alaska, he played an important role in having Glacier Bay set aside as a national monument. He served as a member of the Committee on Preservation of Natural Conditions, National Research Council. He was vice president in 1927, president in 1936, and named Eminent Ecologist in 1963 in the Ecological Society of America. He was awarded the Certificate

of Merit by the Botanical Society of America in 1956. Author of
numerous scientific papers and monographs in botany and geomorphology; one of his more important papers, *The Fundamentals of
Vegetational Change*, 1926, was a clear expression of his concept
of vegetation dynamics, a concept now taken for granted by most
ecologists.

GEORGE SPRUGEL, JR.

American Men of Science (The Physical and Biological Sciences), 11th ed., 1965.
Bulletin of the Ecological Society of America: vol. 44, no. 4, 1963.

COTTAM, CLARENCE (1899–   )

Born January 1, 1899, in St. George, Utah. Brigham Young University, B.S. (biology) 1926, M.S. 1927; George Washington University, Ph.D. 1936. After serving as instructor in biology at Brigham
Young University, 1927–29, he was junior biologist in the Bureau
of Biological Survey, United States Department of Agriculture,
1929–31, assistant biologist, 1931–35, and senior biologist in charge
of food habits, Division of Wildlife Research, 1935–40. He held the
same position in the Fish and Wildlife Service, United States
Department of Interior, 1940–42, and was in charge of economic
wildlife investigations, Division of Wildlife Research, 1942–44,
assistant to the director, 1944, chief of Division of Wildlife
Research, 1944–46, and assistant director, 1946–54. Dean of the
College of Biological and Agricultural Sciences at Brigham Young
University, 1954–55, he has been director, Welder Wildlife Founda-
tion since 1955. He received the honorary award of the Utah
Academy of Sciences, Arts and Letters in 1948, and of Laval
University in 1952; the Aldo Leopold Medal of the Wildlife Society
in 1955; the Distinguished Service Award in Conservation and
Forestry of Utah State University in 1957; the National Audubon
Conservation Distinguished Service Medal in 1961; the Poage
Humanitarian Award, Society of Animal Protection, 1962; Francis
K. Hutchinson Medal for Conservation, Garden Clubs of America,
1962; Paul Bartsch award for contributions to Natural History,

Audubon Naturalist Society, 1962. He was president of the Wildlife Society, 1949–50; president of the Texas Ornithological Society in 1957; and has been president of the National Parks Association since 1960. Author of many scientific papers, he is possibly best known for the book *Food Habits of American Diving Ducks*, 1939.

GEORGE SPRUGEL, JR.

American Men of Science (The Physical and Biological Sciences), 11th ed., 1965. Who's Who in America, 1968–69.

COVILLE, FREDERICK VERNON (1867–1937)

Born March 23, 1867, in Preston, Chenango County, New York. Cornell University, A.B. (botany) 1887. After graduation he served briefly in the geological survey of Arkansas, but returned to Cornell to teach botany until 1888. Thereafter his professional career was with the United States Department of Agriculture, becoming botanist and also curator of the National Herbarium. Active in the development of the National Arboretum, he was acting director for a few years. His *Botany of the Death Valley Expedition*, published in 1893, is regarded as a classic on desert vegetation. He was an authority on American *Juncaceae*, and his publications on these grass-like plants were standard references. During his career he pioneered in a number of areas, such as the seed laboratory in the Department of Agriculture, formulation of policy on grazing use on national forest lands, selection and breeding of commercial varieties of blueberries, and founding of Tucson, Arizona desert botanical laboratory of the Carnegie Institution. He was assigned to a cooperative interagency effort with the Department of the Interior in 1897, and in connection with the grazing use of public lands, he has been credited with starting the first sustained national movement toward range management. The following year he began field appraisals in the Northwest, and as an outgrowth of this work, was one of the first to show that proper controls were needed. By 1904 he had outlined proposed regulations, subsequently incorporated in grazing regulations for public lands. Co-author of 1923 edition of

Standardized Plant Names. Active in professional and scientific societies. Died January 9, 1937.

LLOYD W. SWIFT

National Cyclopaedia of American Biography, 1939.
TALBOT, M. W., and CRONEMILLER, F. P. "Some Beginnings of Range Management," *Journal of Range Management,* vol. 14, March 1961.

COX, WILLIAM THOMAS (1878–1961)

Born January 25, 1878, near Glenwood, Minnesota. In June 1901, became a student assistant in United States Department of Agriculture's Bureau of Forestry, and forest assistant in 1905. University of Minnesota, B.S. (forestry) 1906. In 1907 promoted by Bureau of Forestry to rank of assistant forester in charge of silviculture and management. In 1911, at the Minnesota Forestry Board's request he organized state's Forest Service and became Minnesota state forester until 1924. Refuge manager, Upper Mississippi National Wild Life Refuge, 1925–28. Between 1929 and 1931 he assisted Brazil in organizing its National Department of Forestry; also explored its Amazonian forests. From 1931 to 1933 he was Minnesota's Conservation Commissioner. In 1935 he became the Federal Resettlement Administration's regional biologist for Minnesota and the four states surrounding it. Between the activities above listed he worked as a forestry and/or wildlife consultant to private owners of forest property. During World War II, he headed a joint American–British Mission engaged in obtaining from South America supplies of balsa and mahogany needed by the American Navy and the Royal Air Force. From 1946 to 1959 he wrote a column entitled "Wild Animals of Field and Forest," which appeared in St. Paul's bi-weekly newspaper, *The Farmer,* published by the Webb Publishing Company. Fellow, Society of American Foresters; author of *Biennial Reports,* Minnesota State Forest Service, 1912–22, *Wild Animals of Field and Forest,* and *Fearsome Creatures of the Lumberwoods.* In 1952 he was recipient of the National Association of Conservation, Education and Publicity's annual award for "Meritorious Service to State, National and International Progress." Died January 25, 1961.

JOHN H. ALLISON

CRAFTS, EDWARD CLAYTON (1910–)

Born April 14, 1910 at Chicago, Illinois. Attended Dartmouth College; University of Michigan, B.S. (forestry) 1932, M.F. 1936, Ph.D. 1942, Sc.D. 1969. Forest officer for 29 years in the United States Forest Service with assignments in Utah, Arizona, New Mexico, and California before moving to Washington in 1944; chief, Division of Forest Economics Research for a number of years, and assistant chief in charge of program development, legislation, and Congressional relations for ten years. Directed numerous policy studies including a five-year appraisal of the nation's timber supply which was published in 1958 as *Timber Resources for America's Future*. First director of Bureau of Outdoor Recreation, Department of the Interior, 1962–69. Executive director of the President's Council on Recreation and Natural Beauty, executive officer of the Lewis and Clark Trail Commission, and the Secretary of the Interior's alternate representative on the National Advisory Council on Historic Preservation and the National Forest Preservation Commission. Chairman of the federal interagency study team which explored all resource potentials of the North Cascade Mountains to determine how these federal lands could best serve the public interest; the findings and recommendations for management and administration of the area appear in the North Cascades Study Report published in 1965. He holds the Distinguished Service Award of both the Department of the Interior and the Department of Agriculture, and also holds a Distinguished Service Award from the American Institute of Park Executives. Was an official representative to two World Forestry Congresses. Fellow of the Society of American Foresters.

WILLIAM E. TOWELL

Who's Who in America, 1968–69.

CRAIG, JAMES BARKLEY (1912–   )

Born September 30, 1912 in West Hebron, Washington County, New York. Kent State University, A.B. 1936. Began his professional career as a reporter on the Akron (Ohio) *Times Press*, followed by similar experience on the Athens (Ohio) *Messenger* and Cumberland (Md.) *News*. Served in the Pacific Area with the 41st Infantry Division in World War II. Returned to newspaper work with the Cumberland *Times* and became interested in conservation of natural resources. In 1947 he became assistant editor of *American Forests*, published by the American Forestry Association of Washington, D. C. In 1950 he was named manager of the New York City News Bureau of American Forest Industries, Inc. He returned to *American Forests* as editor in 1953 and was elected secretary of the American Forestry Association in 1956. He still serves in both capacities. In 1960 he was named to the Steering Committee of the National Watershed Congress and presently serves as chairman of its Awards Committee. As a result of his extensive travels he has written hundreds of articles on conservation and more than 160 editorials, many of which have been reprinted in periodicals, textbooks, and the *Congressional Record*. His courageous exposé of mining claim abuses led to correction of the situation in the Multiple Use Mining Act of 1955. The weight of his pen has been leveled impartially on fire bugs, grazers, lumbermen, litter-bugs, and pollutors whenever there was just cause. During his editorship *American Forests* grew in readership and in coverage of the entire range of natural resources. In 1959 he was cited by Kent State University for distinguished service in his chosen field.

KENNETH B. POMEROY

Who's Who in America, 1970–71.

DAMTOFT, WALTER JULIUS (1890–   )

Born November 11, 1890 in Southport, Connecticut. Yale University Sheffield Scientific School, Ph.B. 1910; Yale Forest School, M.F. 1911; North Carolina State College at Raleigh, Doctor of Forest

Science (honorary) 1954. Worked for United States Forest Service as field assistant, forest assistant, and forest examiner in Colorado, 1911–12, and in North Carolina, 1913–19, where he appraised lands for Pisgah National Forest under Weeks Law. Joined Champion Paper and Fibre Company, Canton, North Carolina as chief forester in 1920. Served in that capacity with additional duties as assistant secretary, 1933; assistant secretary–treasurer, 1946; and assistant secretary–treasurer and director of general wood and woodlands department, from 1951 until retirement in 1958. The first industrial forester in the South, throughout his career he was spokesman and leader for many forest industry and conservation programs. He took an important part in the organization of Southern Pulpwood Conservation Association in 1939 (president in 1942–43) and the Forest Farmers Association. He was a member of the North Carolina Board of Conservation and Development for many years, and served as its vice chairman and chairman of the Forestry Committee. He was trustee and vice president of American Forest Products Industries; director of the American Pulpwood Association; director and vice president of the American Forestry Association; council member of the Society of American Foresters, 1944–47, of which he was elected a Fellow in 1951, and served many other conservation and industrial organizations in various capacities. In 1951 he was head of Pulp and Paper Branch, Forest Products Division, Economic Stabilization and Administration, Washington, D. C. He received a Certificate of Commendation from Forest Farmers Association in 1959.

ELWOOD L. DEMMON

DANA, SAMUEL TRASK (1883–   )

Born April 21, 1883 in Portland, Maine. Bowdoin College, A.B. 1904; Yale University, M.F. 1907. Honorary doctorates awarded by Syracuse University in 1928, by Bowdoin in 1930, and by Yale University and the University of Michigan in 1953. Entered the United States Forest Service in 1907 where he moved from forest assistant to assistant chief of the Office of Silvics and Forest Investigations. Following service in World War I as a captain in the Army, he returned to the Forest Service and became assistant chief of research in 1920. Forest commissioner of Maine, 1921–23. Returned to the Forest Service as director of the Northeastern Forest Experiment Station, 1923. Appointed dean of the School of Forestry and Conservation at the University of Michigan in 1927 (renamed School of Natural Resources in 1950); pioneered the development of forestry and natural resources education, and retired in 1953 as dean emeritus. He served as treasurer, vice president, and president of the Society of American Foresters; was twice editor-in-chief of the *Journal of Forestry* for a total of six years. Chairman of the American delegation to the First World Forestry Congress; member of the Task Force on Natural Resources of the First Hoover Commission on Reorganization of the Executive Branch of the Federal Government; Presidentially appointed member of the Outdoor Recreation Resources Review Commission. His major books are *Forest and Range Policy*, 1956, *California Lands* (with Myron Krueger), 1958, *Minnesota Lands* (with John H. Allison and Russell N. Cummingham), 1960, *Forestry Education in America* (with Evert W. Johnson), 1963. He has been advisor to the Secretary of Agriculture on strip mining policy; consultant to the United States Forest Service for planning its forest recreation research program; consultant to the American Forestry Association on Redwood National Park policy; consultant to the Bureau of Outdoor Recreation on education in outdoor recreation; and advisor on forestry education to Yale University, the University of Florida, and North Carolina State University. Recipient of the Sir William Schlich Memorial medal of the Society of American Foresters, the American Forest Products Industries award for Distinguished Service to Forest Industry, the medal for outstanding service in international forestry at the Sixth World Forestry Congress, and the sesquicentennial medal of the University of Michigan.

P. KEITH ARNOLD

American Men of Science, 11th ed., 1965.
Who's Who in America, 1962–63.

DARLING, FRANK FRASER (1903–   )

Born June 23, 1903 in Scotland. Midland Agricultural College, national diploma in agriculture; University of Edinburgh, Ph.D. 1930, D.Sc. 1938; University of Glasgow, LL.D. (honorary); Williams College, D.Sc. (honorary). From 1930 to 1934, he served as chief officer of the Imperial Bureau of Animal Genetics. In 1944 he became director of the West Highland Survey and served until 1950. In 1947 the Royal Scottish Geographical Society presented him with the Mungo Park Medal, and in 1950 he became a Rockefeller special research fellow. Beginning in 1953, for five years, he served as senior lecturer on ecology and conservation at the University of Edinburgh. Since 1959 he has been director of research and vice president of the Conservation Foundation, Washington, D. C. In the same year he also became an honorary trustee of the Royal National Parks of Kenya. In 1967 he was elected vice president of the International Union for the Conservation of Nature and Natural Resources. He is a Fellow of the Royal Society of Edinburgh and of the Institute of Biology; a member of the British Ecological Society. He has participated in numerous surveys and studies of wildlife and land use in Africa, Alaska, Great Britain, and elsewhere. The author of numerous scientific publications, he is known for the following books: *Wild Life Conservation*, 1934; *A Herd of Red Deer*, 1937; *Wild Country*, 1938; *Wild Life of Britain*, 1943; *Pelican in the Wilderness: Odyssey of a Naturalist*, 1956; *The Unity of Ecology*, 1963; and *The Nature of a National Park*, 1968.

THE CONSERVATION FOUNDATION

Directory of British Scientists. London, 1964–65.
Who's Who in America, 1968–69.

DARLING, JAY NORWOOD (1876–1962)

Born October 21, 1876 in Norwood, Michigan. Beloit College, Wisconsin, Ph.D. 1900, Litt.D.; Drake University, LL.D. Began his career as a reporter in Sioux City, Iowa, soon drawing sketches to accompany stories. His gift for political cartooning was the basis for a half-century career that gave him fame and fortune with the simple pen name "Ding." In 1906 joined the *Des Moines Register*, an association lasting for most of his career. In 1917 his cartoons were syndicated through the *New York Herald Tribune*, eventually appearing in 130 daily newspapers. For five years was also editorial cartoonist for *Collier's Weekly*. His satirical pen won the Pulitzer Prize for cartooning in 1923 and 1942. His strong interest in conservation of natural resources was often reflected in his drawings which continued to bring national attention to the crises in soil erosion, pollution, and other misuses of land and wildlife resources. He was particularly concerned about wildlife problems and the destruction of irreplaceable waterfowl habitat. This interest caused him to take a leave of absence from newspaper work to serve as chief of the Biological Survey, forerunner of the United States Fish and Wildlife Service, during 1934–35. Was the leading organizer and first president of the National Wildlife Federation, which he conceived as potentially the largest and most broadly interested citizen's conservation organization in the nation. Devised the world-famous wildlife conservation stamps produced by the Federation. Recipient of the the Theodore Roosevelt Gold Medal award and Pulitzer Prize, 1923. Because of his long standing interest, the J. "Ding" Darling Foundation was instrumental in the organization and passage of the Lewis & Clark Trail Commission which is planning means by which the historical trail from St. Joseph, Missouri, to the Pacific coast can be marked and set aside for historical and recreational purposes. Sanibel Island in Florida, one of his favorite bird-watching locations, was set aside and renamed the J. "Ding" Darling Wildlife Refuge honoring his memory. Author of *Ding Goes to Russia*, 1931, and *The Cruise of the Bouncing Betsy*, 1937. Died February 12, 1962.

JAMES D. DAVIS

Who Was Who in America, 1961–68.

DASMANN, RAYMOND FREDRIC (1919–   )

Born May 27, 1919 in San Francisco. University of California at Berkeley, A.B. 1948, M.A. 1951, Ph.D. (zoology) 1954. He worked as a forest guard for the United States Forest Service and the California Division of Forestry, 1939–41, and was with the United States Army in the Southwest Pacific, 1941–45. He was a research assistant and associate at the Museum of Vertebrate Zoology and the School of Forestry, University of California, 1948–55. After teaching biology at the University of Minnesota, Duluth, 1953–54, he served as assistant to the associate professor and head of game management at Humboldt State College, California, 1954–59. From 1959 to 1961, he was a Fulbright research biologist at the National Museums of Southern Rhodesia. Lecturer in zoology at the University of California, Berkeley, in 1961; returned in 1962 to Humboldt State College where he became professor of wildlife management and chairman of the Division of Natural Resources. Since 1966 he has been director of environmental studies for the Conservation Foundation, Washington, D. C. He is a Fellow of the California Academy of Sciences; has been president of the California section, and western regional representative, of the Wildlife Society. He is a member of the American Society of Mammalogists, Ecological Society of America, Faunal Preservation Society, and Association of Tropical Biologists. In 1966–67 he served as a consultant to UNESCO. His writings include the following books: *Environmental Conservation, Wildlife Biology, African Game Ranching, The Last Horizon, The Destruction of California,* and *A Different Kind of Country.*

THE CONSERVATION FOUNDATION

American Men of Science (The Physical and Biological Sciences), 11th ed., 1965.

DAVIS, DEAN WILLIAM (1894–1963)

Born February 15, 1894 in West Plains, Missouri. University of Missouri, B.A. 1915, B.J. 1916. Prior to entering military service during World War I, he was engaged in newspaper work on the

Cleveland (Ohio) *Leader.* After the war, he became a businessman. He first became active in organized conservation work when he served as county chairman during the 1936 campaign of the Conservation Federation of Missouri to take the state Game and Fish Department out of politics. This movement established the Missouri Conservation Commission as a non-political state agency dedicated to management of forest and wildlife resources under a constitutional amendment which established a "model law." He was elected as a director of the Conservation Federation of Missouri in 1938 and served as its president from 1946 to 1949. In 1951 he received Missouri's "Master Conservationist" award. Also active nationally, he served as a member of the Board of Directors of the National Wildlife Federation from 1948 to 1951 and as a vice president during 1952 and 1953. He traveled widely to give state affiliates of the Federation a national viewpoint in the same manner as he had labored to give county chapters in Missouri a statewide outlook. He was particularly effective in opposing construction of dams on clear water streams of the Ozarks and in arousing public support for protection of the Florida Key deer. Died January 30, 1963.

Louis S. Clapper

National Cyclopaedia of American Biography, 1965.

DAVIS, HERBERT SPENCER (1875–1958)

Born March 28, 1875 in Oneida, New York. Wesleyan University, Ph.B. 1899; Harvard University, Ph.D. 1907. He was instructor and assistant professor at Washington State College, 1901–6, and professor of zoology at the University of Florida, 1907–22. He joined the Fish and Wildlife Service as a fish pathologist and became chief of aquaculture investigations in 1929, serving in this capacity until his retirement in 1944. He then was chief fish pathologist for the Oregon State Game Commission, 1945–47, after which he became research associate at the University of California, Berkeley. He was responsible for the establishment of experimental fisheries stations at Leetown, West Virginia; Pittsford, Vermont; and Convict Creek, California. He pioneered early experimental dietary

work with trout in hatcheries and conducted some of the first
research directed toward perfecting superior strains of fishes. His
major work dealt with diseases and parasites of fishes and his
publication *Care and Diseases of Trout*, 1935, became the most
used reference at fish hatcheries throughout the world. His *Culture
and Diseases of Game Fishes*, 1953, was his last and most comprehensive publication. He was president of the American Fisheries
Society, 1932–33. Died July 15, 1958.

RICHARD J. GRAHAM

American Men of Science, 7th ed., 1944.
Transactions of the American Fisheries Society, vol. 88, no. 2, 1959.

DAVIS, KENNETH PICKETT (1906–   )

Born September 2, 1906 in Denver, Colorado. University of Montana, B.S.F. 1928; University of Michigan, M.F. 1932, Ph.D. (forest
management) 1940. After employment as a district ranger in the
United States Forest Service from 1928 to 1931, he then became
silviculturist at the Northern Rocky Mountain Forest and Range
Experiment Station, and in 1940 was transferred to Washington,
D. C. as assistant and then chief of the Division of Forest Management Research. In 1945 he left this post to become dean of the
School of Forestry at Montana State University. In 1949 he was
appointed professor of forest management and in 1950 chairman of
the Department of Forestry at the University of Michigan School
of Natural Resources. Since 1967 he has been professor of forest
land use at the School of Forestry, Yale University. In addition to
his official duties he was president of the Montana Conservation
Council, 1948–49; a member of the Michigan Board of Registration
of Foresters, 1956–62; chairman of the Wood Section, Michigan
Natural Resources Council, 1954–61; and Fulbright lecturer at the
University of Helsinki in 1963. Long active in the Society of American Foresters, he has been chairman of the Washington, Northern
Rocky Mountain, and Wisconsin–Michigan Sections; chairman of
the Forest Practices Committee, 1945–56; acting editor of *Forest
Science*, 1957–58; member of the Council, 1958–61; vice president,

Davis   92

1966–69; and in 1961 he was elected a Fellow. The author of ten
bulletins and 75 published papers, he also wrote the books *American Forest Management: Regulation and Valuation*, 2nd ed., 1966,
and *Forest Fires: Control and Use*, 1959.

SOCIETY OF AMERICAN FORESTERS

American Men of Science (The Physical and Biological Sciences), 11th ed., 1965.
Who's Who in America, 1968–69.

DAVIS, WATERS SMITH, JR. (1899–1958)

Born October 30, 1899 in Galveston, Texas. Graduated Williams
College 1922. His business career began when he was made vice
president of the Comet Rice Company. For a number of years, he
held a seat on the New York Stock Exchange and was a member
of the brokerage firm of Lapham and Davis. In 1940 he returned to
League City, Texas and assumed management of his family's ranch
holdings, League Davis properties, which included extensive operations
in lumber, grain, cotton, and cattle industries. He made
experiments in the management of lands and grasses. In 1944 he
was elected district supervisor of his local Brazoria-Galveston Soil
Conservation District. In 1947 the Texas Association of Soil Conservation
Districts elected him president. He began writing "Texas
Topsoil," probably the first newsletter devoted to the development
of Soil Conservation Districts. In 1950 he was elected president of
the National Association of Soil Conservation Districts, served five
consecutive terms, and until his death was treasurer and director.
In 1954 he began a series of terms as general chairman of five
National Watershed Congresses. He was awarded the Hugh Hammond
Bennett gold medallion in 1958 by Friends of the Land. His
own National Association selected him as "Conservation Man of the
Year" in 1954. He was made an honorary life member of the Soil
Conservation Society of America in 1952. Died November 15, 1958.

DAVID STEWART, JR.

Who's Who in the South and Southwest.

DAY, ALBERT MERRILL (1897–)

Born April 2, 1897 in Humboldt, Nebraska. University of Wyoming, B.S. (biology) 1922. He began as leader in the Division of Predator and Rodent Control, United States Bureau of Biological Survey, in Wyoming from 1918 to 1930, then became assistant chief and chief of that division in Washington, D. C., 1930–38. He was the first chief of the Division of Federal Aid in Wildlife Restoration, 1938–42, and nurtured that agency to its present place of prominence. He served the Fish and Wildlife Service, United States Department of the Interior, through its post-war growth, first as assistant director, 1942–46, then as director, 1946–53. Subsequently, for three years he was director of wildlife research for the Arctic Institute of North America; then director of the Oregon Fish Commission, 1958–60; and executive director of the Pennsylvania Fish Commission, 1960–64. Now a conservation consultant. Served as a member or advisor on several international fisheries commissions; in the United States Section, United Nations Conference on Law of the Sea; and on the Special Advisory Committee to the Secretary of the Interior. National director of the Izaak Walton League of America, 1945–52; an honorary member of the Wildlife Society. A contributor of articles to professional and popular journals; author of *North American Waterfowl*, 1949, and co-author of a chapter in *Waterfowl Tomorrow*, 1964.

PHILIP A. DUMONT

American Men of Science (The Physical and Biological Sciences), 11th ed., 1965.

DAYTON, WILLIAM ADAMS (1885–1958)

Born December 14, 1885 in New York City. Williams College, B.A. 1905, M.A. 1908. Plant ecologist and dendrologist with the Forest Service, United States Department of Agriculture, for more than 45 years, from 1910 to 1955, and adviser after retirement. He pioneered in range research on the national forests, was in charge of range forage investigations, and conducted field work in many parts of the country. Transferring from the West to Washington, D. C., in 1914, he became chief of the new Division of Dendrology and Range Forage Investigations in 1942. Under his supervision the Forest Service herbarium, founded by him in 1910, became the largest collection of range plants in the nation with more than 120,000 specimens. In 1943 he served as dendrologist with a forest survey in Costa Rica. He was an authority on range plants and a leader in standardization of English plant names. Received the gold medal of the Massachusetts Horticultural Society and the Distinguished Service Award of the United States Department of Agriculture. Member of more than twenty scientific societies, serving several as president or other officer. Delegate to the Seventh International Botanical Congress at Stockholm, Sweden, in 1950, and section chairman at the Sixth International Grassland Congress, State College, Pennsylvania, in 1952. Author of *Important Western Browse Plants*, 1931, *Range Plant Handbook* (with others) 1937, *Standardized Plant Names* (2nd ed., with Harlan P. Kelsey) 1942, *The Forests of Costa Rica* (with others) 1943, *Notes on Western Range Forbs*, 1960, also more than 150 scientific articles, bulletins, notes, and reviews. Died October 20, 1958.

ELBERT L. LITTLE, JR.

American Men of Science, 9th ed., 1955.
Taxon 8: 185–187; portrait, 1959.
Who Was Who in America, 1951–60.

DILG, WILL H. (1867–1927)

Born in 1867 in Milwaukee, Wisconsin. A writer for outdoor magazines, he was the founder of the Izaak Walton League of America in Chicago in January 1922. Originally established by a group of 54 men, the League was started with the object of improving land and water conservation in the public interest. Among its first projects was a fight to preserve clean waterways and to combat stream pollution. Now a national organization of 55,000 members with active local chapters throughout the country, the League works to advance the management of all resources and the total quality of the environment. As the League's first president until 1926, Dilg helped save from commercial exploitation that portion of the Superior National Forest in Minnesota now included in the Boundary Waters Canoe Area. He also conceived the plan for creating the Upper Mississippi Wild Life and Game Refuge and set up the Izaak Walton League fund to save the starving elk in Jackson Hole, Wyoming. In 1952 the League dedicated the Will H. Dilg memorial, now in Prairie Island City Park, Minnesota.

ROBERT L. HERBST

DIXON, JOSEPH SCATTERGOOD   (1884–1952)

Born March 5, 1884 in Cherokee County, Kansas. Educated in biological sciences at Throop Academy, graduating in 1908; graduate studies at Stanford University and the University of California, Berkeley. He was a member of the Alexander expedition to Alaska during 1907–8, and of the Harvard expedition to Alaska and Siberia during 1913–14, collecting biological data. Assistant curator of mammals at the Museum of Vertebrate Zoology at Berkeley, 1915–18, and economic mammalogist at the Museum, 1918–31. In 1931 he joined with George Melendez Wright to start the Wildlife Division in the National Park Service, Department of the Interior, in which he was field naturalist from 1931 to 1946, when he retired. He was a member of the Ornithologists Union; an honorary member of the Cooper Ornithological Club; vice president, president, and a member of the Board of Governors of the American Society of Mammalogists; a member of the Wildlife Society, a Fellow of the California Academy of Sciences, and vice president in 1937. He was a regional director of the First North American Wildlife Conference in 1936 which led to the founding of the National Wildlife Federation. He published numerous scientific articles on economic mammalogy, ornithology, and ecology, and was author of the *Birds and Mammals of Mount McKinley National Park*, No. 3 of the National Park Service's *Fauna Series* and co-author of

Fauna Series 1; he collaborated with Joseph Grinnell and Jean M. Linsdale in the *Fur-Bearing Mammals of California*, 1937, and was co-author with Lowell Sumner of *Birds and Mammals of the Sierra Nevada*, 1953. Died June 23, 1952.

BEN H. THOMPSON

American Men of Science, 8th ed., 1949.

DODGE, MARCELLUS HARTLEY (1881–1963)

Born 1881. Columbia University, A.B. 1903. He served as president and chairman of the board of Remington Arms Company, maintaining a close personal interest in conservation affairs throughout his life. He was a member of the American Game Protective Association, a member of the board of directors of the American Wildlife Institute from 1935 through 1945, and trustee of the North American Wildlife Foundation from 1946 to 1963. He was largely responsible for rallying support of the sporting arms and manufacturing industry for the Pittman-Robertson Federal Aid in Wildlife Restoration Act, a major factor in the enactment of that milestone legislation. Support of the industry for retention of the 11 per cent excise tax on sporting firearms and ammunition and its application to wildlife conservation was a vital consideration when the act was being considered by Congress in 1937. In 1959 he suggested the creation of a national wildlife refuge to be created in the Great Swamp of Morris County, New Jersey, and donated substantial funds to the North American Wildlife Foundation to initiate the project. Acquisition of the land and its donation to the federal government were completed in 1964 by the North American Wildlife Foundation; the refuge was dedicated in May 1964. Died December 25, 1963.

JAMES B. TREFETHEN

Who Was Who in America, 1961–68.
Who's Who in America, 1962–63.

DOREMUS, THOMAS EDWARD (1874–1962)

Born in 1874. An industrialist and officer for many years of the du Pont Company who devoted much of his time to furthering the cause of conservation. In 1911 he was one of the founding members of the American Game Protective and Propagation Association and became a member of its board of directors in 1912. From 1935 to 1945, he was a trustee of the American Wildlife Institute, the predecessor of the Wildlife Management Institute and the North American Wildlife Foundation. With the establishment of the latter organization in 1945, he became treasurer, serving in this capacity until his death. In 1935, he was instrumental in launching the National Wildlife Federation. He also helped obtain private funds with which to start the Cooperative Wildlife Research Unit Program, a student training program involving the Department of the Interior, state conservation agencies, land-grant colleges, and the American Wildlife Institute (late Wildlife Management Institute). He played a prominent role in the passage of the Federal Aid in Wildlife Restoration Act of 1937 by developing support for its enactment among the members of the sporting arms and ammunition manufacturers. He was awarded the Nash Conservation Award for exceptional service to conservation in 1955. Died September 23, 1962.

JAMES B. TREFETHEN

DOUGLAS, PHILIP ARNETT (1917–   )

Born December 1, 1917 at Detroit, Michigan. University of Arizona, B.S. 1941; University of Michigan, M.S. (fisheries biology) 1948. He began his professional career in fish conservation with the California Department of Fish and Game in 1948; was promoted in 1950 to assistant fisheries biologist, and in 1952 to district fisheries biologist in Southern California where he worked on the establishment of a saltwater gamefish sport fishery in the Salton Sea project, and, during the later stages of its development, served as chairman of the Salton Sea Advisory Committee. During 1956–57, he was special consultant to the California Wildlife Conservation Board, as the southern representative to secure fishing access to both marine and fresh water areas, then transferred to the staff of the Wildlife Conservation Board to help administer a special state conservation fund for access to and development of fishing and hunting areas. Since 1961, he has been executive secretary of the Sport Fishing Institute, Washington, D. C. He has served on many committees of various conservation groups, and has helped organize important seminars, symposia, and national workshops on fish conservation subjects including access to recreational waters, water quality standards to protect aquatic life, and thermal pollution. He is a member of Phi Sigma Biological Honorary Society, as well as several professional and scientific societies in the natural resources field, and is certified by the American Fisheries Society as a qualified fishery scientist. He has been a trustee and treasurer of the Sport Fishery Research Foundation since its inception in 1962.

R. H. STROUD

DRAKE, GEORGE LINCOLN (1889–)

Born April 7, 1889 in Laconia, New Hampshire. Pennsylvania State University, B.S. (forestry) 1912. From 1912 to 1930 was with the United States Forest Service in Alaska, Oregon, and Washington as forest examiner, deputy supervisor, logging engineer, and assistant regional forester. Employed by Simpson Logging Company in 1930 as its first professional forester; served as general superintendent of logging and forestry work, retiring as vice president in 1954. He joined the Society of American Foresters in 1918, was president, 1952–53, and was elected a Fellow in 1953. As a representative of the West Coast Lumbermen's Association and the Pacific Northwest Loggers Association he helped draw up the forest practice rules under the National Industrial Recovery Act of 1933. These rules initiated the application of forestry on the industrial timberlands of the West. Among his many activities and offices in behalf of improved forest management, he was a member of the board of the

Washington Forest Fire Association, 1930–54; director of the Pacific Logging Congress, 1932–37 (president during latter year); member of the Western Forestry and Conservation Association for four decades, and president in 1948. He was the originator of the Shelton Cooperative Sustained Yield Unit, a pooling of private and national forest totaling 260,000 acres under a coordinated management plan for the period 1947–2047. He was a founder and vice president of the South Olympic Tree Farm established in 1941. Recipient of awards from Washington State University in 1950, the American Forestry Association in 1954, and the Pennsylvania State University in 1957.

HENRY CLEPPER

DRURY, NEWTON BISHOP (1889–   )

Born April 9, 1889 in San Francisco, California. University of California, B.L. 1912, LL.D. 1947. From 1912 to 1918, he was an instructor in English at the University of California. Following military service in World War I, he opened a public relations firm in San Francisco. In 1919 he was instrumental in founding the Save-the-Redwoods League which he served as executive secretary from 1919 to 1940. It was through his early leadership that the crusade to preserve the coastal groves became a national movement. In 1927, he helped write the legislation creating the California State Park Commission, and from 1929 to 1940, concurrent with his duties in the League, he served as the Commission's acquisition officer and executive secretary. During this period, 56 state parks were established. In 1940, he was appointed director of the National Park Service, a position he held until 1951. During his administration, he became widely known in conservation circles for his tenacious opposition to special interest demands, especially during the critical years of World War II. From 1951 to 1959, he was chief of the California Division of Beaches and Parks. Following his retirement in 1959, he returned to the Save-the-Redwoods League as secretary. Awards received for his accomplishments in conservation and park development include: the Conservation Award of the Trustees of Public Reservations; the Pugsley Gold Medal of the American Scenic and Historic Preservation Society; Distinguished Service Award of the American Forestry Association; Conservation Award of the National Audubon Society; the Francis K. Hutchinson Medal of the Garden Club of America; honorary member of the American Society of Landscape Architects and of the Society of American Foresters; Fellow, American Institute of Park Executives; and honorary vice president of the Sierra Club. Two California redwood groves have been designated as living memorials to him: the Drury Brothers Grove in Prairie Creek State Park and the Newton B. Drury Grove in Humbolt Redwoods State Park.

HOLT BODINSON

SHANKLAND, ROBERT. *Steve Mather of the National Parks.* New York: Alfred A. Knopf, 1951.
Who's Who in America, 1968–69.
Who's Who in the West, 1969.

DULEY, FRANK LESLIE (1888–)

Born December 21, 1888 in Grant City, Missouri. University of Missouri, B.S.A. 1914, A.M. 1915; University of Wisconsin, Ph.D. 1923. At the University of Missouri, where he was on the faculty from 1915 to 1925, he helped in 1917 to set up the first plots in this country to study the effects of cropping systems on runoff and erosion. Still maintained, these plots along with the Old Sandborn experimental field were designated in 1965 by the United States Department of the Interior as a national monument. From 1925 to 1933, he was professor of agronomy at Kansas State College. He was then made regional director in Kansas of one of the first groups of soil erosion projects started in the United States; after three years with the Soil Conservation Service, United States Department of Agriculture, in Kansas, he became leader of a research team in soil and moisture conservation at Lincoln, Nebraska, retiring from federal service in December 1958. From 1959 to 1964, he was employed by Colorado State University and assigned to a project of the Agency for International Development at the University of Peshawar, West Pakistan, where he also served as principal of its new agricultural college. He is a Fellow of the American Association for the Advancement of Science, the American Society of Agronomy, and the Soil Conservation Society of America (president in 1947). The United States Department of Agriculture conferred on him the Superior Service Award in 1955 for his work in originating and developing the stubble mulch system of farming for water and wind erosion control. He is the author of numerous articles on soil and water conservation.

D. E. HUTCHINSON

American Men of Science (The Physical and Biological Sciences), 11th ed., 1965.

DUNN, PAUL MILLARD (1898–)

Born October 15, 1898 in Lennox, South Dakota. Iowa State College, B.S. 1923, M.S. (forestry) 1933. He was assistant and associate state forester in Missouri from 1926 to 1931, and then joined the faculty of the Utah State University School of Forest Range and Wildlife Management where he was dean from 1938 to 1942 and also state forester-firewarden for Utah. While dean of the School of Forestry at Oregon State College from 1942 to 1954, he was also director, Oregon Forest Products Laboratory, 1942–53, and director of the College Forest Experiment Station, 1950–54. During 1952–53 he took leave of absence on an assignment with the Food and Agriculture Organization of the United Nations to assist the government of Chile to establish a curriculum in forestry at the University of Chile. He joined the St. Regis Paper Company as technical director of forestry in 1955 and in 1962 was advanced to vice president (forestry and timberlands) which position he held until his retirement in 1968, though continuing as a forestry consultant thereafter. In the Society of American Foresters he served as chairman of the Intermountain and Columbia River Sections, and the Division of Education; as a member of the Council, 1946–

49; as president, 1962–63; he was elected a Fellow in 1959. He is also a Fellow of the American Association for the Advancement of Science. He was president of the Forest History Society in 1967–68, and was president of the American Forestry Association, 1968–70. He is past president of the Southern Pulpwood Conservation Association and was a director of the American Pulpwood Association. He has been a member of the Cooperative Forestry Research Advisory Committee for the United States Department of Agriculture since 1964.

SOCIETY OF AMERICAN FORESTERS

American Men of Science (The Physical and Biological Sciences), 11th ed., 1965.
Journal of Forestry. Forestry News, vol. 65:912, 1967.
Who's Who in America, 1968–69.

DUTCHER, WILLIAM (1846–1920)

Born January 20, 1846 in Stelton, New Jersey. Following education in local public schools, he engaged in the insurance business. His avocation was wildlife, especially bird, conservation in which cause he made a notable and lasting contribution. Joining the American Ornithologists' Union in 1883, he became, one year later, a member of its Committee on Bird Protection which in 1886 drew up a prototype state law for the protection of non-game birds. He was made chairman of this committee in 1896, the year that marks the beginning of the existing Audubon movement. By 1903 the Audubon law protecting song birds had been passed in 26 states. Having encouraged the formation of regional Audubon societies, which by 1905 had increased to more than 40, he founded in that year the National Association of Audubon Societies, now the National Audubon Society, and was elected president of the organization, an unsalaried post he held until his death. This society, which 65 years later is one of the nation's largest and most influential citizens' bodies devoted to the preservation and wise use of all natural resources, has 80,000 members and a strong network of chapters throughout the United States. For years he was an indefatigable worker for laws to protect bird life, and through many personal visits to state legislatures he obtained the enactment of legislation regulating or prohibiting market hunting and the killing of song and insectivorous birds. He was the administrator of a fund to employ wardens to protect seabirds and plumed herons. In 1910 he was successful in obtaining passage of the New York Plumage Act which closed the state, center of the millinery trade, to all American wild bird plumage and to foreign plumage from birds of the same families. This law was the precursor of the Weeks-McLean Act passed by Congress in 1913 and of the Migratory Bird Treaty Act of 1918 which saved untold millions of birds from market hunting for their plumage and which prohibited their importation into the United States. Although a crusader without scientific education in biology, he was recognized by scientific societies for his work. Active in the New York Zoological Society, he was elected also to the New York Academy of Sciences and was a Fellow of the American Association for the Advancement of Science. The Camp Fire Club of America presented him with its gold medal for his accomplishments in bird conservation. Died July 2, 1920.

JEANNE GOODWIN

Bird Lore, September–October, 1920.
New York Times. Obituary, 21:4, July 4, 1920.
The Auk, October, 1921.
Who Was Who in America, 1897–1942.

DUTTON, WALT LEROY (1889–   )

Born May 1, 1889 near Alliance, Nebraska. Oregon Agricultural College (now Oregon State University), B.S. (forestry) 1913. Entered the United States Forest Service that year in the Pacific Northwest and advanced successively through the positions of forest guard, assistant forest ranger, forest ranger, grazing examiner, assistant forest supervisor, forest supervisor, and district forest inspector. Transferred to the Washington office in 1936 as chief (now director) of the Division of Range Management. In this position he made an outstanding record in stopping destructive grazing use and improving range and watershed conditions on the national forests through reduction in numbers of permitted livestock, better handling of the grazing animals, installation or structural range improvements, and range reseeding. Much of the reduction in grazing use was accomplished in the face of opposition from the organized livestock industry and hostile committees of Congress. Retired in 1953 and spent eighteen months with the British Colonial Service as range and forestry consultant in the African colonies. In 1955 was a member of a United Nations team making an economic survey of possibilities for increasing agricultural production in Argentina. In 1948–49 served two years on the three-man Pan American Committee on Conservation Awards. In 1949 received the United States Department of Agriculture Superior Service Award "for outstanding service to public welfare through effective administration and leadership in the field of range management, resulting in critically needed improvement of range land in the national forests with respect to forage, water run-off, and soil conservation." Also in 1949 received the United States Department of Agriculture Certificate of Merit in which he was "commended for performance substantially exceeding the requirements of his position." In 1951 he was assigned to the Army of Occupation in Japan as special advisor on pasture and forestry activities. A life member and one of the founders of the American Society of Range Management, he served on its board of directors, 1949–51. A member of the Society of American Foresters since 1918.

LLOYD W. SWIFT

EDDY, SAMUEL (1897–)

Born March 29, 1897 in Decatur, Illinois. James Millikin University, A.B. 1924; University of Illinois, A.M. 1925, Ph.D. (zoology) 1929. Instructor and assistant professor at James Millikin University, 1924–26; teaching assistant in zoology at the University of Illinois and assistant aquatic biologist for the Illinois Natural History Survey, Urbana, 1926–29. From assistant professor of zoology University of Minnesota, 1929–38, he became associate professor, 1938–44, professor, 1944–64, and has been honorary curator of fishes at James Ford Bell Museum of Natural History, University of Minnesota, since 1964. He was in charge of fisheries research for the Minnesota Department of Conservation and was consultant for biological surveys for the Minnesota Division of Game and Fish, 1937–40. He was vice president of the Ecological Society of America in 1953. His books include two textbooks on comparative anatomy; he is co-author of *Taxonomic Keys to Common Animals of North Central States*, 1950, and is author of *How to Know the Fresh-Water Fishes of the United States*, 1957. He has conducted surveys in Illinois and Minnesota, and has worked in areas of fish taxonomy and growth.

LAWRENCE A. JAHN

American Men of Science (The Physical and Biological Sciences), 11th ed., 1965.
Who's Who in America, 1964–65.
World Who's Who in Science, 1968.

EDGE, MABEL ROSALIE (1877–1962)

Born November 3, 1877 in New York City. Private school education; Wagner College, Staten Island, New York, Litt.D. (honorary) 1948. Active in the votes-for-women movement, she became interested in conservation following adoption of the women suffrage amendment in 1920. One of her early concerns was for wild birds, and she launched a successful personal campaign within the National Audubon Society for a change in the society's leadership. In 1929 she created the Emergency Conservation Committee of which for three decades she was the crusading chairman. Supported by many small contributions, it published more than one million copies of a hundred pamphlets on many resource issues. Under the aegis of this Committee, she campaigned for waterfowl hunting laws and regulations, against the United States Biological Survey's policies of predator poisoning, and for creation of Olympic and Kings Canyon National Parks. One of her most notable reforms was the establishment of Hawk Mountain Sanctuary in southeastern Pennsylvania. In 1934, having solicited the necessary funds, she obtained a one-year lease on Hawk Mountain where for decades shooters had annually slaughtered thousands of migrating birds of prey. Later she was able to exercise an option to purchase some two square miles of wooded property which became the nucleus of the present sanctuary, the first created for birds of prey. It is now administered by the Hawk Mountain Sanctuary Association, which she organized in 1936 and of which she was a director and president until her death. A militant activist in the conservation movement of the middle twentieth century, she also helped obtain the victory that abolished baiting and the use of live decoys in waterfowl hunting and resulted in other reforms in wildlife management. Died November 30, 1962.

JEANNE GOODWIN

Hawks Aloft: The Story of Hawk Mountain. New York: Dodd, Mead Company, 1947.
New York Times. Obituary, December 1, 1962.
The New Yorker, April 17, 1948.
Who's Who in America, 1954–55.

EDMINSTER, FRANK CUSTER (1903–)

Born December 26, 1903 in Ithaca, New York. Cornell University, B.S. 1926, M.S. (ornithology) 1930. Then for seven years he was research biologist with New York State Conservation Department. He was an instructor in game management at Cornell University, 1936–37. Joining the Soil Conservation Service in 1937 as regional biologist, he advanced to New York state conservationist and finally to recreation specialist. Retired in 1966 from the United States Department of Agriculture after 28 years of distinguished service during which he gained a national reputation in the integrated fields of land management and wildlife management. He pioneered in the management of farm ponds for fish production and in the use of shrubs as tools of land management. He was chairman of the Northeast Board of Agricultural Examiners for the United States Civil Service Commission, 1946–57. He served as secretary of the Wildlife Society, 1940–42, and in 1947 was a co-recipient of the society's award for outstanding wildlife publication of the year. He is a Fellow of the Soil Conservation Society of America and was chairman of the Society's Committee on Wetland Management. Following retirement from government service he has served as consulting ecologist. He is the author of more than 100 scientific and popular publications. His major books include *The Ruffed Grouse*, 1947, *Fish Ponds for the Farm*, 1947, and *American Game Birds of Field and Forest*, 1954.

LAWRENCE V. COMPTON

American Men of Science (The Physical and Biological Sciences), 11th ed., 1965.

ELDREDGE, INMAN FOWLER (1883–1963)

Born March 24, 1883 in Camden, South Carolina. Attended Clemson College, Biltmore Forest School, Bachelor of Forestry 1909; North Carolina State College, Doctor of Forest Science (honorary). In 1905 entered the United States Forest Service as a student assistant; appointed forest assistant in 1906, and in 1909 was made forest examiner assigned to timber sales. Later that year he became supervisor of the newly created national forests in Florida, and for eight years administered one-half million acres of government timberland. During this period he developed new techniques of conservative turpentining, now in general use throughout the naval stores region. In 1917, at the outbreak of World War I, was commissioned in the Army and served as captain in the 10th Engineers (Forestry) in France. After the war returned to the Forest Service as chief of the Division of Timber Management in the Eastern Region; subsequently forest inspector of management and timber sales on all national forests on the chief forester's staff in Washington, D. C. His Forest Service career was interrupted in 1926 when he took industrial employment to manage the Suwanee Forest in the long-leaf pine region of southeast Georgia. Returned to the Forest Service in 1932 as regional director of the forest survey of the South at the Southern Forest Experiment Station in New Orleans. In 1944 he retired from the Forest Service but continued work as a private forest consultant. Member of the Board of the Charles Lathrop Pack Foundation, and the Southern Division of the Natural Resources Planning Board. Member, Society of American Foresters, 1911; Fellow, 1942; Gifford Pinchot Medal, 1956; member of the Council, 1940–43. Died April 15, 1963.

SOCIETY OF AMERICAN FORESTERS

Journal of Forestry. Obituary, 61:470, 1963.

EMBODY, GEORGE CHARLES (1876–1939)

Born November 23, 1876 in Auburn, New York. Colgate University, M.S. (aquatic biology) 1901; Cornell University, Ph.D. (biology) 1910. A teacher of science at Delaware Literary Institute, New York, early in his career, he was then a high school teacher at Bradford, Pennsylvania, professor of science at Butler College, professor of biology at Randolph-Macon College, and later was assistant professor in aquaculture at Cornell University. He served as conservation biologist for the New Jersey Fish Commission, then became biologist-advisor in fisheries for the New York Conservation Department. In 1932 he was the biologist in charge of trout investigations in California. He was president of the American Fisheries Society in 1924. Among his many papers on fisheries, he will be remembered most for his work in fish culture and trout field studies. He was a pioneer in the area of fish population harvest and dynamics and is recognized as one of the foremost early leaders in fisheries ecology. Died February 17, 1939.

ELWOOD A. SEAMAN

Who Was Who in America, 1897–1942.

ENGLISH, PENNOYER FRANCIS (1894–1958)

Born February 21, 1894 in Farmington, Washington. Oregon State
College, B.S. (zoology) 1919; Texas A. and M. College, M.S. 1925;
University of Michigan, Ph.D. (wildlife management) 1934; also
graduate work at University of Chicago and Ohio State University.
Nearly all his professional career was spent as a university educator.
He was assistant in zoology at Oregon State College, 1919–21;
assistant professor of biology at Texas A. and M. College, 1921–24;
professor of biology at St. Teresa College, Minnesota, 1924–26;
associate professor of biology at Texas A. and M. College, 1926–31;
biologist for the Michigan Department of Conservation, 1933–35;
associate professor of wildlife management at the University of
Connecticut, 1935–38; and professor of wildlife management at the
Pennsylvania State University, 1938–58. He was a charter member of the Wildlife Society, its secretary from 1943 to 1946, its tenth
president in 1946, and was elected an honorary member in 1956.
Other professional affiliations included the Society of American
Mammalogists, Cooper Ornithological Society, Wilson Ornithological Club, and American Ornithologists' Union. He was author of
more than 50 scientific papers on wildlife management and conservation. As a teacher and research worker he guided and directed the
graduate programs of some 60 wildlife management students. One
of the first men in the United States to be trained in wildlife
management, he helped found the wildlife profession. Died October
8, 1958.

ROBERT G. WINGARD

American Men of Science (The Physical and Biological Sciences), 10th ed., 1955.
Journal of Wildlife Management. Obituary, vol. 23, July 1959.

ERRINGTON, PAUL LESTER (1902–62)

Born June 14, 1902 in Bruce, South Dakota. South Dakota State
College, B.S. 1930; University of Wisconsin, Ph.D. (zoology) 1932.
He was employed by Iowa State University during his entire pro-

fessional career; as research assistant professor of zoology, 1932–38; research associate professor of zoology, 1938–48; and professor of zoology, 1948–62. His major research concerned the food habits of avian and mammalian predators, the effects of predation on prey populations, and the automatically adjusting trends in population mechanisms of vertebrates. He spent a year, 1958–59, in Scandinavia under the auspices of the Swedish government, the Guggenheim Foundation, and the National Science Foundation. He was selected twice by the Wildlife Society for the outstanding writing on terrestrial wildlife, in 1941 for *The Great Horned Owl and Its Prey in North-Central United States*, 1940—a bulletin of the Iowa Agricultural Experiment Station, with Frances Hamerstrom and F. N. Hamerstrom, Jr.—and in 1947 for "Predation and Vertebrate Populations," 1946 in *Quarterly Review of Biology*. In 1962, he was awarded the Aldo Leopold Medal by the Wildlife Society, the highest honor the society can bestow, and an especially fitting one since he had received his graduate training under the supervision of Professor Leopold at the University of Wisconsin. A memorial fund at Iowa State University in his name supports lectures by distinguished scientists. There are over 200 titles in his bibliography. His other better known publications are: *Of Men and Marshes*, 1957; *Muskrats and Marsh Management*, 1961; *Muskrat Populations*, 1963; *Predation and Life*, 1967. Died November 5, 1962.

THOMAS G. SCOTT

American Men of Science (The Physical and Biological Sciences), 10th ed., 1955.
Iowa State Journal of Science. Bibliography, 38(4):447–58, 1964.
Journal of Wildlife Management. Obituary, 27(2):321–24, 1963.

ESCHMEYER, REUBEN WILLIAM (1905–55)

Born June 29, 1905 in New Knoxville, Ohio. Heidelberg College, Tiffin, Ohio, A.B. 1927; University of Michigan, A.M. 1931, Ph.D. (fisheries) 1937. He began his professional career as fishery biologist for the Institute of Fisheries Research, Michigan Conservation Department, where he was in charge of lake investigations for eight years until 1938, and pioneered in the use of rotenone as a management tool for improving fishing in public waters by eliminating existing fish populations and starting over, and in the improvement of lake and pond fish habitat. In 1938 he joined the staff of the Biological Readjustment Division (later renamed Fish and Game Branch) Tennessee Valley Authority, as associate aquatic biologist in charge of fisheries work, and remained there for 12 years, becoming assistant chief of that Division (later Branch) in 1947. He organized and directed the research program that resulted, in 1944, in abandoning the closed season on warmwater game fishes in the multi-purpose TVA reservoirs, and in a near-doubling of total catch without harm to future supply, a concept which has since been applied to varying extent in most of the states. In 1950 he was selected as the first executive vice president of the Sport Fishing Institute, Washington, D. C., a newly organized, national conservation organization, and developed a program emphasizing conservation education, research in fishery biology, and improvement of professional standards in fishery science. Understanding the close dependence of fish on proper soil and forest conditions, he showed conservationists and sportsmen the basic similarity between managing fish populations and managing land crops. He was consulted by state fish and conservation commissions for advice on modernizing their state fishery programs. He was founding editor of the Sport Fishing Institute's monthly *Bulletin,* wrote important essays on fish conservation subjects, particularly those grouped together in "Fish Conservation Fundamentals," "Land, Water and Fishing," and "Conservation Chart and Text." In addition to a series of 10 children's conservation books, he was author or co-author of more than 50 scientific fishery papers and conservation textbook chapters on fish conservation as well as junior author (with Carl L. Hubbs) of *The Improvement of Lakes for Fishing,* 1938, and senior author (with George S. Fichter) of *Good Fishing,* 1959. Died May 21, 1955. He was installed posthumously in the Ohio Conservation Hall of Fame in August, 1967.

R. H. STROUD

American Men of Science, 8th ed., 1949.
Journal of Wildlife Management. Obituary, 19(4):483–84, October 1955.
Sport Fishing Institute Bulletin. Obituary, 44:1–2, July 1955.

EVANS, CHARLES FLOYD (1885–1963)

Born February 26, 1885 at Muscoda, Wisconsin. University of Wisconsin, B.A. 1909; Yale University School of Forestry, M.F. 1912. Reported for duty with the United States Forest Service in 1912 and was assigned to the Targhee National Forest at St. Anthony, Idaho for two years and at Vernal, Utah for three years. Was forest supervisor of the Challis National Forest at Mackay, Idaho 1918–22, and then assistant chief of operation in the Ogden, Utah regional office. He moved to New Orleans, Louisiana in March 1927 as a district inspector for the Division of State Cooperation of the Forest Service, administering the fire protection and tree seedling provisions of the Clarke-McNary Act. From 1929 through June 1934, he served in similar capacity for the southeastern states from Asheville, North Carolina. When the southern regional office of the Forest Service opened in Atlanta, Georgia in July 1934 he became assistant regional forester in charge of the State and Private Forestry Division for eleven states, performing outstanding service in this position until retirement in 1950. During this period, he provided leadership and guidance in these programs. An active worker in Society of American Foresters from 1921 until after retirement; served as chairman of the Gulf States, Appalachian, and Southeastern Sections; was a national councilman, vice president, and president during 1950–51; elected to grade of Fellow in 1950. The American Forestry Association honored him in 1950 with its Distinguished Service to Conservation Award. Died September 7, 1963.

JOHN W. COOPER

Journal of Forestry. Obituary, November 1963.

EVENDEN, FREDERICK GEORGE (1921–)

Born April 11, 1921 in Woodburn, Oregon. Oregon State University, B.S. 1943, Ph.D. (zoology) 1949. In 1948 he was appointed research biologist in the United States Fish and Wildlife Service Office of River Basin Studies, Sacramento, California. In 1943 he became executive director of the California Junior Museum in Sacramento. During the years 1956 to 1963, while in private business, he was an active conservationist. He created the Conservation Committee for the Golden Empire Council, Boy Scouts of America, and served as its chairman for several years, was on the Chamber of Commerce Natural Resources Committee, and was president of the Audubon Society. In 1963 he was selected by the Wildlife Society, Washington, D. C. as its first full-time executive secretary, becoming executive director in 1968, and was editor of *The Wildlife News*, 1964–69. He has since served as chairman of the International Association of Game Fish and Conservation Commissioners Professional Improvement Committee, 1966–68, the American Ornithologists' Union's Committee on Conservation, 1966–69, and on the Boy Scouts National Conservation Committee since 1963 where he was instrumental in creation of the Conservation of Natural Resources and Mammalogy merit badges. He has been a member of the Board of Consulting Experts on the Rachel Carson Trust for Living Environment since 1967, and a member of the Advisory Board of the Sierra Club Atlantic Chapter since 1965. He is a Fellow of the American Association for the Advancement of Science, was recipient of the California Conservation Council Honor Award in 1958, and the Boy Scouts Silver Beaver award in 1959. Author of numerous scientific articles and notes on natural resources subjects. Currently he is affiliated with more than thirty national and regional conservation organizations.

HENRY CLEPPER

American Men of Science, 11th ed., 1965.
Who's Who in America, 1968–69.

EVERMANN, BARTON WARREN (1853–1932)

Born October 24, 1853 in Albia, Monroe County, Iowa. Indiana University, B.S. 1886, A.M. 1888, Ph.D. 1891, LL.D. 1927; University of Utah, LL.D. 1922. From 1886 to 1891, he was professor of biology at Indiana State Normal School. Joining the United

States Bureau of Fisheries in 1891, he was advanced to chief of the Division of Statistics and Methods of Fisheries in 1902, then became assistant in charge of scientific inquiry the following year, and was in charge of the Alaska Fisheries Service, 1910–14; he then retired from federal service. While with the government he served as United States fur seal commissioner in 1892; was a special lecturer at Stanford University, 1893–94; and was a lecturer on fish and game protection at Cornell University, 1900–1903, and at Yale University, 1903–6. In 1914 he became director of the California Academy of Sciences, San Francisco, and in 1922, director of the Steinhart Aquarium, offices he held until his death. He was co-author with David Starr Jordan of *The Fishes of North and Middle America* 4 vols., 1896–1900; *American Food and Game Fishes*, 1902; *A Checklist of the Fishes and Fishlike Vertebrates of North and Middle America*, 1896. He wrote or contributed to 196 publications on fishes, some of the others being *Fishes of the Philippines*, 1906; *The Golden Trout of the Southern High Sierras*, 1906; *The Fishes of Alaska*, 1907; and the *Fishes of Peru*, 1915. His wide interest as a naturalist is revealed in 191 other publications including 59 on birds. Management policies that he advocated for the Alaska seal herd have helped conserve this valuable species, once almost on the verge of extinction. Died September 27, 1932.

ROBERT V. THURSTON

Dictionary of American Biography, 1944.
National Cyclopaedia of American Biography, 1906.
Webster's Bibliographical Dictionary, 1961.
Who Was Who in America, 1897–1943.
World Who's Who in Science, 1968.

FARQUHAR, FRANCIS PELOUBET (1887–)

Born December 31, 1887 in Newton, Massachusetts. Harvard University, A.B. 1909; University of California, LL.D. (honorary) 1967. He was in professional practice as a certified public accountant from 1918 to 1959. He worked for the enlargement of Sequoia National Park from 1919 to 1926, and as the representative of the

Sierra Club he appeared in behalf of this movement before Congressional committees. He was president of the Sierra Club, 1933–35, and 1948–49, served on the Board of Directors, 1924–51, was appointed honorary vice president in 1951, and honorary president in 1969; and was the recipient of the Club's John Muir Conservation Award in 1965. From 1936 to 1950, he served on the Committee on Registration of Historic Sites for the California Department of Natural Resources. He was editor of the *Sierra Club Bulletin*, 1926–46; of the *American Alpine Journal*, 1956–59; of *Up and Down California* (1860–1864), *The Journal of William H. Brewer*, 1930; and of *Mountaineering in the Sierra Nevada* by Clarence King, 1935. He is the author of *Place Names of the High Sierra*, 1926; *Yosemite, The Big Trees and the High Sierra: A Selective Bibliography*, 1948; *History of the Sierra Nevada*, 1965. In addition, he has written numerous articles on western mountains and history, including several for *Encyclopedia Britannica*. He received the Henry T. Wagner Medal from the California Historical Society in 1965 for mountaineering. He is a director of Save-the-Redwoods League.

LUELLA K. SAWYER

Sierra Club Handbook, 1967.

FELL, GEORGE BRADY (1916–)

Born September 27, 1916, in Elgin, Illinois. University of Illinois, B.A. 1938; University of Michigan, M.S. 1940. He taught public school during 1940–41. He was a bacteriologist and serologist for the Rockford, Illinois, City Health Department from 1946 to 1948. For the next year he was a soil conservationist for the United States Soil Conservation Service. He helped found the Nature Conservancy and was its executive director from 1950 to 1958. He has been director of the Natural Land Institute since 1958, and is currently chairman of the Citizens Committee for Nature Conservation and is secretary of the Nature Preserves Commission of Illinois. He is a member of numerous conservation groups, including the Wildlife Society, the Ecological Society of America, and the Soil Conservation Society. He is noted for his work in the methods of preserving and maintaining natural areas and in analysis and management of natural vegetation.

MARY JEAN CLEVELAND

American Men of Science (The Physical and Biological Sciences), 10th ed., 1955.

FERNOW, BERNHARD EDUARD (1851–1923)

Born January 7, 1851 in the province of Posen, Prussia. Studied law at the University of Konigsberg; then completed the prescribed curriculum in forestry for government service at Hanover-Muenden Academy and was licensed in 1869; University of Wisconsin, LL.D. 1896; Queen's University, LL.D. 1903; University of Toronto, LL.D. 1920. Prior to his arrival in the United States in 1876, he had been with the Prussian Forest Service. From 1878 to 1885, he managed a large private forest in Pennsylvania and became active in public forestry causes, and from 1883 to 1895, he was also secretary of the American Forestry Association. In 1886 he was appointed chief of the Division of Forestry, United States Department of Agriculture, and served until 1898. He was largely responsible for the law of 1891 that authorized the President to set apart portions of the timbered public domain as forest reserves; this was the basic act from which the present national forest system evolved. As chief forester he laid the foundations on which were built the present organization of the United States Forest Service. In addition, he created an intelligent public interest in forestry and in the need for education and research. From 1898 to 1903, he was director of the New York State College of Forestry at Cornell University, where he organized the first professional forestry curriculum in the Western Hemisphere. In 1904 he gave a series of lectures on forestry at Yale University, engaged also in consulting practice, and in 1907 helped start the Department of Forestry at Pennsylvania State College. He then went to the University of Toronto in 1907 where he organized the Faculty of Forestry, and in 1919 retired with emeritus status.

In 1902, while at Cornell, he was responsible for the establishment of *Forestry Quarterly* of which he was editor from 1903 to 1916. After its merger with the *Proceedings* of the Society of American Foresters to become the *Journal of Forestry* he was editor-in-chief from 1917 to 1923. His contributions to the literature of forestry were exceptional in number and quality; his bibliography totals 250 published papers, bulletins, and three books: *Economics of Forestry*, 1902; *A Brief History of Forestry*, 1913; and *Care of Trees*, 1910. Fernow Hall at Cornell was named for him and dedicated in his honor in 1922. One of the pioneer leaders of the profession of forestry in America, he had a dominant role as administrator, educator, author, and editor. He gave the New World its start in education for the profession and remained the educational leader for as long as he lived. Died February 6, 1923.

HENRY CLEPPER

Dictionary of American Biography. 1931.
Journal of Forestry. Obituary, 21:306–37. 1923.
RODGERS, ANDREW DENNY, III, *Bernhard Eduard Fernow: A Study of North American Forestry*, Princeton, N.J.: 1951.

FISHER, JOSEPH LYMAN (1914–)

Born January 11, 1914 in Pawtucket, Rhode Island. Bowdoin College, B.S. 1935; Harvard University, M.A. 1938, Ph.D. (economics) 1947; George Washington University, M.A. (education) 1951. He taught economics at Allegheny College, 1938–40. From 1939 to 1943, he was a planning technician with the National Resources Planning Board, in field offices, and in the latter year was an economist with the Department of State. After service in the Army, 1943–46, he was instructor in economics at Harvard for a year, then was economist and executive officer of the Council of Economic Advisers in the Executive Office of the President, 1947–53. Appointed associate director of Resources for the Future, Inc., Washington, D. C. in 1954, he became president in 1959. Resources for the Future, a nonprofit research and educational foundation concerned with the development of natural resources, is an affiliate

of the Ford Foundation. Writer, lecturer, and consultant on
economic problems of resource development and regional growth;
author or co-author of several books including *Resources in America's Future*, 1963, *World Prospects for Natural Resources*, 1964,
and of numerous professional articles. A director of the American
Forestry Association, he has been active in the American Association for the Advancement of Science, the American Economic
Association, the American Society for Public Administration, the
Arctic Institute of North America, and the Regional Science Association. He is president of the Metropolitan Washington Council of
Governments, and a trustee of the United Planning Organization
for the Washington, D. C. area.

HENRY CLEPPER

American Men of Science (The Social and Behavioral Sciences), 1968.
Who's Who in America, 1968–69.

FORBES, STEPHEN ALFRED   (1844–1930)

Born May 29, 1844 in Stephenson County, Illinois. Attended Rush
Medical College in Chicago but did not take his degree. Indiana
University awarded him a doctorate in 1884 "by thesis and examination." His first publications appeared in 1870. In 1872 he was
appointed curator of the museum established by the State Natural
History Society at Normal, Illinois; when it became the State
Laboratory of Natural History in 1877 he was appointed its head.
In 1885 he became professor of zoology and entomology at the
University of Illinois, director of the State Laboratory of Natural
History, and state entomologist. He was professor of zoology for
25 years, concurrently professor of entomology for 13 years and
dean of the College of Science for 16 years. When the State
Laboratory of Natural History and the State Entomologist's Office
were united in 1917 to form the Illinois Natural History Survey, he
became the first chief, a position he held throughout his lifetime.
Often called the father of ecology, his interests covered all biology.
Altogether he wrote more than 50 papers and reports on such

diverse subjects as crustacea, foods of fishes, foods of birds, ornithology, taxonomy and distribution of fishes, economic entomology, elm trees, forestry survey, and river biology. His best known works are *The Lake as a Microcosm*, Illinois Natural History Survey Bulletin 15(9):537–50, and the two-volume work with R. E. Richardson entitled *The Fishes of Illinois*.

GEORGE W. BENNETT

"A Century of Biological Research," *Illinois Natural History Bulletin* 27(2):94–97.

FORBUSH, EDWARD HOWE (1858–1929)

Born April 24, 1858 in Quincy, Massachusetts. His formal education was limited, and he learned ornithology and taxidermy by working. At the age of 16 he was appointed curator of ornithology of the Worcester Massachusetts Natural History Museum. Following collecting expeditions in Florida, he was co-founder of the Naturalists' Exchange. In 1888 he led a collecting expedition to the Pacific Northwest, Western Canada, and Alaska. In 1893 he served on a committee of the Massachusetts Board of Agriculture studying the destructive gypsy moth, and in 1903 was designated ornithologist to the Board. In 1908 he was named state ornithologist, and in 1920 was appointed as the first director of the Division of Ornithology in the Massachusetts Department of Agriculture. He retired in 1928. His investigations contributed much to scientific knowledge of the control by birds of insects injurious to agricultural and tree crops. Among his lasting contributions were the Massachusetts wildlife and conservation laws which he inspired and which served as models for legislation in other states. A founder of the Massachusetts Audubon Society, he was also a Fellow of the American Ornithologists' Union. He was on the Advisory Board of the United States Department of Agriculture for the migratory bird treaty of 1913 between Canada and the United States. Among his important writings are *Useful Birds and Their Protection*, 1907, and his monumental *Birds of Massachusetts and Other New England States,* 1925 and 1927. Died March 7, 1929.

NATIONAL AUDUBON SOCIETY

"Edward Howe Forbush: A Biographical Sketch," Proceedings of the Boston Society of Natural History, 39(2):33–72, 1928.
"In Memoriam: Edward Howe Forbush," *The Auk,* 47(2):137–46, April 1930.
National Cyclopaedia of American Biography, 1931.
Who Was Who in America, 1897–1942.

FORESTER, FRANK. Pseudonym of Henry William Herbert

FOX, ADRIAN CASPER (1905–)

Born January 28, 1905 near Leeds, North Dakota. Educated in agriculture, forestry, botany, and entomology at North Dakota State College, M.S. 1932. Began his career as assistant county agent before joining the Soil Conservation Service, United States Department of Agriculture, in 1935 as assistant forester at Huron, South Dakota. In 1935 became biologist at Park River, North Dakota where he directed wildlife conservation and game management programs in SCS demonstration projects and Civilian Conservation Corps camps throughout the state. Served from 1942 to 1955, except for 33 months in military service, as head of educational relation work for a seven-state region consisting of Montana, Wyoming, Colorado, North Dakota, South Dakota, Nebraska, and Kansas. In 1955 transferred to the Washington office of SCS in charge of this work nationally where he served until his retirement in December, 1965. Served on the board of directors of the Conservation Education Association and the American Nature Study Society; was advisor to the youth programs and education committees of the

National Association of Soil and Water Conservation Districts, and
a member of the Conservation Education Committee for the Soil
Conservation Society of America, the Izaak Walton League, and
the National Association of Biology Teachers. Received the
Nebraska Conservation Trophy in 1949 and the Award of Merit
from the National Association of Conservation and Publicity in
1950. In 1964 he was awarded the American Motors Conservation
Award for professional conservationists. Author of numerous articles and publications; co-author of *Teaching Soil and Water Conservation* of which a million and a half copies have been distributed
to teachers and other youth leaders by the United States Department of Agriculture.

ALBERT B. FOSTER

FRANK, BERNARD (1902–64)

Born March 7, 1902 in New York City. Cornell University, B.S.
(forestry) 1925, M.F. 1929. The first year of his career was spent
as forester for a pulp and paper company in Quebec, and in 1926
he was an assistant in forest utilization at Cornell. Entering the
United States Forest Service in 1927, he was assigned to economic
studies, and in 1931 was transferred to the Lake States Forest
Experiment Station at St. Paul for research. From 1934 to 1948, he
was on the forestry staff of the Tennessee Valley Authority, then
returned to the Forest Service in Washington, D. C., where from
1945 onward he was assistant chief of the Division of Watershed
Management Research until his retirement in January 1959. He
next set up a program of watershed management research in India
on an assignment for the Food and Agriculture Organization of the
United Nations. Then in 1960 he joined the faculty of the School
of Forestry at Colorado State University as professor of watershed
management. A charter member of the Wilderness Society, founded
in 1935, he was on its Governing Council from its inception. He
was a Fellow of the Society of American Foresters and of the Soil
Conservation Society of America as well as a member of the edi-

torial board of the *Journal of Soil and Water Conservation*, and
was active in other scientific and conservation bodies. Co-author of
Water, Land and People, 1950, he was author of *Our National
Forests*, 1955, and in addition wrote more than one hundred papers
and bulletins on all aspects of forestry management, recreation,
soil erosion, and flood control. Died November 15, 1964.

MICHAEL NADEL

The Living Wilderness, Winter 1964–65, no. 87.

FREDERICK, KARL TELFORD (1881–1963)

Born February 2, 1881 in Chateaugay, New York. Princeton University, A.B. 1903, A.M. (economics) 1904; Harvard Law School,
LL.B. 1908. He was editor of *The Harvard Law Review*, 1906–8,
was admitted to the New York Bar in 1909, and practiced law
throughout his active career. As a member of the United States
pistol and revolver teams, he won the individual pistol champion-
ship of the world at the 1920 Olympic Games in Belgium. He was a
founder of the New York State Conservation Council, serving as its
president from 1935 to 1942, and thereafter until his death as
chairman of its Board of Directors. For 26 years he was a director of
the American Forestry Association and chairman of its Executive
Committee for most of that period. Long active in the Campfire
Club of America, he was its vice president in 1926 and president in
1927 and 1928, and received the Club's Medal of Honor in 1956. He
was a founder of the American Game Protective Association and
an early leader of the National Wildlife Federation, serving as a
director from 1939 to 1948 and as vice president from 1949 to 1953.
In 1927 he was elected to the Board of Directors of the National
Rifle Association, to its presidency from 1934 to 1936, and to its
Executive Council in 1937; and was awarded honorary life membership in 1958. For many years he was a member of the American
Olympic Committee. As a member of the National Crime Commis-

sion's Committee on Firearms, he devoted much study to the formulation of the Uniform Pistol Law which was approved by the American Bar Association and adopted by a number of states. Frederick Peak in Yellowstone National Park was named for him in 1966. Died February 11, 1963.

RICHARD PARDO

FREDINE, CLARENCE GORDON (1909–)

Born August 15, 1909 in St. Paul, Minnesota. Hamline University, St. Paul, B.S. (biology) 1932; graduate study at University of Minnesota, 1932–35, and Purdue University, 1941–43. After working as a biologist with the National Park Service in 1934 and the Minnesota Conservation Department from 1935 to 1941, he was assistant professor in wildlife at Purdue University from 1941 to 1947. He joined the Department of the Interior as regional supervisor of the Fish and Wildlife Service's Office of River Basin Studies, and from 1947 to 1952 made a significant contribution to knowledge about the continent's resources through analysis of America's wetlands habitats. After serving as wildlife research biologist supervisor in Washington, 1952–55, he transferred in 1956 to the National Park Service as principal naturalist where his interest in application of ecological principles influenced the Service's research and wildlife management programs. As principal park planner he helped carry the Mission 66 program to its successful conclusion. He was chief of park extension services, 1962–64, and has been chief of international affairs since 1964. He organized and expanded the Student Conservation Program and helped develop the Service's policy leading to increased international activities. He assisted in establishment of a Latin American Committee on National Parks and an Inter-American Conference on Renewable Natural Resources and a Joint United States–Japan Park Management Panel. He was executive secretary of the Wildlife Society, 1960–63, was its vice president, 1966–67, and was elected an

honorary member in 1964. He was honored with the United States
Department of the Interior Distinguished Service Award in 1967. He
authored wildlife science articles and several United States
Government bulletins including *Wetlands of the United States/
Their Extent and Their Value to Waterfowl and Other Wildlife*,
1956.

FRED G. EVENDEN

American Men of Science (The Physical and Biological Sciences), 11th ed., 1965.
Who's Who in America, 1968–69.

FRITZ, EMANUEL (1886–   )

Born October 29, 1886 in Baltimore, Maryland. Cornell University,
M.E. 1908; Yale University, M.F. 1914. Began his professional
career in forestry under the state forester of New Hampshire.
Joined the United States Forest Service in 1915 in the Northern
Rocky Mountain Region; transferred in 1916 to the Fort Valley
Forest Experiment Station in Arizona. Then followed two years
with the Army Air Service in France as officer with 639th Aero
Squadron (mechanics). He joined the faculty of the University of
California School of Forestry in 1919 and taught wood technology
and forest products. He then began a half century of study of the
ecology of the California redwoods and the silvicultural practices
and economics of the redwood industry. As forestry adviser to the
California Redwood Association he influenced the adoption of
selective cutting practices by the industry. Long a member of the
Society of American Foresters he was a member of its Council,
1934–36; associate editor, 1928–30; chief editor, 1930–33; elected
a Fellow in 1951. In 1955 he received the distinguished achievement award from the Western Forestry and Conservation Association. A founder of the Redwood Region Logging Congress, he was
its manager for 22 years. Served as councillor of the Save-the-Red-
wood League since 1933. Currently a director of the Forest History
Society, Inc. The author of nearly 200 articles on forestry, forest
policy, wood technology, and lumbering, he wrote the book *Cali-*

fornia Coast Redwood, an annotated bibliography published in
1957. Retired from the University in 1954.

Paul Casamajor

American Men of Science (The Physical and Biological Sciences), 11th ed., 1965.
Who's Who in the West.

FROME, MICHAEL (1920–   )

Born May 25, 1920 in New York City. Studied at City College,
New York; George Washington University; and Pan-American Air-
ways School, University of Miami. Following service as a first
lieutenant in the United States Army Air Corps, 1942–45, he was
a staff writer on the *Washington* (D. C.) *Post,* 1945–46, and
worked in public relations for the American Automobile Association, 1947–57. On becoming a free lance writer in 1958, he first
devoted much attention to tourism, then enlarged his horizons to
studies and articles about natural resources, people, and their
environment. In 1967 he began contributing monthly articles to
American Forests magazine and a year later to *Field and Stream.*
In addition, his writings appear frequently in other nationally
known periodicals. Among his books are *Whose Woods These Are*:
the Story of the National Forests, 1962; *Strangers in High Places*:
the Story of the Great Smoky Mountains, 1966; the Rand-McNally
Park Guide, 1967; *The National Forests of America* (co-author with
Orville L. Freeman), 1968; and *The Varmints,* 1969. A lucid interpreter of natural resources and a defender of the endangered
environment, he has written knowledgeably about forests, soil,
water, wildlife, and outdoor recreation as they relate to human
culture. In 1967 he received the Thomas Wolfe Literary Award
from the Western North Carolina Historical Society. He is a director of Defenders of Wildlife; trustee, America the Beautiful Fund
of the Natural Areas Council; past president and chairman of the
Committee on Conservation and Preservation, Society of American
Travel Writers; and past honorary vice president of the American

Forestry Association. He is a leading author and critic of contemporary policies, public and private, that affect America's resource heritage.

HENRY CLEPPER

GABRIELSON, IRA NOEL (1889–)

Born September 27, 1889 at Sioux Rapids, Iowa. Morningside College, B.A. (biology) 1912, LL.D. 1941; Oregon State College, D.Sc. 1936; Middlebury College, D.Sc. 1959; Colby College, D.Sc. 1969. After teaching high school biology at Marshalltown, Iowa, 1912–15, he joined the Bureau of Biological Survey in the United States Department of Agriculture, and worked mainly in the West for the next two decades in field and supervisory positions involving economic ornithology, food habits research, rodent control, and game management. In 1935 he transferred to Washington, D. C., as the assistant chief of the Division of Wildlife Research, becoming chief of the Bureau of Biological Survey that same year; then in 1940 was appointed as the first director of the Fish and Wildlife Service in the United States Department of the Interior. He served as deputy coordinator of fisheries during World War II, with the responsibility of sustaining seafood production essential to the conduct of the war. Appointed as a United States Delegate to the International Whaling Conference by the Department of State in 1946, he resigned government service that same year to assume presidency of the Wildlife Management Institute. In 1948 as United States delegate he helped found the International Union for the Conservation of Nature and Natural Resources. In 1961 he helped to organize and became president of the World Wildlife Fund (United States) and is a trustee of the World Wildlife Fund (International). He served on the advisory committee of the Outdoor Recreation Resources Review Commission; was a member of the Secretary of the Interior's Advisory Committee on Fish and Wildlife for many years, and more recently a member of the Secretary's Advisory Board on Wildlife Management. Chairman of the Citizens

Committee on Natural Resources; chairman of the Coordinating Committee on the Potomac River Valley; member of the National Conservation Committee, Boy Scouts of America; and member, Committee on Pest Control and Wildlife Relationships, National Academy of Sciences-National Research Council. He has directed staff studies of the organization and operation of wildlife departments in 31 states and two Canadian provinces. He is author of *Western American Alpines,* 1932; *Wildlife Conservation,* 1941; *Wildlife Refuges,* 1943; *Wildlife Management,* 1951; co-author of *Birds of Oregon,* 1940; *The Birds of Alaska,* 1958; *Birds: A Guide to the Most Familiar American Birds,* 1949; and editor of the *Fisherman's Encyclopedia,* 1951, and the *New Fish Encyclopedia,* 1964. He received the Distinguished Service Medal of the Department of the Interior in 1948; the Aldo Leopold Memorial Award Medal of the Wildlife Society in 1953; the Audubon Medal of the National Audubon Society in 1949; the Hugh H. Bennett Medal of Friends of the Land in 1958; the Distinguished Service Award of the American Forestry Association in 1962; and the Department of the Interior's Conservation Service Award in 1964.

DANIEL A. POOLE

American Men of Science (The Physical and Biological Sciences), 11th ed., 1965.
Who's Who in America, 1968–69.

GANNETT, HENRY (1846–1914)

Born August 24, 1846 in Bath, Maine. Harvard University, S.B. 1869, M.E. 1870; Bowdoin College, LL.D. 1899. A topographer on geographical surveys in the West, 1872–79, he became chief geographer in 1882 for the Geographical Survey, Department of the Interior, with which bureau he served with distinction until his death. He was chairman for twenty years of the United States Geographic Board, established in 1890. He aided in the formation of the National Geographic Society in 1883, was its first secretary, and was president, 1910–14. He was also a founder of the Geographical Society of America and associate editor of the Society's

Bulletin, and a founder of the Association of America Geographers. Following passage of the act of 1897 that provided for the administration and protection of the forest reserves, then under jurisdiction of the Department of the Interior, he was put in charge of their mapping and classification. His duties included making an estimate of the timber stand which was reported to be 1.39 billion board feet in the twelfth census of 1900. Assigned by President Theodore Roosevelt to supervise the compilation of the first inventory of natural resources ever made in the United States, he edited the National Conservation Commission's monumental three-volume report published in 1909. He was author of books on geography, including a *Manual of Topographic Surveying*, and of several statistical atlases of the United States. Died November 5, 1914.

HENRY CLEPPER

Dictionary of American Biography, 1931.
National Geographic Magazine. Obituary, 26(6):609–13, December 1914.
Who Was Who in America, 1897–42.

GARRATT, GEORGE ALFRED (1898–   )

Born May 7, 1898 in Brooklyn, New York. Michigan Agricultural College, B.S. 1920; Yale University, M.F. 1923, Ph.D. 1933; University of the South, D.Sc. 1957. His career has been largely devoted to teaching and educational administration, including 41 years on the faculty of Yale University. He taught forestry at Michigan Agricultural College, 1921–22; and at the University of the South, 1923–25. In 1925 he joined the faculty of Yale School of Forestry where his specialty was wood technology; became Manufacturers' Association professor of lumbering in 1939, and Pinchot professor of forestry in 1955. He was assistant dean, 1936–39, and dean from 1945 until 1965. He retired in 1966. During World War II he was chief of the division of technical service training at the Forest Products Laboratory of the United States Forest Service in Madison, Wisconsin and later director of the packaging training center, United States Transportation Corps in Paris, France, with the rank of colonel. For the latter service he was awarded the United States Medal of Freedom. Member of Connecticut State Park and Forest Commission since 1949 (chairman since 1950), and of Connecticut State Council on Agriculture and Natural Resources, since 1959 (chairman 1961–65). On national forestry research advisory committee, United States Department of Agriculture, 1958–64. Member of program planning committees of Third, Fourth, and Fifth American Forest Congresses. Charter member Forest Products Research Society (vice president 1948, president 1949). Fellow, Society of American Foresters (vice president 1956–57, president 1958–59, Council member 1960–61). Charter member, Society of Wood Science and Technology. Has served as associate editor *Journal of Forestry.* Currently director of a study of forestry education in Canada sponsored by the Canadian Institute of Forestry. He received the Sir William Schlich Medal of the Society of American Foresters in 1966; and in 1967 the distinguished service award of American Forest Products Industries, Inc. Author of *Mechanical Properties of Wood,* 1931; and with G. M. Hunt of *Wood Preservation,* 1938 and later editions.

JESSE H. BUELL

American Men of Science (The Physical and Biological Sciences), 11th ed., 1965.
Yale Forest School News, Deanship Succession, vol. 53, April, 1965.

GIFFORD, JOHN CLAYTON (1870–1949)

Born February 8, 1870 at Mays Landing, New Jersey. Swarthmore College, B.S. 1890; graduate studies in botany at University of Michigan and Johns Hopkins University; University of Munich, Bavaria, D.Oec. (economics) 1899. He taught botany at Swarthmore College, 1890–94. While employed as forester for the New Jersey Geological Survey during 1895–96, he was founding editor of the magazine *New Jersey Forester,* subsequently named *American Forests,* which became the official organ of the American Forestry Association. In 1900 he joined the faculty of the New York State College of Forestry at Cornell University, the first collegiate institution in America to offer a professional curriculum in forestry. When it was discontinued three years later he became a special agent for the United States Bureau of Forestry (now the Forest Service) on a survey of the forests of Puerto Rico. Subsequently, he traveled in the West Indies, Central and South America, and Mexico, studying tropical forests and fruit-bearing trees. For two decades he was professor of tropical forestry and conservation at the University of Miami; in addition to his university teaching, he lectured widely in public schools and before civic organizations. Joined the Society of American Foresters in 1902; elected a Fellow in 1942. He was a Fellow also of the American Association for the Advancement of Science. The author of one of the first books on forest management—*Practical Forestry*, 1901—he wrote many articles and several books thereafter on agriculture, forestry, and horticulture, among them *The Everglades of Florida*, 1911, and his last, *Living by the Land*, 1945. Died June 25, 1949.

HENRY CLEPPER

Journal of Forestry, 45(6):455–56, June 1947.
Who Was Who in America, 1943–50.

GILL, THOMAS HARVEY (1891–   )

Born January 21, 1891 in Philadelphia. University of Pennsylvania, B.A. 1913; Yale University, M.F. 1915; University of the Andes, Venezuela, honorary doctorate 1953. Joined United States Forest Service in Wyoming in 1915 as assistant ranger; ranger, 1916–17; supervisor, 1922; in charge of public relations in Washington, D. C. office, 1922–25. Forester for the American Forestry Association and associate editor *American Forests and Forest Life*, 1925. Appointed 1926, as executive director of the Charles Lathrop Pack Forestry Foundation, continuing until its liquidation in 1960. First lieutenant, United States Army Air Service during World War I. Long active in the Society of American Foresters, he was chairman of the Committee on International Relations for seven years; elected Fellow in 1948; and awarded the Sir William Schlich memorial medal in 1954 for outstanding contributions to forestry. International services include membership (1944) on the Technical Committee on Forestry and Forest Products of the United Nations Interim Commission on Food and Agriculture, and advisor on forestry (1945) at the FAO organizing conference in Quebec. Delegate to all six World Forestry Congresses: Rome 1926, Budapest 1936, Helsinki 1949, India 1954, Seattle (member of Organizing Committee) 1960, and Madrid 1966. Other international bodies have sought his advice on forests and related natural resources, including Japan 1951, Formosa 1952, and the Philippines 1959. President since 1950 of the International Society of Tropical Foresters; currently executive director of the International Union of Societies of Foresters. Awarded Merito Civico Forestal by Mexico; Distinguished Service Cross by Germany; Chevalier, Merite Agricole, by France; honorary diploma by the Mexican Institute of Renewable Resources, and the Bernhard E. Fernow Award by the American Forestry Association and Deutscher Forstverein. Author of numerous articles on forestry and natural resources, and of the books *Forests and Mankind* (co-author), 1929; *Tropical Forests of the Caribbean*, 1931; *The Forestry Directory* (co-editor) 1943 and 1949; *Land Hunger in Mexico*, 1951; and other works including fiction.

HENRY CLEPPER

Who's Who in America, 1968–69.

GILLETT, CHARLES ALTON (1904–   )

Born October 24, 1904 in Auburn, New York. Cornell University, B.S. 1925, M.S. 1929. Appointed extension forester in North Dakota in 1925, he served two years, then became extension forester in Arkansas in 1929. In 1933 as the first state forester of Arkansas, he built up a forestry organization and a fire control system during the next six years. In 1939 he was employed by the Seaboard Air Line Railroad as industrial forester, engaging in educational work with landowners, schools, and youth organizations in the area served by the railroad. American Forest Products Industries, Inc., which had been founded three years earlier in Washington, D. C. by the forest industries as a medium for public education, engaged him in 1944 as chief forester. AFPI's primary purpose was to inform the American people about the economic contributions of forest products to the general welfare and about progress in private forestry under free enterprise. After three years as chief forester Gillett was promoted to the position of managing director. Under his administration the tree farm movement, started in 1941, grew to 70 million acres. The 32,000 tree farms in the system formed the world's greatest voluntary forest-growing enterprise. In addition, he successfully directed the "Keep America Green" fire prevention campaign, together with a cooperative 4-H club forestry program under which more than one million boys and girls conducted 4-H forestry projects. Thus for two decades he was a national exponent of industrial forestry policy and an interpreter of private forestry progress. Retiring in July 1967, as managing director, he continued for two years as a consultant to the organization, renamed the American Forest Institute.

HENRY CLEPPER

"Charles A. Gillett, Profile of a Forester," *American Forests*, July 1967.

GLASCOCK, HARDIN ROADS, JR. (1921–)

Born November 7, 1921 in Muncie, Indiana. University of Washington, B.S. (forest management) 1947. Following graduation, he was employed by forest owners and the forest products industry in the State of Washington, then in 1951 became district forester for the Industrial Forestry Association, helping advance the tree farm program in western Oregon. In 1958 he was appointed forest counsel for the Western Forestry and Conservation Association at Portland, Oregon, an organization which promotes cooperation in forestry and related conservation developments in western Canada and western United States. It is supported by industries, protection associations, and individuals. He was named in 1966 to his present position, executive secretary of the Society of American Foresters, Washington, D. C., a 17,000-member organization representing the profession of forestry in the United States. He is also editor-in-chief of the *Journal of Forestry*, as well as director and secretary of the Foundation for Professional Forestry. He serves as forestry adviser to the Food and Agriculture Organization of the United Nations. Previously, he had been on the Department of the Interior Advisory Committee for the Oregon and California Revested Land Grant Administration, the Advisory Committee for the U. S. Forest Service's Pacific Northwest Forest and Range Experiment Station, and the Natural Resources Committee of the U. S. Chamber of Commerce. Active in several national conservation organizations, he is currently on the Task Force for a National Program for Wildfire Control, set up in 1967 by the American Forestry Association, and the Trees for People Task Force organized in 1969 to raise the general level of timber production on non-industry private forest lands. He has written numerous articles interpreting land use policies and the multiple use of natural resources and writes a monthly column for the *Journal of Forestry*. He led the development of *Forest Policies*, a comprehensive statement of principles approved by the membership of the Society of American Foresters in 1967.

HENRY CLEPPER

Journal of Forestry, 63(10):808, October 1965.

GLICK, PHILIP MILTON (1905–)

Born December 9, 1905, in Kiev, Russia; brought to the United States in 1912. University of Chicago, Ph.B. 1928, the Law School, J.D. 1930. In 1934 at the age of 28, he became the youngest general counsel in the federal government, for the Federal Subsistence Homesteads Corporation, United States Department of the Interior, then transferred the same year to the United States Department of Agriculture as chief of the Land Policy Division, and later became assistant solicitor, in the Office of the Solicitor, where until 1942 he headed the legal work of the Soil Conservation Service, the Forest

Service, and the Office of Land Use Coordination. He drafted the Standard State Soil Conservation Districts Law; and between 1937 and 1947 all states passed laws patterned after his draft. He assisted in developing the methods and procedures under which the Department of Agriculture and its agencies cooperate with soil conservation districts organized under state legislation. From 1942 to 1953 he served successively as general counsel for the War Relocation Authority, the Federal Public Housing Authority, the Institute of Inter-American Affairs, and the Technical Cooperation Administration, Department of State. From 1953 to 1955, while visiting professor in economic development and cultural change at the University of Chicago, he wrote *The Administration of Technical Assistance*, published by the University of Chicago Press, 1957. From 1955 to 1967, he practiced law in Washington as a member of the firm of Dorfman and Glick. From 1958 to 1967 he was retained by the National Association of Soil and Water Conservation Districts as general counsel, and from 1967 has been assistant director for policy and legal advisor to federal Water Resources Council. He is an honorary member of the Soil Conservation Society of America.

F. GLENNON LOYD

Who's Who in America, 1968–69.

GODDARD, MAURICE KIMBALL (1912–   )

Born September 13, 1912 in Lowell, Massachusetts. University of Maine, B.S. (forestry) 1935, Sc.D. (honorary) 1966; University of California, M.S. 1938; Waynesburg College, Sc.D. (honorary) 1959. Became an instructor in forestry at the Pennsylvania State College in 1935. Was in military service, 1942–46; awarded Legion of Merit, Bronze Star, separated as lieutenant colonel. He was appointed director of the Mont Alto Branch of the Penn State School of Forestry in 1946 and was named director of the School of Forestry at Pennsylvania State University in 1952. As Secretary, Department of Forests and Waters, Commonwealth of Pennsylvania, since 1955, he obtained much favorable resource-use legislation with impact on timber, minerals, water, recreation, and wildlife; promoted a state-wide park program and a $70 million bond issue to support it. In his position as Secretary of Forest and Waters, he is chairman of the State Forestry Commission, the Water and Power Resource Board, the Geographic Board, the Governor's Executive Board, Sanitary Water Board, and several other official boards and councils. He is a director of the American Forestry Association, a director of the Pennsylvania Forestry Association, a member of the Commonwealth Industrial Research Corporation, and four river basin committees and several other commissions and boards, and a member of the President's Public Land Law Review Commission. In the Society of American Foresters, he became a member in 1935, Fellow in 1963, was chairman of the Allegheny Section in 1951, chairman, Committee on Civil Service, 1952–53, and member of Council for two terms, 1956–59.

SOCIETY OF AMERICAN FORESTERS

Society of American Foresters: biographical summary of candidates elected to grade of Fellow, 1963. Other biographical information on file.

GORDON, SETH EDWIN (1890–)

Born April 2, 1890 in Richfield, Pennsylvania. Graduated Pennsylvania Business College, 1911; University of Michigan, D.Sc. (honorary) 1953. After a brief career in teaching and business, he joined the Pennsylvania Game Commission as a game protector in 1913, was appointed assistant secretary of the Commission in 1915, and became secretary and chief game protector in 1919. He resigned in 1926 to become conservation director of the Izaak Walton League of America. He was president of the American Game Association, 1931–34, and was secretary of the American Wildlife Institute in 1935. In 1936 he returned to Pennsylvania as executive director of the Game Commission, serving until 1948 when he became a private conservation consultant. In this capacity he was engaged by the California Wildlife Conservation Board to advise on funds allocated to the California Department of Fish and

Game; then was appointed director of the Department in 1951, serving until 1959. He was a member of the Forest Research Advisory Committee to the Secretary of Agriculture, 1952–62, and a member of the President's Water Pollution Control Advisory Board to the Surgeon General of the United States, 1958–61. He has been a trustee of the North American Wildlife Foundation since 1947, a member of the Conservation Committee of the Boy Scouts of America since 1956, and general counsel (also honorary life member and past president) of the International Association of Game, Fish and Conservation Commissioners since 1964. He is an honorary member and past president of the American Fisheries Society; a past vice president of the American Forestry Association; director of the National Rifle Association since 1958; an honorary member of the Outdoor Writers Association of America; and from 1960 to 1962 was an honorary national president of the Izaak Walton League of America. He is recipient of Founders of the Izaak Walton League and of the Aldo Leopold Memorial Medal of the Wildlife Society (1967). He has had one of the longest continuous careers in conservation of any living American. Among his greatest contributions was his participation in the drafting of the Model Game Law of 1934, which established criteria for modern wildlife administrative agencies. He was one of the first state wildlife administrators to develop realistic hunting regulations for deer and was instrumental in obtaining general public acceptance of modern principles of game management.

JAMES B. TREFETHEN

Who's Who in America, 1968–69.

GOTTSCHALK, JOHN SIMISON (1912–   )

Born September 27, 1912 in Berne, Indiana. Earlham College, A.B. 1934, LL.D. 1966; University of Indiana, M.A. 1943. His first employment was as naturalist and conservation education specialist with the Indiana Conservation Department; later he was superintendent of fisheries, initiating the state's first formal program of fisheries management. During World War II, he served as a senior bacteriologist for Schenley Laboratories, a manufacturer of penicillin. He began his federal career as a fishery biologist preparing plans for the reservoirs of the Missouri River Basin for the United States Fish and Wildlife Service. He was made responsible for the organization of the Federal Aid in Fish Restoration program in 1951, and was promoted to the position of chief of the Division of Sport Fisheries following the reorganization of the Fish and Wildlife Service in 1957. Two years later he became regional director for all Bureau of Sport Fisheries and Wildlife activities in the 11 northeastern states. In 1964 he was appointed director of the Bureau of Sport Fisheries and Wildlife. He has represented the Department of the Interior at numerous international meetings, and serves as a member of the Ecology Commission of the International Union for the Conservation of Nature and Natural Resources, and as a member of the International Migratory Bird Committee. He was president of the American Fisheries Society, 1963–64, received the Conservation Award of the American Motors Corporation in 1953, and was granted the John Pearce Award of the Northeast Wildlife Society for outstanding public service.

ELWOOD A. SEAMAN

American Men of Science (The Physical and Biological Sciences), 11th ed., 1966.

GRAHAM, EDWARD HARRISON (1902–66)

Born November 30, 1902 in New Brighton, Pennsylvania. University of Pittsburgh, B.S. 1927, Ph.D. (botany) 1932. For three years he was curator of botany at Carnegie Museum, Pittsburgh. He then joined the Soil Conservation Service, United States Department of Agriculture in 1937, and advanced successively from biologist to chief of the Division of Biology, and finally assistant administrator for international programs. He retired in 1964 from the federal government after 27 years of distinguished service, during which he was an active leader in the conservation and scientific community. He was a lecturer in land management ecology in the Graduate

School of the United States Department of Agriculture, 1942–52, at Harvard University in 1949, and was a Guggenheim Fellow in 1954. He represented the United States at numerous scientific conferences in Mexico, Venezuela, Denmark, France, Scotland, and Greece. He served as president of the Soil Conservation Society of America; was a consultant to the Nature Conservancy of Great Britain; chairman of the Commission on Ecology of the International Union for the Conservation of Nature and Natural Resources; and a member of the United States National Committee for the International Biological Program. Following his retirement from government service he was a consultant to the Ford Foundation and a senior associate of the Conservation Foundation. The author of numerous scientific papers and monographs, he will long be remembered for his two books *The Land and Wildlife*, 1947, and *Natural Principles of Land Use*, 1944. Died May 16, 1966.

HENRY CLEPPER

American Men of Science (The Physical and Biologial Sciences), 10th ed., 1965.
Journal of Wildlife Management. Obituary, vol. 30, July 1966.

GRANGER, CHRISTOPHER MABLEY (1885–1967)

Born 1885 in Detroit, Michigan. Michigan State University, B.S. (forestry); doctor of forestry (honorary) 1932. Began career of nearly 45 years with the Forest Service, United States Department of Agriculture, as forest assistant on the Sequoia National Forest in California. After assignments as deputy supervisor and supervisor of various national forests in Colorado and Wyoming, he became assistant regional forester for operation in Denver in 1916. After serving as a major in the Army Engineers' forestry unit during World War I, he became regional forester for the Pacific Northwest Region in 1919, with its important national forest and state and private forestry cooperative programs. Transferred to Washington, D. C. in 1930, he developed the nationwide forest survey authorized by the 1928 McSweeney-McNary Act, which produces the basic forest resource information for private forestry enterprise and for public forest policy. In 1933 he administered the Forest Service's part of the Civilian Conservation Corps program. In 1935 he was named assistant chief of the Forest Service for administration of the national forests. In 1952, he received the Department of Agriculture's Distinguished Service Award. Michigan State University conferred its Alumni Award for Distinguished Service in 1949. Chief of the American delegation and co-president of the Third World Forestry Conference in Helsinki in 1949. President of the Society of American Foresters 1932–34. Remained active after retirement in 1952 in promoting forest conservation affairs. Died November 21, 1967.

GORDEN D. FOX

American Men of Science (The Physical and Biological Sciences), 10th ed., 1955.

GRANT, KENNETH ELVARD (1920–)

Born March 19, 1920 in Rollinsford, New Hampshire. University of New Hampshire, B.S. (agriculture) 1941; Harvard University, M.P.A. 1964. He became a Soil Conservation Service employee in March 1946, after serving in the United States Army Air Corps from December 1941 to October 1945. In New Hampshire he rose from a junior soil scientist to state conservationist in 12 years, serving as head of the agency's work there from January 1959 until he enrolled in Harvard's Littauer School of Public Administration in 1963. He was promoted and transferred to Indiana as state conservationist in 1964. He transferred to Washington, D. C., as associate administrator of the agency in 1967, becoming its administrator in January 1969. He was in the forefront of the agency's efforts to apply its farm-proven techniques of soil and water conservation and development to achieve environmental improvement, to assist urbanizing areas with acute land and water management problems, and to assist multi-county areas to gain economic and social betterment. He helped initiate the nation's first resource conservation and development project (Lincoln Hills) in southern Indiana. While heading the agency's work in New Hampshire, he also served as the United States Department of Agriculture's representative on the Connecticut River Basin Comprehensive Study. During his Indiana assignment, he had the leadership for the Department's part of the Ohio River Basin Comprehensive Framework Survey, the first of its kind completed in the United States, as well as leadership in the Wabash River Basin Comprehensive Study. He was a member of a team that made trips to West Pakistan in 1967 and 1968 to advise the government of Pakistan on erosion, sedimentation, and water management. He holds the United States Department of Agriculture's Distinguished Service Award (1969); is a Fellow in the Soil Conservation Society of America (1969); is a member of the American Society for Public Administration; and the Conservation Committee of the Boy Scouts of America.

F. GLENNON LOYD

GRAVES, HENRY SOLON (1871–1951)

Born May 3, 1871 in Marietta, Ohio. Yale College, B.A. 1892, after which he studied forestry in Europe, the second native American to prepare for a forestry career. Yale University, M.A. 1900, LL.D. 1940; Harvard University, M.A. 1911; Lincoln Memorial University, LL.D. 1923; Syracuse University, LL.D. 1923. Appointed in 1898 as assistant chief of the Division of Forestry, United States Department of Agriculture (now the Forest Service), under Gifford Pinchot. Resigned in 1900 to become director of the Yale University School of Forestry. Returning to the Forest Service as chief forester in 1910, he held the post until 1920. When the United States entered World War I, he was commissioned temporary lieutenant colonel, Corps of Engineers, to set up forestry operations for production of the Army's timber needs in France. Returning to Yale in 1922 as dean of the Yale School of Forestry, he won recognition as the foremost forestry educator in America. He retired as dean emeritus in 1939. From 1929 to 1931 he directed the Forest Education Inquiry which established standards of professional instruction. He was twice president of the American Forestry Asso-

141   Greeley

ciation, 1923–24, and 1934–36; and president of the Society of American Foresters, 1912. In 1944 the Society awarded him the Sir William Schlich Memorial Medal and in 1950 the Gifford Pinchot Medal. He was chairman of the Committee on Forestry and Forest Products that planned for the inclusion of forestry in the work program of the Food and Agriculture Organization of the United Nations. The French government honored him with the medal of the Order *Merite Agricole* in recognition of his distinguished service to forestry. Author of *Forest Mensuration*, 1906, and *Principles of Handling Woodlands*, 1911, both pioneer textbooks; co-author of *Forest Education*, 1932, and *Problems and Progress of Forestry in the United States*, 1947. Died March 7, 1951.

HENRY CLEPPER

"Henry Solon Graves, 1871–1951," *Journal of Forestry*, May 1951.
Who Was Who in America, 1951–60.

GREELEY, ARTHUR WHITE (1912–   )

Born August 1, 1912 in Washington, D. C. University of Washington, B.S. (forestry) 1934; Yale University School of Forestry, M.F. 1935. Starting his career in the United States Forest Service as a ranger on the St. Joe National Forest in Idaho in 1935, he worked up through the ranks to become supervisor of the Lassen National Forest in California. In 1951 he was appointed assistant director of the Pacific Northwest Forest and Range Experiment Station at Portland, Oregon. From 1953 to 56, he was regional forester of the Alaska Region at Juneau, and from 1956 to 1959 was regional forester of the North Central Region at Milwaukee, Wisconsin. Assigned to the Washington, D. C. office in 1959 as assistant chief of the Forest Service, he was responsible for fire control, engineering, and lands activities. In 1962 he was made deputy chief in charge of national forest resource management with responsibility for range management, recreation and land uses, timber management, watershed management, and wildlife management on the country's 151 national forests comprising 181 million acres. Since

March 1966 he has been associate chief, the second ranking officer of the Forest Service. He has been a member of the President's Quetico-Superior Committee since 1956. He is active in the Society of American Foresters, the Soil Conservation Society of America, and the American Society of Range Management.

HENRY CLEPPER

Who's Who in America, 1968–69.

GREELEY, WILLIAM BUCKHOUT (1879–1955)

Born September 6, 1879 in Oswego, New York. University of California, B.S. 1901, LL.D. 1927; Yale University, M.F. 1904, M.A. 1927. Entered Bureau of Forestry (now the Forest Service) in 1904; successively promoted to supervisor of Sequoia National Forest, 1906; regional forester, Northern Rocky Mountain Region, 1908; chief, Branch of Forest Management, Washington, D. C. office, 1911. During World War I, major, later lieutenant colonel, in charge of forestry operations for American Expeditionary Forces in France. Returned to Forest Service in 1919, and a year later was appointed chief. During the eight years of his administration, under the Clarke-McNary law of 1928, the fundamental forest policy of the United States was established, providing for federal-state cooperation in fire control, reforestation, and farm forestry extension. The net area of the national forests was enlarged to nearly 160 million acres. In May 1928 he became secretary-manager of the West Coast Lumbermen's Association at Seattle. While in this position he was influential in advancing forest management and protection on lands of the forest industries. He retired in 1946, but continued leadership in forestry by chairmanship of the board of American Forest Products Industries, Inc. He was president of the Society of American Foresters in 1915, was elected a Fellow in 1918, and received the Sir William Schlich memorial medal for distinguished service to forestry in 1946. He was a director of the American Forestry Association for 34 years. The author of *Forests and Men*, 1951, and

Forest Policy, 1953, he was a frequent contributor to scientific and popular magazines on natural resources subjects. Died November 30, 1955.

HENRY CLEPPER

MORGAN, GEORGE T., JR., *William B. Greeley, a Practical Forester, 1879–1955*. St. Paul, Minn.: Forest History Society, Inc., 1961.
"William Buckhout Greeley, 1879–1955," *Journal of Forestry*, January 1956.

GREEN, SAMUEL BOWDLEAR (1859–1910)

Born September 15, 1859 in Chelsea, Massachusetts. Massachusetts Agricultural College at Amherst, B.S. 1879, graduate student in horticulture, 1880–81. He was horticulturist for the Houghton Farm Agricultural Experiment Station at Cornwall, New York, 1881–84, and superintendent of horticulture at Massachusetts Agricultural College, 1886–88. In 1888 he became horticulturist for the University of Minnesota's Agricultural Experiment Station, and professor of horticulture and forestry in 1897 at the University. A member of the executive board of the Minnesota Horticultural Society, 1892–1910, he served as president of the Society, 1907–10. He also served as president of the board of administration of the Farmers' Institutes of Minnesota and as a member of the executive committee of the Minnesota State Forestry Association. In 1899 he became a member of the Minnesota State Forestry Board which the legislature had authorized to oversee state forest lands. He successfully worked toward the creation of the Division of Forestry in the University of Minnesota (1903), the transfer of administration and protection of Itasca Park to the State Forestry Board (1907), and the creation of Cloquet Experimental Forest (1909). He was appointed professor of forestry and dean of the College of Forestry at the University of Minnesota in 1910. He wrote many books and articles including *Forestry in Minnesota*, 1898, and *Principles of American Forestry*, 1903. He was associate editor of *Farm and Fireside* from 1888 until his death. He early recognized the need for the practice of forestry and was largely responsible for the introduction of higher education for forestry and horticulture in Minnesota. Died July 11, 1910.

ELWOOD R. MAUNDER

ALLISON, JOHN H., "The Story of Samuel Green," *Conservation Volunteer*, September/ October, November/December, 1967.
Dictionary of American Biography, 1960.
Who Was Who in America, 1897–1942.

GRIFFITH, GEORGE ALLISON (1901–   )

Born March 19, 1901 in Vaughnsville, Ohio. Graduated from International College, Fort Wayne, Indiana in 1921. Most of his business career was with Wayne Knitting Mills of Fort Wayne, where he lived until 1944 at which time he moved to Grayling, Michigan. Dedicated nonprofessional conservationist with a particular interest in preserving trouts and their environment, and in the perpetuation of the sport of trout angling, he was effective in promoting improved methods for trout and stream management as a member of the Izaak Walton League and the Federation of Sportsmans Clubs in Indiana and Michigan, and was active also in the International Association of Fish and Game Commissioners and the American Fisheries Society. In recognition of his conservation activities, the governor of Michigan in 1950 appointed him to the Michigan Conservation Commission in which capacity he served until 1961; during 1954 he was chairman of the Commission, and chairman of its Fish Conservation Committee from 1955 to 1961. On July 16, 1959 on the Au Sable River in Grayling, Michigan, he founded Trout Unlimited, a national, nonprofit, nonpolitical organization of conservation-minded fishermen dedicated to preserving clean waters, and to continuing and improving high quality fishing by supporting and encouraging legislation, regulations, and research programs based on sound biological and ecological knowledge. In 1961 he was elected president of Trout Unlimited, an office he held until 1964 when he became its chairman of the board. As a result of his realistic leadership and enthusiasm, Trout Unlimited has grown to an organization with an international membership in excess of eight thousand. In 1963 he was appointed to a special commission to study the functions and structure of the Michigan Conservation Department; recommendations resulting from this study were responsible for reorganizing the Department into a highly efficient operation of the state government. He has written numerous articles dealing with water quality and trout management for *Trout Magazine*, the official organ of Trout Unlimited.

RAYMOND A. KOTRLA

Who's Who in America—Midwest, 1967–1968.

GRINNELL, GEORGE BIRD   (1849–1938)

Born September 20, 1849 in Brooklyn, New York. Yale University, A.B. 1870, Ph.D. (osteology) 1880, Litt.D. (honorary) 1921. Between 1870 and 1875 he was a member of important scientific and exploratory expeditions in the West, including an expedition through the Black Hills in 1874 and a reconnaisance of Yellowstone National Park in 1875. During these missions, he became interested in the culture and welfare of the American Indian, returning to the West annually for many years to enlarge his knowledge. In 1876 he became an editor of *Forest and Stream* magazine, rising to senior editor and publisher in 1880, positions he held until 1911. In this capacity in 1876 he launched a sustained campaign against market hunting and for realistic game laws. This movement culminated in the enactment of the Migratory Bird Treaty with Great Britain in 1916 and with the adoption of strong regulatory control of hunting in all states. In the winter of 1893 he had an investigation made of game poaching in Yellowstone National Park; the resulting articles led directly to the enactment by Congress of the Yellowstone Park Protection Act of 1894, a keystone of national park legislation. In the summer of 1885, he explored the country in Montana now known as Glacier National Park, and through his writings he was largely responsible for its inclusion in 1910 in the national park system. A quiet and modest man who preferred to work behind the scenes, he had a clear influence on much of the pioneer legislation affecting national parks, national forests, and wildlife. In 1886 he founded the Audubon Society of New York, the first such state organization in America and the forerunner of the National Audubon Society which he served as director for 26 years. He was a founding member of the Boone and Crockett Club in 1887, was president from 1918 to 1927, and in 1927 was named honorary president for life. He served on the first advisory board for Federal Migratory Bird Law. A Fellow of the American Ornithologists Union, he was also president of the National Parks Association, and a trustee of the American Museum of Natural History. In 1925 he was awarded the Theodore Roosevelt Gold Medal of Honor for his contribution to the cause of conservation. He was the author and co-author of nearly 30 volumes, ranging from adventure books for boys to scholarly works on Indian life and customs. Died April 11, 1938.

JAMES B. TREFETHEN

Dictionary of American Biography, vol. 22, supp. 2, 1958.
Who Was Who in America, 1897–1942.

GUTERMUTH, CLINTON RAYMOND (1900–   )

Born August 16, 1900 at Fort Wayne, Indiana. Attended the University of Notre Dame, 1918–19. Graduate of the American Institute of Banking in 1927, postgraduate 1928. He was director of the Division of Education, Indiana Department of Conservation, 1934–40, and director of the Division of Fish and Game, 1940–42. He served as executive secretary, American Wildlife Institute in Washington, D. C., 1945–46; and has been vice president of the Wildlife Management Institute since 1946. A founder and first secretary (1946–57) of the National Resources Council of America, he was chairman from 1959 to 1961. A founder of the National Watershed Congress, he has been a member of the steering committee since 1954; chairman from 1958 to 1962. He was a member of the Secretary of the Interior's Advisory Committee on Fish and Wildlife, 1949–53 and 1957–61; and has been a member of the Secretary of Agriculture's Committee on Wildlife since 1965. He was

appointed to the National Advisory Council, Public Land Law
Review Commission, 1965. He has served in the following capaci-
ties since the year indicated: trustee and secretary, North American
Wildlife Foundation, 1945; secretary, director, subsequently treasurer, World Wildlife Fund, 1961; director and secretary, Wildfowl
Foundation, Inc., 1956; director and executive committee member,
Citizens Committee on Natural Resources, 1954; director, American
Committee for International Wild Life Protection, 1950; vice president, 1969 and trustee, the Wildlife Society, 1951–66 and 1967;
director, National Rifle Association of America, 1963. As secretary
of the North American Wildlife Foundation, he initiated campaigns
that secured nearly $3 million in private donations for acquiring
lands that were deeded to the federal government for establishing
the Great Swamp (New Jersey), Key Deer (Florida), and Cedar
Point (Ohio) National Wildlife Refuges. Published numerous articles on conservation subjects, including statewide survey report,
Where To Go in Indiana: Official Lake Guide, 1938; first editor of
the Wildlife Management Institute's bi-weekly *Outdoor News Bulletin*, 1947–48; and contributing author, *The Fisherman's Encyclopedia*, 1950, and *The Standard Book of Fishing*, 1950. Program
chairman of the annual North American Wildlife and Natural
Resources Conference since 1946. Recipient of the Aldo Leopold
Memorial Award Medal of the Wildlife Society, 1957; Distinguished
Service Award, National Association of Soil and Water Conservation
Districts, 1958; Fishing Hall of Fame Award, 1958; Watershed Man
of the Year Award, National Watershed Congress, 1963; National
Service Award, Keep America Beautiful, 1965; and Meritorious
Service Award, Michigan United Conservation Clubs, 1968.

DANIEL A. POOLE

Who's Who in America, 1968–69.

HAFENRICHTER, ATLEE LAWRENCE (1897–   )

Born October 12, 1897 near Plainfield, Illinois. Northwestern College, A.B. 1922; University of Illinois, Ph.D. 1926. In 1926 he became
head of the Department of Botany and Bacteriology at Baker Uni-

versity and, simultaneously, served as investigator for the Division of Ecology, Carnegie Institution of Washington. From 1929 to 1933 he was assistant professor of farm crops and assistant in the Agricultural Experiment Station at Washington State University. His career in conservation began in 1933 when he was appointed as agronomist in the United States Department of Interior Soil Erosion Service, which became the Soil Conservation Service in the United States Department of Agriculture in 1935. Shortly after his transfer he became chief of the Regional Nursery Division and progressed steadily until he was regional plant materials specialist for the 13 western states, including Alaska and Hawaii; he was technically responsible for testing vegetation of all kinds in eight plant materials centers, in field evaluation plantings, and on farms and ranches under actual use. More than 100 new species and varieties are in use and in commercial production from 25,000 plants that were tested. He is author of numerous scientific papers, state experiment station and federal bulletins, monographs, and chapters in textbooks and United States Department of Agriculture yearbooks. He presented papers to the Sixth and Seventh International Grassland Congresses, served as chairman of a section at the Eighth Congress, and was co-author of a paper given at the Ninth. In 1947 he received the Superior Service Award and in 1963 the Distinguished Service Award from the United States Department of Agriculture. In 1955 he was elected a Fellow of the American Society of Agronomy, and in 1964 an Honorary Member of the Soil Conservation Society of America. He retired in 1967.

H. WAYNE PRITCHARD

American Men of Science (The Physical and Biological Sciences), 11th ed., 1965.
Who's Who in the West, 1963–64.

HAGENSTEIN, WILLIAM DAVID (1915–   )

Born March 8, 1915 in Seattle, Washington. University of Washington, B.S.F. 1938; Duke University, M.F. 1941. After working as an entomological field aide for the United States Department of Agriculture in 1938, he was logging superintendent for the Eagle Logging Company in 1939, and Civilian Conservation Corps foreman, United States Forest Service, in 1940. He was forester for the West Coast Lumbermen's Association, 1941–43 and 1945–49, with interim service during World War II as senior forester in the Foreign Economic Administration, attached to construction units of the United States Army in Guadalcanal and the United States Navy in Guam. He spent the last six months of World War II in Costa Rica in developing the American quinine plantation. Since 1949 he has been manager of the Industrial Forestry Association, Portland, Oregon and executive vice president since 1956. In addition, he has served variously as consulting forest engineer for the United States Navy in the Philippines in 1952; was MacMillan lecturer in forestry at the University of British Columbia in 1952, and Benson memorial lecturer at the University of Missouri in 1966. He has been on the Executive Committee of the Northwest Forest Pest Action Council since 1949 and has been chairman of the Council's Timber Disaster Committee since 1962. A trustee of the Washington State Forestry Conference since 1948, he has been also an advisory trustee of the Keep Washington Green Association and a trustee of the Keep Oregon Green Association, both since 1958. He has served on the Advisory Committee of the Pacific Northwest Forest and Range Experiment Station since 1954, was a director of the Foundation for American Resource Management, 1963–67, and has been a vice president and on the Executive Committee of the Western Forestry Center since 1965. A life member of the American Forestry Association, he was honorary vice president, 1966–69. In the Society of American Foresters he has been chairman of the Division of Private Forestry, 1955; associate editor of the *Journal of Forestry*, 1946–53; Council member, 1958–63; president, 1966–69; and in 1963 he was elected a Fellow. The author of numerous articles and other publications on forestry, he is co-author of the textbook *Harvesting Timber Crops*, 2nd ed. He received the Forest Products Industry National Award for forest management in 1968 from the National Forest Products Association.

Society of American Foresters

Society of American Foresters; biographical sketches of candidates, October 16, 1967.

HALL, WILLIAM LOGAN (1873–1960)

Born May 28, 1873 in Holden, Missouri. Kansas State College, B.S. 1898, M.S. (horticulture and forestry) 1899. Joining the Bureau of Forestry, (now the Forest Service), United States Department of Agriculture, in 1899, he served a succession of assignments including supervision of tree planting, making a forest survey in Hawaii, directing the Branch of Forest Products, and becoming the first district (now regional) forester in the eastern United States. He was influential in securing the establishment in 1910 of the Forest Products Laboratory at Madison, Wisconsin. During World War I, he served in the Army Corps of Engineers, and in 1919 returned to the Forest Service and worked on plans that culminated in the Clarke-McNary Act of 1924. Late in 1919 he resigned from the Forest Service and entered private business as a consultant. He served numerous lumber and paper companies in the South and West, and concurrently built up an extensive timber property in Arkansas. Thus, he contributed significantly to the advancement of both public and private forestry in the United States during the formative decades of the forest conservation movement. His professional career spanned sixty years. A charter member of the Society of American Foresters in 1900, he served it as secretary–treasurer, 1903–7; as president in 1913; and as a member of the Council, 1918–19. He was elected a Fellow of the Society in 1939 and was presented with the Gifford Pinchot medal for distinguished service to forestry in 1954. Died October 2, 1960.

SOCIETY OF AMERICAN FORESTERS

Journal of Forestry, 43:771, 1945.
Journal of Forestry. Obituary, 58:904, 1960.

HAMILTON, WILLIAM JOHN, JR. (1902–   )

Born December 11, 1902, at Corona, New York. Cornell University, B.S. 1926, M.S. 1928, Ph.D. (zoology) in 1930. Appointed assistant biologist at Cornell in 1926, he had advanced to professor of zoology in the Department of Conservation by 1947, and retired as emeritus professor in 1963. He had concurrent appointment as research associate in mammalogy at the American Museum of Natural History. Has been chairman of the Science Advisory Committee of the Edward Niles Huyck Biological Station since 1939. He was member of the Advisory Committee for Environmental Biology, National Science Foundation, 1956–58. He served as vice president of the American Society of Mammalogists, 1949–50 and as president, 1950–51. He was secretary of the Ecological Society of America, 1939–41 and president in 1955. His chief research interests were in the fields of mammalogy and herpetology with emphasis on the food habits of North American vertebrates, vertebrate populations, and life histories, and he was a strong advocate of basing conservation practice on the results of sound scientific studies. A prolific writer, his scientific publications number more than 150 plus many review articles. He was the author of *Mammals of Eastern United States*, 1943, and a co-author of the book *Conservation in the United States*, 1939. His *American Mammals*, 1939, was the first definitive treatment in a single book of all mammal families of the North American continent, and served for many years as the bible of American mammalogy.

GEORGE SPRUGEL, JR.

American Men of Science (The Physical and Biological Sciences), 11th ed., 1966; supp. 3, 1967.
Bulletin of the Ecological Society of America, vol. 35, no. 4, 1954.

HARDTNER, HENRY ERNEST (1870–1935)

Born September 10, 1870 in Pineville, Louisiana. Educated in bookkeeping at Soules' College. Began a life-long career in forestry in 1892 as part owner and secretary-treasurer of Nugent-Hardtner and Company, Nugent, Louisiana. During the succeeding decade he experienced the ups and downs of contemporary American lumbermen as he bought one tract after another of virgin timber, cut each one, and moved on to another. Then he organized the Urania Lumber Company, became interested in growing trees as a crop and gradually became known as "The Father of Southern Forestry." In

December 1908 he was designated Louisiana delegate to the Joint Conference on Conservation, Washington, D. C. The experience made him an active advocate for the Louisiana Commission on Natural Resources, the first in the South. Hardtner became the first chairman. He also was named chairman of the newly organized Conservation Commission. Elected to the state legislature in 1910, he became a strong force for pioneering forestry legislation. Lands devoted to forestry were valued at one dollar per acre for 40 years for taxation purposes. Another law established a severance tax on timber. Meanwhile he pioneered in fire prevention by organizing a fire protection system on 90,000 acres belonging to his company. He launched a great reforestation program by planting 30,000 acres of cutover land around Urania. A long-time member of the American Forestry Association, he cooperated with the Forest Service in early research experiments, became the host of the Yale School of Forestry for its annual spring field classes. He was an associate member of the Society of American Foresters; president, Southern Forestry Congress; president, Louisiana Forestry Association; chairman, forestry committee, Southern Pine Association; chairman, Southern Forest Research Advisory Committee; and a member of the conference committee on Article X of the Lumber Code, 1934. Died August 7, 1935.

KENNETH B. POMEROY

Forests and People, 13(1):56–57, 124–25, 1963.
Journal of Forestry, 33:885–86, 1935.

HARPER, VERNE LESTER (1902–   )

Born August 13, 1902 in Monroe, South Dakota. University of California, B.S. 1926, M.S. 1927; Duke University, Ph.D. 1943; North Carolina State University, D.Sc. (honorary) 1967. Began Forest Service career in gum naval stores research in Florida in 1927; division chief, forest management, Southern Forest Experiment Station, New Orleans, 1935–36; promoted to division chief, forest management research, Washington, D. C. 1937–44; director,

Northeastern Forest Experiment Station, Philadelphia, Pennsylvania, 1945–50; deputy chief (research), Washington, D. C., 1951–65. Became professor of forestry, University of Florida, 1966. Member of the United States delegation to conferences of the United Nations Food and Agriculture Organization in 1951, 1953, 1957, 1959, and 1965; chairman Latin-American Forestry Research Commission, 1958–61; chairman, executive committee, Fifth World Forestry Congress, Seattle, Washington, 1960; vice-chairman, United States delegation to Sixth World Forestry Congress, Madrid, Spain, 1966. Member, International Union of Forest Research Organizations, 1956–62; vice president, 1962–65. As a member of the Society of American Foresters Committee on International Relations from 1953 to 1966 (chairman in 1956), he obtained funds to compile the English portion of a multilingual forestry terminology and grants to assist American foresters in attending foreign schools. Primarily responsible for establishment of the North American Forestry Commission in FAO. His work with Latin-American officials in 1954 resulted in establishment of the Latin-American Research and Training Institute at Merida, Venezuela. Elected an honorary member of the Finnish Society of Foresters and a Fellow of the American Society of Foresters; awarded the Distinguished Service Award, United States Department of Agriculture, and Bernhard E. Fernow Award for Distinguished Service to International Forestry. He is the author of numerous scientific articles dealing with turpentine production of southern pines, forest management, silviculture, timber resources, range management, watershed management, wood utilization, and international relations in forestry.

KENNETH B. POMEROY

American Men of Science, 1960.
Who's Who in America, 1968–69.

HARTZOG, GEORGE BENJAMIN, JR. (1920–)

Born March 17, 1920 in Colleton County, South Carolina. American University, B.S. (business administration) 1953. Read law under supervision of Hon. J. M. Moorer, 1939–42. Admitted to practice before Supreme Court of South Carolina, 1942; Supreme Court of the United States, 1949; Supreme Court of Missouri, 1963. United States Army, 1940–41 and 1943–46, private to first lieutenant. Appointed attorney and administrator with the Department of the Interior, Bureau of Land Management and National Park Service, 1946; assistant superintendent of Rocky Mountain National Park, 1955–57, and Great Smoky National Park, 1957–59; superintendent of Jefferson National Expansion Memorial, St. Louis, 1959–62. Private employment as executive director, Downtown St. Louis, 1962–63. Assistant director of the National Park Service, 1963; director since January 8, 1964. Author of three volumes of National Park Service administrative manual series. Received Meritorious Award Certificate from William A. Jump Memorial Foundation, 1956; Special Service Award of Greater St. Louis Federal Business Association, 1962; Distinguished Service Award of the Department of the Interior, 1962; Cornelius Amory Pugsley Gold Medal Award, 1967. Active member of National Conference of State Parks; Sierra Club; Nature Conservancy; Board of Trustees, National Trust for Historic Preservation; Board of Trustees, National Recreation and Park Association; Advisory Council on Historic Preservation.

WILLIAM E. TOWELL

Who's Who in America, 1968–69.

HAWES, AUSTIN FOSTER (1879–1962)

Born March 17, 1879 in Danvers, Massachusetts. Tufts College, B.A. 1901; Yale University, M.F. 1903. Attracted to the federal Bureau of Forestry (now the Forest Service), he was among the early student assistants in that organization. He was appointed state forester of Connecticut in 1904, and was state forester of Vermont from 1909 to 1917. He returned to the Forest Service during World War I, serving in various capacities related to the war effort. He became state forester of Connecticut again in 1921, retiring from that position in 1944. He organized a statewide system of fire protection, promoted the acquisition of extensive state forests, provided for their management for wood production and recreation, and fostered a successful program of extension work resulting in intelligent and favorable public sentiment toward forestry generally throughout the state. From 1933 to 1941, using the Civilian Conservation Corps to a degree exceeding most other states, he carried out forest improvement work over large areas of state forest lands. He retired as state forester in 1944. Active in the Association of State Foresters, he was president in 1927. He was elected Fellow of the Society of American Foresters in 1939 in recognition of his leadership in the advancement of sound state forestry administration in the public interest. He was co-author of *Forestry in New England* (with R. C. Hawley), 1912; and *Manual of Forestry* (with R. C. Hawley), 1918. Died May 10, 1962.

JESSE H. BUELL

Journal of Forestry. Obituary, September 1962.
Yale Forest School News, "Austin F. Hawes Retires", April 1944.

HAWLEY, RALPH CHIPMAN (1880–1971)

Born March 5, 1880 in Atlanta, Georgia. Amherst College, A.B. 1901; Yale University, M.F. 1904. After a year with the United States Bureau of Forestry and another as assistant state forester of Massachusetts, he joined the faculty of Yale Forest School in 1906 and began a lifetime career in teaching at a strategic period when the forestry movement was gaining momentum in the United States and there was great need for technically trained foresters. His major work at Yale was in silviculture and forest protection. He succeeded in 1933 to the Morris K. Jesup professorship of silviculture and held that position until his retirement in 1948. He recognized the importance of field work in the training of foresters and was instrumental in making arrangements with the New Haven Water Company whereby the Yale School of Forestry cooperatively managed its forest lands, eventually covering 20,000 acres, and used them for training and research. He was chairman of a committee of the Society of American Foresters which designated and described the forest types recognized in the United States; and of a committee of the same society which published a book *Forestry Terminology*. He was elected a Fellow of the Society of American Foresters in 1942. He served 12 years as associate editor of the *Journal of Forestry*. He is author of *Forestry in New England* (with A. F. Hawes), 1912; *Manual of Forestry* (with Hawes), 1918; *Practice of Silviculture*, 1921 and later editions; and *Forest Protection*, 1937. Died January 19, 1971.

JESSE H. BUELL

American Men of Science (The Physical and Biological Sciences), 10th ed., 1955. "Ralph Hawley Retires," *Yale Forest School News*, October, 1948.

HAZZARD, ALBERT SIDNEY (1901–)

Born July 30, 1901 in Buchanan, New York. Cornell University, A.B. 1924, Ph.D. (zoology) 1931. Instructor in zoology at Cornell from 1924 to 1931, he was then appointed associate aquatic biologist in the United States Bureau of Fisheries. He was chief fisheries biologist and director of the Institute for Fisheries Research, Michigan Department of Conservation, 1935–55; and assistant executive director of the Pennsylvania Fish Commission, 1955–63. Since then he has been a fisheries consultant, living in Cadosia, New York. He served as president of the American Fisheries Society in 1951 and is active in the Society of Ichthyologists and Herpetologists. He is author of numerous scientific papers and of *Natural History of Fishes, Ecology of Fishes, Fish Management Methods*, and the bulletin *Pennsylvania Fishes*.

ROBERT E. OLSON

American Men of Science (The Physical and Biological Sciences), 11th ed., 1966.

HEALD, WELDON F. (1901–67)

Born May 1, 1901 Milford, New Hampshire. Graduated with degree in architecture from Massachusetts Institute of Technology, but turned to writing as a career, concentrating on conservation. He was the author of 754 pieces of literature which appeared in 146 different publications. His specialties were history, ecology, preservation of mountains, wilderness, deserts, state and national parks and monuments, and national forests. As a director of the Sierra Club, 1945–46 and 1947–49, he organized its first Conservation Committee; he was also a member of the Conservation Committee of the American Alpine Club. A consultant on national parks and monuments to the Secretary of the Interior from 1961 until his death, he made field inspections and reports for the National Park Service and the same for the Forest Service on wilderness and recreational areas as part of his assignments. He represented the National Parks Association at Congressional hearings and conferences as a trustee of that group. He donated the Laura G. Heald Grove in Prairie Creek Redwoods State Park in California to the State Park Commission. He established the Great Basin National Park Association in 1955 when Lehman Caves National Monument in Nevada was threatened with deletion from the National Park System. During World War II he served in the Army as a climatologist. He was famed for his snowfall predictions in the Sierra, based on his knowledge of glaciers. He was a member of advisory boards of the Desert Protective Council, the Trailfinders, and Friends of the Three Sisters Wilderness. He was a staff reporter for *National Wildlife News*. Among publications in which his work appeared were the *Sierra Club Bulletin, National Parks Magazine, Western Outdoor Quarterly*, and *Westways*. Died July 28, 1967.

MICHAEL McCLOSKEY

HEINTZLEMAN, B FRANK (1888–1965)

Born December 3, 1888 at Fayetteville, Pennsylvania. Pennsylvania State Forest Academy at Mont Alto, B.F. 1907; Yale Forest School, M.F. 1910. Entered the United States Forest Service at Portland,

Oregon as a forest assistant in 1910; transferred in 1918 to the Tongass National Forest in Alaska; and later became assistant regional forester. During the period 1934–36, he was assigned to cooperative forestry work with the timber industry in Washington, D. C. For one year was deputy administrator in charge of forest conservation, Lumber Division, National Industrial Recovery Administration. Appointed regional forester for the Alaska Region of the Forest Service, with headquarters in Juneau, in 1937. Negotiated the establishment of the two large pulp mills at Ketchikan and Sitka. Served as commissioner for the Department of Agriculture in the territory, as representative of the Federal Power Commission, and as chairman of the Alaska Planning Council. During World War II, he directed the Alaska spruce log program, cooperatively with the War Production Board. In 1953, following his retirement from the Forest Service, he was appointed governor of the Territory of Alaska by President Eisenhower; served four years, resigning in 1957, in anticipation of the passage of the Statehood Enabling Act of 1958. In recognition of his contributions to the advancement of forestry, he was elected a Fellow of the Society of American Foresters in 1951; and was awarded the Sir William Schlich Memorial Medal for distinguished service to forestry in 1958; he had been a member of the Society for 50 years. Died June 24, 1965.

SOCIETY OF AMERICAN FORESTERS

Journal of Forestry. Obituary, vol. 63:654, 1965.
Who's Who in America, 1956–57.

HEPTING, GEORGE HENRY (1907–   )

Born September 1, 1907 in Brooklyn, New York. Cornell University, B.S. (forestry) 1929, Ph.D. (plant pathology) 1933. He began his career in forest disease research in 1931 with the Bureau of Plant Industry, United States Department of Agriculture, and since 1933 has been associated with the Southeastern Forest Experiment Station at Asheville, North Carolina. In 1934 he was assigned responsibility for all forest pathology studies of the Forest Service in the

Southeastern United States. Named chief of the Division of Forest Disease Research at the Southeastern Station in 1953, he was made principal scientist in forest disease research for the entire Forest Service in 1961. He was associate editor of *Phytopathology*, 1937–39, of the *Journal of Forestry*, 1950–52, and of *Forest Science*, 1959–65. In 1963 he received the Barrington Moore award from the Society of American Foresters for achievement in biological research, and was elected a Fellow in 1965. In 1954 he received the Department of Agriculture superior service award, and in 1969 was elected to the National Academy of Sciences. He is the author of more than 150 scientific and professional publications on tree diseases and on the effect of air pollution on tree growth, a field of research in which he pioneered.

HENRY CLEPPER

American Men of Science (The Physical and Biological Sciences), 11th ed., 1966.
Journal of Forestry, 67(7):510, July 1969.
World Who's Who in Science, 1968.

HERBERT, HENRY WILLIAM   (1807–58)
(Frank Forester)

Born April 7, 1807 in London, England. Cambridge University (Caius College), B.A. 1830. Immigrating to the United States in 1831, he taught classical languages for eight years at a private school for boys in New York City. In 1833 he founded the magazine *American Monthly*, but retired as editor two years later. An ardent hunter and fisherman, he began writing about the sports of forest and stream and gave up teaching for a literary career in which he became successful. A prolific writer, as well as an artist skillful at drawing with the pen, he wrote historical novels and poetry in addition to articles and books about sports. His novels and poetry were published over his own name; his sports writings, which he considered of less literary merit, appeared over the pseudonym Frank Forester. The valuation he put on his works has been reversed by time; those about the sporting scene have been of more lasting worth than his romantic fiction. Among his outdoor books that had considerable vogue during the mid-1800s were *The Warwick Woodlands*, 1845; *My Shooting Box*, 1846; *The Deerstalkers*, 1849; *Frank Forester's Field Sports*, 2 vols., 1849; *Frank Forester's Fish and Fishing of the United States and British Provinces of North America*, 1850; and *The Complete Manual for Young Sportsmen*, 1856. Although wordy according to contemporary fashion, they were well written, with accurate descriptions of forest and field. His books were important because they extolled the code of the gentleman in sports and the significance of sportsmanship. The pioneer American writer in this genre, he influenced the development of American authorship about outdoor themes. Died May 17, 1858.

HENRY CLEPPER

Dictionary of American Biography, 1932.
Dictionary of National Biography, 1949–50.
Who Was Who in American History (Historical Volume), *1607–1896*, 1967.

HERBERT, PAUL ANTHONY (1899–   )

Born August 21, 1899 in Brooklyn, New York. Cornell University, B.S. 1921, M.F. 1922; University of Michigan, Ph.D. (land use planning) 1941. Following teaching as assistant professor of forestry at Michigan State University, 1922–26, he was senior forest economist in the United States Forest Service, 1926–30, and lecturer at the Yale University School of Forestry, 1930–31. Appointed professor of forestry and head of the Department of Forestry at Michigan State University in 1931, he was director of the University's Division of Conservation, 1950–56. After serving as chief of research for the Michigan Department of Economic Development, 1957–67, he is now consultant to the Michigan United Conservation Clubs. He served in the Army of the United States, 1918–19, and was a captain of ordnance, 1942–44. Elected vice president of the National Wildlife Federation, 1952–60, he was president, 1961–62; the magazine *National Wildlife* was initiated during his tenure.

From 1931 to 1935, he was associate editor (forest economics and policy) of the *Journal of Forestry*, published by the Society of American Foresters; and was editor of *Michigan Out-of-Doors*, 1947–53. He is a former member of the Board of Governors of Nature Conservancy, and is active in the American Forestry Association, National Parks Association, Soil Conservation Society of America, and the Wildlife Society. He is the author of numerous papers on forest economics, land use planning, and general conservation.

National Wildlife Federation

American Men of Science (The Physical and Biological Sciences), 11th ed., 1968.
Who's Who in America, 1964–65.

HERBST, ROBERT LEROY (1935–   )

Born October 5, 1935 in Minneapolis, Minnesota. University of Minnesota, B.S. (forestry) 1957. From 1957 to 1963, he was assistant area forest supervisor for the Minnesota Department of Conservation, responsible for the management and protection of state lands in 20 north central counties. Appointed executive secretary of Keep Minnesota Green, Inc. in 1963, he was executive officer of this nonprofit conservation organization for three years, promoting public education in conservation, and also supervising the State's tree farm program. In 1966 he was appointed deputy commissioner of the Minnesota Department of Conservation; in this position he was vice administrator of a comprehensive governmental agency that provided protection from fire to 17 million acres of land; management of 6 million acres of state forests, parks, and wildlife units; custodianship of forest, fish, game, mineral resources, and public waters; and advice and assistance to private landowners in resources management. In 1967 he was presented with the Governor's award as Conservationist of the Year, and also represented the Governor on the Public Land Law Review Commission. In April, 1969 he became executive director of the Izaak Walton League of America, one of the nation's largest and foremost conservation organizations. Organized in 1922, the League, with a membership of 56,000 is dedicated to sound resource management in the public interest; it promotes public education in the conservation of forests, soil, water, and other resources and the proper management of these resources for recreation and utilization. The author of many articles and bulletins on conservation subjects, he is an effective public speaker. In 1971 he was appointed commissioner of the Minnesota Department of Natural Resources.

HENRY CLEPPER

HERR, CLARENCE STUMPF (1901–   )

Born September 26, 1901 in Maytown, Pennsylvania. Pennsylvania State University, B.S. (forestry) 1925; Harvard University, M.F. 1930. Employed by United States Forest Service on Allegheny National Forest, 1925–28; in the latter year he entered the New Hampshire Forestry Department as white pine blister rust agent, and in 1930 the University of New Hampshire appointed him extension forester for the northern part of the state. In 1943 he became chief forester for the Brown Company of Berlin, New Hampshire, a corporation manufacturing pulp and paper, veneer, chemicals, and other forest products. Advanced to assistant woods manager in 1945, he became woods manager in 1948, and company vice president (Woodlands Division) in 1952. Brown Company together with its subsidaries owns or controls 4.5 million acres of timberland in the United States and Canada. During World War II he served with the pulpwood unit of the War Production Board and with the Office of Price Control. He was a member of the Council of the Society of American Foresters and vice president, 1950–51. He was president of the American Pulpwood Association, 1964–65. He was long a member of the Forestry and Wood Industries Committee of the New England Council, and a member of the national Forest Industries Council since 1964. One of the influential corporation foresters in the Northeast, he has been a leader in industry's application of scientific management to its woodlands. For twenty-five years he was president of the New Hampshire Timberland Owners Association. The author of numerous articles on forestry, he wrote *The Development of Industrial Forestry in the Northeast,* 1959.

HENRY CLEPPER

"Clarence S. Herr, Industrial Forester," *Journal of Forestry,* December 1956. *Who's Who in America,* 1968–69.

HEWITT, OLIVER HAROLD (1916–)

Born May 21, 1916 at Blind River, Ontario, Canada; naturalized United States citizen in 1954. McMaster University, B.A. (biology and chemistry) 1939; Cornell University, M.S. 1941, Ph.D. 1944. Instructor in wildlife management and ornithology at Cornell, 1942–44. Appointed wildlife management officer with the Canadian Wildlife Service in 1944; promoted to chief federal migratory bird officer and held this position until 1949 when he returned to Cornell as assistant professor of wildlife management; associate professor, 1952–57; professor since 1957. He served as associate editor of *The Journal of Wildlife Management,* 1951–53, and editor-in-chief 1953–56; also served on the committee which prepared the Wildlife Society's *Manual of Wildlife Investigational Techniques*; and was editor of the Society's *The Wild Turkey and Its Management.* The author of more than 50 publications and scientific journals on ornithology and wildlife management, his research interests have included development of techniques; waterfowl ecology, population estimation, and control; marsh and marine ecology. He taught wildlife management at the University of Pretoria, Republic of South Africa, for the academic year, 1967–68. In addition to serving on several Wildlife Society committees, he also served as secretary-general of the International Union for Applied Ornithology.

DANIEL Q. THOMPSON

American Men of Science (The Physical and Biological Sciences), 11th ed., 1965.

HICKEY, JOSEPH JAMES (1907–   )

Born April 16, 1907, in New York City. New York University, B.S. (history) 1930; University of Wisconsin, M.S. (wildlife management) 1943; University of Michigan, Ph.D. (zoology) 1949. He served as a research assistant in the Wisconsin Soil Conservation Commission, 1941–43, and was a Guggenheim Fellow in 1946–47. He has taught wildlife ecology and game management at the University of Wisconsin since 1948; has been professor, Department of Wildlife Ecology, since 1958; and represented the University at conservation conferences in France and England. Editor of *The Journal of Wildlife Management* for three years, 1956–59, he was also an associate editor of the *Proceedings* of the Thirteenth International Ornithological Congress. He organized an international conference on the peregrine falcons, and edited the results of the symposium published as *Peregrine Falcon Populations, Their Biology and Decline* by the University of Wisconsin Press, 1968. Served as officer of several ornithological societies and as collaborator, United States Fish and Wildlife Service. Elected a Fellow of American Ornithologists' Union in 1954, he has served on its council and its Bird Protection Committee. He is an honorary life member of the Linnaean Society of New York and of the Wisconsin Society for Ornithology, a member of the Board of Governors of the Nature Conservancy, and of the Conservation Committee of the Wilson Ornithological Society. He is the author of many publications on the ecology of birds, on pesticide-wildlife relationships, and on population dynamics and conservation of waterfowl. Notable are his ecological studies of songbird mortality caused by DDT in the control of Dutch elm disease in Wisconsin, and of the pesticidal pollution of Lake Michigan that documented the build-up of pesticidal residues in gulls, fish, and aquatic invertebrates. His book *A Guide to Bird Watching*, 1943, is a noteworthy contribution to avian ecology.

JAMES O. STEVENSON

American Men of Science (The Physical and Biological Sciences), 11th ed., 1966. *Who's Who in America*, 1968–69.

HILE, RALPH OSCAR (1904–)

Born March 18, 1904, in Plaineville, Indiana. Indiana Central College, B.A. 1924, LL.D. 1961; Indiana University, Ph.D. (zoology) 1930. He taught in Indiana public schools, 1924–26 and at Indiana University, 1926–30. Joining the United States Department of the Interior Bureau of Fisheries in 1930, he advanced successively from assistant aquatic biologist through position of assistant laboratory director (1958–61) to senior scientist with the Bureau of Commercial Fisheries, and since 1965 has been technical editor, Division of Biological Research. Recipient of the Department of the Interior's Distinguished Service Award, he served on the Council of the Great Lakes Research Institute, as associate, Institute of Human Biology; and as research associate, Department of Fisheries and Zoology of the University of Michigan. He is active in many professional societies including the American Fisheries Society, American Institute of Fishery Research Biologists, Biometrics Society, American Society of Limnology and Oceanography, and International Limnological Society. Editor of *Transactions of the American Fisheries Society*, 1946–49, he was president of the Society in 1952–53, and is now an honorary member. He is the author or co-author of 48 publications. Best known for his work as a biometrician, his primary interest has been in study of environmental effects on fish morphology and population dynamics. He was an early leader in the study of factors of age, growth, abundance, and distribution of fishes of the Great Lakes. He is now a counselor for analysis, interpretation, and reporting of fishery research findings for the United States Department of the Interior.

JACK D. LARMOYEUX

American Men of Science (The Physical and Biological Sciences), 11th ed., 1966.

HILL, ROBERT R. (1885–)

Born March 18, 1885 in Bruning, Nebraska. Graduated from University of Nebraska in forestry in 1910. During that year he was appointed to the Forest Service, United States Department of Agriculture, and was assigned to Fort Valley Forest Experiment Station in Arizona to investigate the effect of livestock grazing on ponderosa pine reproduction. This was a relatively new field of study, and techniques for measuring soil and plant conditions and responses were worked out. The data showed the extent of damage to the range and the pine reproduction and the need for reduced livestock use. In 1911 he was placed in charge of the first party to do range survey work, wherein the forage types were mapped and carrying capacity calculated. Some of the first range management plans on federal land evolved from these surveys. He was appointed director of the Santa Rita Range Experiment Station in Arizona in 1918, where original work established means of determining the best grazing use and management to maintain and improve range conditions. To cut down on the time consumed in detailed mapping of vegetation in small plots, a field pantograph was developed. He served as range inspector for the California Region of Forest Service, 1921–26. Transferred to the Washington, D. C. office in 1927 as inspector of grazing, he drafted a plan for study of range economic conditions and distribution problems on the western national forests, which eventually led to studies of grazing use and stability of permits and to policy changes. His last assignment in the Forest Service was as director of the Division of Recreation, Wildlife and Range Management, in the regional office at Milwaukee, a position from which he retired in 1945. Throughout his career he advocated conservative use of range lands, and was ahead of most of his contemporaries in recognizing, and urging correction of, the damage being done to watersheds through overuse by livestock. He counseled against the Department's program of attempting to increase meat production through heavier stocking on range lands during World War I. In 1936 he declared the authors of *The Western Range* were unrealistic in their recommendation that national forest range lands needed only a 6.3 per cent reduction in stocking to reach safe capacity and start range conditions on an upward trend. In testimony to the soundness of his declaration, the present stocking has been reduced by more than 50 per cent.

LLOYD W. SWIFT

HOCKENSMITH, ROY DOUGLAS (1905–)

Born February 27, 1905 in Gallatin, Missouri. University of Missouri, B.S. (agriculture) 1927, M.S. (soils) 1928. He was assistant professor of agronomy, 1929–30, and associate professor of agronomy in charge of soils, 1930–34, at Colorado State University; then became a soils specialist with the Federal Land Bank, 1934–37. Appointed regional soil scientist for the Soil Conservation Service in Amarillo, Texas, in 1937; he became assistant chief, Soil Conservation Surveys Division, Washington, D. C., 1939–46; division chief, 1946–52; and, since 1952, director of SCS Soil Survey Operations. He is a Fellow of the Soil Conservation Society of America (president in 1962); also a Fellow of the American Society of Agronomy and of the American Association for the Advancement of Science. He is a member of the International Society of Soil Science and chairman of the Soil Technology Commission, 1950–54; a member of the Soil Science Society of America and of the American Society of Range Management. He has been a participant in many international conferences including the United Nations Scientific Conference on Conservation and Utilization of Resources in 1949, and the FAO Conference on Land and Water Utilization and Conservation in 1950. He was United States advisor on agriculture to the Caribbean Commission in 1950; United States delegate to the Fourth International Congress of Soil Science in 1950, and participant in the Fifth International Congress in 1954. He was United States delegate to the First Pan-American Soil Conservation Congress in 1966, and participated in soil studies to locate new areas of settlement in Brazil during special assignments in 1963–66 and 1968. He received the Superior Service Award of the United States Department of Agriculture in 1959 and the Department's Certificate of Merit in 1967.

F. GLENNON LLOYD

American Men of Science (The Physical and Biological Sciences), 11th ed., 1967.

HOLBROOK, STEWART HALL (1893–1964)

Born August 22, 1893 in Newport, Vermont. Colebrook New Hampshire Academy; Pacific University, D.H.L. 1957; Willamette University, Litt.D. (honorary) 1959. United States Army, 1917–19; first sergeant, two battle stars. Associate editor, *The Lumber News,* Portland, Oregon, 1923–25; editor, 1926–34. His first book, *Holy Old Mackinaw,* a natural history of the American lumberjack, was published in 1938. A year later he was appointed director of the "Keep Washington Green" program to promote forest fire prevention and reforestation. In 1943 his book, *Burning an Empire,* the story of American forest fires, became a classic in its field. During the next two decades he wrote a series of books on historical themes and conservation subjects, including a juvenile, *Tall Timber,* and several histories of forest products companies, including *Green Commonwealth,* a history of the Simpson Logging Company, and *Yankee Loggers,* an account of International Paper Company. In all, he wrote 40 books and hundreds of newspaper and magazine articles, many of which treated of natural resource protection and management. He was an effective interpreter of conservation needs and progress whose writings received wide public acceptance. Although best known as a popularizer of national and regional history, his contributions to the literature of forest conservation were valuable in advancing the movement because they reached a class of readers not generally interested in technical and scientific works. Received Distinguished Service Award from American Forest Products Industries in 1963. Died September 3, 1964.

JAMES B. CRAIG

HOLMES, JOSEPH AUSTIN (1859–1915)

Born November 23, 1859 in Laurens, South Carolina. Cornell University, B.S. 1881; University of Pittsburgh, D.Sc.; University of North Carolina, LL.D. Beginning in 1881 he was professor of geology and natural history at the University of North Carolina until 1891 when he was appointed state geologist, the first in the nation, on the establishment of the North Carolina Geological Survey. Directed also to investigate the state's timber resources, in 1892 he employed W. W. Ashe (*q.v.*) who was thus one of the country's first state forestry employees, and who made one of the earliest state forest surveys ever published. In 1899 Holmes was a founder of the Appalachian National Park Association, later named Appalachian National Forest Reserve Association, and was one of the first persons to propose federal acquisition of woodland in the southern Appalachians for forest and park purposes, a proposal consummated with the passage of the Weeks Law of 1911, the genesis of which may be credited to him, and the subsequent acquisition of 1.5 million acres of national forests and parks in North Carolina. He went with the United States Geological Survey in 1904, was appointed chief of the technological branch investigating mine accidents in 1907, and in 1910 became director of the newly created Bureau of Mines. He worked with Gifford Pinchot and others to bring about the transfer, in 1905, of the forest reserves from the Department of the Interior to the Department of Agriculture, where they have become the present 188-million-acre national forest system. As secretary of the Section on Minerals of the National Conservation Commission, he helped compile the first inventory of the nation's natural resources. Died July 12, 1915.

HENRY CLEPPER

Dictionary of American Biography, 1932.
Who Was Who in America, 1897–1942.

HORNADAY, FRED EUGENE (1900–   )

Born June 18, 1900 in Indianapolis, Indiana. Wharton School of Finance and Commerce, University of Pennsylvania, B.S. (journalism) 1924. Field secretary, Chamber of Commerce of the United States, 1924–26; with Advertising Department, *United States Daily* (later *U. S. News and World Report*), 1926–28. Business manager, the American Forestry Association, 1928–45; inaugurated promotional and advertising programs for the association's magazine,

American Forests; secretary, 1945–56; executive vice president, 1956–66; special consultant, 1967–68; retired December 31, 1968, having served the association for 40 years, the longest service of any association employee. A staunch defender of national forests and parks, an enthusiastic outdoorsman and participant in the association's Trail Riders of the Wilderness program. Conducted the pioneer trip in the Bob Marshall Wilderness Area in 1933 and conducted 12 other trips in western wilderness areas. He was acquainted with more members of the American Forestry Association than any other staff member, having planned its annual meetings from 1929 to 1966. He is a member of the Society of American Foresters; member, Conservation Committee, and member-at-large of the National Council, Boy Scouts of America. He served as chairman, National Advisory Council Steering Committee, Keep America Beautiful, Inc., 1967, receiving its plaque for meritorious service. Chairman, Natural Resources Council of America, 1966–67; member of the Tree Committee of the D. C. Commissioners' Planning and Urban Renewal Advisory Council; served on President Eisenhower's Council for Youth Fitness; participant in Sixth World Forestry Congress, Madrid, Spain, 1966.

KENNETH B. POMEROY

HORNADAY, WILLIAM TEMPLE (1854–1937)

Born December 1, 1854 near Plainfield, Indiana. Educated at Oskaloosa College, and Iowa State Agricultural College; University of Pittsburgh, Sc.D. 1906; Yale University, 1917; Iowa State College, Ph.M. 1923. At Ward's Natural Science Establishment in Rochester, New York, which supplied mounted specimens for museums, he became a scientific taxidermist, collected vertebrate animals in different parts of the world, and on one early trip established definitely the previously disputed existence of the Florida crocodile. In 1882 he became chief taxidermist of the U. S. National Museum in Washington, D. C. Instrumental in starting the National Zoological Park in Washington, he served as its superintendent for two years until he resigned from government service in 1890 after a dispute with superiors over plans for its future. He then engaged in private business at Buffalo, New York until called upon in 1896 to become the first director and builder of the New York Zoological Park. World renowned as a zookeeper, he became equally famous as a champion of wildlife protection, a cause in which he remained active and articulate after his retirement from zoo administration in 1926. With caustic tongue and pen, he denounced hunting for sport and inveighed against what he regarded as the malevolent influence of the manufacturers of sporting arms and ammunition. He worked for laws against the sale of wild game and the importation of wild bird plumage, and for hunting bag limits. His efforts were credited with helping to save the American bison, the pronghorn antelope, and the Alaskan fur seal from threatened extinction. He established the Permanent Wild Life Fund in 1913, and served as its trustee and chief administrator until his death, March 6, 1937. Of some 20 books, two of his better known volumes are *Our Vanishing Wild Life*, 1913, and *30 Years' War for Wildlife*, 1913.

CHARLES H. CALLISON

Dictionary of American Biography, supp. 2, 1958.
National Cyclopaedia of American Biography, 1897.
New York Herald Tribune. Obituary, March 8, 1937.
New York Times. Obituary, March 7, 1937.
Who Was Who in America, 1897–1942.

HOSMER, RALPH SHELDON (1874–1963)

Born March 4, 1874 at Deerfield, Massachusetts. Harvard University, B.S. (agriculture) 1894; Yale University, M.F. 1902, a member of the first graduating class in the School of Forestry. Entered government service in the Division of Soils, United States Department of Agriculture in 1896; after two years he transferred to the Division of Forestry, recently reorganized under Gifford Pinchot. Became the first superintendent of the Division of Forestry of the Territory of Hawaii in 1904. As territorial forester he obtained establishment of a system of forest reserves and put the Division of

Forestry on a sound operating basis. He was an advisor at the White House Conference of Governors in 1908 and chairman of the Territorial Conservation Commission of Hawaii, 1908–14. In 1914 he became professor of forestry and head of the Department of Forestry at New York State College of Agriculture at Cornell University. He retired from this position in July 1942 as professor of forestry, emeritus. Member of the Research Council of the North-eastern Forest Experiment Station, 1926–42; secretary of the Forestry Section, International Congress of Plant Sciences, 1926; member of the New York State Conservation Advisory Council, 1932–41; honorary life member of the Empire State Forest Products Association, 1924; and a member of the American Forestry Association. He was a Fellow of the American Association for the Advancement of Science and of the Forest History Society. A Charter Member of the Society of American Foresters, he served as president in 1923, Councilman, 1930–33, held many other offices and committee assignments, was elected a Fellow in 1932, and was awarded the Sir William Schlich Memorial Medal in 1950. He was the author of many articles, bulletins and books; especially noteworthy are *Impressions of European Forestry*, 1921; *The Cornell Plantations—A History*, 1947; *The Society of American Foresters—An Historical Summary*, 1940 and 1950; and *Forestry at Cornell*, 1950. Died July 19, 1963.

SOCIETY OF AMERICAN FORESTERS

American Men of Science (The Physical and Biological Sciences), 10th ed., 1955.
Journal of Forestry, 61(9):686, September 1963.

HOUGH, FRANKLIN BENJAMIN (1822–85)

Born July 22, 1822 in Martinsburg, New York. Union College, graduated 1843; Western Reserve Medical College, M.D. 1848. While practicing medicine in New York State, he was also director of the state census of 1854. During the Civil War he was a surgeon in the Union Army. Resuming his medical practice in Lowville, New York, he was superintendent of the state census of 1865, and of the United States census of 1870. His findings as a census administrator alerted him to the extent of depletion of the country's timber lands. At the 1873 meeting of the American Association for the Advancement of Science in Portland, Maine, he presented a paper "On the Duty of Governments in the Preservation of Forests." The association appointed a committee of which he was chairman to memorialize Congress on the importance of promoting the cultivation of timber and the preservation of forests. In August 1876 Congress appropriated $2,000 to the Commissioner of Agriculture to employ an agent to investigate the consumption of timber and other forest products and the best means for the renewal of the forests. Hough was given the assignment on August 30, 1876. Thus began the first action by the federal government toward a forest policy. His modest office became the Division of Forestry in 1881, the Bureau of Forestry in 1901, and the present United States Forest Service in 1905. A fluent writer of papers and speeches, he published his first *Report upon Forestry* in 1887, and his second in 1880. In his third report of 1882, he described European systems of forestry which he had studied in person. Superseded as head of the Division of Forestry in 1883, but not dismissed, he remained on duty to write the fourth official report of 1885. In 1882 he published a book, *Elements of Forestry*, and started the *American Journal of Forestry*, which was discontinued after one year for lack of support. One of his last contributions to the advancement of forestry was his drafting of legislation in 1885 for a forestry commission in New York State. Died June 11, 1885.

HENRY CLEPPER

Dictionary of American Biography, 1933.
Who's Who in American History (Historical Volume), 1607–1896.
JACOBSEN, EDNA L. "Franklin B. Hough, a pioneer in Scientific Forestry in America," *New York History* XV. New York State Library, Albany, July 1934, pp. 317–21.

HOWARD, WILLIAM GIBBS (1887–1948)

Born February 17, 1887 in Medford, Massachusetts. Harvard University, A.B. 1907, M.F. 1908. Entered the United States Forest Service in 1908 as forest assistant, and in 1909 joined the New

York State Forest Fish and Game Commission as forester. He became assistant head of the Division of Lands and Forests in the successor New York Conservation Commission in 1910, and director of that Division in the succeeding New York Conservation Department in 1927, which position he held until his death. He organized in New York one of the first effective state forest fire control organizations, which became a model for numerous other states, and directly supervised it until he became the head of the Division of Lands and Forests. In addition, he carried on an expanding program of development of New York's forest preserve in the Adirondack and Catskill regions for public recreation, and fathered many of the policies for the administration of the preserve. He was a leading spirit in the program of acquiring and reforesting abandoned agricultural lands and in the enactment of the New York Forest Practice Act which provides technical forestry assistance to woodland owners. From 1911 until his death, he was active in the Society of American Foresters and served that organization as vice president, member of the Council and chairman of the New York Section; he was elected a Fellow of the society in 1942. He was one of the founders of the National Association of State Foresters in 1920 and president of the Association in 1933. Died October 30, 1948.

W. D. MULHOLLAND

HOWE, SIDNEY (1928–   )

Born May 12, 1928 in Waterbury, Connecticut. Graduated from the Loomis School in 1945; exchange student at Radley College, England, 1946; Yale University, B.A. (sociology) 1949; University of Michigan School of Natural Resources, M.S. (conservation) 1954. He served in the United States Army, 1950–52, and was with Aluminium Limited in Canada, 1954–57. Then for seven years he was executive director of the Farmington River Watershed Association, a citizens' organization in Connecticut. In April 1965 he joined the Conservation Foundation, Washington, D. C., as director of conservation services, was appointed acting director of the association in February 1969, and in June 1969 was elected president, a trustee, and a member of the executive committee of this research, education, and information organization. A member of the Board of Directors of the National Audubon Society, he is also a member of the Executive Committee of the Natural Resources Council of America, a member of the Advisory Council of the Center for Information on America, Washington, Connecticut, and is president of Rockywold-Deephaven Camps, Inc., a family business in New Hampshire.

RAYMOND F. DASMANN

HUBACHEK, FRANK BROOKES (1894–   )

Born August 10, 1894 in Minneapolis, Minnesota. University of Minnesota, A.B. 1915, LL.B. 1922; Harvard Law School, 1915–17; Cornell College, L.H.D. (honorary) 1962; Beloit College, LL.D. 1970. Engaged in practice of law beginning in 1922; now a partner of Hubachek, Kelly, Rauch & Kirby, Chicago. In World War I he was a Navy Air Corps pilot (lt. j.g.); in World War II in the Office of Price Administration. Since 1926 he has been active in the protection and management of wilderness areas, particularly the Quetico-Superior region along the Minnesota-Ontario border. In 1948 he established the Quetico-Superior Wilderness Research Center, dedicated to investigations concerned with the maintenance of wilderness areas and their utilization for the benefit of science and humanity. In 1957 he created and endowed the Wilderness Research Foundation, a nonprofit Illinois corporation of which he is trustee and president, to sponsor scientific research in wilderness ecology. Located on Basswood Lake, north of Ely, Minnesota, the Center provides research facilities for visiting scientists and a permanent staff. It is operated under the advisory guidance of university scientists, the United States Forest Service, and other agencies concerned with wilderness ecology. Recipient of the American Forestry Association's Conservation Award in 1957; later served as an association director. He was elected an Honorary Member of the Society of American Foresters in 1953. In recognition of his leadership in advancing scientific knowledge of wilderness ecology, in 1968 he was recipient of the American Motors Conservation Award.

HENRY CLEPPER

HUBBS, CARL LEAVITT (1894–)

Born October 18, 1894 in Williams, Arizona. Stanford University, A.B. 1916, A.M. 1917; University of Michigan, Ph.D. (zoology) 1927. For four years assistant curator of ichthyology and herpetology at the Field Museum of Natural History, Chicago, he joined the staff of the Museum of Zoology, University of Michigan, in 1920, and rose from instructor to professor of zoology and curator of fishes. Since 1944 at Scripps Institution of Oceanography (University of California at San Diego), he is now research biologist and emeritus professor. Founder of the Michigan Department of Conservation's Institute for Fisheries Research in 1930, he has been active in conservation work for almost 40 years. In 1939–40 he was field representative for the United States Department of the Interior in Alaska and in the same year was vice president of the Wildlife Society. He was instrumental in getting the unique habitat of the Devils Hole pupfish (*Cyprinodon diabolis*) added to Death Valley National Monument in 1952 and in having a refuge area developed for native fishes of Owens Valley, California, in 1967. Similar efforts to conserve Torrey Pines and Mission Bay, near San Diego, were successfully concluded. In 1963 he was invited by the Japan Fisheries Resource Conservation Association to lecture in Japan. In 1964 he received the Leidy Award and Medal of the Academy of Natural Sciences of Philadelphia; in 1966, the Fellows Medal of the California Academy of Sciences; and in 1965 he was elected a foreign member of the Linnaean Society of London. From 1964 through 1967 he served as vice president for conservation and chairman of the Committee on Conservation of the American Society of Ichthyologists and Herpetologists. His achievements were recognized by his election to the National Academy of Sciences in 1952. The author of more than 600 scientific publications and reviews, he is senior author of *Fishes of the Great Lakes Region*, 1941–64.

ROBERT RUSH MILLER

American Men of Science (The Physical and Biological Sciences), 11th ed., 1966.

HUBODA, MICHAEL (1913–)

Born August 1, 1913 in Struthers, Ohio. Following eight years employment with the Reconstruction Finance Corporation, he became active in national conservation affairs when he was appointed in 1945 as Washington, D. C. editor and columnist for *Sports Afield*. Since then he has written this magazine's monthly "Report from Washington" dealing with natural resource developments in the federal government. He was one of the first Washington-based writers to involve sportsmen—hunters and fishermen—in actively supporting improved management of the basic soil and water resources. During the past quarter-century, he has been a leading exponent of conservation viewpoints not regularly covered by writers representing the scientific, technical, and professional resource journals. In addition to his magazine reporting, he has served on numerous conservation committee and advisory bodies. Beginning in 1949 he served on various committees dealing with resources in the Department of the Interior, including the chairmanship of the Secretary's Advisory Committee on Conservation, 1957–61; and in 1957 was on the Advisory Committee on Conservation to the Secretary of the Navy. From 1949 to 1951, he was representative of the Izaak Walton League of America in Washington, D. C., and received the League's public relations honor roll award in 1951 together with life membership. Since 1953 he has been on the Board of Trustees of the National Parks Association. He was secretary and conservation director of the Outdoor Writers Association of America, 1948–53; was recipient of the 1954 award of the National Association of Conservation Education and Publicity; and in 1956 was presented with the Wildlife Society's national award in conservation education. He was a member of the Editorial Committee that compiled the book *America's Natural Resources*, 1957, revised 1967, sponsored by the Natural Resources Council of America. Indicative of his standing among magazine and newspaper reporters was his election as president of the National Press Club of Washington, D. C., for 1970.

HENRY CLEPPER

HUTTON, ROBERT FRANKLIN (1921–)

Born July 18, 1921 in Red Lion, Pennsylvania. University of Miami, B.S. (biological sciences) 1949, M.S. 1961; University of London, Ph.D. 1954. During 1954–55, he headed the research program on the Florida red tide for the University of Miami. In 1955 he joined the staff of the University of Florida as an assistant professor and served as director of the University's field station at St. Petersburg. Later (1955–62) he was biologist-in-charge and parasitologist for the Florida State Board of Conservation Marine Laboratory at St. Petersburg. From 1962 until 1965, he was chief marine biologist and assistant director of the Division of Marine Fisheries, Department of Natural Resources, Boston, Massachusetts. In 1965 he received the Massachusetts Governor's Award as conservationist of the year. Also in 1965, he became the first executive secretary of the American Fisheries Society. He was elected treasurer of the Natural Resources Council in 1966, 1967, and 1968. He has served as chairman of the Statistical Needs Committee of the Atlantic States Marine Fisheries Commission, and on both the Biological Committee and the Estuarine Committee of the Commission. He directed research on problems such as parasite and disease investigations, fish taxonomy and ecology, shrimp and oyster investigations, red tide, seagrass ecology, algae taxonomy, dredge and fill studies, bulkhead line investigations, artificial reef studies, shellfish depuration, lobster culture and ecology, and estuarine fisheries studies. A new larval trematode, *Gigantobilharzia huttoni*, and a new trematode,

Neostictodora huttoni, were named in his honor. Author of many papers on estuaries, parasites and diseases, and ecology, he holds professional certification as a Fisheries Scientist in the American Fisheries Society, and is a Fellow of the American Association for the Advancement of Science.

ELWOOD A. SEAMAN

American Men of Science (The Physical and Biological Sciences), 11th ed., 1966. *Leaders in American Science,* 7th ed., 1966–67.

ILLICK, JOSEPH SIMON (1884–1967)

Born September 16, 1884 near Easton, Pennsylvania. Lafayette College, B.A. (biology) 1907, D.Sc. (honorary) 1925; Biltmore Forest School, North Carolina, B.F. (forestry) 1911, F.E. (forest engineering) 1913; Juniata College, Sc.M. (honorary) 1925; Syracuse University, LL.D. 1952. He began his teaching career at the Pennsylvania State Forest Academy at Mont Alto in 1907, advanced to professor of silviculture, and left in 1919 to become chief of the Bureau of Silviculture and later director of research for the Pennsylvania Department of Forests and Waters. He was state forester of Pennsylvania, 1927–31. In the latter year he went to New York State College of Forestry at Syracuse University as head of the Department of Forest Engineering and Management, and was appointed dean of the College in 1945. He retired in 1952 as dean emeritus. He was a former chairman of the Division of Education in the Society of American Foresters, served on the Society's Council, 1954–57, and was elected a Fellow in 1957. He was the first chairman of the Council of Forestry School Executives organized in 1948, and was a member of the board of trustees of the Charles Lathrop Pack Forestry Foundation. He was a Fellow of the American Association for the Advancement of Science. The author of 12 books, 10 major bulletins, and many articles on forestry and education, he wrote *Pennsylvania Trees,* 1913 (four later editions); *Tree Habits: How to Know the Hardwoods,* 1924; and *Outline of General Forestry,* 3rd edition 1939. He was one of America's outstanding forestry educators and a leader in the development of education in related fields of natural resources. Died August 31, 1967.

HENRY CLEPPER

Journal of Forestry. Obituary, 65(11):848–49, November 1967.

JAMES, HARLEAN (1877–1969)

Born July 18, 1877 in Mattoon, Illinois. Stanford University, A.B. (history) 1898; graduate studies at the University of Chicago and Columbia University. Following secretarial work in Hawaii, she became executive secretary of the Women's Civic League in Baltimore during 1911–16, then was with the National Defense Council and the Department of Labor during World War I. She was executive secretary of the American Civic Association, 1921–35, and of the American Planning and Civic Association, 1935–58. She served also as executive secretary of the National Conference on State Parks, 1935–57, and on her retirement was made a member of the Board of Directors; the Conference is now a unit of the National Recreation and Parks Association. At various times she was a collaborator with the National Park Service on recreational planning, and was on the Advisory Committee of the Department of the Interior. The American Scenic and Historic Preservation Society presented her with the bronze medal in 1943 and the gold medal in 1953. She was an honorary vice president of the American Forestry Association, and honorary corresponding member of the American Association of Landscape Architects. The author of several books, she wrote *Land Planning in the United States for the City, State and Nation*, 1926, and *Romance of the National Parks*, 1939. She was editor of the American Planning and Civic Association *Annuals* during 1927–57, and of *Yearbook of Park and Recreation Progress*, 1942. Died November 15, 1969.

HENRY CLEPPER

The Evening Star, Washington, D.C. Obituary, November 19, 1969.
Who's Who of American Women, 1961–62.

JARDINE, JAMES TERTIUS (1881–1954)

Born November 28, 1881, Cherry Creek, Oneida County, Idaho. Utah Agricultural College, B.S. 1905; studied at University of Chicago summers of 1905 and 1906. Taught English at Utah two years; then employed by the Forest Service, United States Department of Agriculture, until 1920. During this period he became the first chief of studies for this bureau of grazing use and management on western range lands resulting in several publications, of which the classic bulletin *Range Management on the National Forests*, 1919, was issued with Mark Anderson as junior author. A contribution of the bulletin was a method devised by Jardine for estimating the forage supply and grazing capacity of range lands. It summarized the basic principles of range management on numbers of livestock, grazing seasons, and other matters, and this publication is regarded as the foundation statement of the science and art of range management. He was director of the Oregon Agricultural Experiment Station from 1920 to 1931. Returning to the Department of Agriculture, Washington, D. C., he was chief officer of experiment stations beginning in 1931, and from 1936 to 1941 was director of research for the department. A pioneer in the field of range and livestock management, through his keen analytical mind and command of English he made a major contribution to the principles of grazing use of western public lands. He was awarded honorary D.Sc. degrees from three American colleges. Perhaps more than any other man, he initiated the science of range management. As chief of grazing studies in the Forest Service he exercised strong leadership, organizing the work into projects, and proceeding with the establishment of field stations, of which the Great Basin Experiment Station in Utah, where studies on plant succession were conducted, is an example. Died October 24, 1954.

LLOYD W. SWIFT

American Men of Science, 7th ed.,
TALBOT, M. W., and CRONEMILLER, F. P., "Some of the Beginnings of Range Management," *Journal of Range Management*, vol. 14, March, 1961.

JEMISON, GEORGE MEREDITH (1908–)

Born July 11, 1908 in Spokane, Washington. University of Idaho, B.S. 1931; Yale University, M.F. 1936; Duke University, Ph.D. (tree physiology) 1942. Entering the United States Forest Service in 1931 as a junior forester assigned to fire danger measurement studies at the Northern Rocky Mountain Forest and Range Experiment Station, Missoula, Montana, he continued in research and was transferred in 1937 to the Southeastern Forest Experiment Station at Asheville, North Carolina where he engaged in forest fire and forest management research. He was made director of the Northern Rocky Mountain Station in 1950; then from 1954 to 1957 was director of the Pacific Southwest Forest and Range Experiment Station at Berkeley, California. In 1957 he was assigned to the Washington, D. C. office of the Forest Service as assistant chief of the Branch of Research, and in 1966 was appointed deputy chief in charge of research. Retiring from government service in 1969, he became professor of forest management at Oregon State University. He was a member of the Council of the Society of American Foresters, 1962–66, having been elected a Fellow in 1961. He serves as president from 1968 to 1971 of the International Union of Forest Research Organizations. His research publications include 50 papers on forest fire behavior, fire control techniques, and the silviculture of pines and hardwoods. In 1959 he was leader of a group of foresters sent by the United States to the USSR to observe forest conditions and forestry practices in Russia.

HENRY CLEPPER

American Men of Science (The Physical and Biological Sciences), 11th ed., 1966. "Jemison Joins Oregon Faculty," Journal of Forestry, 67(6):424, June 1969.

JENKINS, ROBERT MERLE (1923–)

Born June 18, 1923 in Kansas City, Missouri. University of Oklahoma, B.S. 1948, M.S. (fisheries biology) 1949. He began his professional career with the Oklahoma Game and Fish Department in 1949, managing selected ponds and small lakes in northeastern

Oklahoma for improved sport fishing, and also conducted field investigations of the sport fishery of 46,000-acre Grand Lake. In 1952 he joined the staff of the Oklahoma Fishery Research Laboratory, a joint venture of the University of Oklahoma and the Oklahoma Game and Fish Department (later renamed the Oklahoma Department of Wildlife Conservation), and in 1953 was appointed director. From 1958 to 1963, he was assistant executive vice president for the Sport Fishing Institute and co-editor of the Institute's monthly *SFI Bulletin* and of its biennial review series *Fish Conservation Highlights*. His studies of research needs for better understanding of the ecology of large reservoirs having contributed to the development within the United States Bureau of Sport Fisheries and Wildlife of a National Reservoir Research Program, he was designated as the Program's first director in 1963. As chairman of the Reservoir Committee, Southern Division, American Fisheries Society, he was a principal organizer of the first Reservoir Fishery Resources Symposium, at the University of Georgia in 1967. He has published over 40 scientific papers on fishery resource subjects, as well as numerous popular articles, including *Bibliography on Reservoir Fishery Biology in North America,* 1965. He was second vice president of the American Fisheries Society in 1967, first vice president in 1968, and president-elect in 1969, and is a certified fishery scientist (American Fisheries Society). One of the original trustees of the Sport Fishery Research Foundation, he served as its first secretary during 1962–63.

R. H. STROUD

JORDAN, DAVID STARR   (1851–1931)

Born January 19, 1851 in Gainesville, New York. Cornell University, M.S. 1872; Indiana Medical College, M.D. 1875; Butler University, Ph.D. 1878. Awarded LL.D. by Cornell University, 1886; Johns Hopkins University, 1902; Illinois College, 1903; Indiana University, 1909; University of California, 1913; and Western Reserve University, 1915. He taught at various schools including Cornell University, Butler University, and Indiana University from 1871 to 1885. He was in charge of fishery investigations of the United States Fish Commission for the Pacific Coast in 1880; of fur seals in the Bering Sea, 1896–97; Japan, 1900; Hawaii, 1901; Samoa, 1902; and Alaska, 1903. He was president of Indiana University, 1885–91; president of Stanford University, 1891–1913; and chancellor of Stanford University, 1913–16. Elected president of California Academy of Sciences 1896–1904 and 1908–12. The dominant ichthyologist of his time by virtue of his work and influence on associates and students, he wrote over 600 ichthyological papers and was author and co-author of many books including *A Manual of Vertebrate Animals of Northern U. S.*, 1876–1929; *Synopsis of Fishes of North America*, 1883; *Fishes of North and Middle America*, 1896–1900; *American Food and Game Fishes*, 1902; *A Guide to the Study of Fishes*, 1905; *The Genera of Fishes*, 1917–20; *Classification of Fishes*, 1923; and *Check List of the Fishes and Fishlike Vertebrates of North and Middle America North of Venezuela and Columbia*, 1930. Died September 19, 1931.

WILLIAM R. GOULD

American Men of Science, 4th ed.
Copeia, no. 1, 1964.
Dictionary of American Biography, 1933.
Who Was Who in America, 1897–1942.
World Who's Who in Science, 1968.

JUDAY, CHANCEY (1871–1944)

Born May 5, 1871, near Millersburg, Indiana. University of Indiana, A.B. 1896, A.M. 1897, LL.D. (honorary) 1933. Biologist, Wisconsin Geological and Natural History Survey, 1900–1901 and 1905–31. At the University of Wisconsin, from 1908 to 1931, he served as lecturer in limnology and plankton organisms and directed the training of graduate students specializing in limnology, and from 1931–42 he was professor of limnology. Although he retired from teaching in 1942, the University retained him as a research associate to prepare a comprehensive review of Wisconsin limnology. He held

185   Judd

many high positions in scientific organizations: president, American
Microscopical Society, 1923; president, Ecological Society of America, 1927; president, Wisconsin Academy of Sciences, Arts and
Letters for two years and secretary for nine years. The major
motivating force in the formation of the Limnological Society of
America, he was elected as the first president in 1935 and reelected
in 1936. A fellow of the American Association for the Advancement
of Science, he belonged also to the American Society of Zoologists,
the American Society of Naturalists, and the International Limnological Society. In 1943 he was awarded the Leidy Medal of Honor
by the Academy of Natural Sciences of Philadelphia. His publications number over 100 and include papers on the smaller crusta-
ceans, the diurnal movements of plankton, anaerobic organisms of
lake bottoms, chemistry of lake waters, growth of fresh water fish,
photosynthesis, and many other aspects of limnology. Among his
best known and larger works are *Hydrography and Morphometry of
the Lakes* in the series *Inland Lakes in Wisconsin* and the two extensive reports (published jointly with E. A. Birge) on the dissolved
gases and the plankton of Wisconsin lakes. He attracted many col-
laborators, and his advice and cooperation were sought by state
and federal conservation agencies. Died March 29, 1944.

EDWARD SCHNEBERGER

American Men of Science, 7th ed., 1944.
FREY, DAVID G. *Limnology in North America*. Madison: University of Wisconsin
Press, 1963.
NOLAND, LOWELL E. "Chancey Juday," *Limnological Society of America*. Special
Publication No. 16, pp. 1–3.

JUDD, BENJAMIN IRA (1904–   )

Born December 8, 1904 in Granite, Utah. Utah State University,
B.S. 1928, M.Sc. 1929; University of Nebraska, Ph.D. (agronomy)
1936. Appointed assistant scientist in the Resettlement Administration in 1936; the following year named assistant soil conservationist
in the Soil Conservation Service, United States Department of
Agriculture. Professor of agronomy at Arizona State University

(Tempe) since 1937; head of the Department of Agronomy from 1937 to 1950. Has studied conservation and served as a consultant in Central America, Jamaica, Mexico, Virgin Islands. Was visiting professor in Puerto Rico, 1963–64. Sponsored the Arizona Conservation Club and was named Arizona Conservation Educator of the Year, 1965. Has written widely on agronomy, tropical agriculture, conservation, soil science, and range management. Active member of the American Association for the Advancement of Science, Conservation Education Association (Board of Directors), Ecological Society of America, American Society of Agronomy, American Society of Range Management, and Soil Conservation Society of America. He has been a leading influence in conservation education for youth and adults alike.

WAYNE KESSLER

American Men of Science (The Physical and Biological Sciences), 11th ed., 1965.

KALMBACH, EDWIN RICHARD (1884–)

Born April 29, 1884 in Grand Rapids, Michigan. Self-educated in the higher biological sciences of ornithology, mammalogy, entomology, botany, and ecology. Honorary doctorate awarded him by the University of Colorado, 1955. His career in wildlife economics and conservation began as assistant director of the Kent Scientific Museum in 1903. In 1910 he joined the United States Bureau of Biological Survey in Washington, D. C., as assistant biologist and advanced to biologist (1924), senior biologist (1928), and director of the Wildlife Research Laboratory, Denver, Colorado under the United States Fish and Wildlife Service in 1934. Retired from that position in 1954. Represented the government's interest in wildlife conservation and management at numerous scientific conferences. Active in the affairs of many societies of the biological sciences such as the American Ornithologists' Union, Society of Mammalogists, Wildlife Society, and the Cooper and Wilson Ornithological Societies. Instrumental in founding and developing the government's series of duck stamps and United States postage stamps displaying wildlife species. Designed the 1941–42 duck stamp (ruddy duck). Among many conservation honors: the Department of the Interior Distinguished Service Award, 1955; the Aldo Leopold Award, 1958; and the Founders Day Award, Izaak Walton League, 1958. Widely recognized for his research on economic ornithology and mammalogy, botulism, and as a wildlife artist. Author of numerous publications and reports which helped guide the government's policies and practices relating to the conservation and management of the nation's wildlife resources, for example: *The Armadillo*; *Botulism—A Recurring Hazard*; and *Wildlife in a Developing Hemisphere*.

CECIL S. WILLIAMS

American Men of Science (The Physical and Biological Sciences), 10th ed., 1955.

KAUFERT, FRANK HENRY (1905–   )

Born December 2, 1905 in Princeton, Minnesota. University of Minnesota, B.S. (forestry) 1928, M.S. 1930, Ph.D. (forest pathology) 1935. After a year of teaching in the University of Minnesota School of Forestry, in 1936 he joined the firm of E. I. du Pont de Nemours as a research technologist in forest pest control. Returning to the University of Minnesota in 1940 as associate professor of forestry, he went on leave during World War II to serve as senior wood technologist in the Forest Products Laboratory, operated by the United States Forest Service in Madison, Wisconsin. In 1946 he was advanced to professor and in 1947 to director of the School of Forestry, University of Minnesota, his present position. In 1954 he was director of the Society of American Foresters forestry research project, and was senior author of the project's book report, *Forestry and Related Research in North America*, 1955. A member of the Council of the Society of American Foresters, 1950–53, he was elected a Fellow in 1955, and was chairman of the Committee for the Advancement of Forestry Education, 1959–63. President of the Forest History Society, 1956–57 and 1963–64, he was also president of the Forest Products Research Society, 1957–58, and of the Association of State College and University Research Organizations, 1966–68. For 16 years he was president of Keep Minnesota Green, Inc. He was assistant administrator of the United States Department of Agriculture Cooperative State Research Service during 1963–64, and since then has served on the Department's Cooperative Research Advisory Committee. Currently, he is a director of the American Forestry Association and a trustee of the Wilderness Research Foundation.

HENRY CLEPPER

American Men of Science (The Physical and Biological Sciences), 11th ed., 1966. *Who's Who in America*, 1968–69.

KEEN, FREDERICK PAUL (1890–)

Born November 20, 1890, in San Diego, California. University of California, Berkeley, B.S. (agricultural sciences) 1914. Subsequently appointed entomological ranger, Bureau of Entomology, United States Department of Agriculture, Ashland, Oregon. Advanced successively to more responsible positions, including senior entomologist, in charge, Forest Insect Laboratories, Portland, Oregon, and Berkeley, California. Appointed special assistant to chief, Division of Forest Insect Investigations, Bureau of Entomology and Plant Quarantine, in 1952. Except for two years military service during World War I, served continuously and with distinction in the Department of Agriculture until his retirement January 1, 1956. Studied intensively climatic cycles as evidenced by tree rings and their interrelationship to outbreaks of western pine beetle. From these and related studies he developed a relative susceptibility classification of ponderosa pines to bark beetle attack. This led to use of the tree-classification system in managing interior-type pine stands. He supervised bark beetle survey and control operations in Arizona, California, and Oregon, and performed research in many phases of forest insects in the western United States. He is author of more than 50 scientific publications on forest insects and their control, including such definitive ones as *Insect Enemies of Western Forests*, United States Department of Agriculture Miscellaneous

Publication 273, revised, 1952; *Biology and Control of the Western Pine Beetle*, United States Department of Agriculture Miscellaneous Publication 800; and *Cone and Seed Insects of Western Forest Trees*, Technical Bulletin No. 1169, United States Department of Agriculture, 1958. He received an award for superior service, United States Department of Agriculture, 1947, and the first award for distinguished service in forestry from Western Forestry and Conservation Association in 1953. He also received the Conservation Award, American Forestry Association in 1954. He served on the Society of American Foresters Council, 1942–45, and was elected a Fellow in 1955. He was president, Pacific Coast Entomological Society, 1946.

J. W. BONBERG

American Men of Science (The Physical and Biological Sciences), 11th ed., 1965.

KELLEY, CLAUDE DONAHUE (1907–   )

Born September 22, 1907 in Pine Hill, Alabama. Educated in public schools in Alabama, he began a career in accounting, banking, and finance. In addition to his business interests, he spent much of his time in conservation endeavors starting in 1940 when he was elected president of a local wildlife federation in Alabama. He served as regional director of the Alabama Wildlife Federation and later as its president, and is now a permanent member of the advisory committee. In 1948 he was elected to his first term as a director and in 1950 became president of the National Wildlife Federation, continuing in office for the next ten years. During his administration, the Federation expanded to include affiliated organizations in each of the states with all operations consolidated in Washington, D. C., the National Wildlife Federation Endowment was organized to provide a solid financial structure for the organization, and a permanent headquarters building was constructed in the District of Columbia. In addition, the Federation initiated an annual Conservation Conference, initiated the new publication *National Wildlife*, and organized youth education programs. In 1962 he was appointed director of the Alabama Department of Conservation and continued as administrator of this agency until 1968. He then was appointed as southeastern field representative of the National Wildlife Federation in 1969.

NATIONAL WILDLIFE FEDERATION

KELLEY, EVAN WILLIAM (1882–1966)

Born on October 19, 1882 in Sierra City, California. No formal education beyond elementary school; received an honorary masters degree in forest engineering from Montana State University in 1940. Entered the United States Forest Service in California as a guard on the Yuba Forest Reserve in 1906; in 1910 he became the first forest supervisor of the Eldorado National Forest. His outstanding work running a sawmill in France for the United States Army won him decorations and promotion to the rank of major. After the war, he served from 1920 to 1925 as a fire control inspector in the Washington, D. C. office of the Forest Service; in 1925 he was named regional forester for the Eastern Region and in 1929 for the Northern Region (Montana, northern Idaho, and northeastern Washington) where he gained wide recognition for his work in reorganizing and developing fire control methods. During his administration, the innovations included the construction of an intensive system of motor truck trails by means of the then-new crawler tractors and bulldozers, greatly intensified detection of fires, faster initial attack, a highly organized system for the rapid build-up and supply of forces on large fires, an active part in the development and use of portable two-way radios, and the development of "smokejumping" by specially trained and equipped parachutists. During World War II he was in charge of the emergency rubber project in California. Member of the Society of American Foresters since 1920 and elected Fellow, 1949. Died October 3, 1966.

SOCIETY OF AMERICAN FORESTERS

"We Present Evan W. Kelley," *Journal of Forestry*, vol. 48:499–500, 1950.
Journal of Forestry. Obituary, vol. 65:72, 1967.

KIMBALL, THOMAS LLOYD (1918–   )

Born February 21, 1918, in Los Angeles, California. Attended Phoenix Junior College; Brigham Young University, B.S. (soil conservation) 1939. Except for four years spent as a pilot in the Air Force during World War II, he was employed by the Arizona Game and Fish Department from 1939 to 1952. During this tenure, he served as a wildlife project leader, federal aid coordinator, chief of game and director during his last five years with the agency. In 1952, he became director of the Colorado Game and Fish Department and served in that capacity until resigning to become executive director of the National Wildlife Federation on September 1, 1960—a position he continues to hold. While in state work, he served for two terms as president of the Western Association of Game and Fish Commissioners and for one term as president of the Midwest Game and Fish Commissioners. He relinquished the position of first vice president of the International Association of Game, Fish and Conservation Commissioners when he left state work. He has had several special assignments, serving as a member of the Advisory Board for Wildlife and Game Management to the Secretary of the Interior; of the Advisory Board on Wildlife, Department of Agriculture; and of the Advisory Board on Water Quality Criteria, Department of Health, Education, and Welfare. He has been a member of the Board of Governors for the National Shooting Sports Foundation; of the Board of Trustees for the Ding Darling Foundation; of the Advisory Board of Keep America Beautiful; and of the National Conservation Committee of the Boy Scouts of America. He has served as a consultant to wildlife agencies in four states. He is the author of numerous articles and technical bulletins on wildlife conservation management and contributes frequently to *National Wildlife* magazine and *Conservation News*. He has been the recipient of several awards: the Nash Motors Certificate of Merit, 1953; Colorado Wildlife Federation, 1962; Colorado Division, Izaak Walton League of America, 1960; Colorado Game and Fish Commission, 1960; Northeast Outdoor Writers Association, 1963; United States Department of the Interior, Conservation Service Award, 1964; University of Arizona's Distinguished Citizen Award, 1964; and Winchester-Western's Outdoorsman's Citation, 1964. He is a member of the Wildlife Society, the American Forestry

Association, and was elected a Fellow of the American Association for the Advancement of Science in 1963.

Louis S. Clapper

KING, RALPH TERENCE (1900–)

Born June 30, 1900 in St. Paul, Kansas. Utah State Agricultural College, B.S. 1924, M.A. (zoology) 1925. He remained there for one year as instructor in zoology, and then did special work at the University of Minnesota, and also served as head of the Department of Biology at the College of St. Thomas at St. Paul, 1925–29. From 1929 to 1932 he held the position of research fellow, and from 1932 to 1937 he was on the faculty of the Department of Economic Zoology of the University of Minnesota. He was also state biologist for the Minnesota Conservation Department from 1932 to 1937. It was during his association with the University of Minnesota that he became well known for his ruffed grouse research. One of the organizers of a professional group that formed the Society of Wildlife Specialists in 1936, he was the first and only president of that organization; in 1937 when it became the Wildlife Society, he was one of its founders. In 1937 he became the chairman of the Department of Forest Zoology at the State University College of Forestry at Syracuse University. He also became the director of the Roosevelt Wildlife Forest Experiment Station located at that same institution. He was awarded two Fulbright lectureships in 1959 and in 1960 in Denmark and Israel. He is a member of the Society of American Foresters and of the Ecological Society of America, and is a Fellow of the American Association for the Advancement of Science. He was elected Honorary Member of the Wildlife Society in 1964. He has written numerous scientific papers and resource articles. He retired from the College of Forestry in 1965.

Maurice M. Alexander

American Men of Science (The Physical and Biological Sciences), 11th ed., 1966.
Who Knows—and What, 1954.

KINNEY, JAY P (1875–   )

Born September 18, 1875, in Snowdon (town of Otsego) New York. Cornell University, A.B. 1902, M.F. 1913, National University, LL.B. 1908. After several years as high school principal, appointed assistant examiner, United States Patent Office, in 1906. In 1910, appointed assistant forester, United States Indian Service, Department of the Interior, with instructions to organize a forestry unit. Under various titles, as head of the unit for 23 years, he developed a strong and effective organization to manage the Indians' forest and range lands, under the principles of sustained yield, for the benefit of the Indian owners. In 1933, became general production supervisor in charge of Civilian Conservation Corps activities on Indian reservations. In 1942, was appointed assistant director of Soil Conservation, Office of Land Utilization, United States Department of the Interior. In 1945, under a special exception to the mandatory requirement of retirement at age 70, appointed advisor in forestry in the United States Department of Justice. In 1954, he retired from full-time duty, but during the next 13 years continued as consultant in the same Department. He retired permanently in 1967, after distinguished service with the federal government over a span of 61 years. While with the Department of Justice, his training in law and in forestry, his long experience as head of the Indian forestry organization, and his lifelong reputation as a man of integrity and moral courage, made him a valuable contributor in the preparation of cases, and as a witness, in claims brought before the United States Court of Claims and the Indian Claims Commission. He is a Fellow of the Society of American Foresters, and active in the Forest History Society. In addition to many magazine articles, he has written four authoritative books of recognized merit in their fields: *The Essentials of American Timber Law*, 1917; *The Development of Forest Law in the United States*, 1917; *A Continent Lost—A Civilization Won*, 1937; and *Indian Forest and Range*, 1950.

GEORGE S. KEPHART

Who's Who Among American Authors, 1933–35 and 1936–39.
Who's Who in Government, 1933.
Who's Who in the Nation's Capital, 1934–35.

KNEIPP, LEON FREDERICK (1880–1966)

Born November 30, 1880 in Chicago, Illinois. Educated in the public schools of Chicago. Began his forestry career as a ranger on a forest reserve in the Territory of Arizona, with the General Land Office, in 1900. When the forest reserves were placed under the United States Department of Agriculture and the Forest Service was established in that Department in 1905, he was one of eight men from various parts of the West brought into Washington, D. C. to draft new rules and procedures for the administration of these reserves, later to be known as national forests. As assistant chief in charge of lands, 1920–46, he was instrumental in adding to the national forest system about 20 million acres east of the Mississippi, and about 5 million acres in the West. A recognized authority on outdoor recreation, in 1924 he served as executive secretary of the Advisory Council of the National Conference of Outdoor Recreation. He pioneered in the movement for the preservation of wilderness tracts and in the development of the Forest Service program for maintenance of designated wilderness areas. He wrote widely on forestry subjects and was the author of important sections of *A National Plan for American Forestry* and *The Western Range*. He retired from the Forest Service in 1946 after nearly 47 years of continuous service. Died October 29, 1966.

SOCIETY OF AMERICAN FORESTERS

Journal of Forestry. Obituary, 65:72–73, January 1967.

LACEY, JOHN FLETCHER (1841–1913)

Born May 30, 1841 in Martinsville, Virginia (now West Virginia). Educated in public and private schools in Virginia and Iowa. Entered the Union Army in 1861 and was discharged with the brevet rank of major in 1865. He was elected to the Congress in 1889 and served through 1907. As chairman of the House Committee on Public Lands he was the author of much of the early legislation affecting national parks, wildlife, and forests. Among the measures he fought through Congress were the Yellowstone Park

Protection Act of 1894, which established the foundation for the National Park Service; the Lacey Act of 1900, which ended market hunting and the interstate shipment of wildlife or wildlife products taken in violation of state law; and the Transfer Act for Forest Reserves of 1905, which established the United States Forest Service. Died September 29, 1913.

JAMES B. TREFETHEN

Biographical Directory of the American Congress, 1961.
Who Was Who in America, 1897–1942.
Who's Who in America, 1912–1913.

LAGLER, KARL FRANK (1912–)

Born November 15, 1912 in Rochester, New York. Rochester University, A.B. 1934; Cornell University, M.S. 1936; University of Michigan, Ph.D. (zoology) 1940. An investigator in fishery management at the University of Michigan from 1937 to 1939, he was instructor in zoology from 1939 to 1944, then became successively assistant professor, associate professor, and in 1955 professor in fisheries and zoology; chairman of the Department of Fisheries, 1950–65. He served as a research associate for the Institute for Fisheries Research, Michigan Department of Conservation, and as an advisor to the United States Operations Mission Kasetsart at the University of Hawaii. He was a technical consultant to the Associated Fishing Tackle Manufacturers from 1948 to 1950, and was a member of the Great Lakes Research Institute, intermittently, from 1948 to 1960. He participated in expeditions to the Upper Great Lakes, western Europe, Alaska, and Southeast Asia, served as fisheries advisor in Thailand in 1964 and 1965, and coordinated African lake projects under the Food and Agricultural Organization of the United Nations in 1966–67. In 1961, he received a gold medal and diploma from the French Academy of Agriculture. He holds memberships in the American Academy of Arts and Sciences, Society of Ichthyologists and Herpetologists, Society of Limnologists and Oceanographers, American Fisheries Society; and is a Fellow in the Academy of Zoology and in the Institute of Fisheries

Research Biologists (president, 1964–65). His published works include *Guide to the Fishes of the Great Lakes and Tributary Waters* (junior author with C. L. Hubbs), 1941; revised as *Fishes of the Great Lakes Region*, 1964; *Freshwater Fishery Biology*, 1956; *Peches Continentales* (co-author with R. Vibert), 1961; and *Ichthyology* (senior author and editor with J. Bardach and R. Miller), 1962. Active in educational television since 1968, he has produced several TV films on aquatic resources. He was elected president of the International Academy of Fisheries Scientists of Rome, Italy, in 1968.

P. A. DOUGLAS

American Men of Science, (The Physical and Biological Sciences), 11th ed., 1967.

LANGLOIS, THOMAS HUXLEY (1898–1968)

Born February 19, 1898 in Detroit, Michigan. University of Michigan, B.S. 1924, M.S. 1925; Ohio State University, Ph.D. 1935. Fisheries biologist, Michigan Department of Conservation, 1924–27, state fish pathologist, 1927–29. As chief of fish propagation and management, Ohio Division of Conservation and Natural Resources, 1930–46, he expanded the fish cultural program, organized a fish management section with a staff of trained biologists, and led a movement for liberalized fishing. Served as professor of zoology at Ohio State University, and as director of the Franz Theodore Stone Institute of Hydrobiology, 1938–56. As director he initiated programs of instruction in limnology and fisheries, emphasizing the ecological approach to aquatic problems. The research that resulted yielded valuable information on Lake Erie. President, American Fisheries Society, 1940; active in the American Society of Limnology and Oceanography. Author of many scientific reports, including *Ecology and Sociology of Fish and People, Ice on Lake Erie,* and *The Western End of Lake Erie and its Ecology.* Died December 5, 1968.

DONALD J. LEEDY

American Men of Science (The Physical and Biological Sciences), 11th ed., 1965.

LATHAM, ROGER MARION (1914–   )

Born January 12, 1914 at Sandy Lake, Pennsylvania. Pennsylvania
State University, B.S. (entomology, zoology) 1950, M.S. (wildlife
management) 1951, Ph.D. (zoology) 1957. He was graduated in
the first class to complete the Pennsylvania Game Commission's
Leffler School of Conservation in 1937, and was assigned as game
protector, 1937–38, then as research technician, 1938–44. During
World War II, he was detailed to a medical research project on
arctic subjects at Cornell University. He returned to the Pennsylvania Game Commission as chief, Division of Research, from 1951
through 1957. Appointed outdoor editor of the *Pittsburgh Press* in
1957, he has since worked in this position. He served as regional
representative for the Wildlife Society for six years; director of
Trout Unlimited; director of Hawk Mountain Sanctuary Association; director of Pennsylvania Roadside Council; president of
Pennsylvania Outdoor Writers Association; and president of the
Outdoor Writers Association of America. He has been active as a
member of the Governor's Advisory Committee of Conservation
(Pennsylvania); Northeast Forest Resources Committee; Pennsyl-
vania Wildlife Resources Committee; Citizens' Advisory Commit-
tee to Outdoor Recreation Resources Review Commission; founder,
Conservation Committee, Allegheny Trails Council, Boy Scouts of
America; associate director, Allegheny County Soil & Water Con-
servation District. Author of *Pennsylvania's Deer Problem*, 1950;
Food of Predaceous Animals in Northeastern United States, 1950;
The Ecology and Economics of Predator Management, 1951; *The
Pennsylvania Bounty System*, 1951; *The Bobwhite Quail in Pennsyl-
vania*, 1952; *The Complete Book of the Wild Turkey*, 1956.
Recipient of the Nash Conservation Award, 1954; Jade of Chiefs,
Outdoor Writers Association of America, 1961; Conservation
Award, Pennsylvania Forestry Association, 1963; Outstanding Con-
servationist Award, Keystone Chapter, Soil Conservation Society of
America, 1965; International Outdoorman of the Year 1968,
Winchester-Western.

RALPH W. ABELE

Pennsylvania Game News, vol. 22, no. 5, August 1951.

LEEDY, DANIEL LONEY (1912–)

Born February 17, 1912 in Butler, Ohio. Miami (Ohio) University, A.B. 1934, B.Sc. 1935; Ohio State University, M.Sc. 1938, Ph.D. (wildlife ecology) 1940. Instructor in wildlife management at Ohio State University, 1940–42. United States Army Air Force, 1942–45; captain. Leader, Ohio cooperative research unit, United States Fish and Wildlife Service, 1945–48; coordinator of wildlife research unit programs in Washington, D. C., 1949–57; chief, Bureau of Wildlife Research, 1957–63. Served as the first chief of the Division of Research, Bureau of Outdoor Recreation, Department of the Interior, 1963–65; since then he has been research scientist in the Office of Water Resources Research, Department of the Interior. A charter member of the Wildlife Society, he was president in 1952, and executive secretary, 1953–57; since 1953 he has been the representative of the Society in the American Institute of Biological Sciences. Recipient of the American Motors Conservation Award in 1958. Fellow of the American Association for the Advancement of Science. Author or co-author of 100 articles in biological and other scientific publications.

LEE E. YEAGER

American Men of Science (The Physical and Biological Sciences), 11th ed., 1965. Who's Who in America, 1968–69.

LEFFLER, ROSS LILLIE (1886–1964)

Born August 7, 1886 in Butte, Montana. Attended University of Michigan School of Engineering. In 1910 began work as timekeeper in the Carnegie Steel Corporation, Duquesne, Pennsylvania; on his retirement in 1957 he was assistant to the executive vice president for operations of the United States Steel Corporation. Appointed by President Eisenhower in 1957 as first assistant secretary of the Department of the Interior for fish and wildlife; was instrumental in establishment of the Arctic Wildlife Range in northeastern Alaska and the Key Largo Coral Reef Preserve off the coast of Florida. Had served previously, 1927–57, as a member of the

Pennsylvania Game Commission and as its president, 1928–44. He claimed as his proudest achievement the establishment of the Commission training school near Brockway, Pennsylvania, later named in his honor. Helped organize the first Pennsylvania chapter of the Izaak Walton League of America, serving as president and later as a director of the national organization. Was one of the founders of the Pennsylvania Federation of Sportsmen's Clubs and served as its first secretary. In 1961 was elected to the board of directors of the National Wildlife Federation; was elected president in 1963 and served one year before ill health necessitated retirement. A member of numerous other conservation organizations, he was a former president of the International Association of Game, Fish and Conservation Commissioners; vice president of the Boone and Crockett Club; director of World Wildlife Fund; and honorary director of the International Wild Waterfowl Association. Devoted many years service to the Boy Scouts of America, was a life member of its executive board, and recipient of Scouting's three highest awards. Died December 14, 1964.

NATIONAL WILDLIFE FEDERATION

Who Was Who in America, 1961–68.

LEONARD, JUSTIN WILKINSON (1909–   )

Born October 28, 1909 in Moulton, Iowa. Grinnell College (Iowa), A.B. 1931; University of Michigan, A.M. 1932, Ph.D. 1937. Employed in the Michigan Department of Conservation from 1934 to 1964, he served successively as fisheries investigator and associate aquatic biologist, 1934–39; director of the Hunt Creek Experiment Station, 1939–42; associate fisheries biologist, 1946–48; fisheries biologist, 1949–50; and assistant deputy director for research, 1951–64. As an Army medical entomologist he was with the Sanitary Corps in the South Pacific, 1943–46. He became professor of natural resources and zoology in the University of Michigan School of Natural Resources in 1964, was chairman of the Department of Wildlife and Fisheries until 1967, and since then has been chairman of the Department of Resource Planning and Conservation. His activity in scientific societies includes service to the American Fisheries Society as associate editor, 1940–55; the Wildlife Society as president in 1956; the American Society of Limnology and Oceanography as vice president in 1951; and the Michigan Academy of Science, Arts, and Letters as president in 1962. Author of over 70 bulletins and journal articles, he is co-author (with his wife) of *Mayflies of Michigan Trout Streams*, 1962; (with S. W. Allen) of *Conserving Natural Resources*, 3rd ed., 1966; and (with S. H. Spurr *et al.*) *Rampart Dam and the Economic Development of Alaska*, vol. 1, summary report, 1966. He served a three-year term on the Board of Directors of the Michigan Rural Rehabilitation Corporation, was Governor's designee for the McIntyre-Stennis Fund, and served on the Governor's Committee on Control of Botulism. Currently he is serving on a National Academy of Sciences study group concerned with biology and renewable resources.

REEVE M. BAILEY

American Men of Science, (The Physical and Biological Sciences), 11th ed., 1967.

LEONARD, RICHARD MANNING (1908–   )

Born October 22, 1908 in Elyria, Ohio. University of California Law School, LL.D. 1932. He was admitted to the California bar in 1933, to practice before the United States Supreme Court in 1941, and to the United States Tax Court in 1951. Joined the Sierra Club in 1930; has been a member of the Board of Directors since 1938; president, 1953–55; secretary, 1946–53, and 1963–65; and treasurer, 1957–59. He was founder of the Conservation Law Society in 1963, an organization established to use law to aid conservation and wilderness projects; for this accomplishment he received an American Motors Conservation Award in 1964. In addition, he was a founder of Trustees for Conservation; founder-secretary of *American Conservation Films*, vice chairman of the Committee on Legislation for the International Union for the Conservation of Nature; a member of the Board of Directors of the Wilderness Society; vice president of Save-the-Redwoods League since 1966; and was founder of the California Chapter of the Izaak Walton League of America. He helped create Conservation Associates as a nonprofit counseling service to help conservation organizations acquire parks, open spaces, and reserves. The author of technical articles relating to law, check dams, and avalanches, he also wrote *Belaying the Leader*, 1946, and was a contributor to *Manual of Ski Mountaineering*, 1942; *Going Light with Backpack and Burro*, 1951; and *A Climber's Guide to the High Sierras*, 1954.

LUELLA K. SAWYER

Who's Who in the West, 11th ed., 1968.
Sierra Club Handbook, 1967.

LEOPOLD, ALDO (1886–1948)

Born January 11, 1886 in Burlington, Iowa. Yale University, Ph.B. 1908, M.F. 1909. Entered the United States Forest Service in 1909 as a forest assistant in Arizona; was promoted in 1911 to deputy forest supervisor, and in 1912 to supervisor of the Carson National Forest in New Mexico. In 1917 he became assistant district forester for operations of the Southwestern District. A pioneer in wilderness preservation, he interested other forest officers in wilderness ecology, and was mainly responsible for the establishment of the Gila Wilderness Area in New Mexico, the first in the national-forest wilderness system. From 1925 to 1927 he was associate director of the Forest Products Laboratory at Madison, Wisconsin. Leaving government service in 1928, he became game consultant for the Sporting Arms and Ammunition Manufacturers' Institute. The game surveys he made during this time were published in 1931 with the title, *Report on a Game Survey of the North Central States*. This report was one of the first intensive studies of game populations ever undertaken in America and won for him the *Outdoor Life* medal. During a year of private practice as a consulting forester, he completed his book *Game Management*, 1933, and was appointed

professor of game management at the University of Wisconsin.
This chair, created especially for him, he held with distinction until
his death. He was active in many conservation movements outside
his official duties. He served on the Council of the Society of
American Foresters, 1927–31, and was associate editor of the
Journal of Forestry, 1936–47. At various times he was a director of
the National Audubon Society and vice president of the American
Forestry Association. One of the organizers of the Wilderness Society in 1935, he served on its Council thereafter and was vice president in 1945. He was an organizer of the Wildlife Society in 1937,
and served as its president in 1939. Active also in the Ecological
Society of America, he was president in 1947. He was appointed
by President Franklin D. Roosevelt to the Special Committee on
Wild Life Restoration in 1934. From 1943 until his death he was a
member of the Wisconsin Conservation Commission. His best known
book, *A Sand County Almanac*, was published posthumously in
1949. The Aldo Leopold Memorial Medal, established in his honor
by the Wildlife Society, has been awarded annually since 1950.
Died April 21, 1948.

HENRY CLEPPER

American Forests, Biography. August and December, 1954.
Dictionary of American Biography, 1941–50. In press, 1970.
Journal of Forestry. Obituary, August 1948.
Journal of Wildlife Management, Obituary, October 1948.
National Wildlife, Biography, April–May, 1965.
Who Was Who in America, 1950.

LEOPOLD, ALDO STARKER (1913–   )

Born October 22, 1913 in Burlington, Iowa. University of Wisconsin,
B.S. (agriculture) 1936; Yale University School of Forestry, 1936–37;
University of California, Ph.D. (zoology) 1944. In 1934 he began
his career as a junior biologist for the Soil Erosion Service of the
United States Department of Agriculture, in Wisconsin. He then
served five years as a field biologist for the Missouri State Conservation Commission, 1939–44. He became director of field research

for the conservation section of the Pan-American Union in Mexico in 1944. In 1946 he became an instructor at the University of California at Berkeley and by 1957 had advanced to professor; then for eleven years was associate director of the University Museum of Vertebrate Zoology; and in 1968 he joined the School of Forestry and Conservation. He was a Guggenheim Fellow, 1947–48; president of the Wildlife Society, 1957–58. He also served as president of the California Academy of Sciences and as advisor on conservation and fauna for the National Park Service and the United States Fish and Wildlife Service. Recipient of the Audubon Medal from the National Audubon Society in 1966; awarded the Aldo Leopold Medal by the Wildlife Society in 1965. He is a member of many conservation and wildlife organizations. Author of numerous publications, he wrote *Wildlife in Mexico*, 1959; was co-author of *Wildlife in Alaska*, 1952; and author with the editors of *Life* of *The Desert*, 1961.

THE CONSERVATION FOUNDATION

American Men of Science (The Physical and Biological Sciences), 11th ed., 1965.
Who's Who in America, 1968–69.

LEOPOLD, LUNA BERGERE (1915–   )

Born on October 8, 1915 in Albuquerque, New Mexico. University of Wisconsin, B.S. (zoology) 1936; University of California at Los Angeles, M.A.; Harvard University, Ph.D. (geology) 1950. From 1936 to 1938, he advanced to associate engineer from junior engineer with the Soil Conservation Service, United States Department of Agriculture, in New Mexico. He was in the United States Engineers office in Los Angeles, 1941–42, and during World War II was a captain in the United States Air Force's air weather service for three years. In 1946 he was with the Bureau of Reclamation, United States Department of the Interior, then was engaged in 1947 as head meteorologist for the Pineapple Research Institute in Hawaii. In 1950 he began as hydraulic engineer for the United States Geological Survey, and since 1966 has been senior research hydrologist. In 1958 the Department of Interior presented him with a distinguished service award and the Geological Society of America gave him the Kirk Bryan award. In 1963 he received the Royal Netherlands Geographical Society Veth Medal. Long active in the Sierra Club, he became a member of its Board of Directors in 1968. A member of the American Society of Civil Engineers, American Meteorological Society, American Geological Society, American Geophysical Union, and the National Academy of Sciences. Co-author of *The Flood Control Controversy*, 1954; the *Fluvial Processes in Geomorphology*, 1964; and *Water*, 1966.

THE CONSERVATION FOUNDATION

American Men of Science (The Physical and Biological Sciences), 11th ed., 1965. *Who's Who in America*, 1968–69.

LIEBER, RICHARD (1869–1944)

Born September 5, 1869 in Germany. Educated at the Royal Lyceum, Duesseldorf; Wabash College, D.Sc. (honorary) 1938. Immigrated to the United States in 1891; became a naturalized citizen in 1901. From 1892 to 1900, he was employed by newspapers in Indianapolis, Indiana, then was associated with a firm of importers in Indianapolis, 1905–18. He early developed an interest in conservation and parks. He was chairman of the Board of Governors for the Fourth National Conservation Congress in 1912; was chairman of the Indiana State Park Commission, 1915–19; and was secretary of the Indiana Board of Forestry, 1917–19. In 1919, when all conservation agencies of the state government of Indiana were combined in the Department of Conservation, he was elected to the office of director of the Department, and served until his resignation in 1933. In addition to his work in Indiana, he was active in the National Conference on State Parks, formed in 1921, was president from 1930 to 1939, and chairman of its board thereafter. He was also vice president and a director of the American Planning and Civic Association, and was a member of the Advisory Board and a consultant for the National Park Service. Author of *America's Natural Wealth: A Story of the Use and Abuse of Our Natural Resources*, 1942; contributor to the *American Planning and Civic Annual*, 1935–43. Among the honors accorded him was the Pugsley gold medal awarded in 1933 by the American Scenic and Historic Preservation Society. During the previous year a monument was dedicated in his honor at Turkey Run State Park, Indiana. Died April 15, 1944.

BARRY S. TINDALL

LIEBER, EMMA. *Richard Lieber.* Indianapolis, Ind.: Privately printed, 1947.
Parks (National Conference on State Parks, Washington, D. C.), 6(10):1–5, October 1966.
Planning and Civic Comment, April 1944, pp. 45–46.
Who Was Who in America, 1943–50.

LINCOLN, FREDERICK CHARLES (1892–1960)

Born May 5, 1892 in Denver, Colorado. University of Colorado, Sc.D. (honorary), 1956. After serving as curator of birds in the Colorado Museum of Natural History at Denver, he joined United States Biological Survey in March 1920. In this and its successor agency, the Bureau of Sport Fisheries and Wildlife of the United States Department of the Interior, he worked until his death. As chief of the Section of Distribution and Migration of Birds, he organized and directed the bird banding program to study the movements and population dynamics of migratory birds. He headed a continental investigation of the status of migratory waterfowl; developed the concept of four continental flyways now the basis for formulating hunting regulations for migratory birds; and devised the Lincoln Index, a formula for estimating total populations of waterfowl from recoveries of banded birds. In his last years of government service, he served as special assistant to the director of the Bureau of Sport Fisheries and Wildlife. Recipient of the highest honor of the Department of the Interior, its Distinguished Service Award, in 1956, he was elected a Fellow of the American

Ornithologists' Union in 1934 and served as its treasurer from 1945 to 1947. Author of 300 scientific and popular articles, he was co-author with John C. Phillips of *American Waterfowl*, 1930; author of *Bird Migration*, 1939; co-author with Ira N. Gabrielson of *Birds of Alaska*, 1959. Died September 16, 1960.

JOHN W. ALDRICH

American Men of Science, 9th ed.,
GABRIELSON, IRA N. Obituary. *The Auk*, vol. 79 (3), 1962.

LINDUSKA, JOSEPH PAUL (1913–   )

Born July 25, 1913, in Butte, Montana. University of Montana, A.B. (zoology) 1936, M.A. 1939; Michigan State University, Ph.D. 1950. Carried out research on ecology and land-use relationships of small mammals on southern Michigan farmland. Served as fishery biologist in Yellowstone National Park; as research entomologist on war-associated projects at the Orlando laboratory of the Department of Agriculture; and as game biologist with the Michigan Department of Conservation. In 1947 he became project leader and carried out pioneering studies on the effects of pesticides on wildlife at the Patuxent Research Refuge of the Fish and Wildlife Service. Was appointed assistant chief of the Service's Branch of Wildlife Research in 1949 and chief of the Branch of Game Management in 1951. In 1956 he joined Remington Arms Company as director of wildlife management and four years later was promoted to director of public relations and wildlife management. Returning to government service in 1966, he was appointed associate director of the Bureau of Sport Fisheries and Wildlife. Served as executive secretary of the Wildlife Society for three years and as president, 1967–68. Was a member of board of directors of Outdoor Writers Association of America and chairman of that organization's Conservation Council; also a member of the board of directors of the Wildlife Management Institute. He was presented the Wildlife Society Conservation Education Award in 1963, and also in that

year the Jade of Chiefs award of the Outdoor Writers Association
of America for service to conservation. He received the Conservation Service Award of the Department of the Interior in 1964. Well
known for technical and popular writings in wildlife biology and
conservation, he is editor of *Waterfowl Tomorrow*, published by the
Bureau of Sport Fisheries and Wildlife in 1964.

DURWOOD L. ALLEN

American Men of Science (The Physical and Biological Sciences), 11th ed., 1965.

LOVEJOY, PARRISH STORRS (1884–1942)

Born January 23, 1884 in Princeton, Illinois. University of Michigan
Department of Forestry, 1903–5. Entered the United States Forest
Service in 1905; became supervisor of the Cheyenne (now the
Medicine Bow) National Forest in Wyoming in 1909, and of the
Olympic National Forest in Washington in 1910. Leaving federal
service in 1912, he returned to the University of Michigan as
assistant professor of forestry. In 1920 he was employed as a staff
writer by the Curtis Publishing Company; his articles in *The Country Gentleman* promoted improved land use, the restoration of cutover forests, and farm forestry. Because these writings, together
with his articles published in other periodicals, were given national
circulation, he was one of the most influential contemporary spokesman for a rational land-use policy. He was commissioned in 1923
to organize the Michigan Land Economic Survey, the first of its
kind in the United States, and the forerunner of land planning
studies by other states. This work for the Michigan Department of
Conservation led to the creation of the state game refuge system of
which he took charge in 1925 as the first chief of the Game and Fur
Division. Because of ill health he retired from active work in 1930,
but continued as adviser to the Department on land policy. He was
an early proponent of the utilization and management of wildlands
for wildlife, applying forestry practices for this purpose. In June,
1942 a bronze tablet in commemoration of his services to conserva-

tion was dedicated in the Pigeon River State Forest of Michigan. He defined conservation as reason applied to environment. Died January 20, 1942.

HENRY CLEPPER

LEOPOLD, ALDO. "P. S. Lovejoy," *Journal of Wildlife Management*, 7(1):125–28, January 1943.
Journal of Forestry. Obituary, 40(4):337, April 1942.

LOWDERMILK, WALTER CLAY (1888–)

Born July 1, 1888 in Liberty, North Carolina. Oxford University, A.B. (Rhodes scholar) 1915; University of California, Ph.D. 1929; Israel Institute of Technology, Dr. Tech. Sci. (honorary) 1952. He was employed by the United States Forest Service, 1915–17, and 1919–22, then was research professor of forestry at the University of Nanking, China, 1922–27. He was project leader for erosion streamflow research for the Forest Service's California Forest and Range Experiment Station, 1927–33, and designed and supervised the establishment of the San Diemas Hydrological Station. From 1933 to 1947, he was with the Soil Conservation Service, United States Department of Agriculture (initially the Soil Erosion Service, Department of the Interior) as assistant chief, associate chief, and chief of research. Representing the Department of Agriculture, he made soil and water conservation surveys in Europe, North Africa, and the Mid-East. From 1947 to 1957, he served as consultant to the French colonial governments in Algeria, Morocco, and Tunisia; to the British Colonial Office in eleven African colonies; and was adviser on flood control in Japan. For the United Nations Food and Agriculture Organization he developed a soil and water conservation program in Israel and a curriculum in agricultural engineering (The Lowdermilk School of Agricultural Engineering) at Technion University; from Israel he received the Medallion of Valor Award in 1961 and the Macabee Award in 1964. He was president of the American Geophysical Union of Earth Sciences,

1941–44. Elected a Fellow of the Soil Conservation Society of America (president from 1941 to 1943), and a Fellow of the Society of American Foresters. He is the author of many publications, including *Conquest of the Land Through 7000 Years*, 1939, and *Palestine, Land of Promise*, 1940.

JOHN S. BARNES

American Men of Science (The Physical and Biological Sciences), 10th ed., 1955.
The Bancroft Library, University of California at Berkeley, has a two-volume oral history of his lifetime activities.
International Who's Who, London, 1968–69.
World Who's Who in Science, 1968.

McARDLE, RICHARD EDWIN (1899–   )

Born February 25, 1899 in Lexington, Kentucky. University of Michigan, B.S. (forestry) 1923, M.S. 1924, Ph.D. 1930, Sc.D. (honorary) 1953; Syracuse University, LL.D. 1961; University of Maine, Sc.D. (honorary) 1962. Junior forester to silviculturist, Pacific Northwest Forest and Range Experiment Station, 1924–34; dean, University of Idaho School of Forestry, 1934–35; director, Rocky Mountain Forest and Range Experiment Station, 1935–38; and Appalachian Forest Experiment Station, 1938–44. Was appointed assistant chief of the Forest Service in charge of cooperative programs (state and private), 1944–52; chief, 1952–62. Executive director of National Institute of Public Affairs, 1962–64. Recipient of the United States Department of Agriculture's Distinguished Service Award, 1957; the Rockefeller Public Service Award, 1960; the President's Gold Medal for Distinguished Federal Civilian Service, 1961; the Sir William Schlich Memorial Medal of the Society of American Foresters, 1962; the Knight Commander Order of Merit, Germany, 1962; and from Mexico the Order of Merit for Forestry of Miguel de Quevedo. He was president of the Fifth World Forestry Congress in Seattle in 1960, and a member of the United States delegation to the Sixth World Forestry Congress in Madrid in 1966. He is a Fellow of the Society of American Foresters and a three-term member of the Council. Since 1958 he has been a director of the American Forestry Association. He was a founder of the North American Forestry Commission of the Food and Agriculture Organization of the United Nations.

HENRY CLEPPER

American Men of Science (The Physical and Biological Sciences), 11th ed., 1965. *Who's Who in America*, 1968–69.

McATEE, WALDO LEE (1883–1962)

Born January 21, 1883 in Japala, Indiana. University of Indiana, A.M. (biology) 1904, Sc.D. (honorary) 1961. His entire professional career (1904–47) was with the Biological Survey of the United States Department of Agriculture and its successor agency, the Fish and Wildlife Service of the United States Department of the Interior. He contributed much to research in the food of birds and mammals, and developed and became director of the Biological Survey's Division of Food Habits Research. He served for many years as treasurer of the American Ornithologists' Union, and was instrumental in the creation of the Wildlife Society and the establishment of its *Journal of Wildlife Management*, of which he was the initial editor. A versatile and proficient entomologist, for 27 years he held the position of acting curator of Hemiptera in the United States National Museum. Late in his career he served as technical adviser to the chief of the Biological Survey and the director of the Fish and Wildlife Service. His extensive knowledge of the food of birds led to his publishing critiques of protective coloration and certain Darwinian theories. A monumental typescript, the work of a lifelong project, the compilation of "American Bird Names, Their Histories and Meanings," remains unpublished in the Fuertes Library at Cornell University. His writings exceed 1200 items, exclusive of abstracts and similar notes. A member of many scientific societies, he was a Fellow of the American Association for the Advancement of Science. He received the Distinguished Service Award with gold medal from the Department of the Interior. He was one of the outstanding biologists and leading conservationists of his times. Died January 7, 1962.

E. R. KALMBACH

KALMBACH, E. R. "In Memoriam: W. L. McAtee." *The Auk*, 80(4):474–85, October 1963.
TERRES, JOHN K. "McAtee, Food Analyst of the Birds." *Audubon Magazine*, November–December, 1946, 362–68.
———. "W. L. McAtee, 1883–1962." *Journal of Wildlife Management*, 27(3):494–99, July 1963.

McCLELLAN, JAMES CHARLES (1908–   )

Born March 11, 1908 in Hannibal, New York. New York State College of Forestry at Syracuse, B.S. (forest utilization) 1929. Entered the United States Forest Service in 1933; assigned to timber management on the Allegheny National Forest in Pennsylvania three years later, and in 1941 to the Monongahela National Forest in West Virginia. In 1944 he was employed as forester by the National Lumber Manufacturers Association in Washington, D. C., where he promoted improved management on the industry's woodlands and edited the Association's *Conservation News Digest*. American Forest Products Industries, Inc. (renamed the American Forest Institute in 1968) appointed him assistant forester in 1946 and in 1948 chief forester. This institute is a nonprofit conservation educational organization supported by the forest industries to encourage the practice of tree farming by private landowners. As director of the Tree Farm Program, he has given national leadership to this popular movement to put private land under productive management. The number of tree farms, the first of which was established in 1941 in the state of Washington, has grown to 33,500 and about 75 million acres in 48 states, representing the most extensive voluntary application of forestry to private lands ever undertaken anywhere in the world. In 1956 he directed the first national survey of recreational use of forest industry lands, and has since guided industrial owners of commercial timberlands in making their holdings available for public recreation. Brought up to date in 1968, the survey showed that some 60 million acres were open for various forms of recreational use. He has also been an exponent of industrial employment of wildlife managers and the application of fee hunting, and of the protection of scenic values particularly where industrial forests border public roads.

HENRY CLEPPER

McCLOSKEY, JOHN MICHAEL (1934–   )

Born April 21, 1934 in Eugene, Oregon. Harvard University, B.A. magna cum laude (American government) 1956; University of Oregon, LL.B. 1961. Artillery captain in United States Army, 1956–58. From 1961 to 1964, he represented the Sierra Club and the Federation of Western Outdoor Clubs on conservation matters in the Pacific Northwest. Appointed assistant to the president of the Sierra Club in 1965, he then became conservation director, and in May 1969 was made chief of staff, his present position. He is the author of articles on conservation policy published in the *Sierra Club Bulletin, Western Outdoor Quarterly, American West*, legal journals, and other periodicals. Active in support of the Wilderness Preservation Act of 1964, he directed the club's staff work in successful pursuit of establishment of a North Cascades and Redwood National Park. He is a director of the North Cascades Conservation Council and a member of the Citizens Committee on Natural Resources.

SIERRA CLUB

Dictionary of International Biography, 1969.
Who's Who in California, 1969.
Who's Who in the West, 1969–70.

McGEE, W(ILLIAM) J(OHN) (1853–1912)

Born April 17, 1853 near Farley, Iowa. Largely self-educated in anthropology, geology, and hydrology; honorary doctorate awarded by Cornell College, Iowa, 1901. He joined the United States Geo-

logical Survey in July 1883, but resigned in 1893 to become ethnol-
ogist in the Bureau of American Ethnology. He served as the first
director of the St. Louis Public Museum, 1905–7. Following creation by President Theodore Roosevelt of the Inland Waterways
Commission on March 14, 1907, he was elected vice chairman and
secretary. On March 23, 1907 he was appointed as an expert on soil
waters in the United States Department of Agriculture Bureau of
Soils. He served on the committee with Gifford Pinchot that
arranged the Governors Conference on the Conservation of Natural
Resources, held in the White House in May, 1908. As secretary of
the Section of Waters for the National Conservation Commission,
he helped compile the first inventory of the nation's natural resources in 1908, and was recording secretary of the Joint Conservation Conference, Washington, D. C., December, 1908. He was
president of the American Association for the Advancement of Science, 1897, and was a founder of the Geological Society of America,
and as editor established its *Bulletin.* Author of more than 100 scientific publications; wrote the monograph *Soil Erosion,* 1911, one of
the early treatises on this subject. He was one of the principal
founders of the conservation movement at the turn of the century.
Died September 4, 1912.

HENRY CLEPPER

McGEE, EMMA R. *Life of W J McGee.* Farley, Iowa: Privately printed, 1915.
Who Was Who in America, 1897–1942.

McGREGOR, LOUIS DILLMOR (1901–   )

Born January 9, 1901 in Linden, Michigan. Educated at Detroit
Teachers College (now Wayne State University) and Michigan
State Normal College, he received an LL.B. degree from Detroit
College of Law. After employment as a school teacher and high
school principal, he became a practicing attorney. Admitted to the
Michigan Bar in 1925, he served from 1959 to 1964 as circuit judge
of the Seventh Judicial Circuit of Michigan, and in 1964 was elected
to the newly created Michigan Court of Appeals where he is now an

appellate judge. Active for many years in conservation affairs, he served as president of the Michigan United Conservation Clubs, 1949–51, and is currently a member of the Board of Directors. Elected to the Board of Directors, National Wildlife Federation in 1953; he was president from March 1964 to March 1967, and is presently a trustee of the National Wildlife Federation Endowment, Inc. In 1963 he was appointed by the governor of Michigan to the Special Conservation Study Committee, and served as chairman of the subcommittee to study the need for codification and simplification of the state's conservation laws and regulations. He is presently serving as a member of the Governor's Task Force on Water Rights, Use and Pollution Control. He was named Sportsman of the Year in 1950 by the Detroit Sportsman's Congress, and received the Award of Merit in 1953 from the Michigan United Conservation Clubs. In 1963 he organized and incorporated the Michigan Wildlife Foundation. An honorary member of the Detroit Sportsmen's Congress and Flushing Sportsman's Clubs, he also holds memberships in the Wilderness Society, National Audubon Society, and National Rifle Association.

NATIONAL WILDLIFE FEDERATION

Who's Who in the Midwest, 11th ed., 1969–70.

MacKAYE, BENTON (1879–   )

Born March 6, 1879 in Stamford, Connecticut. Harvard University, A.B. 1900; A.M. (forestry) 1905. He was a research forester in the United States Forest Service from 1905 to 1918, making field examinations of timberlands. He prepared a forest management plan for private land in the Adirondacks, and made watershed investigations of areas for acquisition as national forests under the Weeks Law of 1910. In 1918–19 he was a specialist in land colonization for the United States Department of Labor. For several years he was instructor in forestry at the Harvard Forest in Massachusetts. Active in promoting a 2,050-mile footpath stretching from Maine to Georgia, he wrote an article on the subject in 1921 for the *Journal* of the

American Institute of Architects that earned him the sobriquet of Father of the Appalachian Trail. In 1928 he made a regional survey of Massachusetts for the Governor's Committee on Open Spaces. In 1933 he was a consultant to the Indian Service in a planning study for reservations in South Dakota, New Mexico, and Arizona. He was on the regional planning staff of the Tennessee Valley Authority from 1934 to 1936. In 1937 he made the plan known as the Bay Circuit Project for developing the series of state parks encircling Boston, Massachusetts. He was a consultant of the United States Department of Agriculture from 1938 to 1941 on flood-control policies of the Forest Service, and on the staff of the Rural Electrification Administration in 1942 and 1943. In 1944 and 1945 he made a study of possible development under the proposed Missouri Valley Authority. He was one of the key organizers of the Wilderness Society in 1935, a member of its governing Council, president from 1945 to 1950, and honorary president since 1950. After World War I he wrote a publication *Employment and Natural Resources* for the United States Department of Labor, and in 1928 a book *The New Exploration: a Philosophy of Regional Planning*, reprinted in 1962. His published works include *From Geography to Geotechnics*, 1968, and *Expedition Nine: A Return to a Region*, 1969. The latter work is a selection of his essays published by the Wilderness Society and presented to him on his ninetieth birthday. In 1966 he received the Conservation Service Award of the Department of the Interior.

MICHAEL NADEL

Congressional Record, H4867–4877, June 11, 1968.
Journal of Forestry, 45:295–96, April 1947.
Who's Who In America, 1946–47.

McNARY, CHARLES LINZA   (1874–1944)

Born June 12, 1874 near Salem, Oregon. He attended Leland Stanford Junior University; studied law; was admitted to the Oregon bar in 1898, and began practice in Salem. Was deputy district attorney of the third judicial district, 1906–13; dean of the law department of Willamette University, 1908–13; associate justice of the Oregon State Supreme Court, 1913–15. Appointed United States senator to fill an unexpired term in May 1917, he was elected in his own right in 1918, and served continuously until his death. His chief senatorial interests were agriculture, reforestation, irrigation, reclamation, and water power development. He was influential in the construction of Bonneville Dam on the Columbia River in Oregon. As chairman of the Senate's Select Committee on Reforestation (1923), he conducted a series of hearings across the nation to acquire information on the problems of public and private forestry. These hearings were a major factor in the enactment of the Clarke-McNary Act of 1924 which established the tradition of federal-state-private cooperation in forest protection and provided substantial financial assistance to state forestry agencies. The McNary-Woodruff Act of 1928 provided additional funds for public purchase of private forest land, and the McSweeney-McNary Act of 1928 established a broad program of federal forest research and provided for forest inventories. He was made chairman of Senate Committee on Agriculture and Forestry in 1926. Died February 25, 1944.

ELWOOD R. MAUNDER

Biographical Directory of the American Congress, 1774–1961, Washington, D.C., 1961.
National Cyclopaedia of American Biography, 1945.
Who Was Who in America, 1943–50.

MALSBERGER, HENRY JAMES (1902–)

Born October 15, 1902 in Pottstown, Pennsylvania. Pennsylvania State University, B.S. (forestry) 1925. He began his forestry career with a lumber company in Florida, then in 1928 joined the newly organized Florida Forest Service. He was advanced to district forester in 1931, to assistant state forester in 1934, and became director of forests and parks in 1937, a position later changed to state forester and park executive. During his period with the Florida

Forest Service, he helped train camp superintendents for the Civilian Conservation Corps and wrote a textbook on the state's forest resources for the school system. In 1945 he was appointed forester and manager for the Southern Pulpwood Conservation Association at Atlanta, an organization founded in 1939 by the pulp and paper industry in the South to stimulate improvement in forest practices and to encourage the growing of trees. He built up a field force of professional foresters who conducted field demonstrations of tree planting, conservative harvesting, and proper forest management. The association sponsored popular forestry education, and established training camps for boys with joint sponsorship by the industry and public agencies. Under his direction much forestry literature and many documentary films on fire prevention and forest conservation were distributed for public information. He was vice president of the Society of American Foresters, 1958–61, and was elected a Fellow in the latter year. In 1965 he was the recipient of the American Motors conservation award. He retired in 1968.

HENRY CLEPPER

Journal of Forestry. Biography, 48:432–33, June 1950; 66(5):427, May 1968.

MARSH, GEORGE PERKINS (1801–82)

Born March 15, 1801 in Woodstock, Vermont. Dartmouth College, graduated 1820, LL.D. (honorary) 1886; Harvard University, LL.D. 1856. During most of his life he held public office. He was on the Vermont Governor's Council in 1835; was a member of the United States House of Representatives, 1843–49; and was minister to Turkey, 1849–53. Fish commissioner of Vermont, 1857–59, he then re-entered diplomatic service as minister to Italy, 1861–82. Throughout his career he was a student of science, particularly of natural history. He wrote several books on grammar and linguistics, and an early one on a zoological topic—*The Camel*, 1856. Among natural scientists he was best known for his monumental *Man and Nature*, 1864. One of the most significant books on natural resources by an American published during the nineteenth century, it delineated for the first time the basic principles of conservation, principles that have endured for more than a century. A scholar with wide-ranging interests, he painstakingly explained the relationship of soil, water, and vegetative cover, and demonstrated by hundreds of references to European scientific knowledge that destruction of grass and forest cover causes alteration in soil and water, and that man himself was changing the physical condition of the earth. In the 1874 edition the book was titled *The Earth as Modified by Human Action*. He assembled an impressive body of data showing how the cutting of forests, fire, and overgrazing contributed to the decline of agriculture, of water supplies, of cities, and indeed of whole civilizations, and pointed for proof to the extensive areas of once productive land that had become desert in China, Europe, and north Africa. He presented the case for forest preservation as the support of American civilization. Died July 23, 1882.

HENRY CLEPPER

Biographical Directory of the American Congress. Washington, D.C.: United States Government Printing Office, 1961.
Dictionary of American Biography. 1933.
HART, JAMES D., ed. *The Oxford Companion to American Literature*, 4th ed. New York: Oxford University Press, 1965.
LOWENTHAL, DAVID. *George Perkins Marsh, Versatile Vermonter*. New York: Columbia University Press, 1958.
Who Was Who in America (Historical Volume), 1607–1896.

MARSHALL, GEORGE (1904–   )

Born February 11, 1904 in New York City. Columbia University, B.A. 1926, M.A. 1927; Robert Brookings Graduate School of Economics and Government, Ph.D. 1930. He was assistant editor of the *Encyclopedia of the Social Sciences*, 1921–31. He was an economist in the National Recovery Administration, Washington, D. C., 1934–37. Instrumental in the formation of the Wilderness Society, he has served on its Council since 1936, and was managing editor of *The Living Wilderness*, 1957–61. He is editor of *Arctic*

Wilderness, writings by his brother, the late Robert Marshall (1956; new edition by the University of California Press, 1970). Joining the Sierra Club in 1950, he was elected to the Board of Directors in 1959, and was president in 1966–67. A strong supporter of the Wilderness Preservation Act of 1964, he has written widely for conservation magazines on wilderness and related subjects. He is a director of Trustees for Conservation, the Sierra Club Foundation, and the California Conservation Council; was a charter member of the Adirondack Mountain Club, and is active in the Federation of Western Outdoor Clubs.

SIERRA CLUB

Sierra Club Handbook, 1967.
Who's Who in America, 1968–69.

MARSHALL, ROBERT (1901–39)

Born January 2, 1901 in New York City. New York State College of Forestry, B.S. 1924; Harvard Forest School, M.F. 1925; Johns Hopkins University, Ph.D. (plant physiology) 1930. From 1925 to 1928, he was a research silviculturist with the United States Forest Service's Northern Rocky Mountain Forest and Range Experiment Station in Montana. Then he spent two years studying tree growth, climate, geography, and social conditions in arctic Alaska. In 1933 he was appointed director of forestry in the Office (now Bureau) of Indian Affairs, United States Department of the Interior, and was effective in stimulating a higher degree of participation by the Indians in the management of their forest and range resources. In 1927 he returned to the Forest Service as chief of the Division of Recreation and Lands, and was influential in advancing the Service's policies on recreation and the preservation of wilderness areas. In addition to his official duties, he was a founder of the Wilderness Society in 1935, and served on its Council and Executive Committee. One of the leaders of a group of foresters and fellow conservationists who advocated socialization (public ownership) of the nation's commercial timber lands, he delineated his views in the pamphlet *The Social Management of American Forests*, 1930, and in the book *The People's Forests*, 1933. He wrote also *Arctic Village*, 1933; *Doonerak or Bust*, 1938; and *North to Doonerak, Amawk and Apoon*, 1939. In addition, he was the author of articles on silviculture, forest recreation, and the social management of woodland, and contributed a section on recreation to *A National Plan for American Forestry* (Senate Document No. 12), 1933. Died November 30, 1939.

HENRY CLEPPER

Journal of Forestry. Obituary, 38(1):61–62, January 1940.

MARTIN, CLYDE SAYERS (1884–1963)

Born September 19, 1884 in Waynesburg, Pennsylvania. DePauw University, B.Sc. 1905; Yale University, M.F. 1907. During the period 1907–20, he was employed by Weyerhaeuser Timber Company as a timber cruiser and forest engineer. Appointed consulting forest engineer for the government of India, he served in that capacity, and later as chief forest engineer for the government of Madras from 1920 to 1930. Returning to the United States, he engaged in saw-milling for three years in western Oregon, became chief forester for the Western Pine Association in 1934, and five years later returned to Weyerhaeuser Timber Company as chief forester. Under his direction, the Weyerhaeuser Company established the Clemons Tree Farm in 1941; it marked the start of the national tree farm movement. Pioneered numerous other developments for the advancement of industrial forestry. As a trustee of American Forest Products Industries, he helped to expand the industry's program for improved forest protection and practices. A member of the Society of American Foresters since 1918, he participated actively in its affairs—chairman of the Columbia River Section, 1935–46; of the Puget Sound Section, 1943–44; member of the Committee on Private Forestry; elected vice president for the term 1946–47; elected Fellow in 1947; president, 1948–49. Died February 10, 1963.

SOCIETY OF AMERICAN FORESTERS

Journal of Forestry. Obituary, vol. 61:320, 1963.

MASON, DAVID TOWNSEND (1883–)

Born March 11, 1883 in Newark, New Jersey. Rutgers University, B.S. (civil engineering) 1905; Yale University, M.F. 1907, M.S. 1908. From 1907 to 1915 he worked for the United States Forest Service, then after Army service as a major in World War I he taught until 1919 at the University of California School of Forestry. During 1919 he prepared regulations for the Timber Valuation Section, Bureau of Internal Revenue. He began work as a consulting forester in 1921 in Portland, Oregon, and has continued until the present except from 1931 to 1935 when he was manager of the Western Pine Association. During his professional life he has been a persistent advocate of sustained yield management in American forestry and in so doing influenced or actually wrote much of the legislation which brought sustained yield into widespread practice. He was a member of the Timber Conservation Board in 1931 and was executive officer of the Lumber Code Authority under the National Recovery Act in 1934. Since 1938 he has served as chairman of the Advisory Committee to the Bureau of Land Management for the Oregon & California Revested Lands, and also as a member of the Research Advisory Committee of the Pacific Northwest Forest and Range Experiment Station. He was elected a Fellow of the Society of American Foresters in 1948 and of the Forest History Society in 1966. He received the Conservation Award from the American Forestry Association in 1957; the Forestry Award from Western Forestry & Conservation Association in 1961; the Conservation Service Award from the Department of Interior in 1954, and its Appreciation Award in 1963; and the Distinguished Service Award from Oregon State University in 1966. In 1966 the

David T. Mason Professorship of Forest Land Use was endowed in his honor at the Yale University School of Forestry by Louis W. and Maud Hill Family Foundation.

CARL A. NEWPORT

LOEHR, RODNEY C. *Forests for the Future, the Diaries of David T. Mason.* St. Paul, Minn.: The Forest Products History Foundation, 1952.

MATHER, STEPHEN TYNG (1867–1930)

Born July 4, 1867, in San Francisco, California. University of California, Bachelor of Letters 1887, LL.D. 1924; George Washington University, LL.D. 1921. From 1887 to 1893, he was a reporter for the *New York Sun.* Then he engaged in the production and marketing of borax until his partial retirement in 1913. Publicly critical of the early management of the national parks for their lack of central administration, adequate appropriations, accommodations, roads, and personnel, he was challenged by Franklin K. Lane, Secretary of the Interior, to come to Washington and "run them yourself." On January 21, 1915, he was appointed assistant to the Secretary. When the National Park Service was created, he became its first director in May 1917, and served in this office until forced to retire by illness in November 1928. During his administration of the Park Service, seven national parks (Acadia, Bryce Canyon, Grand Canyon, Hawaii, Lassen Volcanic, Mount McKinley, Zion) and fourteen national monuments were established. Studies initiated under his direction resulted in the later creation of the Great Smoky Mountains, Shenandoah, and Mammoth Cave National Parks. In January 1921 he was the leader in the organization of the National Conference on State Parks, which was largely responsible for the creation of state parks and recreation areas in nearly all states. He was a member of the National Capital Park and Planning Commission from its creation in 1924 until his retirement from government service. In 1927 he received the Pugsley Gold Medal of the American Scenic and Historic Preservation Society. Memorials to him are numerous. A ranger district in Yosemite National Park bears his name. A high pass in the Sierra Nevadas, traversed by the John

Muir Trail, is Mather Pass. A peak in the Alaskan Range is Mount
Mather. Across the Cascades and through Mount Rainier National
Park runs the Mather Memorial Highway. The canyon of the
Potomac River below Great Falls has been named and dedicated
as Mather Gorge. Died January 22, 1930.

HORACE M. ALBRIGHT
HOLT BODINSON

Who Was Who in America, 1897–1942.
SHANKLAND, ROBERT. Steve Mather of the National Parks. New York: Alfred A.
Knopf, 1951.

MATTISON, CHARLES WESLEY (1904–   )

Born May 11, 1904 in Hankins, New York. Cornell University, B.S.
(forestry) 1928. Joined the United States Forest Service in 1933,
and served in various capacities and in several states. Until 1942
he worked with the Civilian Conservation Corps; then was assigned
to the Washington office of the Forest Service, serving as chief of
the Division of Education until his retirement in 1960. Since then
he has served years as a consultant to the New York State Conservation Department in its extensive land acquisition program, and as
liaison officer with the Bureau of Outdoor Recreation, United States
Department of the Interior. Over the years, he was active in several
organizations, notably the National Committee on Policies in Conservation Education; its successor organization the Conservation
Education Association (director, 1953–57; president, 1957–61);
and the Society of American Foresters. He also served on several
committees of other conservation organizations. His articles
appeared in a variety of journals and magazines, and his more
formal works include significant contributions on forestry in
Encyclopedia Americana, sections of The Challenge of Science
Education (Philosophical Library, 1959), and co-authorship of
Man and His Resources in Today's World (The Creative Education Society, 1967).

WILSON F. CLARK

MAUNDER, ELWOOD RONDEAU (1917–)

Born April 11, 1917 in Bottineau, North Dakota. University of Minnesota, B.A. 1939; Washington University at St. Louis, M.A. (modern European history) 1947; London School of Economics and Political Science, 1948. He was a reporter and feature writer for Minneapolis newspapers, 1939–41, then served as a combat correspondent in the Coast Guard during World War II, and did public relations work for the Methodist Church, 1948–52. Since 1952 he has been secretary and executive director of the Forest History Society, Inc., with headquarters in Santa Cruz, California, and since 1957 editor of the quarterly journal *Forest History*. From 1964 to 1969, he was curator of forest history at Yale University Library. Under his leadership, the Forest History Society had been internationally effective in stimulating scholarly research and writing in the annals of forestry and natural resource conservation generally; 46 repositories and archival centers have been established in the United States and Canada at universities and libraries for collecting and preserving of documents relating to forest history. As a writer and editor he has made significant contributions to this hitherto neglected aspect of history, and in recognition of his services the Society of American Foresters elected him an honorary member in 1968. He is also a founding director of the International Oral History Society, and is an active member of the Agricultural History Society, the American Academy of Political and Social Science, the American Historical Association, the Organization of American Historians, the Oral History Association, the Society of American Archivists, and the American Forestry Association.

HENRY CLEPPER

Directory of American Scholars, vol. 1, "History," 5th ed., 1969.
Who's Who in the East, 10th ed., 1965.

MAXWELL, GEORGE HEBARD (1860–1946)

Born June 3, 1860 in Sonoma, California. Educated at St. Matthew's Hall, San Mateo, California. He began his law career as a court stenographer in 1879, was admitted to the bar in 1882, and prac-

ticed law until 1899. In that year he organized the National Irrigation Association and as executive secretary led the movement for a
national irrigation policy. It culminated in the passage of the
Reclamation Act in 1902. In 1903 he organized the nation's first
water users association in Arizona. Thereafter he was a foremost
exponent of a governmental policy on river regulation and flood
control, and was active in the National Flood Prevention and River
Regulation Commission. At the first Conservation Congress held in
Washington, D. C., in 1905, he launched a public attack against
land grabbers and antiquated laws that permitted them to despoil
the public domain. His last great achievement was the starting in
1930 of the Muskingum Conservancy District in Ohio, the precursor
of the Tennessee Valley Authority type of land and water administration. He was also a pioneer advocate of contour plowing, later
effectively promoted by the Soil Conservation Service. The author
of several books, now out of print, he is to be remembered for
Golden Rivers and Treasure Valleys. During the era of conservation development he was recognized as the leader and father of
the irrigation movement. Died December 1, 1946.

HENRY CLEPPER

Journal of Forestry. Obituary, 45(4):286–87, April 1947.
Who Was Who in America, vol. 2, 1943–50.

MERRIAM, CLINTON HART   (1855–1942)

Born December 15, 1855 in New York City. Yale University
Sheffield Scientific School, 1874–77; Columbia University College
of Physicians and Surgeons, M.D. 1879. He practiced medicine
until 1885 when he was appointed the first head of the Division of
Economic Ornithology and Mammalogy, which in 1905 became the
Bureau of Biological Survey, in the United States Department of
Agriculture. One of the earliest advocates of laws for bird protection, he helped prepare model legislation for the states. Upon his
retirement from the Biological Survey in 1910, he became affiliated
with the Smithsonian Institution as a research associate, and for

three decades conducted investigations in botany, zoology, and ethnology. During and subsequent to his association with the Smithsonian, he devoted himself to the study of fauna and flora and the Indian tribes of the West, particularly in California and Nevada. He made exploring trips through all the states and Bermuda. His long list of contributions to natural history and conservation includes service as president of the American Ornithologists' Union, 1900–1902; president of the Biological Section of the Washington Academy of Sciences, 1891–92; chairman of the United States Geographic Board, 1917–25; president of the American Society of Mammalogists, 1919–21; and president of the American Society of Naturalists, 1924–25. He was a member of the National Academy of Sciences, and was associate editor of *National Geographic Mazagine* and zoological editor of *Science*. The author of more than 400 papers on biological and ethnological subjects, he wrote 29 books and book-length reports including *Birds of Connecticut*, 1877; *Mammals of the Adirondacks*, 1882–84; and *Life Zones and Crop Zones of the United States*, 1898. Died March 19, 1942.

EVE HERBST

National Cyclopaedia of American Biography, 1906.
New York Times. Obituary, March 20, 1942.
Who Was Who in America, 1943–50.

MICHAUD, HOWARD HENRY (1902–)

Born October 12, 1902, in Berne, Indiana. Bluffton College, B.A. (biological science) 1925; Indiana University, (zoology) 1930. For twenty years he was a teacher in the public school system of Fort Wayne, Indiana, and served during the summers as chief naturalist with the Indiana State Parks system. From 1945 to the present has been professor of conservation at Purdue University in the Department of Forestry and Conservation. Delegate to the United Nations Conference on World Resources in 1948. Active in local, state, and national conservation organizations, he served as president of the Conservation Education Association, 1956–57, and has held other positions as officer or director repeatedly. His work with the Soil Conservation Society lead to an honorary membership in 1961. He has served the Indiana Division of the Izaak Walton League of America many years, and was president in 1953. President in 1948 of the National Association of Biology Teachers. Recipient of the Charles S. Osborn award for conservation from Purdue University, 1959. In 1961 he received a Merit Award from the National Wildlife Federation. In his writings, he has contributed numerous articles to *School Science and Mathematics, American Biology Teacher*, the *Indiana Academy of Sciences Bulletin*, and numerous conference reports, including the *Proceedings* of the International Union for Conservation of Nature and Natural Resources. Beyond articles he has made a number of major writing contributions, including authorship of a section of the 1966 World Topics Yearbook, Indiana State publications on the state parks system, and bibliographies of several forms. He served as editor of a series of five booklets on conservation topics for the Indiana Department of Public Instruction. Perhaps his most important contribution, however, lies in the many students he has instructed and guided in his professional teaching career.

WILSON F. CLARK

American Men of Science (The Physical and Biological Sciences), 11th ed., 1965. *Who's Who in America*, 1968–69.

MILLER, ALDEN HOLMES (1906–65)

Born February 4, 1906 in Los Angeles, California. University of California at Los Angeles, A.B. 1927; University of California, Berkeley, M.A. 1928, Ph.D. 1930. From instructor in zoology at the University of California in 1931, he advanced to professor in 1945. He became curator of birds at the University's Museum of Vertebrate Zoology in 1939 and was named director in 1940. In 1960 he was also appointed curator of birds in the Museum of Paleontology. During his career he made field studies of vertebrates in the western United States, Central America, South America, and Australia. He was awarded the William Brewster memorial medal of the

American Ornithologists' Union in 1943, and served as the Union's president, 1953–56. He was a member of the National Academy of Sciences and a Fellow of the American Association for the Advancement of Science. For many years he served on the Committee on Classification and Nomenclature of North American Birds and on the International Committee on Zoological Nomenclature. He was editor of *The Condor* from 1939 onward. Author of numerous scientific papers and other writings on birds, animal ecology, and evolution, he published his last book, *Lives of Desert Animals*, in 1964. Died October 9, 1965.

NATIONAL AUDUBON SOCIETY

Who Was Who in America, 1961–68.

MOFFETT, JAMES WILLIAM (1908–67)

Born August 3, 1908, in American Fork, Utah. University of Utah, A.B. 1933, M.A. 1935; University of Michigan, Ph.D. (zoology and limnology) 1939. He served the Michigan Department of Conservation as aquatic biologist in the Institute for Fishery Research, 1939–41. Joining the Fish and Wildlife Service in 1941, he was assigned to California for work on lakes of the Sierras and later became chief of Central Valley Investigations. In 1950, he became chief of Great Lake Fishery Investigations, Bureau of Commercial Fisheries, in Ann Arbor, Michigan where he was nationally and internationally known for planning and supervision of research for control of the sea lamprey which had ruined commercial and sport fishing for lake trout and other valuable species in the Great Lakes. The sea lamprey control accomplishment was recognized in 1959 by the United States Department of the Interior Unit Award. Member of the United States delegation in negotiations with Canada on Great Lakes fishery treaty, 1952–55; acting executive secretary of the Great Lakes Fishery Commission, 1956–57. He became laboratory director, Bureau of Commercial Fisheries Great Lakes Research Laboratory, in 1959 and in this capacity reorganized fishery and limnological research programs for greater effectiveness.

He was president of the American Fisheries Society, 1959–60, and a founder of American Institute of Fishery Research Biologists. Author of numerous scientific articles and papers. Received the Department of the Interior Distinguished Service Award, 1968, posthumously. Died June 6, 1967.

DONALD J. LEEDY

American Men of Science (The Physical and Biological Sciences), 11th ed., 1966.

MOORE, EMMELINE (1872–1963)

Born April 29, 1872 in Batavia, New York. Wellesley College, A.M. 1906; Cornell University, Ph.D. (aquatic botany) 1914; Hobart College, Sc.D. (honorary) 1939. She taught in public schools and normal schools; was a substitute professor in botany at Huguenot University, and a teacher at Wellington College, Cape Colony, South Africa; then was an instructor and assistant professor at Vassar College. Starting as a research biologist, she was promoted to chief aquatic biologist and director of the New York Conservation Department State Biological Survey. She was New York's first investigator-biologist in the field of fish culture; in 1958 a New York state marine research vessel was named for her (*The Emmeline M.*), which she christened. Her leadership of the New York biological survey of aquatic resources in the state can be viewed as a classic accomplishment, possibly the best early state survey carried out. In retirement she served as Honorary Fellow at the University of Wisconsin and as a research assistant at the Yale University Laboratory of Oceanography. She was the first woman president of American Fisheries Society in 1928. The author of numerous scientific papers and monographs, she will be remembered for her contributions in fish disease studies and pollution surveys. Died September 12, 1963.

ELWOOD A. SEAMAN

American Men of Science (The Physical and Biological Sciences), 10th ed., 1955.

MORTON, JULIUS STERLING (1832–1902)

Born April 22, 1832 in Adams, New York. University of Michigan, A.B. 1854; Union College, New York, A.B. 1856. He then became a farmer and newspaper editor in Nebraska. From 1858 to 1861, he was secretary of the Territory of Nebraska, was later a member of the Territorial legislature and of the Board of Agriculture. Tree planting was his hobby, and in 1872 he offered a resolution to the Board of Agriculture that it set aside April 10 as "tree planting day." It was so proclaimed by the governor, and in 1885 the legislature designated April 22, Morton's birthday, as Arbor Day, a legal holiday. Other states followed Nebraska's example, and Arbor Day is now observed in all the states and in many nations throughout the world. He was influential in inducing Congress to pass the Timber Culture Act of 1873; this law offered free land to settlers who would plant trees on their claims. The act helped stimulate tree planting, but it was not generally successful, and was repealed in 1891. He served as United States Secretary of Agriculture, 1893–97, and during part of this period was also president of the American Forestry Association. The creation of Arbor Day was the conservation achievement of his life and career. Died April 27, 1902.

HENRY CLEPPER

Dictionary of American Biography, 1934.
Who Was Who in America, 1897–1942.

MUIR, JOHN (1838–1914)

Born April 21, 1838 in Dunbar, Scotland; immigrated to the United States in 1849. Majored in chemistry and geology at the University of Wisconsin, (no degree) 1863, LL.D. (honorary) 1897; Harvard University, A.M. (honorary) 1896; Yale University, Litt.D. 1911; University of California LL.D. 1913. At the age of 29, he walked 1,000 miles from Indiana to the Gulf of Mexico, then took ship to California, arriving in 1868. He made geological studies in the Yosemite Valley and the Sierra Nevada, and during 1871–72 his first writings on Yosemite were published in the *Overland Monthly* and the New York *Daily Tribune.* He turned from geologist to conservationist as he observed the results of land and water despoilation by business monopoly. His concern for the forests and mountains resulted in his helping to start the magazine, *Picturesque California.* After a Yosemite trip in 1889, he wrote a series of articles for the San Francisco *Bulletin,* describing the destruction of forests and urging federal management for watershed protection. An act of 1891 created the Sierra Forest Reserve of 4 million acres; Yosemite Park became a reality in 1906. Meanwhile, in 1892 he was a founder and first president (1892–1914) of the Sierra Club. His plans for a national park system were submitted to President Taft in 1911, but he did not live to see the National Park Service established in 1916. He was a Fellow of the American Association for the Advancement of Science and president of the American Alpine Club. The author of a dozen books, among his most influential were *The Mountains of California,* 1894; *The Yosemite,* 1912; *Our National Parks,* 1901; and *Travels in Alaska,* 1915. Died December 24, 1914.

MICHAEL McCLOSKEY

Dictionary of American Biography, 1934.
National Cyclopaedia of American Biography, 1907.
Who Was Who in America, 1897–1942.

MULAIK, STANLEY B (1902–   )

Born September 30, 1902 in Pittsburgh, Pennsylvania. Pennsylvania State Teachers College, B.S. 1928; Cornell University, M.S. 1931; University of Utah, Ph.D. 1954. Supervisor of nature and conservation education, Edinburg Junior College (Texas), 1932–39. Joined faculty of University of Utah as instructor in biology in 1939; assistant professor, 1955–59; associate professor of zoology and entomology since 1959. He has been affiliated with the Conservation Education Association as director and vice president; the National Association of Biology Teachers as a director; the American Nature Study Society as director and president; the Soil Conservation Society as a member of its Education Committee; the Utah Nature Study Society as president and currently as executive secretary; the Utah Audubon Society as president; and the American Association for the Advancement of Science as Fellow and life member. Has contributed about 50 articles to various zoology and science education journals. Editor of *Nature News-Notes* of the Utah Nature Study Society from 1954 to 1958; since 1954 has been the editor of the quarterly Nature Study of the American Nature Study Society. Has several monographs issued by the Natural History Society of Mexico. One of his major contributions has been through work with youth groups and in-service teachers, as well as with his own students at the University of Utah. He rates as one of those rather rare all-round field naturalists and inspiring teachers who have left their distinct marks on national conservation education efforts.

WILSON F. CLARK

American Men of Science (The Physical and Biological Sciences), 11th ed., 1965. Who's Who in American Education, vol. 23, 1967–68, Hattiesburg, Miss.

MULFORD, WALTER (1877–1955)

Born September 16, 1877 in Millville, New Jersey. Cornell University, B.S. (agriculture) 1899, F.E. (forest engineer) 1901; University of Michigan, Sc.D. (honorary) 1938. Established the state forestry program in Connecticut in 1901; the first man in America to hold the title of state forester. During 1904–5 he held brief assignments with the United States Bureau of Forestry and served as assistant in the Yale School of Forestry. From 1905 to 1911 he taught silviculture at the University of Michigan; then returned to Cornell in 1911 to rebuild instruction in forestry there and supervise the construction of Fernow Hall. In 1914 he became head of the Division of Forestry, University of California at Berkeley, where he directed its development into a Department in 1939, and the School of Forestry in 1946, retiring as dean in 1947. He planned and supervised the construction of the forestry building in 1948, now designated Mulford Hall. He was an inspiring teacher and an effective writer on silviculture and forest management. He made notable contributions to the development of strong forest policies in California as a member of the State Board of Forestry and of the State Chamber of Commerce. A dedicated member of the Society of American Foresters, he served as president in 1924, and contributed many articles to the *Journal of Forestry*. Elected as Fellow of the Society, he also had similar distinction as Fellow of the American Association for the Advancement of Science. From 1933 to 1950 he was consulting editor of the American Forestry Series (McGraw-Hill Book Company) which under his leadership grew to 23 volumes of technical forestry subject matter. He was vice president of the First World Forestry Congress at Rome in 1926; president of the trustees of the Institute of Forest Genetics, 1932–33; and in 1942 was appointed as advisor to the National Bureau of Forestry Research of China. Died September 7, 1955.

WOODBRIDGE METCALF

Journal of Forestry. Obituary, 53:852, 1955.
Who's Who in America, 1952–53.

MURIE, OLAUS JOHANN (1889–1963)

Born March 1, 1889 in Moorhead, Minnesota. Pacific University, Oregon, A.B. 1912, D.Sc. (honorary) 1949; University of Michigan, M.S. 1927. He was a conservation officer with the Oregon State Game Commission, 1912–14, and field naturalist and curator of mammals at Carnegie Museum in Pittsburgh, 1914–17. From 1920 to 1926 he conducted field research in Alaska for the Biological Survey, United States Department of Agriculture, and in 1927 he started a study of the elk of North America. As field naturalist for the Biological Survey he conducted research expeditions to British Columbia and made special inspections of national forests, Indian reservations, and other public lands as a basis for land-management recommendations. He conducted a biological survey of the Aleutian Islands, 1936–37, and led a scientific expedition to New Zealand during 1948–49, on invitation of the New Zealand government, to make recommendations on the problems of introduced wapiti. In 1956 he led an expedition to the Brooks Range in Alaska under the sponsorship of the Wilderness Society, the New York Zoological Society, and the Conservation Foundation; the Arctic Wildlife Range was established in this area in 1960. Awarded the Aldo Leopold Memorial Medal in 1952 by the Wildlife Society in recognition of his contribution to the cause of wildlife conservation, he received the Cornelius Amory Pugsley Bronze Medal of the American Scenic and Historic Preservation Society in 1954, and in the same year the Conservation Award of the American Forestry Association. In 1959 he was awarded the Audubon Medal by the National Audubon Society, and the John Muir Award of the Sierra Club in 1963. Elected to the Council of the Wilderness Society when it was incorporated in 1937, he remained on the Council until his death. He became director of the society in 1945, and was president from 1950 to 1957. He was one of five trustees of the Robert Marshall Wilderness Fund set up by the late Robert Marshall to promote wilderness preservation. A member of many scientific and conserva- tion organizations, he was a past president of the Wildlife Society, a national director of the Izaak Walton League of America, and a member of the American Committee for International Wildlife Protection. The author of many contributions to technical and general periodicals, his writings include *The Elk of North America*, published in 1951. Considered the definitive work on this subject, it received the Wildlife Society's 1961 award for an outstanding ecological publication. He was author also of *A Field Guide to Animal Tracks*, 1954; *Alaska-Yukon Caribou*; *Food Habits of the Coyote in Jackson Hole, Wyoming*; *Fauna of the Aleutian Islands and Alaska Peninsula*; and *Jackson Hole with a Naturalist*, 1963. *Wapiti Wilderness* was published posthumously in 1966 with Margaret Murie as co-author. Died October 21, 1963.

MICHAEL NADEL

The Living Wilderness, Summer–Fall 1963 (no. 84).
Who Was Who in America, 1961–68.

MURPHY, ROBERT CUSHMAN (1887–   )

Born April 29, 1887 in Brooklyn, New York. Brown University, Ph.B. 1911, Sc.D. (honorary) 1941; Columbia University, A.M. 1918; San Marcos University (Lima, Peru), honorary doctorate 1925; Long Island University, Sc.D. (honorary) 1964. In 1911 he became curator of mammals and birds at the Brooklyn Museum, and in 1917 was named head of its Department of Natural Science. Joining the staff of the American Museum of Natural History in 1921 as associate curator of birds, he served as assistant director, 1924–26, as curator of oceanic birds, 1924–42, as chairman of the Department of Birds, 1942–54, as Lamont curator, 1949–55, and as curator emeritus and research associate thereafter. From 1940 to 1952, he was president of the Biological Laboratory at Cold Spring Harbor, Long Island, New York. Over a period of three decades he led ornithological expeditions to foreign regions, particularly to tropical and subantarctic America. A pioneer in the ecology of oceanic birds, he was a consultant to several South American governments on conservation and economic aspects of bird populations. He was a member of numerous scientific commissions, including the Pacific Science Board and the National Research Council. Awards and medals were conferred on him for his scientific contributions. He received the bronze medal of the John Burroughs Association in 1938, the Cullum medal of the American Geographical Society in 1940, the Frances Hutchinson medal of the Garden Club of America in 1941, and the Elliott medal of the National Academy of Sciences in 1943. He was president of the American Ornithologists' Union, 1948–50, having received the Union's William Brewster memorial medal in 1937, and is honorary president of the National Audubon Society. His writings are extensive, and include the books *Oceanic Birds of South America*, 2 vol., 1936; *Land Birds of America* (co-author), 1953; and *Rare and Exotic Birds*, 1964. His career has been notable for his influence on the advancement of ecological knowledge about birds, especially oceanic birds, and for his investigations of the economic importance of certain species.

NATIONAL AUDUBON SOCIETY

American Men of Science (The Physical and Biological Sciences), 11th ed., 1966.
World's Who's Who in Science, 1968.

NADEL, MICHAEL (1901–   )

Born February 20, 1901 in Glasgow, Scotland. At the College of the City of New York he majored in literature and writing. He served for four years as a member of the New York State Conservation Commissioner's Advisory Committee on Fish and Game; was vice president and board member of the New York State Conservation Council and editor of its *Bulletin*; and was first vice president of the Sportsmen's Council of the Marine District of New York. For two years he was contributing editor of *Game Breeder and Sportsman* conducting a monthly department on wildlife restoration. For ten years he conducted conservation activities for urban children in a voluntary program that he initiated in 1944. His major conservation activities from 1944 to 1954 were centered in the preservation of the wilderness of New York State's Forest Preserve. His long concern with wilderness led to his appointment in 1955 as assistant executive secretary of the Wilderness Society in Washington, D. C.; in 1964 he became editor of *The Living Wilderness* and was elected secretary of the society. He prepared the original distribution of materials which alerted the country to the proposal for a national wilderness preservation system, culminating in the Wilderness Act of 1964. In addition to his writings for various publications on conservation subjects, he contributed a chapter on "Scenic, Historic, and Natural Sites" for *Origins of American Conservation*, 1966, and the revised chapter on "Parks and Wilderness" for *America's Natural Resources*, 1967, publications of the Natural Resources Council of America. His additional affiliations, past and present, include the Wildlife Society, American Fisheries Society, Outdoor Writers Association of America, Audubon Naturalist Society of the Central Atlantic States, Nature Conservancy, and the Thoreau Society.

THE WILDERNESS SOCIETY

NEEDHAM, JAMES GEORGE (1868–1957)

Born March 16, 1868 in Virginia, Illinois. Knox College, B.S. and M.S.; Cornell University, Ph.D., 1898; Lake Forest University, Litt.D. (honorary) 1921, D.Sc. 1929. Awarded King Memorial Gold Medal by Peking Society of Natural History, 1930. In 1907 he was appointed assistant professor of limnology (full professor in 1911) formally establishing for the first time in an American university the subject of limnology as a field for instruction and research. Previously he had conducted investigations for the state of New York on aquatic life in the Adirondack mountains, the purpose of which was to develop methods for maintaining and increasing the food supply of native fishes. His life-long interest was in the ecology of the fresh water environment and he made a significant contribution to knowledge in three major groups of aquatic insects, the Eppemeroptera, Plecoptera, and Odonata. Three comprehensive books resulted from this special interest: *A Monograph of the Plecoptera or Stone-flies of America, North of Mexico*, 1925; *The Biology of Mayflies*, 1935; and *A Manual of the Dragonflies of North America*, 1954. He was author or co-author of more than a dozen books and numerous popular and scientific papers. *The Life of Inland Waters*, 1915, and the companion laboratory manual *A Guide to the Study of Freshwater Biology*, 1927, were indispensible texts for many early students of limnology. Two additional titles give some notion of the breadth of his understanding and interest in the biology and ecology of the total environment: *About Ourselves*, a survey of human nature from the zoological standpoint, 1941; and *The Natural History of the Farm*, a guide to the practical study of the sources of our wild living in wild nature, 1913. He was president of the Entomological Society, 1923; one of the founders of the Limnological Society and its second president in 1937; and vice president of the Ecological Society, 1936. Died July 24, 1957.

DWIGHT A. WEBSTER

American Men of Science, 9th ed., 1955.

NELSON, DeWITT (1901–   )

Born January 13, 1901 in Madrid, Iowa. Iowa State College, B.S. (forestry) 1925. Joined the United States Forest Service in California and during the next nine years served as ranger on the Tahoe National Forest, then assistant supervisor and supervisor of both the Trinity and the Shasta National Forests. In 1934 he became supervisor of the San Bernardino National Forest, then was Forest Service liaison officer with the Civilian Conservation Corps for the Army's Ninth Corps Area. Between 1936 and 1944 he was supervisor of the Tahoe and San Bernardino Forests. In 1944 he was appointed California's state forester, and in 1953 director of the Department of Natural Resources. In 1961 he was named director of the newly formed Department of Conservation where he supervised 5,000 employees and an annual budget of $40 million until his retirement in 1966 after 41 years of public service. During 1966–67 he was visiting professor of forestry at Iowa State University, and in 1968 was Regents' professor at the University of California and visiting professor of forestry at Oregon State University. Since then he has been professor of forestry at Iowa State University. At various times he was president of the Society of American Foresters (1956–57) and of the National Association of State Foresters (1951); director and honorary vice president of the American Forestry Association; member of the Secretary of Agriculture's Advisory Committee on Soil and Water Conservation; member of the Advisory Committee to the President's Commission on Outdoor Recreation Resources Review; and chairman of the Western Governors' Mining Advisory Council. The Swedish Royal Academy of Science honored him with the Greater Linneaus Medal in 1954. He is a Fellow of the Society of American Foresters.

PAUL CASAMAJOR

Who's Who in America, 1968–69.
Who's Who in the West, 11th ed., 1968.

NELSON, JESSE W. (1874–1958)

Born April 28, 1874 in rural Indiana. After three years of business college, his first employment was on Colonel William F. Cody's horse ranch in Wyoming and as a participant in Cody's Wild West Show. Appointed Ranger of the Yellowstone Park Timber Reserve, Department of the Interior, in 1901, he was thus one of the first men to join in the protection and administration of the public lands that were the forerunner of the national forests. He occupied successively the positions of ranger and forest supervisor in Wyoming; chief of grazing, Rocky Mountain Region (Denver); inspector of grazing, Washington, D. C. office; and for 14 years, chief of the Division of Range and Wildlife Management in the California Region. His final assignment was as superintendent of the newly established San Joaquin Experimental Range in California, from which he retired in 1942 after 41 years of government service. One of the early leaders in the administration of public lands, he was a man of integrity with a sense of fairness and a desire to work for the welfare of both the resource and the local people. These personal characteristics made it possible for him to deal with grazing and other users of public land who had a history of opposition to regulation and management of their activities on timber reserves and national forests. The fact that few of his many decisions were appealed to higher authority was proof of his ability to gain the confidence of the users in his life-long objective of sound wild land administration. Although not technically trained, he had an appreciation of scientific methods. As a keen judge of men he sought out promising young professionals and helped advance their careers. Died April 15, 1958.

LLOYD W. SWIFT

TALBOT, M. W. "Buffalo Bill's Top Hand," *American Forests Magazine*, vol. 66, May, 1960.

NEWELL, FREDERICK HAYNES (1862–1932)

Born March 5, 1862 in Bradford, Pennsylvania. Massachusetts Institute of Technology, B.Sc. (mining engineering) 1885. Joined the Geological Survey, United States Department of the Interior, in 1888 as a hydraulic engineer; became a hydrographer in 1890 and for the next decade made surveys for irrigation projects in the arid West. On passage of the Reclamation Act in 1902 he was made chief (reclamation) engineer in the Geological Survey, and when the Reclamation Service (now the Bureau of Reclamation) became an independent bureau in 1907 he was named director of it, serving until 1914. After being head of the Department of Civil Engineering at the University of Illinois, 1915–19, he was then founding president of Research Service, an organization of engineering consultants. He helped organize the American Society of Civil Engineers (president in 1919), and was secretary of the National Geographic Society. He was influential in conservation affairs; appointed to the United States Public Land Commission in 1903, he participated in the report to President Theodore Roosevelt that helped bring about transfer of the forest reserves from the Department of the Interior to the Department of Agriculture, making possible their subsequent administration as national forests by the Forest Service. A member of the Inland Waterways Commission, he proposed that President Roosevelt call the nation-wide meeting on natural resources that resulted in the historic White House Conference of Governors in May 1908. Among his books were *Hydrography of Arid Regions*, 1891; *Agriculture by Irrigation*, 1894; *The Public Lands of the United States and their Water Supply*, 1895; *Irrigation in the United States*, 1902; and *Water Resources, Present and Future Uses*, 1919. For his contributions he was awarded the Cullum Gold Medal by the American Geographical Society. Died July 5, 1932.

HENRY CLEPPER

Dictionary of American Biography, 1934.
Who Was Who in America, 1897–1942.

OBERHOLTZER, ERNEST C. (1884–)

Born 1884 in Davenport, Iowa. Harvard College, A.B. 1907, graduate studies in landscape architecture; Northern Michigan University of Marquette, L.H.D. (honorary). From 1908 onward he made
many canoe explorations in the Canadian wilderness, from the
Rainy Lake watershed of Minnesota and Ontario to the Barren
Lands of Northwest Canada. His studies of geography, wildlife,
and the Indians have been presented in numerous lectures and
articles. In 1926 he fought a proposal for a series of dams that would
have damaged the water level of the lakes along the international
boundary from Rainy Lake to Pigeon River, thus destroying the
beauty of the canoe country. The battle resulted in the formation
of the Quetico-Superior Council of which he became president in
1927 and which, supported by conservation groups, was dedicated
to the conservation of the forests, wildlife, and related natural
resources of the Minnesota-Ontario border lakeland. In 1934 President Franklin D. Roosevelt appointed the President's Quetico-Superior Committee of five members; Oberholtzer became the executive
secretary. He helped bring about passage of the Shipstead-Newton-
Nolan Act as well as an air space reservation over the roadless area
of the Superior National Forest, now the well-known Boundary
Waters Canoe Area. He is author of many articles on the scientific
and recreational aspects of the area. One of the founders of the
Wilderness Society, he was a member of its governing Council from
its inception in 1935 to 1968, and since then has been an honorary
vice president. Among his honors is the Department of the Interior's
Conservation Award in 1967.

MICHAEL NADEL

Minneapolis Tribune, April 28, 1967.
The Wilderness Society, biographical files.

OLMSTED, FREDERICK ERSKINE (1872–1925)

Born November 8, 1872 in Hartford, Connecticut. Graduated from the Sheffield Scientific School of Yale University in 1894 and entered the United States Geological Survey. While on field work with the Survey he met Gifford Pinchot who inspired him to seek further training in the field of forestry. Following this advice he studied under Sir Dietrich Brandeis in Germany and India during 1899 and 1900, returning to join Pinchot as agent in the United States Division of Forestry on July 1, 1900. Between 1902 and 1905 he directed the important work of locating boundaries of vast areas of public forest lands which became the present system of national forests, and was made assistant forester in 1903. After the Transfer Act of 1905, his first work in the newly created Forest Service was to develop an effective inspection system of which he became chief inspector in 1906. Here he began the fight for decentralized administration, and when western inspection districts were created he became chief inspector of the California District in 1907. The following year he was made the first district forester in California, and during the following three years he brought the new district to a high state of efficiency. Wishing to be closer to the woods and in a position to promote good forest management by private timber owners, he resigned from the Forest Service in June 1911 and joined Fisher and Bryant in a firm of consulting foresters in Boston, Massachusetts. In 1914 he opened an office as consulting forester in San Francisco where he organized and became directing head of the Tamalpais Fire Protective Association in Marin County, one of the first of such districts for watershed protection. He was also employed as forester by the Diamond Match Company to introduce conservative cutting and good management of its forest areas in California. A dedicated member of the Society of American Foresters, he was president in 1919. During his later years he wrote many articles promoting effective fire protection and good forest management on all forest lands in the United States. He died in 1925.

WOODBRIDGE METCALF

Journal of Forestry. Obituary, 23:337–39, April 1925.

OLMSTED, FREDERICK LAW, SR.   (1822–1903)

Born April 26, 1822 in Hartford, Connecticut. Yale University, honorary member class of 1847, LL.D. 1893; Amherst College, A.M. 1867; Harvard University, LL.D. 1893. Considered the principal founder of landscape architecture in the United States; spent his early years in farming, a nursery business, and active participation promoting the creation of parks as playgrounds for the nation. He was the driving force behind the establishment and layout of Central Park in New York City, and was appointed superintendent of the park in 1857. He was secretary of United States Sanitary Commission, 1861–63, and founded the Urban League Club upon his resignation to carry out his work. After the Civil War he traveled to California where he became the first Commissioner of Yosemite State Park, formulating enduring conservation and park-use policies. He engaged in landscape planning for the University of California, Johns Hopkins, Stanford, Amherst, Trinity, West Point, Yale, Smith, and Harvard. He helped plan the Arnold Arboretum and worked on George W. Vanderbilt's Biltmore estate near Asheville, North Carolina. He designed public parks for New York City; Brooklyn, New York; Boston, Massachusetts; Trenton, New Jersey; and other cities including the United States Capitol grounds and terraces, the World's Fair in Chicago (1893); and created the nation's first planned garden suburb, Riverside, Chicago. An authoritative writer on landscaping and park planning, he had an editorial interest in the magazine, *Garden and Forest*. The most notable landscape designer of his era, he had a national influence on the development of parks and the beautification of the urban environment. Died August 28, 1903.

MARY DiGIULIAN

Dictionary of American Biography, 1934.
MILDE, GORDON T., and WENMAYR, V. MICHAEL. *Frederick Law Olmsted, Sr.* Amherst, Mass.: University of Massachusetts Press, 1968.
Who Was Who in America, 1897–1942.

OLSON, SIGURD FERDINAND (1899–   )

Born April 4, 1899 in Chicago, Illinois. University of Wisconsin, B.S. (biology) 1920; University of Illinois, M.S. 1931; Hamline University, L.H.D. 1961; Northland College, Sc.D. 1961; Macalester College, Sc.D. 1963; Carleton College, Sc.D. 1965. He served as head of the Biology Department at Ely (Minnesota) Junior College, 1922–35, and as dean, 1935–45. He was instructor in zoology at the United States Army University, England in 1945 and lecturer, United States Army in Germany, Italy, France, and Austria in 1946. He has been wilderness ecologist for the Izaak Walton League of America since 1947, and a lecturer and free lance writer urging wilderness preservation in the United States. He has been consultant to the President's Quetico-Superior Committee since 1947, and to the Secretary of the Interior and the director of the National Park Service since 1962. He was a member of the Advisory Board on Parks, Monuments, and Historic Sites, United States Department of the Interior, 1960–66. A member of Council of the Wilderness Society since 1956, he was vice president, 1963–68, and president since 1968. He was President of the National Parks Association, 1953–58. Recipient of numerous additional honors including the Frances K. Hutchinson Medal by the Garden Club of America; the Horace M. Albright Medal by the American Scenic and Historic Preservation Society; admittance to the Izaak Walton League of America Hall of Fame; the John Muir Award of the Sierra Club; and election as Fellow of the Association of Interpretive Naturalists. Author of many popular and scientific articles, his best known books include *The Singing Wilderness*, 1956; *Listening Point*, 1958; *The Lonely Land*, 1961; *Runes of the North*, 1963; *Open Horizons*, 1969; and with Les Blacklock, *The Hidden Forest*, 1969.

GEORGE SPRUGEL, JR.

American Men of Science (The Physical and Biological Sciences), 11th ed., 1966.
The Living Wilderness, vol. 32, no. 101, 1968.
Who's Who in America, 1968–69.

ORDWAY, SAMUEL HANSON, JR. (1900–)

Born on January 20, 1900 in New York City. Harvard University, A.B. 1921, LL.B. 1924. He was admitted to the New York State bar in 1925. From 1937 to 1939, he was a member of the United States Civil Service Commission, and during 1940–41 he was president of the National Civil Service Reform League and a consultant to the National Roster of Scientific and Professional Personnel. He has served as a trustee for the Association for Protection of the Adirondacks since 1935 and as treasurer for two years. He became vice president of the Conservation Foundation in 1949, served as executive vice president, 1948–61, then as president, 1961–65, and has also been a trustee since 1962. He is a trustee of the Open Space Action Committee, and of the American Conservation Association. He was chairman of the Natural Resources Council of America in 1954. In 1964 he became co-chairman of the Board of Governors of the Pinchot Institute for Conservation Studies. For two terms he has been a member of the Secretary of Interior's Advisory Committee on Conservation. Author of numerous reports and articles, including an Alaska Program Analysis for the Department of Interior, he has also written several books: *A Conservation Handbook*, *Resources and the American Dream*, and *Prosperity Beyond Tomorrow*.

THE CONSERVATION FOUNDATION

Who's Who in America, vol. 35, 1968–69.

ORELL, BERNARD LEO (1914–)

Born January 26, 1914 in Portland, Oregon. Oregon State University, B.S. (forestry) 1939, B.S. (education) and M.F. 1941; Dakota Wesleyan University, Dr. Bus. Adms. (honorary) 1963. Training officer for the Oregon State Forestry Department, 1941–42. United States Army, 1942–46, 1st Lieutenant. Protection inspector, Oregon State Forestry Department, 1946–47. Assistant professor of forestry at the University of Washington College of Forestry, 1947–49; then state forester of Washington, 1949–53. He joined the Weyerhaeuser Sales Company in St. Paul, Minnesota in 1953 as vice president, handling public and industry relations. Then he was elected vice president in 1958 and transferred to Tacoma, Washington to direct and coordinate resource relations and public affairs activities of Weyerhaeuser Company and its subsidiaries. In 1959 he was elected a Fellow of the Society of American Foresters. He is a past president of the Forest History Society, a director of the National Recreation Association, a director of the American Forestry Association, and a member of the Executive Committee of the National Association of Manufacturers. During his presidency of American Forest Products Industries, Inc., 1964–67, he initiated its transition to the American Forest Institute, and serves on that organization's board of directors and executive committee. Appointed in 1959 as a member of the President's Outdoor Recreation Resources Review Commission. At present he is a member of the Advisory Council to the Public Land Law Review Commission. He is a past chairman of the Forest Industries Council; a member of the Forestry Affairs Committee and past chairman of the Forest Management Committee of the National Forest Products Association; received the 1968 Industry Statesmanship Award from that organization.

WILSON B. SAYERS

Who's Who in America, 1968–69.

OSBORN, FAIRFIELD (1887–1969)

Born on January 15, 1887, in Princeton, New Jersey. Princeton University, A.B. 1909, Sc.D. (honorary) 1957; Cambridge University, 1909–10; New York University, D.Sc. 1955, Kenyon College, LL.D. 1959; University of Buffalo, D.Sc. 1962; Hofstra University, LL.D. 1966. He became a member of the Board of Trustees and of the Executive Committee of the New York Zoological Society in 1923, served as secretary for four years, and in 1940 became president and chairman of the Board. After World War II he took the lead in organizing the Conservation Foundation and in 1948 he became its first president, serving until 1962 when he became chairman of the Board. He was awarded the Medal of Honor from the Theodore Roosevelt Memorial Association in 1949, and the Frances K. Hutchinson Medal from the Garden Club of America in 1952. The Institut Oceanographique of France presented him the Prix Manley Bendall in 1957. Three years later he received the Medal of Honor of the City of New York. These awards were followed by the Louis Bromfield Memorial Medal in 1963 from the Friends of the Land, and the Gold Medal of the New York Zoological Society and the First Conservation Medal of the San Diego Zoological Society, both in 1966. He was chosen honorary vice president of the Fauna Preservation Society in London and of the American Forestry Association. In 1952 he was a member of the Secretary of the Interior's Advisory Committee on Conservation. He was a Foreign Fellow of the Zoological Society of London and a Fellow of the New York Academy of Sciences. He was a member of the American Committee of International Council of Museums, the Council of the Save-the-Redwoods League, and the International Committee for Bird Preservation. He was the author of *Our Plundered Planet*, 1948, for which he received the Gutenberg Award and the National Education Award; known also for his book *Limits of the Earth*, 1953. He was editor of *The Pacific World*, 1944, and *Our Crowded Planet*, 1962. Died September 16, 1969.

THE CONSERVATION FOUNDATION

Who's Who in America, 1968–69.

PACK, ARTHUR NEWTON (1893–   )

Born February 20, 1893 in Cleveland, Ohio. Williams College, B.A. 1914. Harvard Graduate School of Business Administration, 1914–15. University of Arizona, D.Sc. (honorary) 1959. University of New Mexico, LL.D. (honorary) 1960. Honorary Member, Society of American Foresters. Special commissioner, American Forestry Association, 1921, studying European forestry organizations and methods in England, France, Germany, and Belgium. With his

father, Charles Lathrop Pack, organized the American Tree Association in 1922, with the primary purpose of encouraging tree planting, and arousing an appreciation of the importance of forests to
the economic welfare of the United States. The greatest tree-planting drive of the Association culminated in 1932 with the George
Washington Memorial Tree-Planting Campaign, resulting in the
planting of over 27 million trees. Organized the American Nature
Association and served as its president, 1926–46. Editor of the
Association's magazine, *Nature*, devoted to stimulating public
interest in the conservation of both wildlife and forests. In 1930
became editor of a section of the magazine entitled *Conservation*.
Joint trustee of the Charles Lathrop Pack Forestry Trust, founded
in 1924 as a financial means of supporting forestry education and
research. The trust contributed to several forestry projects later
carried on by the Charles Lathrop Pack Forestry Foundation. President of the Charles Lathrop Pack Forestry Foundation, 1956 to
date, during which time he directed the efforts of the Foundation
chiefly to problems of the arid Southwest. President emeritus of the
Arizona-Senora Desert Museum, and trustee of the Ghost Ranch
Museum, an outdoor interpretive project in New Mexico, combining
the facilities of zoo, botanical garden, and museum. Author of
Our Vanishing Forests, 1923; *The Nature Almanac* (with E.
Laurence Palmer), 1927; *Forestry—An Economic Challenge*, 1933;
The Ghost Ranch Story, 1960.

Tom Gill

Butler, Ovid. "A Foundation for the Forest." *American Forests*, 1948.
The Pack Organization. Washington, D.C.: published by the Charles Lathrop Pack
    Forestry Foundation.
Who's Who in America, 1968–69.

PACK, CHARLES LATHROP   (1857–1937)

Born May 7, 1857 in Lexington, Michigan. Educated at Brooks
School, Cleveland; Trinity College, LL.D. 1918; Syracuse University,
Dr. Bus. Adm. 1925; Oberlin College, LL.D. 1926; Rutgers Univer-
sity, Sc.D. 1930. Attended the White House Conference of Gov-

ernors in 1908 as a forester advisor. President Theodore Roosevelt appointed him a member of the National Conservation Commission, 1908. President, American Forestry Association, 1916–20. President, National Conservation Congress, 1913. Awarded the Order *Merite Agricole* France, 1919. After World War I, was active in the reforestation of England, France, and Italy. President, American Nature Association, 1922. With his son, Arthur Newton Pack, organized the American Tree Association in 1922. Served as its president until 1937. Founded the Charles Lathrop Pack Forestry Foundation in 1930, then the only privately endowed foundation dedicated to forestry; its purpose was to promote scientific and professional management of forests through granting of individual fellowships for advanced training, through scientific publications, and a program of specific large-scale projects. Created demonstration forests at Yale, Cornell, Washington, and Michigan universities and the New York State College of Forestry at Syracuse, to show the possibilities of forest management. Endowed professional chairs of forestry at four colleges. Provided numerous scholarships in forestry and endowed twelve colleges with funds to award annual prizes for essays and articles on forestry. A pioneer in forestry education, he established, within the foundation, the Pack Education Board which granted awards for specific studies in conservation in the United States and abroad. In 1908, with Gifford Pinchot, helped form the National Conservation Foundation, which emphasized the concept of conservation through judicious use of the timberlands. Established foundations at Yale and the University of Michigan. In 1923, founded and published the *Forestry News Digest*. Author: *Schoolbook of Forestry*, 1922; *Trees as Good Citizens*, 1923; *Forestry Primer*, 1926; *Forestry and Mankind* (with Tom Gill), 1929; *Forest Facts for Schools* (with Tom Gill), 1931. Died June 14, 1937.

Tom Gill

Butler, Ovid. "Foundation for the Forest." *American Forests*, 1948.
Dictionary of American Biography, vol. 22, supp. 2.,
Evans, Mary, comp. *Biological References*. University of Illinois Library School.
Gill, Tom. "Charles Lathrop Pack." *Journal of Forestry*, 35:622–23, 1937.
Who Was Who in America, 1897–1942.

PACK, RANDOLPH GREENE (1890–1956)

Born June 8, 1890 in Cleveland, Ohio. Williams College, 1909–11; attended Pennsylvania State College as a special forestry student (no degree). University of Michigan, D.Sc. (honorary) 1953. Director, Friends of the Land and the New England Forest Foundation. Member of the American Citizens Committee for United Nations Scientific Conference on Conservation and Utilization of Resources. Honorary Member, Society of American Foresters. Vice President, American Nature Association and American Forestry Association. Director and member of Executive Board of the Conservation Foundation. Became president of the Charles Lathrop Pack Forestry Foundation in 1937, a position he held until his death. During this time, he initiated a number of important studies and concentrated the efforts of the Foundation on specific fields of forestry. At his direction, the Foundation published a number of research findings which, through lack of federal appropriations, might have been delayed for years. He authorized the publication and wide distribution of the report of the Forestry Committee of the Food and Agriculture Organization of the United Nations. He extended the activities of the Pack Foundation beyond the United States through studies of the tropical timber resources of the Caribbean. Under his authorization, the foundation created and for a number of years supported the Mexican Institute of Renewable Natural Resources. In recognition of his international contributions, the United States Government invited him to take part in three international conferences. In 1950, initiated a project to provide scholarships in the School of Public Administration at Harvard, to enable federal and state government conservation workers to study the lag between knowledge and performance in the entire field of conservation. Died December 25, 1956.

TOM GILL

BUTLER, OVID. "A Foundation for the Forest." *American Forests*, 1948.
GILL, TOM. *Ten Years of Fact-Finding*. Charles Lathrop Pack Forestry Foundation.
The Pack Foundation. Charles Lathrop Pack Forestry Foundation.
Who Was Who in America, 1951–60.

PALMER, EPHRAIM LAURENCE (1888–)

Born July 8, 1888, in McGraw, New York. Cornell University, M.A. 1911, Ph.D. 1917. Taught botany and natural science at Iowa State Teachers College, 1913–19. Then joined the faculty of Cornell University in 1919, and until his retirement in 1952 he was involved heavily in nature and conservation education, directed many graduate students, and had a profound influence on science education. One of the more prolific writers in the past half century, he wrote the quarterly Cornell Rural School Leaflets from 1919 to 1952, wrote six articles a year and served as nature editor for *Nature* Magazine from 1925 to 1959, was a contributing editor to *Natural History* Magazine from 1960 through 1962, and wrote many other articles which appeared in numerous journals and publications. His *Fieldbook of Natural History* is considered a classic. In relation to national organizations, he contributed in many ways as a consultant in nature education to the National Wildlife Federation, 1950–57; the Boy Scouts of America, the American Nature Study Society, president, 1936–37; the Ecological Society of America; the National Council of Nature Study Supervisors of the Department of Science Education of the National Education Association; the National Association of Biology Teachers, president, 1947; the National Audubon Society, director, 1943–49; the International Union for the Conservation of Nature and Natural Resources, (Hornaday Gold Medal, 1961); and the National Committee on Policies in Conservation Education. Recipient of Nash Conservation Award, 1954. Throughout his long and productive professional career, he was instrumental in the education of many present-day conservation educators, and in this probably his influence on conservation education as such in the United States will be felt for many years to come.

WILSON F. CLARK

American Men of Science (The Physical and Biological Sciences), 11th ed., 1965. *Who's Who in America*, 1968–69.

PARKER, LANSING ARTHUR (1912–65)

Born June 17, 1912 in Minneapolis, Minnesota. University of Minnesota School of Forestry, B.S. 1935. His career began in 1935 as a project forester in the Soil Conservation Service, United States Department of Agriculture, in Minnesota, and from 1938 to 1944 he was area biologist. In 1945 he joined the Fish and Wildlife Service which later became the Bureau of Sport Fisheries and Wildlife, Department of the Interior. He served first in the Division of Federal Aid, the unit that administers the federal funds made available to the states for cooperative programs in the restoration of wildlife resources, and in 1948 was advanced to assistant chief of the division. In 1957 he was appointed assistant director of the Bureau in charge of all cooperative services, and in 1963 he was made associate director. From 1960 to 1965, he was associate editor for forest wildlife management and recreation of the *Journal of Forestry*. He was a charter member of the Wildlife Society, and an honorary member of the International Wild Waterfowl Association. In 1966 the Department of the Interior conferred on him, posthumously, its highest honor, the Distinguished Service Award "in recognition of an admirable and public spirited career." Died October 25, 1965.

HENRY CLEPPER

PARTAIN, LLOYD ELMER (1906–)

Born February 3, 1906 in Waldron, Arkansas. Oklahoma A & M College, School of Agriculture, B.S. (agricultural education) 1931. From 1928 to 1935, he was a high school teacher and instructor at Oklahoma State University. Joined the Soil Conservation Service, United States Department of Agriculture, in 1935 as information officer and assistant state coordinator in Oklahoma; became extension soil conservationist in the States Relations Division, Washington, D. C., 1937–42. He then transferred to the War Savings Division of the Treasury Department, and in 1943 joined the Curtis Publishing Company in Philadelphia, where he served variously during the next two decades in editorial, sales, marketing, and

research assignments. In 1962 he returned to the Soil Conservation
Service, where he is assistant to the administrator for environmental
development. He is past president (1949–50), and a Fellow of the
Soil Conservation Society of America, and past president (1956–62)
of the Pennsylvania Forestry Association. Since 1947 he has been a
director (now vice president) of the American Forestry Association,
and since 1961 has been a member of the Board of Directors of the
National Audubon Society. From 1958 to 1962, he was a member of
the Advisory Council for the Outdoor Recreation Resources Review
Commission, and more recently has been on the Commission on
Education in Agriculture and Natural Resources for the National
Research Council-National Academy of Sciences. Since 1953 he has
been a member of the National Council and Conservation Committee for the Boy Scouts of America. Long prominent as a conservation lecturer and writer, he has been an interpreter of the relationships of business, industry, and natural resources, and an exponent of
outdoor recreation, natural beauty, and the quality of the environment.

HENRY CLEPPER

PEARSON, GUSTAF ADOLPH (1880–1949)

Born November 14, 1880 in Holdredge, Nebraska. University of
Nebraska, M.A. (botany and forestry) 1907. He became a forest
assistant, Forest Service, United States Department of Agriculture,
in 1907, and was in charge of the Fort Valley Forest Experiment
Station, Flagstaff, Arizona, 1909–29. He was director of the Forest
Service's Southwestern Forest and Range Experiment Station,
1930–35, then relinquished the directorship in 1935 and, as a senior
silviculturist, took over the management and development of the
Fort Valley Experimental Forest. He retired in 1944, but continued
as a Forest Service collaborator. His research in reforestation, forest
meteorology, forest ecology, and silviculture brought about the
development and adoption of procedures used in the management
of *Pinus ponderosa* which are materially increasing the productivity

of this valuable species. He was a trustee of the Northern Arizona Society of Science and Art; and a Fellow of the American Association for the Advancement of Science and of the Society of American Foresters. Author of *Natural Reproduction of Western Yellow Pine*, 1923; *Forest Types in the Southwest as Determined by Climate and Soil*, 1931; *Timber Growing and Logging Practice* (with R. E. Marsh) 1935; and *Forest Land Use*, 1940; also author of government bulletins and contributions to technical journals. He received the 1944 award of Society of American Foresters for best article on forestry. Died January 31, 1949.

JOHN H. ALLISON

Who Was Who in America, 1943–50.

PEARSON, THOMAS GILBERT (1873–1943)

Born November 10, 1873 in Tuscola, Illinois. Guilford College, B.S. 1897; University of North Carolina, B.S. 1899, LL.D. 1924; graduate study at Harvard University. While teaching biology at Guilford College, 1899–1901 and at the North Carolina State Normal and Industrial College for Women, 1901–4, he became alarmed at the widespread slaughter of birds and game animals which were then without legal protection. In 1902 he organized and incorporated the Audubon Society of North Carolina which was granted the authority of a state law enforcement agency, and as secretary of the society he functioned as state game commissioner, 1903–10. He became secretary of the National Association of Audubon Societies whose name was later changed to the National Audubon Society when it was organized in 1905. He was appointed its executive officer in 1910, was president from 1922 to 1934, and president emeritus thereafter, retiring officially in 1942. He is credited with the development of the Audubon Society into one of the nation's largest and most influential bodies devoted to the conservation of wildlife and all resources. For years he was the author of much of the educational material distributed by the society. In 1922 he founded the International Committee for Bird Preservation and was its chairman until 1938. He was also founder and chairman of the National Committee on Wildlife Legislation, was a member of the Advisory Board on the Migratory Bird Treaty Act for 20 years, was a national director of the Izaak Walton League of America, and an official collaborator of the National Park Service and the Fish and Wildlife Service, United States Department of the Interior. Recipient of decorations for his international activities in bird conservation from Luxembourg in 1925 and from France in 1937; awarded the John Burrough's medal in 1939 for his contributions to American conservation. He wrote numerous articles on ornithological and conservation subjects for scientific and popular magazines, and was author of several books including *Stories of Bird Life*, 1901; *The Bird Study Book*, 1917; and *Adventures in Bird Protection*, an autobiography, 1937. In addition he was editor-in-chief of *Birds of America*, 3 vols., 1917, and was co-editor of *The Book of Birds*, 1937. Died September 3, 1943.

NATIONAL AUDUBON SOCIETY

Audubon Magazine, 45:26–29 and 45:370–71, 1943.
National Cyclopaedia of American Biography, 1947.
Who Was Who in America, 1943–50.

PENFOLD, JOSEPH WELLER (1907–   )

Born November 18, 1907 in Marinette, Wisconsin. Yale University, 1926–30; University of Denver, 1942–45. Variously employed from 1930 to 1933 in farming, logging, and the merchant marine; in the latter year he was appointed supervisor of federal relief programs in Tennessee, and in 1935 became conservation director of the National Youth Administration in Ohio. During World War II, he was executive officer for the Office of Price Administration at Denver, Colorado and during 1945–48 was a field representative for the United Nations Relief and Rehabilitation Administration in China. His professional career in conservation began in 1949 when he was named western representative of the Izaak Walton League of America in Denver. Since 1957 he has been the league's conservation director in Washington, D. C. Among his outstanding services to conservation, one is especially significant because of its multiple effects: he conceived and drafted the legislation, enacted by Congress in 1958, that created the Outdoor Recreation Resources Review Commission, and served on the Commission by presidential appointment. The Commission's report in 1962 led to the establishment of the Bureau of Outdoor Recreation in the Department of the Interior and the Land and Water Conservation Fund. It also influenced the creation of the Recreation Advisory Council, and the President's Advisory Committee on Recreation and Natural Beauty. Long an officer of the Natural Resources Council, he was its secretary, 1957–65, vice chairman in 1966, and chairman, 1967–69. He has been advisor to the Department of the Interior in the development of the National Fisheries Center and Aquarium, and is a member of the master plan team for the Yellowstone and Teton National Parks. For two decades he has been one of America's most respected and influential conservation leaders.

HENRY CLEPPER

PETERSON, ROGER TORY (1908–   )

Born August 28, 1908 in Jamestown, New York. Art Students' League, 1927; National Academy of Design, 1928–31; Franklin and Marshall College, D.Sc. 1952; Ohio State University, D.Sc. 1962; Allegheny College, D.Sc. 1967; Fairfield University, D.Sc. 1967. From 1931 to 1934, he was an art teacher; then in 1934 he became affiliated with the National Audubon Society as an education specialist and as art editor of *Audubon Magazine*. Following service in the United States Army during World War II, in 1946 he again became associated with the Audubon Society as lecturer with its wildlife film series. Since then he has served the society as artist, officer, and writer; he was a director, 1958–60; secretary, 1960–64; and has again served as director since 1965. In addition, he has been an officer and committee member of other organizations of conservationists and artists. He was president of the American Nature Study Society, 1948–49, has been on the Board of Directors of the World Wildlife Fund since 1962, and is a Fellow of the American Association for the Advancement of Science. For his notable contributions to art and literature, he has received many honors, including the William Brewster memorial medal of the American Ornithologists' Union in 1944; the John Burroughs medal in 1950; the Geoffrey St.-Hilaire gold medal of the National History Society of France in 1957; the gold medal of the New York Zoological Society in 1961; and the Arthur A. Allen medal of the Laboratory of Ornithology at Cornell University in 1967. Since 1946 he has been editor of the Houghton Mifflin Field Guide Series of books; and since 1951 has been art director for the National Wildlife Federation. A prolific and authoritative writer, as well as artist, he is best known for *A Field Guide to the Birds*, a popular work first published in 1934. His companion volume, *A Field Guide to Western Birds*, 1941, was followed by five other bird books. In addition, he is the illustrator of five additional bird guides and is co-author of six more. His influence on the spread of popular education about birds and the conservation of wildlife is international in scope, and he is one of America's best known exponents of nature preservation.

NATIONAL AUDUBON SOCIETY

International Who's Who, 32nd ed., 1968–69.
Twentieth Century Authors, 1st supp. New York: H. W. Wilson Co., 1955.
Who's Who in America, 1968–69.

PETTIT, TED S. (1914–)

Born June 3, 1914 at Far Rockaway, New York. Bard College, B.A. (economics) 1937; Columbia University, graduate work in biology and science education, 1938–42. From 1937 to 1941, he was employed by the National Audubon Society. In 1942 he went to the Boy Scouts of America as assistant director of editorial service; since 1954 he has been director of conservation. For a decade,

1954–64, he was author of a monthly column in the *Pennsylvania Game News*. He has been a frequent contributor to *Boys' Life* and to *Scouting* magazines. Currently, he writes a weekly column on conservation and nature topics for the Somerset County, New Jersey, *Messenger-Gazette*. He is author of the following books: *Book of Nature Hobbies*, 1947; *Birds in Your Backyard*, 1949; *Book of Small Mammals*, 1958; *Web of Nature*, 1959; *Animal Signs and Signals*, 1960; *Guide to Nature Projects*, 1966; and *Boys' Life Book of Conservation*, 1970. Received the Wildlife Society education award in 1955, the American Motors award for conservation in 1966, the Keep American Beautiful citation in 1967, and a citation from the New Jersey Department of Conservation and Economic Development in 1968. In consequence of his work in Scouting and the guidance he has provided millions of American youths during his years of service with the Boy Scout movement, he is one of the nation's most widely known conservation leaders.

HENRY CLEPPER

PHILLIPS, ARTHUR MORTON, JR. (1914–   )

Born June 18, 1914 at Rochester, New York. Cornell University, B.S. 1936, Ph.D. (fisheries) 1939. Initially employed in 1939 as laboratory assistant for fish nutrition and biochemistry, New York Conservation Department, in 1941 he became assistant aquatic biologist, United States Fish and Wildlife Service, leading to associate to chief of Fish Nutrition Investigations, Cortland (N. Y.) laboratory. He taught fish nutrition at Cortland hatchery for in-service biologists, hatchery men, and students of fisheries from Cornell University. His special studies center around vitamin requirements, metabolism, blood analysis, and physiology of fishes. He published numerous papers on nutrition, metabolism, and basic physiology of fishes; outstanding and well known among them are his studies of wild trout versus hatchery trout physiology. His "Cortland No. 6" trout food diet has been accepted throughout the world as the basis of hatchery fish production. He is a member of the American

Association for the Advancement of Science, American Fisheries Society, and the Ecological Society of America.

ELWOOD A. SEAMAN

American Men of Science (The Physical and Biological Sciences), 11th ed., 1967.

PINCHOT, GIFFORD   (1865–1946)

Born August 11, 1865 in Simsbury, Connecticut. Yale University, A.B. 1889; A.M. 1901, LL.D. 1925; Princeton University, A.M. 1904; Michigan Agricultural College, Sc.D. 1907; McGill University, LL.D. 1909; Pennsylvania Military College, LL.D. 1923; Temple University, LL.D. 1931. The first native American to receive formal instruction in forestry, he studied at the National School of Waters and Forests, Nancy, France, in 1900; no academic institution in the United States offered forestry courses. In January 1892 he began the first systematic forest management on the Biltmore forest in North Carolina. He was in private consulting practice for several years thereafter, and in 1896 was a member of the Forest Commission appointed by the National Academy of Sciences that recommended creation of the forest reserve (now the national forests) from the public domain, and that was responsible for the Forest Reserve Act of 1897 that provided for their administration and protection. In 1898 he was appointed chief of the Division of Forestry, United States Department of Agriculture; it became the Bureau of Forestry in 1901 and the present Forest Service in 1905. Also in 1905 the forest reserves were transferred from the Department of the Interior to the Department of Agriculture, and in 1907 were renamed the national forests. During his administration of the national forests they were increased from 51 million acres in area in 1901 to 175 million acres by 1910. He was an organizer of the White House Governors' Conference on Natural Resources of May 1908, and was chairman of the subsequent National Conservation Commission that compiled the first inventory of the country's natural resources. Dismissed as chief of the Forest Service by President Taft in 1910, he organized and became president of the National

Conservation Association, formed to continue the fight for his conservation ideas. From 1920 to 1922, he was commissioner of the Department of Forestry, later secretary of the Department of Forests and Waters, in Pennsylvania; governor of Pennsylvania, 1923–27 and 1931–35. In 1900 he founded the School of Forestry at Yale University and also the Society of American Foresters of which he was the first president. He was the author of numerous papers and reports on conservation topics, including the books *A Primer of Forestry*, 1899; *The Fight for Conservation*, 1909; *The Training of a Forester*, 1914; and *Breaking New Ground*, his autobiography, 1947. The foremost conservationist of his era, he was largely responsible for "conservation" becoming widely known and supported by the public and an established policy of both the federal and state governments. Died October 4, 1946.

HENRY CLEPPER

Journal of Forestry 9 (Gifford Pinchot Commemorative Issue) vol. 63, no. 8, August 1965.
McGREARY, M. NELSON. *Gifford Pinchot, Forester-Politician*. Princeton, N.J.: Princeton University Press, 1960.
PINCHOT, GIFFORD. *Breaking New Ground*. New York: Harcourt, Brace and Co., 1957.
Who Was Who in America, 1943–50.

POMEROY, KENNETH BROWNRIDGE (1907–)

Born May 17, 1907 near Valley Center, Michigan. Michigan State University, B.S. 1928; Duke University, M.F. 1948. Following private employment, he began a 23-year Forest Service career in 1933 as a clerk on the Nicolet National Forest in Wisconsin advancing through line and staff positions in administration, state and private forestry and research to chief of naval stores research, Lake City, Florida and finally chief of timber management research, Northeastern Forest Experiment Station, Philadelphia, Pennsylvania. His research achievements included stimulation of seed production and regeneration of loblolly pine. He became chief forester of the American Forestry Association in 1956 with responsibility for legislative liaison, technical assistance to association members, the Trail Riders of the Wilderness program, and general conservation activities. A member of the Secretary of Agriculture's Forest Research Advisory Committee since 1962; the Secretary of Defense Conservation Award Committee 1968; and the Forest Fire Prevention Committee, Society of American Foresters since 1966; Recreation Committee, Soil Conservation Society of America 1969 and Chairman, National Task Force—Trees For People 1969. He was an official United States Delegate to the Fifth World Forestry Congress in Seattle, 1960, and to the Sixth World Forestry Congress in Madrid, Spain, 1966. Served as secretary, Fifth American Forest Congress, 1963. He is the senior author (with J. G. Yoho) of *North Carolina Lands*, 1964; senior author (with R. W. Cooper) of *Growing Slash Pine*, 1956; contributor to *American Forestry, Six Decades of Growth*, 1960; contributor to *Forestry Handbook*, 1955; and author of 180 articles for scientific and popular magazines.

HENRY CLEPPER

American Men of Science (The Physical and Biological Sciences), 11th ed., 1965.
Who Knows—and What, 1954.
Who's Who in the South and Southwest, 11th ed. In press.

POOLE, DANIEL ARNOLD (1922–   )

Born April 11, 1922 in New York City. Attended Kent State University in 1944 (military service program); University of Montana, B.S. 1950, and M.S. (wildlife management) 1952. Field assistant with the Montana Fish and Game Department in 1949; junior biologist in 1952. Biological aide with the United States Fish and Wildlife Service in California in 1950; Utah, 1951. He joined the Wildlife Management Institute in Washington, D. C. 1952; edited the Institute's bi-weekly *Outdoor News Bulletin*, 1952–69; elected secretary in 1963, president in 1970. Member, board of directors, Outdoor Writers Association of America, 1956–58. Editor of the *Executive News Service* of the Natural Resources Council of America, 1960–65; elected secretary in 1966. He was chairman of the publicity committee for the National Watershed Congress, 1954–62.

He was also a member of the National Mosquito Control, Fish and Wildlife Coordination Committee since 1962; of the board of directors, Citizens Committee on Natural Resources since 1962; and of the Conservation Awards Committee, Department of the Navy, 1963–68. He was elected a trustee of the North American Wildlife Foundation in 1966. His articles on wildlife and natural resources have been published in many newspapers and periodicals. Edited a monthly column on wildlife topics for *The American Rifleman*, 1960–70. He was a special consultant to the Secretary of Agriculture on resources management plan for the Magruder Corridor, Bitterroot National Forest, Montana, 1966–67. In 1967 he was appointed a collaborator to the National Park Service to serve on a master planning team for Yellowstone and Grand Teton National Parks. He received Jade of Chiefs award of the Outdoor Writers Association of America in 1969 for service to conservation.

JAMES B. TREFETHEN

Who's Who in America, 1968–69.

POTTER, ALBERT F. (1859–1944)

Born November 14, 1859 in Lone, California. Educated in the San Francisco Bay area, he moved to Arizona for his health. There he acquired practical knowledge of livestock and range matters, and bought into the sheep business, which he operated profitably and sold in 1900. Through his leadership in the Arizona Woolgrowers Association he was sent to Washington to obtain acceptance of the proposal that sheep should be permitted to graze on forest reserve lands. He guided Gifford Pinchot, head of the Division of Forestry, United States Department of Agriculture, on a field inspection and convinced him that properly managed livestock grazing would not damage the reserves. And thus, over the opposition of most forest officers of that era, official recognition of grazing as a legitimate use of forested lands was established. On Pinchot's recommendation Potter went to Washington in 1901 to work on grazing matters. He made field examinations in Arizona, Utah, and California that led to enlargement or establishment of forest reserves by President Theodore Roosevelt. When the forest reserves were transferred from the Department of the Interior in 1905 and set up as the national forests in the Department of Agriculture, Potter was made chief of grazing. He was promoted to associate forester in 1910, and resigned in 1920. More than any other person, he was the architect of the grazing policy of the Forest Service; the basic philosophy he established has largely been continued. Through his practical knowledge of the sheep and cattle industry associated with the use of public lands in the West, he recognized the signs of overuse and understood the complexities of working out proper stocking with the cattle and sheep growers. Control of grazing use advanced rapidly under his direction; the first regulation was issued July 1, 1905, and grazing fees became effective January 1, 1906. Certain basic principles were followed, i.e., previous users had priority; small homestead-type owners dependent on the forest for forage had preferential status; adjustments in numbers would be made without discontinuing use; stockmen would have a voice in matters affecting their interests. The authority of the Secretary of Agriculture, through the Forest Service, to regulate grazing use and collect fees was challenged by livestock interests who claimed that federal authority could not override state law. Potter believed in the rule of federal power to protect public land, regulate its occupancy, and charge for its use. These questions were settled in the government's favor in the "Fred Light case" by a Supreme Court ruling in 1911, thus confirming Potter's judgment. Died January 1, 1944.

LLOYD W. SWIFT

BARNES, W. C. "Retirement of Albert F. Potter." *Journal of Forestry*, vol. 18:211–13, March, 1920.
ROBERTS, PAUL H., *Hoof Prints on Forest Ranges*. San Antonio, Texas: The Naylor Co., 1963.

POUGH, RICHARD HOOPER (1904–)

Born April 19, 1904 in Brooklyn, New York. Massachusetts Institute of Technology, B.S. 1926; Harvard Graduate School, 1926–27. From 1927 to 1936 he held various engineering positions in business and industry. He joined the research staff of the National Audubon Society in New York City in 1936, and during the next twelve years was a successful popularizer of scientific ornithology. In 1948 he was appointed curator and chairman of the Department of Conservation and General Ecology of the American Museum of Natural History, New York; he helped plan much of the Hall of North American Forests. Since 1957 he has been president of the Natural Area Council. He is active and holds office in numerous national and international conservation organizations, including director of the World Wildlife Fund, and chairman of the Coastal Wetlands Council. He was secretary of the International Council for Bird Preservation, 1950–60; president of the Linnaean Society, 1943–45. He is past president of the Nature Conservancy, past president of the John Burroughs Association, past president and trustee of the American Scenic and Historic Preservation Society, and trustee of the National Parks Association. He is the recipient of the Conservation Award of the American Motors Corporation, 1962; the Horace M. Albright Medal of the American Scenic and Historic Preservation Society, 1963; the Frances K. Hutchinston Medal of the Garden Club of America, 1961. He is the author of numerous scientific papers and magazine articles and the three-volume set of the *Audubon Bird Guides.*

THE NATURE CONSERVANCY

American Men of Science (The Physical and Biological Sciences), 11th ed., 1965.
Who's Who in America, 1968–69.

POWELL, JOHN WESLEY (1834–1902)

Born March 24, 1834 at Mount Morris, New York. Oberlin College and Wheaton College, no degree; Harvard University, LL.D. 1886; University of Heidelberg, Ph.D. 1886; Illinois College, LL.D. 1889; Illinois Wesleyan University, A.M. and Ph.D. After teaching school, he enlisted in the Union Army during the Civil War, and rose to the rank of major. On his return to civil life, he was professor of geology at Illinois Wesleyan College, then later was curator of the museum of Illinois Normal University. In 1867 and 1868 he made natural history studies in the western plains and the Rocky Mountains. In 1869 he led his famous 900-mile boat expedition down the Grand Canyon of the Colorado River under the sponsorship of the Smithsonian Institution. He made additional western explorations in 1871, 1874, and 1875. In 1875 he was made director of United States geological and geographical surveys in the Rocky Mountain region. When the western surveys were consolidated in 1879 under the United States Geological Survey, he became director of the United States Bureau of Ethnology, but returned to the Survey in 1880 as director. He held both positions until 1894, when he was forced out of the directorship of the Geological Survey because of Congressional opposition to his strong advocacy of extensive irrigation projects in the arid West and of forest preservation of the public lands. He continued as director of the Bureau of Ethnology. The results of his early work were published as *Explorations of the Colorado River of the West and Its Tributaries*, 1875; he also published a monograph *Report on the Lands of the Arid Region of the United States*, 1878. In later years he wrote numerous papers and books on scientific subjects. Died September 23, 1902.

HENRY CLEPPER

DARRAH, WILLIAM C. *Powell of the Colorado*. Princeton, N.J.: Princeton University Press, 1951.
Dictionary of American Biography, 1934.
International Encylopedia of the Social Sciences, 1968.
STEGNER, WALLACE. *Beyond the Hundredth Meridian: John Wesley Powell*. Boston: Houghton Mifflin, 1951.
TERRELL, JOHN UPTON. *The Man Who Rediscovered America: a Biography of John Wesley Powell*. New York: Weybright & Talley, 1969.
Who Was Who in America, 1897–1942.

PRESTON, JOHN FREDERICK (1883–1967)

Born February 26, 1883 in Higginsville, Missouri. University of Michigan, A.B. 1907, M.Sc. (forestry) 1915. He began his professional career as a timber cruiser for the United States Forest Service in the Ozarks in 1907. Subsequent assignments took him to the national forests of Montana where he became forest supervisor. In 1920 he transferred to the Washington, D. C. headquarters of the Forest Service as forest inspector of timber sales. In 1925 he joined Hammermill Paper Company at Erie, Pennsylvania as technical advisor in timber land acquisition, harvesting, and reforestation. He returned to the Department of Agriculture in Washington, D. C. in 1936 as chief, Forestry Division, Soil Conservation Service. In this position he supervised a nationwide program to induce farmers to include forestry in integrated farm conservation programs. Upon retirement in 1946 because of ill health he became a free lance writer; and as an instructor in the Department of Agriculture, prepared a correspondence course in farm forestry. He was author of the books *Developing Farm Woodlands* and *Farm Wood Crops*, the bulletin *Woodlands in the Farm Plan*, and many technical and popular articles for magazines. He promoted the principle that growing wood as a farm crop was a distinctly different type of forestry than that practiced in industrial forests and public forests. The Society of American Foresters recognized his contributions to the profession by electing him a Fellow in 1948. He also was a member of Sigma Xi, the American Forestry Association, and Friends of the Land. Died August 24, 1967.

KENNETH B. POMEROY

Cosmos Club, Washington, D. C.
Division of Personnel, Soil Conservation Service, Washington, D. C.

PRICE, OVERTON WESTFELDT (1873–1914)

Born January 27, 1873, in Liverpool, England. Student at Biltmore Forest School in North Carolina, 1895–96. Then studied forestry at the University of Munich for two years, followed by a year of practical experience in European forests. In June, 1899 he entered the Division of Forestry of the United States Department of Agriculture as an agent; was promoted a year later to superintendent of working plans. When the Division became the Bureau of Forestry in 1901 he was advanced to associate forester and continued in this position when the Bureau was named the Forest Service in 1905. Much of the work of establishing national forestry on a sound and permanent basis is credited to his remarkable organizing and executive ability. In 1900 he was one of seven charter members of the Society of American Foresters, first chairman of its executive committee, vice president for five years, and a member of the editorial board of its *Proceedings*. In 1904 he lectured at Yale University on the practice of forestry in the Bureau of Forestry. In 1905 he participated in the American Forest Congress organized by the American Forestry Association. In 1910 he was discharged by President Taft for alleged complicity in the Ballinger-Pinchot controversy. Shortly afterward he became treasurer and vice president of the National Conservation Association, organized by Gifford Pinchot to assist in the "fight" for conservation. Later he was a consultant in organizing the Forest Branch of the Province of British Columbia, served as forester for the Letchworth Park Arboretum, and forestry advisor for the George W. Vanderbilt estate. He wrote *The Land We Live In*, a popular work on conservation for boys, and reports and articles on forestry. Died July 11, 1914.

KENNETH B. POMEROY

American Forestry 20(7):536, July 1914.
Forestry Quarterly 12(3):508–10, September 1914.
Journal of Forestry 38(11): 838, November 1940.

PRITCHARD, HAROLD WAYNE (1916–)

Born March 3, 1916 near Estevan, Saskatchewan, Canada; became a United States citizen in 1929. Iowa State University, B.S. (agricultural education) 1939. Taught vocational agriculture at Greene, Iowa, 1939–40, and at Early, Iowa, 1940–43. Served as public relations N.C.O. in the United States Army Air Force, 1943–45. Taught vocational agriculture at Sac City, Iowa, 1945–49, then was appointed executive secretary of the Iowa State Soil Conservation Committee, 1949–52. He was commended for service to the committee by the Iowa Association of Soil Conservation District Commissioners in 1951. In 1952 he was named executive secretary of the Soil Conservation Society of America, Ankeny, Iowa. After 14 years as executive secretary, during which period he was elected a Fellow, 1959, and received the Society President's citation, he was named executive director of the 12,000-member professional organization. His tenure includes service as editorial director of the *Journal of Soil and Water Conservation*, the Society's official publication. From 1960 to 1967, he was a member of the Forest Service Central States Advisory Council, and of the steering committee for the United States Department of Health, Education and Welfare's National Conference on Water Pollution in 1960. During 1966–67, he was chairman of the National Farm Institute. He was elected secretary of the Pan-American Soil Conservation Commission in 1966, the only member of the commission from North America. He is a co-author of the book *Origins of American Conservation*.

MAX SCHNEPF

Who's Who in America, 1968–69.

RASMUSSEN, BOYD LESTER (1913–   )

Born April 19, 1913 at Glenns Ferry, Idaho. Oregon State University, B.S. (forestry) 1935. Soon thereafter he started his career with the United States Forest Service at the Pacific Northwest Forest and Range Experiment Station in Portland, Oregon. From 1938 to 1942 he was a forest ranger on national forests in Oregon and Washington, then was a timber staff officer until 1950 when he became supervisor of the Siuslaw National Forest at Corvallis, Oregon. In 1952 he was assigned to the Forest Service's Division of Fire Control in Washington, D. C., was reassigned to the Intermountain Region at Ogden, Utah in 1954 as assistant regional forester, and was returned to Washington, D. C. in 1959 as assistant to the deputy chief in charge of national forest resource management. Two years later he was named regional forester of the Northern (Rocky Mountain) Region, at Missoula, Montana. Again he returned to Washington, D. C. in 1964 as deputy chief in charge of the Forest Service's cooperative forestry programs and its insect and disease control projects. In July 1966 he was appointed director of the Department of the Interior's Bureau of Land Management, the sixth director since the formation in 1946 of this bureau which has jurisdiction over 458 million acres, 20 per cent of the nation's total land area. He was granted the Department of the Interior's Honor Award for Distinguished Service in 1968, and serves on the President's Quetico-Superior Committee established in 1934. He is a permanent member of the Forestry Panel of the United States-Japan cooperative program on natural resources development, and is also a member of the task force established by the Secretary of the Interior in 1969 for the strengthening of regulations covering oil drilling and production on Alaska's Arctic North Slope.

HENRY CLEPPER

Who's Who in America, 1968–69.

REDFIELD, ALFRED CLARENCE (1890–)

Born November 15, 1890 in Philadelphia, Pennsylvania. Harvard University, B.S. (biology) 1914, Ph.D. (zoology) 1917; Cambridge 1920–21; Munich, 1930–31; University of Oslo, Ph.D. (honorary) 1956; Lehigh University, Sc.D. 1965; Memorial University of Newfoundland, Sc.D. 1967. After serving as instructor of physiology at Harvard, 1918–19, he was assistant professor of physiology at the University of Toronto, 1919–20, then again at Harvard, 1920–1930, associate professor, 1930–31, professor, 1931–57, and emeritus professor since 1957. He was also director, biological laboratories, at Harvard, 1934–35, and chairman of the Department of Biology, 1935–38. At the Woods Hole Oceanographic Institution he was senior biologist, 1930–36 and 1942–53, trustee since 1936, research associate, 1938–40, associate marine biologist, 1940–42, associate director, 1942–56, senior oceanographer, 1953–56, and emeritus senior oceanographer since 1957. He was managing editor of the *Biological Bulletin* from 1930 to 1942. He was trustee of the Marine Biological Laboratory from 1930 to 1953; has been trustee of the

Bermuda Biological Station since 1944, and was president from 1962 to 1966. The first chairman of the Natural Resources Council, 1946–48, he has been an honorary member since 1948. Member, National Academy of Sciences, Agassiz Medal, 1956; Physiological Society (secretary, 1929–30); Ecological Society of America (vice president, 1944, president 1945, eminent ecologist award, 1966); American Society of Limnology and Oceanography (president, 1956). A prolific writer on a wide range of subjects, one of his significant contributions was a paper, "The Biological Control of Chemical Factors in the Environment," *American Scientist* (46: 205–22). Conservation is one of the many areas in which he demonstrated a remarkable understanding.

GEORGE SPRUGEL, JR.

American Men of Science (The Physical and Biological Sciences), 11th ed., 1967.
Bulletin of the Ecological Society of America, vol. 47: no. 4, 1966; vol. 48: no. 4, 1967.
Who's Who in America, 1968–69.

REED, FRANKLIN WELD (1877–1949)

Born May 11, 1877 in Massachusetts. After two years at Harvard University, he entered the Biltmore Forest School in North Carolina and then studied forestry in Europe. Entering the Bureau of Forestry (now the Forest Service), United States Department of Agriculture, in 1902, he was assigned to making forest management working plans. In July 1910 he was appointed associate district (now regional) forester at Ogden, Utah, and in 1911 returned to the Washington, D. C. office as forest inspector. He resigned in 1913 to become forester for the Indian Service (now the Bureau of Indian Affairs), Department of the Interior, but re-entered the Forest Service a year later and in 1919 was made district forester of a new district embracing the entire eastern United States. Leaving the Forest Service in 1924, he engaged in private consulting practice. In 1926 he was with the National Conference on Outdoor Recreation and two years later became forester for the National Lumber Manufacturers Association. In 1931 he was appointed executive ecretary of the Society of American Foresters and managing editor of the *Journal of Forestry*, the Society's official organ. Following his retirement in 1936, he was made a life member of the Society. During 1931–32, he was also active in the work of the United States Timber Conservation Board, compiling information on the nation's timber supply and the condition of the forest industries. His various assignments in public and private forestry made him one of the well-known foresters of America. Died November 26, 1949.

HENRY CLEPPER

Journal of Forestry. Obituary, 48(1):69, January 1950.

REID, KENNETH ALEXANDER (1895–1956)

Born April 14, 1895 in Connellsville, Pennsylvania. Yale University, Ph.B. 1917. Resources conservation, with emphasis on water pollution abatement and control, and on fish and fishing, was an avocation until 1938, when he became executive director of the Izaak Walton League of America, Chicago. Prior to this he had been appointed to the Pennsylvania Fish Commission in 1932, and was instrumental in the establishment of a trout stream improvement demonstration area on Spring Creek in 1935, which, ironically, had to be closed in 1962 because of pollution. His leadership rebuilt the Izaak Walton League from a depression era weakling into a strong conservation instrument long before illness caused his retirement in the winter of 1948–49. He was a moving force in bringing about enactment of the first federal water pollution control law, Public Law 845 of the Eightieth Congress. He was cofounder of the Izaak Walton League Endowment in 1945, whose chief purpose is the acquisition of private interior holdings in what was then designated the Roadless Area (now the Boundary Waters Canoe Area) of Superior National Forest, Minnesota, to be turned over to the Forest Service in fee. He defended the creation of Jackson Hole National Monument, now a part of Grand Teton National Park, Wyoming; later a peak in the Grand Teton Range was named Mount Reid in his honor. Long an advocate of improved communication between the groups in the conservation movement, he was a cofounder of the Natural Resources Council of America. He had a leading role, for the Izaak Walton League, in opposition to the attempt to secure ownership of vast areas of public lands in the West by a consortium of livestock organization leaders and members of Congress, 1945–48. Author of many articles and editorials, mostly in *Outdoor America*, the magazine of the Izaak Walton League, of which he was editorial director. Memberships included Society of American Foresters, American Fisheries Society, and the Wildlife Society. Died May 21, 1956.

WILLIAM VOIGT, JR.

Who Was Who in America, 1951–56.

REYNOLDS, HARRIS AQUILA (1883–1953)

Born March 30, 1883 in West Newton, Pennsylvania. West Virginia University, Sc.B. (civil engineering) 1909; Harvard University, master of landscape architecture 1911. Soon after beginning the practice of landscape architecture in Boston in 1911, he became secretary of the Massachusetts Forestry Association, organized in 1898; renamed the Massachusetts Forest and Park Association in 1932, it would be the organization through which he would work for national programs in resource management over a period of four decades. In 1913 he studied communal forests in Europe, and returned to America to start the movement for community forests throughout the United States that resulted in the creation of 2,000 community forests embracing 3 million acres during his lifetime. Chairman of the Committee on Community Forests for the Society of American Foresters, he was known in New England as the father of town forests. Along with this movement he helped in the creation of state forests and parks, and promoted roadside beautification and the elimination of billboard advertising along state highways. He was a strong supporter of the Weeks Law of 1911 which resulted in the acquisition of the eastern national forests. In 1913 he was orga-

izing secretary of the American Plant Pest Committee which
elped obtain government appropriations for the control of the
white pine blister rust, Dutch elm disease, and pests of agricultural
crops. He also helped to form the National Conference on State
Parks in 1921. He was secretary of the National Forest Fire Preven-
ion Committee, set up in 1920, that helped with the enactment of
he Clarke-McNary Law of 1924 to provide cooperative fire control
etween the federal government of the states. He was chairman of
he National Committee on Farm Forestry Extension that succeeded
n obtaining legislation by which forestry was included in the activi-
ies of the Agricultural Extension Service. In 1944 he organized
he effective New England Forestry Foundation whose staff of pro-
essional foresters provides complete forestry services to private
owners at cost. He was one of the best known conservationists in
New England and was recognized as one of America's outstanding
conservation association executives. Died October 16, 1953.

HENRY CLEPPER

ournal of Forestry. Biography, 43(5):377, May 1945.

RICHARDS, THOMAS WITWER (1926–)

Born June 30, 1926 in Cumberland, Maryland. Dickinson College,
B.S. 1950; University of Maryland, M.A. 1951; graduate school,
University of Maryland, 1951–53. From 1954 to 1959, he was a geographic intelligence specialist, United States Air Force. From 1958
to 1960 he taught cartography and photo interpretation at George
Washington University. He joined International Business Machines
in 1961 and until 1968 was an advisory engineer; in this capacity
he managed teams conducting analysis and design of geographic
information systems at Air Force bases in Japan, Germany, and
South Carolina. In 1960 he became a member of the Arlington
County Board of Supervisors and was its chairman from 1963 to
1968. He has been a member of the Northern Virginia Regional
Planning Commission, the Northern Virginia Transportation Com-

mission, and chairman of the Land Use Committee of the Metro politan Washington Council of Governments. He is a member o the Audubon Naturalist Society of the Central Atlantic States. Sinc 1967 he has been president of the Nature Conservancy.

MARY JEAN CLEVELANI

RICKER, WILLIAM EDWIN (1908–)

Born August 11, 1908 at Waterdown, Ontario. University of Toronto Ph.D. 1936. In 1938 he was employed by the International Pacific Salmon Fisheries Commission and in 1939 went to the Department of Zoology, Indiana University, as director of the Indiana Lake and Stream Survey and director of the University Biological Station. In 1950 he became editor of the *Journal* of the Fisheries Research Board of Canada; in 1962, biological consultant to the Board; in 1963–64, acting chairman; and since 1965 he has been chief scientist. He has done much to increase the international stature of fisheries science. As the result of his interest in salmon biology and salmon management, he was responsible for important advances in the knowledge of the quantitative relationships between the food of young sockeye salmon, and their growth and mortality. More recently he has brought to light evidence of the balance between growth and mortality of salmon on the high seas—currently a subject of contention in international negotiations concerning high-seas fishing. For a report on new concepts of the relationship between parent stock size and the number of progeny, he received the Wildlife Society citation for the outstanding publication in fish ecology and management in 1953. Further recognition came in 1956 when he was invited to deliver the Edgardo Baldi Memorial Lecture at the Helsinki Congress of the International Association for Theoretical and Applied Limnology. For his *Handbook of Computations for Biological Statistics of Fish Populations*, he was again awarded the Wildlife Society citation in 1959. He has been directly responsible for translation of more than 100 Russian publications for research workers in the western world. An authority on stoneflies,

ne of several groups of insects which have an aquatic phase in
heir life history, he has written more than 20 publications on their
lassification and distribution for entomological and other journals.
n 1966 he was awarded the Gold Medal of the Professional Insti-
ute of the Public Service of Canada "for outstanding achievement
n the field of pure and applied science."

K. S. KETCHEN
P. A. LARKIN

ROCKEFELLER, JOHN DAVIDSON, JR.
1874–1960)

3orn January 29, 1874 in Cleveland, Ohio. Brown University, B.A.
'liberal arts) 1897, M.A. (honorary) 1914, LL.D. 1937. Upon
graduation, he became a business associate of his father. As a knowl-
edgable conservationist he helped preserve much of America's
natural and historical heritage. His early experiences in roadbuild-
ng, landscaping, and resource management on the family proper-
ies left him with an intense interest and appreciation for the
scientific and aesthetic details of conservation programming. His
perspective was both historical and visionary. He understood the
cultural value of environmental and historical preservation and believed that timely private initiative must demonstrate that value
to society and to those who govern it. Throughout his career, he
was concerned with the problems of the emerging National Park
Service. He was one of the individuals who, through the acquisition
and donation of land, were responsible for the establishment of
Acadia National Park. In a tour of the western parks in 1924, he
recognized the necessity of providing quality interpretive services
to the public and made an anonymous gift to the Park Service so
that the Mesa Verde Museum could be completed. Subsequently,
he made pilot funds available to establish museums at Yellowstone,
Grand Canyon, and Yosemite and to conduct general interpretive
studies of numerous park areas. During a second visit to the West in
1926, he undertook the anonymous acquisition of 33,000 acres in

Jackson Hole, Wyoming, which were later given to the federal gov ernment for the expansion and improvement of Grand Teto: National Park, and authorized the acquisition, through the Save the-Redwoods League, of the Bull Creek Grove, later renamed th Rockefeller Redwood Forest in his honor. In 1928, in response t: the cutting of privately owned sugar and yellow pine forests withir Yosemite National Park, he provided matching funds to the federa government to acquire the inholdings. A few years later, he agair came to the rescue of the pines and the *Sequoia giganteas* by assist ing California in the purchase of the Calaveras Groves. During thi same period, the Great Smoky Mountain and the Shenandoah Na tional Parks had been authorized by Congress on the condition tha the states which contained them would purchase all the necessar land. The funds he subsequently made available to Tennessee, Nortl Carolina, and Virginia insured the establishment of those parks Meanwhile, he had acquired and presented to the states of New York and New Jersey the scenic lands along the top of the Palisade escarpment. He had also undertaken the construction of Fort Tryoi Park and the Cloisters Museum for New York City. Active in his toric site preservation, he restored the complete colonial environ ment of Williamsburg, Virginia, the early Dutch manors of the Var Cordlandt and Philipse families, and Washington Irving's home Sunnyside. Although he declined most awards and other forms ol public recognition for his contributions to conservation, he did receive the Conservation Service Award of the Department ol Interior, the Audubon Medal for Distinguished Service to Conserva tion; the Gold Medal of the National Council of State Garden Clubs; honorary membership in the American Institute of Architects; and Fellowship in the Royal Society of Science. Died May 11, 1960.

HOLT BODINSON

FOSDICK, RAYMOND B. *John D. Rockefeller, Jr., a Portrait.* New York: Harper & Row, 1956.
NEWHALL, NANCY; OSBORN, FAIRFIELD; and ALBRIGHT, HORACE M. *A Contribution to the Heritage of Every American: the Conservation Activities of John D. Rocke- feller, Jr.* New York: Alfred A. Knopf, 1957.
Who Was Who in America, 1961–68.

ROCKEFELLER, LAURANCE SPELMAN (1910–)

Born May 26, 1910 in New York City. Princeton University, B.A. (philosophy) 1932. Honorary doctorates received from the State University College of Forestry at Syracuse University, 1961; George Washington University, 1964; Texas Technological College, 1966. In 1935 he began work in the family offices at Rockefeller Center in New York City where he became involved in the conservation and park activities of his father, John D. Rockefeller, Jr., and developed a philosophy of preservation and use which led him into an active conservation career in both the public and private spheres. His introduction to public service came in 1939 when the governor of New York appointed him a commissioner of the Palisades Interstate Park Commission; elected commission secretary in 1941 and vice president in 1960. He also acted as the commission's representative to the New York State Council of Parks and Outdoor Recreation, and in 1963 he was elected chairman of the council. In 1940 he was elected president of the newly formed Jackson Hole Preserve, Inc., the Rockefeller-sponsored nonprofit corporation, which, under his leadership, donated over 33,000 acres of land in Jackson Hole, Wyoming to the federal government in 1949 to be incorporated into the Grand Teton National Park. Later, in 1956, Jackson Hole Preserve, Inc. contributed 5,000 acres on the island of St. John to the government in order to initiate the establishment of the Virgin Islands National Park. To further his conservation goals, he established and became president of the American Conservation Association, Inc. in 1958. In that same year President Eisenhower appointed him chairman of the Outdoor Recreational Resources Review Commission. In 1965 President Johnson asked him to serve as chairman for the White House Conference on Natural Beauty. In 1966 he became the first president of the National Recreation and Park Association, and was appointed to the chairmanship of the President's Citizens' Advisory Committee on Recreation and Natural Beauty. Throughout his career has been associated with the New York Zoological Society and now serves as its president. He is a director of Resources for the Future, Inc. Awards for his contributions to conservation and outdoor recreation include the Medal of Freedom, presented by President Johnson; the Conservation Service Award of the Department of the Interior; the Horace Marden

Albright Scenic Preservation Medal of the American Scenic and Historic Preservation Society; the Fifty-Four Founders Award of the Izaak Walton League of America; the Distinguished Service Medal of the American Forestry Association; the Audubon Medal of the National Audubon Society; the Everly Gold Medal of the National Recreation and Park Association; the Frances K. Hutchinson Medal of the Garden Club of America; and the Gold Medal of the National Institute of the Social Sciences. He served as honorary president of the Izaak Walton League of America in 1963, and is an honorary member of the American Society of Landscape Architects and an honorary vice president of the American Forestry Association.

HOLT BODINSON

International Who's Who, 1968–69.
MORRIS, JOE ALEX. *The Rockefeller Brothers*. New York: Harper & Row, 1953.
Who's Who in America, 1968–69.

ROOSEVELT, THEODORE   (1858–1919)

Born October 27, 1858 in New York City. Graduated Phi Beta Kappa from Harvard University in 1880; awarded many honorary degrees in later years. He was president of the New York Police Board, 1895–97; assistant secretary of the Navy, 1897–98. Served as second in command (lieutenant colonel) of the 1st United States Cavalry Regiment during the war with Spain. He was elected governor of New York in 1898, and vice president of the United States in November 1900. He became president on September 14, 1901, following the assassination of William McKinley. He approved the Newlands Reclamation Act of 1902. He used the prestige of the presidency to assure the transfer of the administration of the federal forest reserves from the General Land Office in the Department of the Interior to the Forest Service in the Department of Agriculture on February 1, 1905. Gifford Pinchot, Roosevelt's friend for many years, was chief of the Forest Service and they worked together to implement a national program for the conservation of natural resources. Roosevelt withdrew a total of 234 million acres of public domain from entry as he created many national forests and mineral and coal reserves. He encouraged the Inland Waterways Commission, which was a prototype for regional, multiple-purpose resource development projects. He sponsored the first White House governors' conference in May 1908, which helped publicize the conservation movement. He was a founding member of the Boone and Crocket Club, associate member of the Society of American Foresters, and an Honorable Fellow of the American Museum of Natural History. He was author of many books, including *Winning the West*, 1889–96. Died January 6, 1919.

ELWOOD R. MAUNDER

Concise Dictionary of American Biography, 1964.
Dictionary of American Biography, 1935.
Facts About the Presidents, 2nd ed. New York: H. W. Wilson Company, 1968.
Who Was Who in America, 1897–1942.

ROTH, FILIBERT (1858–1925)

Born April 20, 1858 at Wilhelmsdorf, Württemberg, Germany. Came to the United States in 1870. University of Michigan, B.S. 1890; Marquette University, LL.D. (honorary) 1923. His microscopic studies of wood led to his appointment in 1893 as special agent and expert in timber physics in the Division of Forestry in the United States Department of Agriculture. He embarked on his career as a teacher in 1898 at the newly established New York State College of Forestry at Cornell University. After brief service in 1901 and 1902 as the first chief of the Forestry Division in the General Land Office in the Department of the Interior, he returned to teaching in 1903 as head of the Department of Forestry at the University of Michigan, the position he occupied until his retirement in 1923. He was the author of numerous articles and of textbooks on forest regulation and forest valuation. Other activities included service as Michigan's state forest warden and a member of its Conservation Commission; as an organizer and later president of the Michigan Forestry Association; and as a representative of the United States at the

International Forestry Congress at Brussels in 1910. He served as president of the Society of American Foresters in 1917 and 1918, and was one of the first six members to be elected a Fellow. A vigorous leader in many aspects of forestry, his outstanding contribution was as the respected and beloved master teacher of the hundreds of students who came under his influence. Died December 4, 1925.

SAMUEL T. DANA

DANA, SAMUEL T. "Filibert Roth—Master Teacher." *Michigan Alumnus Quarterly Review* 61(14): 100–110, 1955.
"Man, Teacher, and Leader—Filibert Roth." *Journal of Forestry* 24:12–18, 1926.
"Memorial." *Journal of Forestry* 24:2–3, 1926.

ROTHROCK, JOSEPH TRIMBLE (1839–1922)

Born April 9, 1839 in McVeytown, Pennsylvania. Preparatory education at Freeland Seminary (now Ursinus College). In 1862 enlisted in the Union Army, advanced to a captaincy in the 20th Regiment, Pennsylvania Volunteer Cavalry. Harvard University, B.S. 1864. University of Pennsylvania, M.D. 1867. Then taught botany at Pennsylvania State Agricultural College for two years. He became an authority in forest mycology, entomology, and medical botany. In 1869 he began the private practice of medicine. As surgeon and botanist for a Corps of Engineers exploratory expedition west of the 100th meridian from 1873 to 1875, he discovered and described numerous species of plants. In 1877 he was appointed F. Andre Michaux lecturer in forestry methods at the University of Strassburg, Germany, and returned home with a conviction of the need for forest conservation in the United States. In 1864 he helped organize the Pennsylvania Forestry Association, serving as its first president. When the governor of Pennsylvania appointed a commission in 1893 to examine forest conditions in the state, Rothrock was one of the commissioners and prepared most of the report. As a result, the legislature of 1895 established the Division of Forestry in the Department of Agriculture. Rothrock became the first commissioner of forestry, serving until 1904. During this period he initiated the acquisition of land for state forests (authorized in 1897). Recognizing the need for trained personnel to manage the forests, he was instrumental in establishing in 1903 the Pennsylvania State Forest Academy at Mont Alto, now a unit of the Pennsylvania State University. During his career, he was a vice president of the American Forestry Association. His long campaign for public education for forest conservation brought international recognition. He participated in the American Forest Congress of 1905 in Washington, D. C. and the Joint Conservation Congress, held in December 1908 in Washington, D. C. Among his many writings was *Areas of Desolation in Pennsylvania*, 1915. His achievements as the "father of forestry in Pennsylvania" were recognized in 1915 when the Society of American Foresters made him an honorary member. Died June 2, 1922.

KENNETH B. POMEROY

ILLICK, JOSEPH S. "Joseph Trimble Rothrock." The Pennsylvania German Society. Reprint from vol. 34, 1929.
Penn State Forestry Alumni Association. *Forestry Education in Pennsylvania*. University Park, Pa.: 1957.

SALYER, JOHN CLARK, II (1902–66)

Born August 16, 1902 in Higgensville, Missouri. Central College, A.B. (biology) 1927; University of Michigan, M.S. 1931. From 1927 to 1930, he was a science teacher in the public schools of Parsons, Kansas; was instructor in biology at Minot, North Dakota, 1932–33; then went to Iowa as the state biologist. In 1934 he entered the employ of the Bureau of Biological Survey, United States Department of Agriculture, predecessor of the Bureau of Sport Fisheries and Wildlife, Department of the Interior. He was head of the Bureau's Division of Wildlife Refuges until 1961 when ill health forced him to accept an advisory assignment in the Bureau. During the years that he headed the Division of Wildlife Refuges, the area dedicated to wildlife purposes rose from 1.5 million acres to nearly 29 million acres in 279 units. He is credited with having had a major role in the salvation of the duck restoration program of 1934–36. Known mainly as the father of the national wildlife refuge system, he received the American Motors Conservation Award in 1956 and the Distinguished Service Award of the Department of the Interior in 1962. Died August 15, 1966.

DANIEL A. POOLE

United States Bureau of Sport Fisheries and Wildlife. News releases and personnel materials on file, Washington, D.C.

SARGENT, CHARLES SPRAGUE (1841–1927)

Born April 24, 1841, in Boston, Massachusetts. Graduated from Harvard in 1862, LL.D. 1907. After service in the army (1862–65), he traveled abroad for three years furthering his knowledge of horticulture and landscape gardening. In 1873 he became the first director of the Arnold Arboretum and developed it into a world famous center for the study of trees and of plant introduction. He gathered together the Morris K. Jessup Collection of American Woods for the American Museum of Natural History (1881). His *Report on the Forests of North America* (1884) prepared for the Tenth Census (1880) was the first authoritative national survey of forest conditions. In 1884–85 he served as chairman of the New York forestry commission whose report led to the establishment of the Adirondack Forest Preserve and the beginnings of forest conservation in the state. He founded and edited the magazine *Garden and Forest* (1887–97), a publication that combined practical and scientific information for gardeners with discussion of forestry problems. In 1896–97 he was made chairman of a committee appointed by the National Academy of Sciences to investigate the inauguration of a forest policy for the United States. The committee's report led to the creation on February 22, 1897, of 13 new forest reserves (21 million acres) and in the following year to the first appropriations for protection and administration of the reserves. He was a Fellow of the American Academy of Arts and Sciences and a member or honorary member of more than 20 scientific societies around the world. In 1920 the Garden Club of America recognized his services to horticulture by presenting him with its first medal of honor. In 1923 he received the Frank N. Meyer horticultural medal from the American Genetics Association for distinguished service in the field of plant introduction. Of his many scientific publications, he is best known for the great *Silva of North America* (14 vols., 1891–1902), which laid the foundation of dendrology in North America. Died March 22, 1927.

JOSEPH A. MILLER

REHDER, ALFRED. "Charles Sprague Sargent" *Journal of the Arnold Arboretum,* vol. 8, April 1927.

SAWYER, ROBERT WILLIAM (1880–1959)

Born May 12, 1880 in Bangor, Maine. Harvard University, A.B. 1902, LL.B. 1905; University of Oregon, LL.D. 1937. Admitted to Massachusetts bar and practiced until 1910. Editor, *Bend* (Oregon) *Bulletin,* 1913–53. Judge of County Court, Deschutes County, Oregon, 1920–27. President, Oregon Reclamation Congress, 1931–37; president, National Reclamation Association, 1946–47; director, the American Forestry Association. An outstanding spokesman on reclamation and conservation affairs, he received in 1958 the American Forestry Association's Distinguished Service Award. A historian of note, his editorials had a great impact on the conservation direction of the nation. He supported sustained-yield forestry and multiple-use management of natural resources. He was responsible for setting aside a portion of the Deschutes River through Bend as a wildlife refuge, and for the establishment of several state parks in Oregon. An original founder of the Order of the Antelope. Active in campaigning against littering woods, streams, and trails. He served as a member of the Hoover Commission Task Force on Water and Power; a member of the United States Forest Service Region Six Advisory Board which wrote Oregon's basic forestry laws in the late 1930s; and chairman, Oregon State Highway Commission. As editor of a daily newspaper he stretched its influence far beyond the boundaries of its circulation area. Died October 13, 1959.

FRED E. HORNADAY

SCHENCK, CARL ALWIN (1868–1955)

Born March 25, 1868 in Darmstadt, Germany. Studied forestry at German universities, 1886–90, and entered the state forest service of Hesse-Darmstadt. Granted Ph.D. by University of Giessen in 1894, and honorary degree of Doctor of Forest Science by North Carolina State College in 1952. On recommendation of Gifford Pinchot, Schenck was appointed forester of the Biltmore estate, a 120,000-acre tract owned by George W. Vanderbilt in North Carolina, in 1895. He started the first American school of applied forestry at Biltmore September 1, 1898. A two-year course, it was never recognized as being of full professional standing, although some of its graduates were able foresters who served capably in government and industry. The school, disbanded in 1913, was comparable to a German "master school"; Schenck taught most of the courses himself. He wrote textbooks on forest management, mensuration, finance, silviculture, and logging and lumbering; these were used not only by Biltmore students, but at other later schools as well. He served in the German army during World War I, then returned to the United States where he lectured on forestry and taught at Montana State University. As one of the first forestry educators in the United States, he was a dominant leader who helped pioneer the new profession of forestry in America. He made his last visit to the United States in 1952 at the age of 84, and died in Lindenfels, Germany, May 15, 1955.

HENRY CLEPPER

The Biltmore Immortals, vol. 2. Privately printed, 1957.
SCHENCK, CARL ALWIN. The Baltimore Story. Edited by Ovid Butler. St. Paul, Minn.: American Forest History Foundation, 1955.

SCHMITZ, HENRY (1892–1965)

Born March 25, 1892, Seattle, Washington. University of Washington, B.S. (forestry) 1915, M.S. 1919; Washington University, St. Louis, Ph.D. 1919; University of Alaska, D.Sc. (honorary) 1955. Appointed instructor in forestry at the University of Idaho in 1919.

Following service in the Navy during World War I, he was promoted to professor of forestry in 1923. Named director of the Division of Forestry, University of Minnesota in 1925, he was advanced to the deanship of the College of Agriculture, Forestry, and Home Economics in 1944. In 1952 he became president of the University of Washington and served until retirement in 1958; then was president emeritus. He was vice president (1939) and a Fellow of the American Association for the Advancement of Science; vice president (1942) of the American Forestry Association; and honorary vice president and an organizer of the Fifth World Forestry Congress held in Seattle in 1960. Member, Botanical Society of America, American Phytopathological Society, and American Wood Preserves Association. He became a member of the Society of American Foresters in 1921; was elected Fellow in 1940; served as associate editor of the *Journal of Forestry* for nine years and editor-in-chief for four; president, 1942–45; recipient of the Sir William Schlich Memorial Medal in 1964. Contributed numerous papers to forestry, educational, and scientific journals on subjects ranging from wood-destroying fungi to higher education. At the time of his death he was writing a history of the College of Forestry, University of Washington. Died January 20, 1965.

SOCIETY OF AMERICAN FORESTERS

American Men of Science (The Physical and Biological Sciences), 10th ed., 1955.
Journal of Forestry. Obituary, vol. 63:230, March 1965.
Who Was Who in America, 1961–68.

SCHURZ, CARL (1829–1906)

Born March 2, 1829, in Liblar, near Cologne, Germany. Entered the University of Bonn in 1846 but was forced to flee before finishing because of his activities in the 1848 revolution. Later received honorary Doctor of Laws degrees from Harvard University, the University of Wisconsin, and Columbia University. Came to the United States in 1852 and settled in Wisconsin. Appointed minister to Spain in 1860 but resigned in 1861 to enter the Union army.

During the Civil War he commanded divisions at Fredericksburg, Gettysburg, and Chattanooga, and was discharged as major general. He was Washington correspondent of the New York *Tribune* (1865–66), editor of the Detroit *Daily Post* (1866–67), editor of the St. Louis *Westliche Post* (1867–68), and editor of the New York *Evening Post* (1881–83). Served as United States Senator from Missouri (1869–75) and Secretary of the Interior (1877–81), the first United States citizen of German birth to sit in a presidential cabinet. As Secretary he vigorously enforced the laws protecting government timber from trespassers and recommended policies of forest conservation—regulated timber sales, forest reserves, a federal forest service, and a national forestry commission. Ever the foe of patronage and corruption, he administered his department strictly on the merit system. He was an influential exponent of reform, high principles of public service, and enlightened citizenship. He was the author of *Speeches* (1865) and *Henry Clay* (1887). Died May 14, 1906.

JOSEPH A. MILLER

FUESS, CLAUDE M. *Carl Schurz, Reformer.* New York: 1932.

SCOTT, JOHN WILLIAM (1871–1956)

Born July 1, 1871 in Lewis County, Missouri. University of Missouri, B.A. 1894, M.A. 1897; University of Chicago, Ph.D. (zoology) 1904. After teaching biology in Kansas City high schools, he joined the Department of Zoology at Kansas State College in 1911. From 1913 until retirement he was head of the Department of Zoology at the University of Wyoming, where he was also professor of zoology and research parasitologist from 1913 to 1945, becoming emeritus professor in 1951. Author of numerous scientific papers with early research interests in marine biology and embryology, he later became interested in parasitology, first of domestic animals (he discovered the insect vector of swamp fever in horses) and then of wildlife. His studies of parasites of the sage grouse led him to a classic investigation of mating behavior in that species. Throughout his career he took an active part in conservation work, beginning in the 1920s. He worked through the Izaak Walton League, of which he was Wyoming state president; national director, 1934–46; and honorary president from 1952 until his death. An advocate of model game and fish laws, he was executive secretary of the Wyoming State Board of Fish and Game, 1937–39, and helped put into effect new policies of game management and conservation. Having traveled extensively in behalf of conservation, after his retirement he became chairman of the National Committee on Policies in Conservation Education and helped found the Conservation Education Association of which he became honorary president in 1953. Died August 15, 1956.

J. P. Scott

American Men of Science, 9th ed., 1955.

SCOTT, THOMAS GEORGE (1912–   )

Born May 22, 1912, at Youngstown, Ohio. Iowa State University, Ph.D. (zoology) 1942. Assistant to the state entomologist of Iowa in 1935. Extension wildlife conservation specialist, 1935–37, and instructor, 1938, at Iowa State University; then leader, Iowa Cooperative Wildlife Research Unit, and biologist, United States Fish and Wildlife Service, 1938–48. Was game specialist and head, Section of Wildlife Research, Illinois State Natural History Survey, 1950–63; adjunct professor of Zoology, Southern Illinois University, 1955–63; professor of zoology and senior staff member, Center of Zoonosis Research, University of Illinois, 1960–63. He then became head, Department of Fisheries and Wildlife, and associate director, Marine Science Center, Oregon State University. Received the Nash Conservation Award Certificate of Merit in 1957; was elected a Fellow of the American Association for the Advancement of Science in 1960; and in 1966 was recipient of the American Motors Professional Conservation Award. Was editor of *The Journal of Wildlife Management*, 1962–65; edited its *Third Ten-Year Index* for 1965–66; and served as president of the Wildlife Society in

1968. His professional affiliations include American Society of Mammalogists, Ecological Society of America, American Ornithologists' Union, and American Fisheries Society. Author of more than 80 titles in ornithology, mammalogy, wildlife management, food habits, conservation, and pesticides. His special research interests are predation, especially of the red fox, and wildlife ecology. Three of his important publications are *Some Food Coactions of the Northern Plains Red Fox*, Ecological Monographs 13, 1943; *Comparative Analysis of Red Fox Feeding Trends on Two Central Iowa Areas*, Iowa State College of Agriculture and Mechanical Arts Research Bulletin 353, 1947; and (senior author) *Red Foxes and a Declining Prey Population*, Southern Illinois University Monograph Series No. 1, 1955.

GLEN C. SANDERSON

American Men of Science (The Physical and Biological Sciences), 11th ed., 1965. *The Wildlife Society News*, 106, October 1966.

SEAMAN, ELWOOD ARMSTRONG (1916–   )

Born August 17, 1916 in Wheeling, West Virginia. College of Wooster, Ohio, B.A. 1939; University of Michigan, graduate work in fisheries biology, 1946–47; Marshall College, M.S. (aquatic biology) 1950. For three years beginning in 1939, he was a fisheries biologist for the Ohio Department of Conservation, then was a field executive with the Boy Scouts of America, 1941–42. During World War II, he served in the Navy and was engaged in research on malaria and filariasis. He was chief of the Division of Fisheries for the West Virginia Conservation Commission, 1946–54, then was head of a biological consulting firm in Pittsburgh, Pennsylvania. In 1956 he became executive secretary of the Sport Fishing Institute, Washington, D. C., and since 1957 he has been a special assistant for natural resources in the United States Department of the Air Force. Long active in the American Fisheries Society, he was secretary-treasurer from 1957 to 1966, vice president, and president in 1968. He originated the society's *Newsletter*, was largely responsible for its present quarterly *Journal*, and established the society's permanent headquarters in Washington, D. C. He is certified by the society as a fisheries scientist. He was associate editor of *Progressive Fish Culture*, 1952–55, and was on the governing board of the American Society of Ichthyologists and Herpetologists in 1957. He is a Fellow of the American Association for the Advancement of Science. In 1967 he was a member of the British Royal Society expedition to Aldabra Island in the Indian Ocean. He is the author of some 40 scientific papers on fish management and related subjects.

ROBERT F. HUTTON

American Men of Science (The Physical and Biological Sciences), 11th ed., 1967.
Who's Who in America, 1966–67.

SEARS, PAUL BIGELOW (1891–   )

Born December 17, 1891 in Bucyrus, Ohio. Ohio Wesleyan University, B.S. 1913, B.A. 1914, D.Sc. 1937; University of Nebraska, M.A. 1915, LL.D. 1957; University of Chicago, Ph.D. (botany) 1922; Marietta College, Litt.D. 1951; University of Arkansas, LL.D. 1957; Bowling Green State College, D.Sc. 1958; Oberlin College, D.Sc. 1958; Wayne State University, LL.D. 1959. Instructor in botany at Ohio State University, 1915–19; then assistant and associate professor at the University of Nebraska, 1919–27. Professor and head of the Botany Department at the University of Oklahoma, 1928–38; served also as botanist for the State Biological Survey of Oklahoma. From 1938 to 1950, he was a professor at Oberlin College, then in 1950 became affiliated with Yale University as a professor of conservation and as chairman of the Conservation Program, where he established the country's first graduate program in conservation of natural resources; became emeritus professor in 1960. For two years, 1953–55, he served also as chairman of the Yale Botany Department. He was president of the Ecological Society of America in 1948, and was president of the American Association for the Advancement of Science in 1956. He was a member of the National

Science Board, 1958–64. For two years he was visiting professor in the Tom Wallace Chair of Conservation at the University of Louisville. He served as president of the American Society of Naturalists and as chairman of the Yale Nature Preserve. He was also chairman of the board and honorary president of the National Audubon Society. The Ecological Society of America presented him the Eminent Ecologist award in 1965. He is the author of ten books, including *Deserts on the March*, 1935; *This is Our World*, 1937; *Life and the Environment*, 1939; *The Living Landscape*, 1964; and *Lands Beyond the Forest*, 1969.

THE CONSERVATION FOUNDATION

American Men of Science (The Physical and Biological Sciences), 11th ed., 1965.
International Who's Who, 30th ed., 1966–67.
World Who's Who in Science, 1968.

SETON, ERNEST THOMPSON (1860–1946)

Born August 19, 1860 in South Shields, Durham, England. He was educated in the Toronto, Canada, Collegiate Institute and the Royal Academy of Arts and Sciences in London. His interest in natural sciences arose from his early life on a Quebec farm. Following his art education abroad, he traveled throughout Canada and the United States, sketching and writing, mostly about wildlife, woodcraft, and nature lore. From 1898 onward, he was a popular lecturer on wildlife and natural resources. He was the cofounder of the Boy Scouts of America, and was the organization's chief scout from 1910 to 1916. Later he founded the Woodcraft League of America, which like the Boy Scouts was intended to inculcate the concepts of nature instruction and knowledge about the out-doors into the training of American youth. A prolific and successful author, he wrote *Wild Animals I Have Known* in 1898; it was followed by 40 additional books, one of the most popular of which was *Lives of Game Animals*, 1925, in four volumes. His last book *The Trail of an Artist Naturalist* was published in 1940. He was awarded the John Burroughs medal in 1928. Prior to his death he was president of the Seton Institute, Santa Fe, New Mexico. Died October 23, 1946.

FRED E. HORNADAY

Twentieth Century Authors. New York: H. W. Wilson Company, 1942.

SHANKLIN, JOHN FERGUSON (1903–)

Born February 9, 1903 on Fishers Island, New York. New York State College of Forestry, Syracuse, B.S. 1924. Privately employed until 1933, when he joined the National Park Service. In 1942 he was appointed a special assistant for land utilization in the office of the Secretary of the Interior; in 1944 he was made assistant director of forests, and director in 1947; forest conservationist in 1950; and chief of land-use management in the Division of Land Utilization in 1951. From 1950 to 1962, he was a forester in several divisions of the office of the Secretary. In 1962 he was named assistant director for federal coordination of the newly created Bureau of Outdoor Recreation. He retired from the Department of the Interior in April 1968, continuing as a consultant. Active in several conservation organizations, he was chairman (1951–52) of the Washington Section, Society of American Foresters, and was chairman (1948–62) of the society's Committee on Natural Areas which seeks to preserve under virgin conditions representative samples of the recognized forest types. He was a member of the Board of Governors of the Nature Conservancy, 1961–66, and since 1968 has been a director of the Forest History Society. For a quarter-century he has been active also in the Boy Scouts of America and since 1962 has been a member of the National Council's Conservation Committee. Author of several conservation publications of the Department of the Interior; co-author of the book *American Forestry: Six Decades of Growth,* 1960. Among the honors accorded him are the Silver Beaver by the Boy Scouts of America, 1957; the merit citation by the National Civil Service League, 1957; the Distinguished Service Award with gold medal by the Secretary of the Interior; and election to the grade of Fellow in the Society of American Foresters, 1961.

HENRY CLEPPER

American Men of Science (The Physical and Biological Sciences), 11th ed., 1965. *Who's Who in America*, 1968–69.

SHELDON, CHARLES (1867–1928)

Born October 17, 1867, at Rutland, Vermont. Yale University, civil engineering degree 1890. In 1898 he was engaged to handle mining and railroad interests in Mexico where he became interested in the desert bighorn sheep and, by the time of his retirement from active business in 1903, became the leading authority on this species. He then devoted full time to exploration and the study of wild sheep of North America. During 1906, 1907, and 1908 he explored the northern slopes of the Alaska Range and particularly Mount McKinley, where he engaged in mapping and collecting scientific specimens for the National Museum and the Bureau of Biological Survey. Largely as a result of his activity, this area was set aside as McKinley National Park. He was the author of the Alaska Game Law Act of 1925, a model for laws of its kind. He was largely instrumental in the calling of the National Conference on Outdoor Recreation by President Calvin Coolidge in 1924. He was active in the organization as well as the inception and conduct of the conference, which functioned until 1929. As a member of the Council of National Parks, Forests and Wildlife, he laid the groundwork for the establishment of Great Smoky Mountains National Park. In his later years he was involved in strengthening legislation for the protection of migratory game birds. He was chairman for many years of the Conservation Committee of the Boone and Crocket Club. From 1912 to 1918 he was a director of the American Game Protection Association. He was a member of the Explorers Club, New York Zoological Society, American Ornothologists' Union,

American Society of Mammalogists, and the Biological Society of Washington. Among his books were *The Wilderness of Denali, The Wilderness of the Upper Yukon,* and *The Wilderness of the North Pacific Coast Islands.* Died September 21, 1928.

JAMES B. TREFETHEN

Who Was Who in America, 1897–1942.
Who's Who in America, 1927–28.

SHELFORD, VICTOR ERNEST (1877–1968)

Born September 22, 1877 in Chemung, New York. University of Chicago, B.S. (biology), 1903, Ph.D. (zoology) 1907. Assistant in zoology at the University of West Virginia, 1900–1901, he then taught at the University of Chicago, 1904–14. Assistant professor at the University of Illinois, 1914–20; advanced to associate professor, 1920–27; professor, 1927–46; and emeritus professor, 1946–68. He was also biologist in charge of research laboratories for the Illinois Natural History Survey, 1914–29; and in charge of marine ecology, Puget Sound Biological Station, alternate years, 1914–30. Editor of the *Naturalists' Guide to the Americas,* 1926; also on the editorial board of *Ecology,* 1920–28. He was a member of the Board, Grasslands Research Foundation and was on the National Research Council's Committee on the Ecology of Grasslands, 1932–39, and the Committee on Wildlife, 1931–36. Vice chairman of the Organizing Committee for the Ecological Society of America, 1914–15, president in 1916, chairman of the Committee on the Preservation of Natural Conditions, 1917–38, and received the Eminent Ecologist Award in 1968. In 1946 he promoted the organization of the Ecologists' Union which later became the Nature Conservancy. Although he did much to establish physiological ecology and population ecology on a firm basis, his major contributions and efforts as well as reputation were in community ecology. The author of many scientific papers, his book, *Animal Communities in Temperate America,* 1913, is generally recognized as furnishing the impetus for getting animal ecology recognized as a distinct biological science. Greatly concerned with use of experimental studies both in the laboratory and in the field, he summarized his ideas, equipment, and methods in a book, *Laboratory and Field Ecology*, 1929. In order to expound his new biome concept he collaborated with Frederick E. Clements in producing a book on *Bio-Ecology*, 1939. His last major book, *The Ecology of North America*, 1963, was an effort to describe all of the biomes and major seral communities in North and Central America both with respect to vegetation and the animal constituents. He is often said to have been the father of animal ecology in the western hemisphere. Died December 27, 1968.

GEORGE SPRUGEL, JR.

American Men of Science, 9th ed., 1955.
Bulletin of the Ecological Society of America; vol. 48, no. 4, 1967; vol. 49, no. 3, 1968; vol. 50, no. 1, 1969.

SHERRARD, THOMAS HERRICK (1874–1941)

Born May 17, 1874 in Brooklyn, Michigan. Yale University, B.A. 1897; graduate work at Harvard University and at the forestry school of the University of Munich, Bavaria. From 1899 to 1907 he held various federal forestry assignments in Washington, D. C., and was appointed supervisor of the Pike National Forest in Colorado in 1907. A year later he became supervisor of the Mount Hood National Forest in Oregon, where he served until 1933. When the Civilian Conservation Corps program was organized in 1933, he was appointed CCC inspector for the North Pacific Region of the Forest Service, in Portland, Oregon. In 1935 he was assigned to the Division of Recreation and Lands, the position he held at the time of his death. He was one of the seven charter members of the Society of American Foresters, November 30, 1900. The Division of Geographic Names, Washington, D. C., in 1947 approved the naming of a viewpoint on Larch Mountain on the Mount Hood National Forest in Oregon in his honor. He was prominently identified in conservation circles as a public lands administrator who emphasized the use of forest lands for recreational purposes. He was also a codesigner of the well-known Forest Service pine tree shield badge. Died January 21, 1941.

ALBERT ARNST

Journal of Forestry. Obituary, 39:330, 1941.

SHIELDS, GEORGE OLIVER (1846–1925)

Born August 26, 1846 at Batavia, Ohio. He attended common school in Delaware County, Iowa; beyond that he was self-educated. He founded the magazine *Recreation* in 1894, continuing as editor and publisher until 1905 when it passed out of his hands; it was merged with *Outdoor Life* in 1927. He then published *Shields' Magazine* from 1905 until 1912. He used his publications to advance conservation causes, such as the Camp Fire Club, which he organized in 1897 and of which he was president from 1897 to 1902, and the League of American Sportsmen, which he founded in 1898 and of which he was the only president. The league declined as his personal fortunes declined after 1908, and it died with him. He crusaded for legal bag limits of game, for banning the automatic shotgun, and for other wildlife protective laws. He helped obtain passage by Congress of the Lacey Act in 1900, the first federal law regulating interstate commerce in and importation of wild birds and game. After the failure of his magazine, he devoted his full time to lecturing and writing on conservation. In his writings he used the pseudonym Coquina. He was the editor of *The Big Game of North America*, 1890, and of *American Game Fishes*, 1892, and was the author of five other books. Died November 10, 1925.

CHARLES H. CALLISON

Dictionary of American Biography, 9(1):106, 1936.
PEARSON, T. GILBERT. *Adventures in Bird Protection*, Chapter 19, pp. 336–45.
Who Was Who in America, 1897–1942.

SHIRLEY, HARDY LOMAX (1900–)

Born November 20, 1900 in Orleans, Indiana. Indiana University, A.B. (science) 1922; Yale University, Ph.D. (botany) 1928; University of Helsinki, honorary doctorate; Syracuse University, D.Sc. (honorary) 1966. After teaching mathematics at the University of Nevada, 1922–25, he was an assistant in biochemistry at the Boyce Thompson Institute of Plant Research, 1927–29. His career with the United States Forest Service began with appointment as silviculturist at the Lake States Forest Experiment at St. Paul, 1929–39; he then advanced to the directorship of the Allegheny (later named the Northeastern) Forest Experiment Station at Philadelphia, 1939–45. In 1945 he was appointed assistant dean of the State University of New York College of Forestry at Syracuse University, was promoted to the deanship in 1952, served in that position until his retirement in 1966, then was designated dean emeritus. His influence on higher education in forestry and related fields of natural resources management has been profound. For years he was chairman of the Advisory Committee in Education in Forestry for the Food and Agriculture Organization of the United Nations. He was a member of the Committee on Forestry for the National Research Council, 1933–37, and was a representative to Council's Division of Biology and Agriculture, 1944–46. He is a Fellow of the American Association for the Advancement of Science and of the Society of American Foresters on whose Council he served during 1944–45 and for which organization he functioned as editor-in-chief of the *Journal of Forestry* from 1946 to 1949. He has written widely on forestry and educational subjects for scientific and technical periodicals, and is author of the book *Forestry and its Career Opportunities*, 1967.

HENRY CLEPPER

American Men of Science (The Physical and Biological Sciences), 11th ed., 1967.
Journal of Forestry, 64(7):484, July 1966.
Who's Who in America, 1968–69.

SHOEMAKER, CARL DAVID (1872–1969)

Born June 20, 1872 in Napoleon, Ohio. Ohio State University, B.A. 1904, LL.B. 1907. After practicing law in Ohio, in 1912 he bought the *Evening News* in Roseburg, Oregon. In 1915, while publishing this newspaper, he was appointed head of the fish and game agency in Oregon, thus initiating a lifelong interest and career in conservation. After ten years as state game warden, he resigned to carry on private conservation work. He was commissioned by the states of Oregon and Washington to go to Washington, D. C., in 1928 in an effort to get an appropriation for the screening of irrigation ditches. In 1929 he was sent back to Washington, D. C., to work on fisheries conservation problems. Then in 1930 when the Special Committee of the Senate on Conservation of Wildlife Resources was established, he was first a special investigator and later secretary, a position he held until the subcommittee was abolished in December 1947. He was one of a group of five persons who prepared the original Coordination Act in 1934. He drafted the original Migratory Bird Hunting Stamp (Duck Stamp), the Pittman-Robertson Federal Aid in Wildlife Restoration Act (1937), and the Dingell-Johnson Federal Aid to Fisheries Act (1950). He joined J. N. (Ding) Darling and others in organizing the National Wildlife Federation in 1936. Long the federation's conservation director, he continued as its conservation consultant after his retirement. During his tenure, the Federation initiated services such as *Conservation News* and *Conservation Report*, which he edited until 1953, and the annual observance of National Wildlife Week. He was appointed as a member of the first Federal Water Pollution Control Advisory Board. He also served as an advisor to both the Departments of Agriculture and the Interior, and was general counsel for the International Association of Game, Fish and Conservation Commissioners from 1952 to 1960. He initiated the *Legislative News Service* for the Natural Resources Council of America and edited the organization's *Executive News Service* through 1960. In 1951 he was awarded the Aldo Leopold Memorial Medal by the Wildlife Society, and in 1953 he received the Department of the Interior's Special Citation for outstanding service. He also was the winner of the medal of honor in the Hunting and Fishing Hall of

Fame. He was an honorary president of the National Wildlife Federation and a life member of the Wildlife Society. Died April 2, 1969.

Louis S. Clapper

Journal of Wildlife Management. Obituary, 33(4):1055–56, October, 1969.

SIMMS, DENTON HARPER (1912–   )

Born December 21, 1912 in Alamogordo, New Mexico. University of Missouri, A.B. and B.J. 1935. He joined the United States Department of Agriculture in December 1935 as a messenger in the Albuquerque, New Mexico, regional office of the Soil Conservation Service. He became a member of the regional Information Division in 1938, head of the regional division in June 1943, and in June 1951 was promoted to director of the Information Division of SCS in Washington, D. C., where he gave meritorious and imaginative leadership in conservation information and education for 17 years. He directed the SCS information program during the period when the agency's responsibility grew from one mainly concerned with erosion control to one directly involved in more than 15 major activities. He retired March 1, 1968. He was elected a Fellow of the Soil Conservation Society of America in 1958, and was awarded Presidential Citations by SCSA in 1959 and again in 1962. Recipient of the American Motors Conservation Award in 1967 and of the United States Department of Agriculture's Superior Service Award in 1959. He is the author of many articles and publications in the field of soil and water conservation and writes and collects in the field of western American history. Author of *The Soil Conservation Service* (in press). He had the leadership for the conception, development, and publication of five conservation education cartoon booklets issued by the Soil Conservation Society of America; more than 8 million copies have been sold by the society's headquarters. Member of Outdoor Writers Association of America, the

Conservation Education Association, the Wilderness Society, the Audubon Naturalist Society, and the Soil Conservation Society of America.

F. GLENNON LOYD

Who's Who in the Southwest, vol. 5, 1956.

SIRI, WILLIAM EMIL (1919–   )

Born January 2, 1919 in Philadelphia, Pennsylvania. University of Chicago, 1937–43; University of California, 1947–50. In 1943 he was employed by the University of California as a research engineer and physicist; since 1945 he has been a bio-physicist on the staff of the university's Donner Laboratory. During the past two decades he has conducted a number of scientific expeditions abroad. He was leader of the California Himalayan Expedition in 1954; field leader of the International Physiological Expedition to Antarctica in 1957–58; leader of the University of California expeditions to Peru (Cordillera Blanca) in 1950 and 1952; and deputy leader of the American Mount Everest Expedition in 1963. A Sierra Club member since 1945, he has been on the Board of Directors since 1956, was president, 1964–66, and treasurer, 1966–69. He is also a director of the Sierra Club Foundation and of the Planning and Conservation League. He was president of the Save-the-Bay Association during the successful campaign to obtain permanent protection of San Francisco Bay from indiscriminate filling and dredging. Received the California Conservation Council Honor Award in 1965, the National Geographic Society Hubbard Medal in 1963, and the Elisha Kent Kane Medal of the Geographic Society of Philadelphia in 1964. Author of *A Rope Length from Eternity*, 1955; contributing photographer and writer for *Everest: The West Ridge*, 1965. He has written for magazines on high altitude physiology, conservation, and climbing.

LUELLA K. SAWYER

Sierra Club Handbook, 1967.
Who's Who in America, 1968–69.
Who's Who in the West, 11th ed., 1968.
World Who's Who in Science, 1968.

SMITH, ANTHONY WAYNE (1906–)

Born February 5, 1906 in Pittsburgh, Pennsylvania. University of Pittsburgh, A.B. 1926; Yale University School of Law, LL.B. 1934. During 1932–33, he was secretary to Governor Gifford Pinchot of Pennsylvania. He then was with a law firm in New York City, and was admitted to practice in the courts of New York State and the District of Columbia. From 1937 to 1956, he was assistant general counsel of the Congress of Industrial Organizations, was executive secretary of its Committee on Regional Development and Conservation, and held other assignments in the CIO. Since 1958 he has been president and general counsel of the National Parks Association, organized in 1919. He directs the Association's business, financial, and legal affairs, and the *National Parks Magazine*, the Association's official publication. A member of the Executive Committee of the Citizen's Committee on Natural Resources, he is also on the Steering Committee of the National Watershed Congress and on the Executive Committee of the Citizens' Conference on the Potomac River Basin. In addition, he is president of the South Central Pennsylvania Citizens' Association, an organization concerned with planning of the Potomac River basin. For two decades he has been active in organizations and movements for improved watershed management, river basin planning, forestry, soil conservation, and wildlife management.

CLARENCE COTTAM

SMITH, GLEN ALBERT (1880–1958)

Born September 15, 1880 near Rich Hill, Missouri. Largely self-educated in forest, range, and wildlife management. In early manhood worked in Kansas, Texas, and Montana on cattle drives, on cattle ranches, and in various capacities for lumber companies. Entered the United States Forest Service in 1907 and retired in 1942; served 35 years in three regions—30 in the Northern, two in the Intermountain, and three in the Rocky Mountain. His assignments were divided among several key administrative positions including ranger, supervisor, and assistant regional forester in charge of range and wildlife management. It is estimated that he traveled 40,000 miles with saddle and packhorses in the course of inspecting these activities. A wise and courageous administrator, he always placed the welfare of the resource above other considerations in dealing with the public or his fellow workers. Nontechnical himself, he knew the need for research and used it in his own work. He held the line against public pressure for increased grazing use of the forests in his region during World War I when damage from such use was continuing unchecked on most other western national forests. As assistant regional forester in the Intermountain Region he brought to light the damage that had been done there for years, and motivated a program working toward better watershed protection and conservative use of range and wildlife resources. He was founder, and for ten years chairman, of the Montana Sportsmen Association. He organized the Dude Ranchers Association. He was a member of the Society of American Foresters, and served on its Council. He was also a member of the American Society of Range Management. Died February 14, 1958.

LLOYD W. SWIFT

SMITH, HERBERT AUGUSTINE (1866–1944)

Born December 6, 1866 in Southampton, Massachusetts. Yale University, B.A. 1889, Ph.D. 1897. Entered the Bureau of Forestry (now the Forest Service) in 1901 in charge of editorial and public educational activities. He was one of the early group who spearheaded the forest conservation movement, and was a pioneer in introducing the study of conservation in the public schools. A student of economic and political history, he was for more than three decades an adviser to successive chiefs of the Forest Service for whom he prepared annual reports and wrote and edited other official papers. In 1908 he became a member of the editorial board of the *Proceedings* of the Society of American Foresters, predecessor publication of the *Journal of Forestry* on which he served as editor-in-chief from 1935 to 1937. One of the best informed men of his era on the history of the conservation movement, he assembled much material on the subject for deposit in the Library of Congress. His technical papers on the history of forestry and conservation set standards of literary quality for the profession. In 1939 he was elected a Fellow of the Society of American Foresters, the highest professional distinction within the power of the society to grant. Following his retirement from the Forest Service in 1937, he aided Gifford Pinchot in writing the latter's personal memoirs of the early history of the Forest Service. Died July 21, 1944.

HENRY CLEPPER

"Herbert A. Smith, 1866–1944," *Journal of Forestry.* 42:625–26, December 1944. *Who Was Who in America*, vol. 2, 1943–50.

SNIESZKO, STANISLAS FRANCIS (1902–   )

Born January 28, 1902 in Krzyz, Poland. Jagiellonian University, M.S. (bacteriology) 1924, Ph.D. 1926. He was awarded a Polish government fellowship in Leipzig in 1928 and a Rockefeller fellowship at the University of Wisconsin during 1930–31. In 1936 he became assistant in bacteriology at the University of Maine, advancing to assistant professor. After United States naturalization in 1944 he served in the United States army during World War II making chemical and biological studies. In 1946 he became chief bacteriologist and laboratory director at the Eastern Fish Disease Laboratory, United States Fish and Wildlife Service, Kearneysville, West Virginia. Chairman of the Fish Disease Committee of the American Fisheries Society for many years, he was elected an Honorary Member of the society in 1966. He is the editor of the *Symposium on Diseases of Fishes and Shellfishes* published by the American Fisheries Society in 1970. Author of more than 100 scientific papers on fish diseases, fish pathology, cellulose decomposition bacteria, and miscellaneous viral and bacterial subjects. His studies have been published in German, French, and Polish journals. He holds professional certification as a fisheries scientist in the American Fisheries Society, is a Fellow of the American Association for the Advancement of Science, and a member of the Society of Microbiologists, Society of Experimental Biologists, and New York Academy of Science.

ELWOOD A. SEAMAN

American Men of Science (The Physical and Biological Sciences), 11th ed., 1967.

SPURR, STEPHEN HOPKINS (1918–   )

Born February 14, 1918, in Washington, D. C. University of Florida, B.S. (botany) 1938; Yale University, M.F. 1940, Ph.D. 1950. His research career began at the Harvard Forest in 1940 where he served as acting director and assistant professor. During 1950–52 he was associate professor of forestry at the University of Minnesota. Since 1952 he has been on the faculty of the University of Michigan as professor of silviculture, dean of the School of Natural Resources (1962–65), and dean of the Horace H. Rackham School of Graduate Studies since 1965. While at Harvard Forest he gained an international reputation in photographic interpretation as the author of *Aerial Photographs in Forestry* (1948), and its revision *Photogrammetry and Photo-interpretation* (1960). From this work with aerial photographs he became involved in various studies of the measurement of significant characteristics of forests, and published *Forest Inventory* (1952). In addition to research in remote sensing and measurements, he carried out a wide range of studies in silviculture and ecology. He was an Oberlaender Trust Fellow in Germany in 1950, became a National Science Foundation Science Fellow at the University of California, Berkeley, during 1957–58; and served as a Fulbright Research Scholar in New Zealand and Australia in 1960. He became the second American to be chosen an honorary member of the New Zealand Institute of Foresters. A National Science Foundation Science faculty fellowship gave him the opportunity for further study and writing, and in 1964 he published *Forest Ecology*. He has held numerous committee and executive assignments, including six years on the Council of the Society of American Foresters; and was the founder and first editor of its journal *Forest Science*. His interest in the social aspects of resource use is reflected in his service as leader of a study team which analyzed the Rampart Dam proposal in Alaska for the National Resources Council. Current studies include organization of higher education in the United States as it pertains to graduate programs and the administration of complex universities. He was one of the founders of the Organization for Tropical Studies and served as its President in 1967 and 1968. He was appointed president of the University of Texas in 1971.

R. KEITH ARNOLD

American Men of Science, 11th ed., 1965.
Who's Who in America, 1968–69.

STAHR, ELVIS JACOB, JR. (1916–   )

Born March 9, 1916 in Hickman, Kentucky. University of Kentucky, A.B. 1936; Oxford University (Rhodes scholar), B.A. 1938, B.C.L. 1939, M.A. 1943. Recipient of 20 honorary degrees. He was appointed president of the National Audubon Society in October, 1968, after a distinguished career as public administrator and educator. He was named one of "Ten Outstanding Young Men of America" by the United States Junior Chamber of Commerce in 1948. His positions included dean of the College of Law and provost of the University of Kentucky; vice chancellor of the University of Pittsburgh; president of West Virginia University; Secretary of the Army, 1961–62; president of Indiana University, 1962–68. He served as special assistant to the Secretary of the Army during much of the Korean War, and in 1956–57 was executive director of President Eisenhower's Committee on Education Beyond High School. Currently, he is a trustee of the Committee for Economic Development of Transylvania University and member of the Boards of the Governmental Affairs Institute and of the National Association of Educational Broadcasters. He is also a trustee of the Association of the United States Army, of which he is chairman and past president. As Audubon president he quickly established new emphasis on the Society's educational programs and in 1969 organized a coalition of conservation organizations to oppose a large jetport at a site near Everglades National Park, Florida.

CHARLES H. CALLISON

National Audubon Society. Staff biographies.
Who's Who in America, 1968–69.

STEPHENS, EDWIN SYDNEY (1881–1948)

Born September 4, 1881 in Columbia, Missouri. University of Missouri, A.B. 1903. After a year at Harvard University, he entered Stephens Publishing Company and became president of the family firm in 1931. For 30 years he was an ardent sportsman. Then, in a wildlife crisis, he led a reform movement in Missouri that would reach from his state to affect wildlife management of all states. He knew that no effective change comes by realignment of titles; in 1935, seeing political wildlife management fail, he demanded new concepts through the Conservation Federation of Missouri which he led in a campaign to amend the state constitution through initiative petition. In the end Missouri adopted a constitutional amendment that gave power to a four-man Conservation Commission. The principle and the legal provisions have survived unchanged since 1936 partly because he accepted the chairmanship of the Commission, and in ten years created a strong tradition of nonpartisan policy-making that did not interfere with professional administration. What he stood for seems obvious now: long-range programs and research, technical skill, nonpolitical decisions; but it was new in 1936. Aldo Leopold wrote of him, "(He) belongs to a group of conservationists . . . who might be called the statesmen of wildlife management . . . because they created the legal, political, and financial framework within which it could operate." He was an honorary life member of the Wildlife Society and the Outdoor Writers Association of America; and honorary life president of the Conservation Federation. Died October 17, 1948.

DAN SAULTS

CALLISON, CHARLES. *Man and Wildlife in Missouri.* Published in 1950. *The Missouri Conservationist,* December 1948 (special edition).

STODDARD, HERBERT LEE, SR. (1889–1970)

Born February 24, 1889 in Rockford, Illinois. Self-educated in ornithology, ecology, and forest-wildlife management. Early in his career he worked as a taxidermist in natural history museums; during 1910–13 and 1920–24 with the ornithology division of Milwaukee Public Museum, Milwaukee, Wisconsin, and during 1913–20 with the Field Museum of Natural History of Chicago. He joined the United States Biological Survey, United States Department of Agriculture, in 1924 as leader of the Cooperative Quail Study Investigation. On completion of this research and after a year in Washington, D. C., where he assisted with the organization of the first game management fellowships, he resigned in 1931 to become director of the Cooperative Quail Study Association at Thomasville, Georgia, a research, service, and consulting organization. Since 1943, when this organization disbanded, he has been a consultant in upland game and forest management in the Deep South. He was active in the organization of the Inland Bird Banding Association, was its first treasurer in 1922, and served for many years on the National Advisory Committee on waterfowl. Author of numerous ornithological and wildlife management papers, his book *The Bobwhite Quail; Its Habits, Preservation and Increase,* 1931, won for him the Brewster Medal awarded by the American Ornithologists' Union in 1936. When Tall Timbers Research, Inc., a privately endowed institution dedicated to biological research, and particularly to the ecology of fire, was established in 1959, he was elected vice president and became president in 1963. He received the *Outdoor Life* award in 1928 for wildlife conservation Eastern Division. He was elected a Life Fellow of the American Ornithologists' Union in 1936, an honorary member of the Wildlife Society in 1940 and of the Wisconsin Society of Ornithologists, Inc. in 1940. Died November 19, 1970.

Roy Kamarek

American Men of Science (The Physical and Biological Sciences), 11th ed., 1965. Stoddard, H. L. Memoirs of a Naturalist. University of Oklahoma Press, 1969.

STROUD, RICHARD HAMILTON (1918–)

Born April 24, 1918 in Dedham, Massachusetts. Bowdoin College, B.S. (biological sciences) 1939; University of New Hampshire, M.S. (zoology and fisheries) 1942; graduate work in ecology at Yale University in 1948 and in education at Boston University in 1949. In 1942 he joined the reservoir research staff of the Biological Readjustment Division (later Fish and Game Branch), Tennessee Valley Authority, where he served until 1947 as a fishery research specialist, interrupted by three years of military services in World War II. In 1949 he joined the Massachusetts Division of Fisheries and Game where he served for five years as that state's first chief aquatic biologist. In August 1953, he became assistant executive vice president of the Sport Fishing Institute, Washington, D. C., and since 1955 has been executive vice president. He has served on many federal, state, and private conservation advisory groups, including the Department of the Interior Advisory Committee on Fish and Wildlife; Technical Subcommittee of the International Commission for the Prevention of Pollution of the Sea by Oil; Board of Consultants, the California Fish and Wildlife Plan; Governing Board, the American Institute of Biological Sciences; United States Public Health Service Advisory Commission on Water Quality Criteria Research; and advisor to United States Delegation to Conference of Plenipotentiaries on Conservation of Atlantic Tunas. A frequent member of the various committees of the American Fisheries Society, he is a fishery expert advisor to the Senate Select Committee on Government Operations, member of the World Panel of Fishery Experts of the United Nations, and a member of the Fishing Industry Advisory Committee of the State Department. He is founder and vice president of Sport Fishery Research Foundation, and is a certified fishery scientist (American Fisheries Society). He served as treasurer of the Natural Resources Council of America from 1961 to 1967, was vice chairman during 1968–1969, and was elected chairman for 1970. He has served continuously since 1956 on the Conservation and Jamboree Committees, Boy Scouts of America, and is a member-at-large of the National Council. He has published more than 30 scientific and semi-technical papers, several of book length on his fishery research findings and fish management activities, as well as several textbook chapters and numerous popular articles on fish conservation. These include "Fish Conservation" in *The Fisherman's Encyclopedia*, 1963, and *Fisheries Report for Some Central, Eastern and Western Massachusetts Lakes, Ponds, and Reservoirs* (1951–52), 1955. He is editor of the *SFI Bulletin* and of *Fish Conservation Highlights*, both published by the Sport Fishing Institute.

P. A. Douglas

American Men of Science (The Physical and Biological Sciences), 11th ed., 1967.

STUART, ROBERT YOUNG (1883–1933)

Born February 13, 1883 in Cumberland County, Pennsylvania. Dickinson College, A.B. 1903, M.A. 1906, D.Sc. (honorary); Yale School of Forestry, M.F. 1906. He was appointed in July 1906 as forest assistant in the United States Forest Service and was assigned to timber sales in Montana. Two years later he was promoted to inspector in the district headquarters at Missoula; in 1910 was advanced to assistant district forester; and in 1912 was transferred to the Washington, D. C. office as assistant to the chief of the Branch of Silviculture. In 1917 he was commissioned captain in the 10th (Forest) Engineers, was sent to France for duty in timber acquisition for the Army, and in 1919 was promoted to major in the 20th (Forest) Engineer Regiment. Returned to the Forest Service in 1919. He was selected in 1920 by Gifford Pinchot, Commissioner of Forestry in Pennsylvania, to be his deputy, and became Commissioner himself in 1922. On the creation of the Pennsylvania Department of Forests and Waters, during Pinchot's governorship, Stuart became its first Secretary, a cabinet position. He re-entered the Forest Service in 1927, and was advanced to chief on May 1, 1928. During the early years of his administration, his leadership kept the Forest Service active and efficient despite pressures for retrenchment in federal expenditures and personnel. With the advent of the Franklin D. Roosevelt administration, he helped prepare the Forest Service for the expanded role it would play under the New Deal. As chairman of the Forest Protection Board, he notably advanced the standards of protection of federal timber lands. He served for eight years on the Council of the Society of American Foresters, was president in 1927, and was elected a Fellow in 1930. Died October 23, 1933.

HENRY CLEPPER

SMITH, HERBERT A. "Robert Young Stuart." *Journal of Forestry*, 29:885–90, December 1933.

SUDWORTH, GEORGE BISHOP (1864–1927)

Born August 31, 1864 in Kingston, Wisconsin. University of Michigan, A.B. 1885. After teaching botany at Michigan Agricultural College during 1885–86, he became botanist in the Division of Forestry, United States Department of Agriculture, 1886–95; was dendrologist in the Bureau of Forestry, 1895–1904; and chief of dendrology in the Forest Service from 1904 until his death. He explored many of the early western forest reserves on foot, and discovered and named numerous new species and varieties of trees and plants. He was the author of scores of publications on dendrology and forestry, and was a leading authority on the subject. His *Check List of North American Forest Trees*, first published in 1898 and reissued since, is a classic reference work of nomenclature and range of native trees. Among his other publications on dendrology are *Forest Flora of the Rocky Mountain Region*, *Forest Flora of Tennessee*, *Nomenclature of the Arborescent Flora of the United*

States, Trees of the United States Important in Forestry, The Forest Nursery, and *Forest Trees of the Pacific Slope*. For the last 15 of his 41 years with the Forest Service he was a member of the Federal Horticultural Board which was responsible for policies relating to the shipment of plants and nursery stock to prevent the spread of plant diseases and insect pests. He was an active member of the Society of American Foresters and of other scientific and botanical organizations. Died May 10, 1927.

HENRY CLEPPER

Journal of Forestry. Obituary, 25:511–12, May 1927.
Who Was Who in America, 1897–1942.

SWANK, WENDELL GEORGE (1917–)

Born September 13, 1917 in Brownsville, Pennsylvania. West Virginia University B.S. (forestry), 1941; University of Michigan, M.S. (wildlife management), 1943; Agricultural and Mechanical College of Texas, Ph.D. 1951. He began his career with the West Virginia Conservation Commission as a research biologist on fur-bearers and forest wildlife from 1945 to 1948. He was instructor in wildlife management at the Agricultural and Mechanical College of Texas, 1948–51; and at the University of Arizona, 1951–52. Joining the Arizona Game and Fish Department in 1952, he led the statewide wildlife research and management project until 1956. As recipient of a Fulbright Award in 1956, he spent a year studying wildlife in Uganda and Kenya. Returning to Arizona in 1957, he was named assistant director of the Department in 1958, and was advanced to director in 1964. In June 1968 he accepted a position as head of the Wildlife Division for the East African Agriculture and Forestry Research Organization of the United Nations at Nairobi, Kenya, supervising and coordinating wildlife management and research work in three East African nations. As regional representative of the Wildlife Society he was instrumental in establishing the New Mexico-Arizona Section and served two terms as president of the parent society from 1962 to 1964. He is a member of the Society of American Mammalogists, the Fauna Preservation Society, and the Wildlife Disease Association. He was a member of the International Association of Game, Fish and Conservation Commissioners, and served on its executive committee, 1966–68. He is the author of the bulletins, *Beaver Ecology and Management in West Virginia* and *The Mule Deer in Arizona Chaparral*, together with other publications on nutria, mourning dove, pheasant, mule deer, and African wildlife.

ROBERT A. JANTZEN

American Men of Science (The Physical and Biological Sciences), 11th ed., 1966.
Who's Who in America, 1968–69.
Who's Who in the West, 17th ed., 1960.
The Wildlife Society News, no. 83, November 1962.

SWANSON, GUSTAV ADOLPH (1910–)

Born February 13, 1910 in Mamre, Minnesota. University of Minnesota, B.S. (education), 1930; M.A. 1932; Ph.D. (biological science) 1937. He served as biologist with the Soil Conservation Service in 1935, and with the Minnesota Conservation Commission during 1935–36. In 1937 he taught game management at the University of Maine, then returned to the University of Minnesota as professor of economic zoology from 1937 to 1944. Joined the United States Fish and Wildlife Service as wildlife biologist in 1944; spent 1946–48 in Washington as chief, Division of Wildlife Research. At Cornell University he was head of the Department of Conservation from 1948 to 1966 and director of the Cornell Laboratory of Ornithology from 1958 to 1961. He has been head of the Department of Fishery and Wildlife Biology at Colorado State University since 1966. He was on leave in Denmark and other Scandinavian countries during 1954–55, and 1961–62, when he also served as consultant to the United Kingdom Nature Conservancy. While at Cornell he served as consultant to several New York State Legislative Committees on matters of conservation and made special contributions in the development of the New York Fish and Wildlife Management Act and in programs of conservation education for citizen leaders. In the Wildlife Society he was vice president in 1945, president during 1954–55, and editor of the *Journal of Wildlife Management*, 1949–53. He served on the Board of Directors of the National Audubon Society from 1950 to 1956. In 1968 he spent six months as visiting professor of conservation at the University of New England, Armidale, New South Wales, Australia. Author of many scientific publications and with Thaddeus Surber and T. S. Roberts of *The Mammals of Minnesota*, 1945. His activity as organizer, consultant and advisor in the field of natural resource conservation is appreciated by colleagues worldwide.

OLIVER H. HEWITT

Who's Who in America, 1966–67.

SWIFT, ERNEST FREMONT (1897–1968)

Born September 15, 1897 in Tracy, Minnesota. Graduated from high school and enlisted in the Army in 1917. In 1926 he was appointed a state conservation warden in Wisconsin. The next 28 years were spent in the service of the Wisconsin Department of Conservation where he rose from the ranks to the directorship, which he held from 1947 to 1954. Under his administration the department employed trained biologists to get information upon which sound programs in fish and game management could be based. In 1954 he was designated assistant director of the United States Fish and Wildlife Service, Washington, D. C., but resigned the following year to become executive director of the National Wildlife Federation, from which position he retired in 1960 though continuing as a consultant. He was the recipient of two score awards and citations, including the Haskell Noyes Conservation Warden Efficiency Award in 1930; the Wildlife Society's Aldo Leopold Medal in 1959; and a Gold Medallion for contributions to the welfare of Wisconsin in 1966. The author of numerous articles on practical conservation topics, as well as *A History of Wisconsin Deer* and *A Conservation Saga*, published in 1967. Died July 24, 1968.

Russ J. Neugebauer

SWIFT, LLOYD WESLEY (1904–)

Born September 5, 1904 in Ione, California. University of California, B.S. 1927, M.S. (forestry) 1928. His career with the United States Forest Service spanned 35 years, beginning with field positions in the West Coast and Rocky Mountain regions. From 1943 to 1963, he was director of the Division of Wildlife Management in the Branch of National Forest Administration, Washington, D. C. In this position he was responsible for the wildlife management program on 180 million acres. Cooperative activities with the state game administrations were much improved; habitat management projects were undertaken, the forest officers gave increasing attention to the rare and vanishing species, and fisheries scientists were employed in all regions. From 1963 to 1966, he was executive director of the World Wildlife Fund, formed in 1961 to undertake worldwide programs for saving rare and endangered species. His foreign assignments in behalf of various international organizations included tours of duty in East and Central Africa, Ethiopia, Israel, Turkey, and Botswana. He was a member of the secretariat for the Fifth World Forestry Congress in Seattle in 1960 and a member of the United States delegation to the Sixth World Forestry Congress in Spain in 1966. In 1967 he became a special consultant for forest recreation and wildlife for the National Wildlife Federation. He was the first chairman of the Division of Wildlife Management, Society of American Foresters. He is a trustee of the Wildlife Society and a director of the World Wildlife Fund. He has contributed technical papers to the *Journal of Wildlife Management*, the *Journal of Mammalogy*, and other publications.

James D. Davis

SWINGLE, HOMER SCOTT (1902–   )

Born July 29, 1902 in Columbus, Ohio. Ohio State University, B.S. 1924, M.S. 1925, D.Sc. (honorary) 1958. He first worked as an entomologist, but in 1934 initiated a program of fisheries research at Auburn University which under his direction has developed into the largest warm-water fisheries research station in the world with 200 experimental ponds comprising 200 surface acres of water. An especially effective teacher, he developed a curriculum in fisheries management and actively participated in training over 100 graduate students from the United States and 20 foreign countries. He was appointed collaborator by the United States Soil Conservation Service in 1937 and by the United States Fish and Wildlife Service in 1946; received the Conservation Service Award of the Department of the Interior in 1951; was appointed United States representative on pondfish culture to the Eighth (1953) and Ninth (1957) Pacific Science Conferences, and served as convenor of the Symposium on Recent Advances on Pondfish Cultures at the Tenth (1961) Conference. He received the Nash Conservation Award for research and teaching contributions to fisheries management in 1954 and was selected Man-of-the-Year in Southern Agriculture by the *Progressive Farmer* in 1958. He served as fisheries consultant to the governments of Israel and Thailand in 1957 and to India in 1961. In 1964 he participated in planning sessions in Rome for the World Symposium on Warm-Water Pondfish Culture, sponsored by the Food and Agriculture Organization of the United Nations, and in 1966 served as the symposium chairman. The Aldo Leopold Memorial Medal was awarded him by the Wildlife Society in 1966. He was president of the American Fisheries Society in 1958, and was elected to Honorary Membership in 1966. In May 1968 Auburn University appointed him alumni research professor of fisheries, the first research chair provided under the program. Currently, he is head of the Department of Fisheries and Allied Aquacultures and director of the International Center for Aquacultures at Auburn University. He has written more than 100 papers relating to fisheries management.

DONOVAN D. MOSS

American Men of Science (The Physical and Biological Sciences), 11th ed., 1967.
Who's Who in the South and Southwest, 1956.

TABOR, PAUL (1893–)

Born March 13, 1893, in Danielsville, Georgia. University of Georgia, B.A. 1914, M.S. (agronomy) 1915. He then served as a field agent for the University of Georgia College of Agriculture, 1915–16; as extension agronomist, 1919–22; and as professor of agronomy, 1922–34. Joined the Soil Conservation Service, United States Department of Agriculture, as agronomist in 1934; worked with soil conserving plants until his retirement in March 1963. During his career, he introduced kobe lespedeza and browntop millet on the Sandy Creek Project near Athens, Georgia, supervised testing of soil conserving plants at nine Soil Conservation Service nurseries in the Southeast, and searched for new plants of practical value in saving soil and water. He assisted in the introduction of tall fescue and bahia grasses and the early distribution of Coastal Bermuda and Pangola grasses throughout the Southeast. His contributions have had extensive value to the conservation programs of the South. He is the author of numerous technical articles in the McGraw-Hill *Encyclopedia of Science and Technology*, of portions of *Grassland Seeds* by Wheeler and Hill, and has made numerous contributions to the *Journal of Soil and Water Conservation, Journal of Agronomy, Soil Conservation, Agricultural History, Crop Science,* and *Progressive Farmer.* A charter member and Fellow of the Soil Conservation Society of America, he is also a Fellow of the American Association for Advancement of Science.

H. WAYNE PRITCHARD

American Men of Science (The Physical and Biological Sciences), 11th ed.,

TARZWELL, CLARENCE MATTHEW (1907–)

Born September 29, 1907 in Deckerville, Michigan. University of Michigan, A.B. 1930, M.S. 1932, Ph.D. (aquatic biology and fishery management) 1936. He was with the Institute for Fisheries Research, Michigan Department of Conservation, 1930–34, then became an aquatic biologist for the United States Bureau of Fisheries, and served as assistant range examiner for the United States Forest

Service from 1934 to 1938. There followed an appointment as an
aquatic biologist in the Biological Readjustment Division, Tennessee
Valley Authority. He left after two years to join the staff of the
United States Public Health Service in Georgia as a sanitary
engineer until 1946. Became chief aquatic biologist at the Environmental Health Center of the Public Health Service in Ohio in 1948,
and was reassigned in 1953 to the Robert A. Taft Engineering
Center, directing a water quality research program until 1965.
During the next two years, he was acting director of the Research
Division of the National Water Quality Laboratory, Federal Water
Pollution Control Administration, Duluth, Minnesota, as well as
director of the National Marine Water Quality Laboratory, Narragansett, Rhode Island, his present position. He has been a member of the Research Committee for the Water Pollution Control
Federation; of the advisory group on waste treatment at the
Engineering Experimental Station of Ohio State University from
1957 to 1959; and of the Committee for Standard Methods since
1968; of the Aquatic Life Advisory Committee for the control of
stream temperature for the Pennsylvania Sanitary Water Board
from 1959 to 1962; of the Advisory Committee for water quality
criteria of the California State Water Pollution Control Board from
1961 to 1963; and also served on the Natural Resources Council of
the National Academy of Sciences from 1961 to 1963. Since 1962
he has been an expert advisor on the Panel for Environmental
Health and a member of the panel of fishery experts for the Food
and Agricultural Organization of the United Nations. He was
chairman of the Subcommittee for Fish, Other Aquatic Life and
Wildlife of the important National Technical Advisory Committee
on Water Quality Criteria. He received the State of Ohio Conservationist of the Year Award in 1961, the American Motors Professional
Conservationist Award in 1962, the Aldo Leopold Medal of the
Wildlife Society in 1963, the Science Director's Meritorious Service
Medal in 1964. He is an honorary member of the American Fisheries Society. He has published more than 200 papers in scientific
journals, and was co-author of *Methods for the Improvement of
Michigan Trout Streams*, 1932.

P. A. DOUGLAS

American Men of Science (The Physical and Biological Sciences), 11th ed., 1967.

ASCHER, WENDELL RUSSELL   (1898–1964)

orn August 31, 1898 in Ashkum, Illinois. University of Illinois, B.S. 924, M.S. 1927; University of Missouri, Ph.D. (genetics) 1929. He ngaged in agronomic research and teaching at the Universities of llinois and Missouri until 1929 when he became county agricultural gent for Osage and Clay counties, Missouri. Then followed an ppointment as extension soil conservationist for the State of Mis- ouri. In 1942 he became extension soil conservationist for the Jnited States Department of Agriculture with headquarters in Vashington, D. C., and served as project leader of extension soil onservation work in the United States and territories, a position he eld until his retirement in 1961. He traveled extensively through- ut the world making a special study of plant genetics. He was ctive in many organizations relating to agriculture and conserva- ion and was the recipient of numerous awards for his outstanding ervice. He assisted in developing the National Goodyear Soil Con- ervation District Awards Program and served as its advisor until is retirement. From its inception in Oklahoma, he originated and as a member of the Advisory Committee for the International and, Pasture and Range Judging Contest. He was a dedicated iember of the Soil Conservation Society of America, having served n many of its technical committees; in 1958 he was among the rst to receive the society's Presidential Citation. He was elected a 'ellow in the society in 1959. As a writer on conservation subjects, e contributed numerous articles to the *Journal of Soil and Water Conservation, Soil Conservation,* and *Extension Service Review.* Ie edited and issued a quarterly publication entitled *Terrain,* istributed to more than 700 workers in conservation education.)ied November 24, 1964.

RUSSELL G. HILL

AYLOR, WALTER PENN   (1888–   )

Born October 31, 1888 at Elkhorn, Wisconsin. University of Cali- ornia, B.S. 1911, Ph.D. (zoology) 1914. For seven years, until 916, he served as assistant curator or curator of mammals at the

University of California Museum of Vertebrate Zoology. He joine
the Biological Survey (later known as Fish and Wildlife Service) i
1916 and advanced from assistant to senior biologist. In coopera
tion with the University of Arizona, he served as professor o
economic zoology at the University of Arizona from 1932 to 193!
then until 1947, still with the federal government, he became th
leader of the Cooperative Wildlife Research Unit at the Texa
Agricultural and Mechanical College at College Station, and du
ing most of this period he also served as head of the Departmen
of Wildlife Management of the College. With the same federa
connections from 1947 to 1951, he served as leader of the Coopera
tive Wildlife Research Unit and professor of zoology at th
Oklahoma Agricultural and Mechanical College, Stillwater. Fro
1954 to 1962 he was professor of conservation education and biolog
at the Claremont Graduate School, and was visiting professor o
zoology at Southern Illinois University, 1957–58. From 1960 t
1968, he served as lecturer at high schools and colleges under th
program sponsored by the American Institute of Biological Science
He was president of the Ecological Society of America in 1934. H
is an honorary member of the American Society of Mammalogis
(president 1941–42), and of the Outdoor Writer's Association
From the Wildlife Society of which he was president in 1943 h
received the Aldo Leopold Award for distinguished service to con
servation (1961), the United States Department of the Interior
Gold Medal Award (1951) for distinguished service, and the Hono
Award from the California Conservation Council (1953). He ha
written 300 scientific papers, bulletins, and notes on zoology, eco
ogy, and conservation, was co-author of *The Birds of the State o
Washington*, 1953, and edited *Deer of North America*, 1956.

CLARENCE COTTAM

American Men of Science (The Physical and Biological Sciences), 11th ed.,

HOMPSON, WILLIAM FRANCIS (1888–1965)

orn April 3, 1888 at St. Cloud, Minnesota. University of Wash-
gton, 1906–9; Stanford University, A.B. 1911, Ph.D. (fisheries)
)30. He served as scientific assistant to David Starr Jordan at
tanford, 1909–15. During 1911–12, he was a scientist for the
alifornia Fish and Game Commission, and from 1912 to 1917 a
:ientific assistant for the Provincial Fisheries Department, British
'olumbia, Canada. From 1917 to 1924 he founded the research
rogram of the California Fish and Game Commission, developing
 pattern of investigation that was carried on for many years by
ie California State Fisheries Laboratory. As director of the Inter-
ational Fisheries Commission, 1924–37, and of the International
acific Salmon Fisheries Commission, 1937–43, he laid the scien-
fic foundation upon which the Commissions' works are based.
lis early work with population dynamics, the overfishing problem,
nd racial studies of halibut and salmon is a landmark in scientific
shery management. He was professor of fisheries, University of
Vashington, 1930–58, and director, School of Fisheries, 1934–47;
ien organized and served as director of the Fisheries Research
istitute at the University, 1947–58. He was a member of the
iology and Research Committee, International North Pacific Fisher-
:s Commission, 1953–59, and was a United States member of the
ifth Pacific Science Congress. He was one of the original organiz-
rs and first president of the American Institute of Fishery Research
iologists. Author of numerous scientific works, many of which
rere distributed as publications of the halibut and salmon com-
iissions. Died November 7, 1965.

CHARLES K. PHENICIE

merican Men of Science (The Physical and Biological Sciences), 10th ed.,
urnal of the Fisheries Research Board of Canada. Obituary, vol. 23, no. 11, 1966.
'ho Was Who in America, 1961–68.

TOUMEY, JAMES WILLIAM (1865–1932)

Born April 17, 1865 in Lawrence, Michigan. Michigan State Agricultural College, Sc.M. 1893, D.For. (honorary) 1927; Syracuse
University, Sc.D. (honorary) 1920. Taught botany at Michigan
State from 1889 to 1891 and at the University of Arizona, 1891 to
1899. He also held the post of botanist in the Arizona State Agricultural Experiment Station. He did special work on the date palm
and became a recognized authority on cacti, establishing a cactus
garden in Tucson. In 1897 he assisted in the arrangement of the
cactus collection in the Kew Garden in England. In 1899 he was
appointed superintendent of tree planting in the Division of Forestry, United States Department of Agriculture. In 1900 he was
called to Yale University where he became an outstanding authority
in dendrology and silviculture. From 1910 to 1922 he served as
dean of the Yale School of Forestry, then retired from the deanship
to pursue his interest in teaching and research at that institution
He materially enlarged the university's endowments and facilities
securing the gift of the building Sage Hall and large accessions to
the library. He donated his personal collection of 2,500 specimens
of American trees and shrubs to the forest herbarium. In 1920 he
was chairman of a Committee on Forest Education of the Society
of American Foresters that had a marked influence in shaping
educational policies of the forestry schools in the United States
Organized the Plant Science Research Club in 1928. In 1929 was a
member of the American delegation to the International Congress
of Forest Experiment Stations at Stockholm, Sweden. Elected a
Fellow of the Society of American Foresters. Author of *Seeding and
Planting in the Practice of Forestry*, 1916 (revised 1931 with C. F
Korstian) and of *Foundations in Silviculture*, 1928; also author of
eight scientific bulletins and many articles for scientific journals
Died May 6, 1932.

KENNETH B. POMEROY

American Forests 38: 366, June 1932.
Journal of Forestry. Obituary, 30: 665–69, October 1932.

OWELL, WILLIAM EARNEST (1916–   )

orn June 11, 1916 at St. James, Missouri. Drury College, Spring-
eld, Missouri, 1933–35; University of Missouri, 1935–36; University
f Michigan, B.S. (forestry) 1937, M.F. (silviculture) 1938.
mployed by Missouri Conservation Commission in July 1938 and
erved it for 28 years as district forester (1938–41), farm forester
1941–42), assistant state forester (1942–56), assistant director
1956–57, and director (1957–67). United States naval intelli-
ence officer during World War II (1943–46) as photo-interpreter
the Pacific theater. Appointed executive vice president of the
merican Forestry Association in January 1967. He was elected
nairman of the Ozark Section, Society of American Foresters, in
)50. Was chairman of various committees in the International
ssociation of Game, Fish and Conservation Commissioners, includ-
g the Endangered Species Committee, the Grants-in-Aid Com-
iittee, the Legislative Committee, (four years), Executive
ommittee (1964), and was president in 1966. Appointed to the
ederal Water Pollution Control Advisory Board by President Ken-
edy in 1963, he served on that board for three years. He was a
ember of the Lewis and Clark Trail Commission, representing the
tate of Missouri (1964–65). Since 1966 has been a member of the
nited States Department of Agriculture Wildlife Advisory Com-
iittee. Currently he is an advisory member of a committee working
1 the interrelationship of agriculture and wildlife with the
ational Academy of Sciences. Member of the Wildlife Society
d the American Fisheries Society. Author of numerous articles in
merican Forests and other conservation publications and speaker
efore many national conservation groups.

HENRY CLEPPER

'ho's Who in the Southeast, 1968.

TRAIN, RUSSELL ERROL (1920–)

Born June 4, 1920, in Jamestown, Rhode Island. Princeton Uni
versity, A.B. 1941; Columbia University, LL.B. 1947. During hi
legal career his professional work dealt with financial and tax mat
ters. As a result of his interest in African wildlife, he founded th
African Wildlife Leadership Foundation in 1961 and became pres
ident and chairman of the Board of Trustees. In 1964 he becam
a trustee and in 1965 president of the Conservation Foundatior
and in 1969 was appointed Under Secretary of the Department o
the Interior. He has served as executive board member of the Inter
national Union for the Conservation of Nature and Natura
Resources, and as director of the American Committee for Interna
tional Wildlife Protection. He has been director and vice presiden
of the World Wildlife Fund; vice president and member of th
executive committee of the Boone and Crockett Club; and consu
tant to the British Fauna Preservation Society. He has served a
trustee of the American Conservation Association and honorar
vice president of the American Forestry Association. The Tanzani:
Kenya, and Uganda National Parks have each made him an honor
ary trustee. In 1967 he was awarded the second annual Conserva
tion Award of the African Safari Club of Washington. He is
member of numerous wildlife and conservation organizations. Hi
publications include *The Role of Foundations and Universities i
Conservation* and *America the Beautiful.*

THE CONSERVATION FOUNDATIO

Who's Who in America, 1968–69.

TRAUTMAN, MILTON BERNARD (1899–)

Born September 7, 1899 in Columbus, Ohio. Mostly self-educate
in ichthyology and ornithology; College of Wooster, D.Sc. (hor
orary) 1951. He began his career in 1930 as assistant in the Burea
of Scientific Research, Ohio Division of Conservation; progressin
in 1934 to assistant curator of the Museum of Zoology, University

3 Trefethen

ichigan. He served as assistant director of the Institute for
sheries Research, 1935–39, Michigan Conservation Department,
lvancing to resident associate, 1935–36. He was a member of
niversity of Michigan zoology expedition to Yucatan in 1936.
esident biologist at Stone Institute of Hydrobiology, Ohio State
niversity in 1939; later became resident associate, lecturer in
ology, and curator of vertebrate collections, Department of
ology and Entomology, Ohio State University, 1955. He was a
ember of the Ohio State University expeditionary institute for
lar studies, Alaska, 1965. He ran summer surveys on salmon in
laska for the Bureau of Commercial Fisheries, 1959–61. He is the
thor of numerous papers in fisheries biology and ornithology, and
ill long be remembered for his two books *The Fishes of Ohio* and
rds of Buckeye Lake.

ELWOOD A. SEAMAN

nerican Men of Science (The Physical and Biological Sciences), 11th ed., 1967.

REFETHEN, JAMES BYRON, JR. (1916–   )

orn on June 3, 1916, in Brockton, Massachusetts. Educated at
ount Hermon School; Northeastern University, B.A. 1940; Univer-
ty of Massachusetts, M.S. (wildlife management) 1953. Joining
e staff of the Wildlife Management Institute on February 1, 1948,
> was editor of *Outdoor News Bulletin*, 1948–51, and has served
> director of publications since 1951. He has been editor of the
ransactions of the North American Wildlife and Natural Resources
onference since 1952, of the *Proceedings* of the National Sym-
osium on Wood Duck Management and Research in 1965, and of
e *Proceedings* of the National Watershed Congress since 1954. He
s been assistant editor, *Executive News Service* of the Natural
esources Council of America since 1968. Author of 100 popular
ticles on conservation, nature, and outdoor recreation published
national magazines, including *American Forests, American Heri-
ge, Audubon Magazine, National Wildlife, Outdoor Life, Sports*

Afield, and *Sports Illustrated.* Contributing editor of *Fisherman's Encyclopedia,* 1951, and *New Fisherman's Encyclopedia,* 1964 Senior editor of *New Hunter's Encyclopedia,* 1966. Author of *Cru sade for Wildlife: Highlights in Conservation Progress,* 1961; *Wild life Management and Conservation,* 1964; *Americans and Their Guns: The National Rifle Association in Nearly a Century of Serv ice to the Nation,* 1967.* Co-editor (with Clarence Cottam), *White wings: The Life History, Status, and Management of the White winged Dove,* 1968. As editor and writer he has been an effectiv exponent of all resource conservation and an expressive interprete of the art and science of wildlife management.

DANIEL A. POOL

TUNISON, ABRAM VORHIS (1909–71)

Born April 16, 1909 in Geneva, New York. Cornell University, B.S 1930, M.S. (biology) 1932. Employed first in 1930 as a techniciaa engaged in trout feeding experiments for General Seafoods Cor poration. Served from 1932 to 1934 as an aquatic nutrition biologis with the New York State Conservation Department. Joined th United States Fish and Wildlife Service in 1944 as assistant chie of branch of game-fish hatcheries; progressed to chief in 1954, t assistant director, to associate director in 1957, thence to deput director in 1964. He was elected Honorary Member of America Fisheries Society in 1964, and served as editor of *The Progressiv Fish-Culturist.* His career has centered around trout nutrition, fis culture, and administrative supervision in fish and wildlife resource He was principally responsible for dietary requirements for trou production in federal hatcheries and was directly responsible fo the establishment of pellet feeding systems now widely used i state, federal, and private hatcheries. Died January 3, 1971.

ELWOOD A. SEAMA

American Men of Science (The Physical and Biological Sciences), 11th ed., 1967.

UDALL, STEWART LEE (1920–)

Born on January 31, 1920 in St. Johns, Arizona. University of Arizona, LL.B. 1948. He became a member of the United States Congress in 1955 and served on the Interior and Insular Affairs Committee. From 1961 to 1968, he was Secretary of the Interior, and since 1969 has engaged in private consulting work in conservation. The 1964 Conservationist of the Year award was presented to him by the National Wildlife Federation; he also received the national award from the National Recreation Association. In 1965 he was honored with the Horace Marden Albright Medal from the American Scenic and Historic Preservation Society, the Outdoorsman of the Year award from the National Rifle Association, honorary citation from the American Institute of Architects, the Frances K. Hutchinson Medal from the Garden Club of America, and the Society Hill Medal from the Society Hill Renewal Association in Philadelphia. In 1966 he received two awards: Outdoor Life grand award from the National Association of Travel Organizations, and the honorary award from the Soil Conservation Society of America. The National Audubon Society presented him the medal for Distinguished Service to Conservation in 1967. The following year he received the Aldo Leopold Memorial Medal from the Wildlife Society. He has received numerous honorary doctor's degrees as well as honorary bachelor of law degrees from universities and colleges across the nation. He is the author of *The Quiet Crisis*, 1963; *Nineteen Seventy Six: Agenda for Tomorrow*, 1968; and is co-author of *National Parks of America*, 1966.

THE CONSERVATION FOUNDATION

The International Who's Who, 30th ed., 1966–67.
Who's Who in America, 1968–69.

VAN OOSTEN, JOHN (1891–1966)

Born December 10, 1891 in Grand Rapids, Michigan. University of Michigan, A.B., M.A., and Ph.D. He served as fishery research biologist for the United States Bureau of Fisheries from 1920 to

1927 when he was appointed chief of Great Lakes fishery investigations. His major interest was research on the life histories of Great Lake fishes and factors affecting the abundance and depletion of important species. He was consulted by fishery administrators of the Great Lakes states, and was chairman of numerous interstate and international committees because of his knowledge of fishery regulation and management. Relinquishing administrative duties in 1949, he devoted full-time to research as senior scientist until his retirement in 1961. He wrote over 90 scientific papers during his career. The United States Department of the Interior conferred on him a Distinguished Service Award in 1962. He served as editor for the American Fisheries Society, 1936–40; was president, 1941–46; and was elected Distinguished Service Honorary Member in 1952. Died January 25, 1966.

DONALD J. LEEDY

American Men of Science (The Physical and Biological Sciences), 10th ed.,

VAUX, HENRY JAMES (1912–   )

Born November 6, 1912 in Bryn Mawr, Pennsylvania. Haverford College, B.S. 1933; University of California, M.S. (forestry) 1935, Ph.D. (agricultural economics) 1948. Instructor in forestry at Oregon State University, 1937-42; associate forest economist at the Agricultural Experiment Station of Louisiana State University, 1942–43. Served in the United States Navy as a lieutenant from 1943 to 1946. Entering the United States Forest Service as a forest economist in 1946, he moved to the University of California School of Forestry at Berkeley where he advanced from lecturer in 1948 to dean in 1965. He was also assistant director of the California Agricultural Experiment Station, 1955–65, and director of the Wildlands Research Center, 1958–65. In 1965 he stepped down as dean at the School of Forestry, but continues teaching and research. He is a Fellow of the American Association for the Advancement of Science and of the Society of American Foresters, and from 1949 to 1955 he was chairman of the society's Steering Committee that conducted a nationwide study of forestry education. The author of many articles on the economics of natural resources use and management and on education, he has been consulting editor of the American Forestry Series of scientific and technical books for McGraw-Hill Book Company since 1952. He is a director of the American Forestry Association, and is active in other scientific and resources organizations.

HENRY CLEPPER

American Men of Science (The Physical and Biological Sciences), 11th ed., 1967.

VOGT, WILLIAM (1902–68)

Born May 15, 1902 in Mineola, New York. Bard College, A.B. (biology) 1925, Sc.D. 1953. Started his career as assistant editor for the New York Academy of Sciences, 1930–32; he was curator of the Jones Beach State Bird Sanctuary, 1932–35. He was with the National Audubon Society as field naturalist and editor of *Bird Lore* from 1935 to 1939. Throughout the next decade he was involved in conservation work in Latin America as conservation ornithologist from the Peruvian Guano Administration, 1939–42; as associate director of the Division of Science and Education, Coordinator of Inter-American Affairs, 1942–43; and as chief of the Conservation Section, Pan American Union, 1943–49. He was national director of the Planned Parenthood Federation of America from 1951 to 1961, and secretary of the Conservation Foundation, 1964–67. At his death he was serving as representative of the International Union for the Conservation of Nature and Natural Resources to the United Nations. Recipient of the field research prize of the Linnaean Society in 1938, he also received the Mary Soper Pope Medal in 1949, and the Lasker Foundation Award in 1951. A contributor of articles and scientific papers to natural history and general magazines, he is remembered for his books *Audubon's Bird of America*, 1937; *Road to Survival*, 1948; *El Hombre y la Tierra*, 1949; and *People*, 1960. Died July 11, 1968.

GEORGE SPRUGEL, JR.

American Men of Science (The Physical and Biological Sciences), 11th ed., 1967.
Who's Who in America, 1968–69.

VOIGT, WILLIAM, JR. (1902–)

Born October 13, 1902 in Atlanta, Georgia. Georgia School of Technology, 1920–21. From 1925 to 1936 he was a reporter on newspapers in Georgia and Oklahoma, was editor-reporter for the Associated Press in Missouri, New York, and Pennsylvania, 1931–36, then engaged in public relations work in Pennsylvania until 1938. During World War II, he served in the Army. Appointed in 1945 as assistant executive director of the Izaak Walton League of America in Chicago, he opened the League's western regional office in Denver in 1947, then became national executive director in 1949, serving until 1955. From 1955 to 1960, he was executive director of the Pennsylvania Fish Commission. Since 1963 he has been executive director of the Interstate Advisory Commission on the Susquehanna River Basin, representing Maryland, New York, and Pennsylvania. He was founding secretary of the National Committee on Policies in Conservation Education from 1945 to 1953, and until 1955 was treasurer of its successor organization, the Conservation Education Association, which has been effective in introducing conservation as a subject in the public schools. He was chairman of the Natural Resources Council of America, 1952–53. Former editor and editorial director of *Outdoor America*, the magazine of the Izaak Walton League, from 1949 to 1955; has written numerous articles about natural resources, particularly on water policy and pollution abatement, and is the author of *National Fishing Guide*, 1946. During his career he has been a forceful exponent and interpreter of the legislative needs for resources, both before Congressional committees and state legislatures.

HENRY CLEPPER

Who's Who in America, 1962–63.

WALCOTT, FREDERIC COLLIN (1869–1949)

Born February 19, 1869 in New York Mills, Oneida County, New York. Yale University, A.B. 1891, A.M. (honorary) 1917; Trinity College, D.Sc. 1928. He rose to national prominence as a member of Herbert Hoover's United States Food Administration during World War I, receiving the Legion of Honor of France and the Officers Cross of Poland for his activities in European relief work. In 1911, he helped found the American Game Protective and Propagation Association, serving on the board of directors of that organization from 1911 until 1935. In 1935 he became president of the American Wildlife Institute and was president of the North American Wildlife Foundation from 1945 to 1948. For seven years he was chairman of the Connecticut Board of Fisheries and Game. He served in the United States Senate from 1929 to 1935 and was chairman of the Special Committee for Wildlife of the Senate from 1930 through 1935. In this capacity he was an author of the Walcott-Kleberg Duck Stamp Act, which provided special funds for wildlife refuges, and assisted in drafting the Forest Wildlife Refuge Act, the Pittman-Robertson Federal Aid in Wildlife Restoration Act, the Whaling Treaty, the Coordination Act of 1934, the enabling act for the Cooperative Wildlife Research Unit Program, and the Migratory Bird Treaty with Mexico. He helped obtain legislation for the establishment of the Patuxent Wildlife Research Center of the Bureau of Biological Survey and for the consolidation of the Bureau of Biological Survey and the Bureau of Sport Fisheries in the new United States Fish and Wildlife Service of the Department of the Interior. In 1935 he was instrumental in convincing President Franklin D. Roosevelt of the need for an international conference on wildlife problems to be called by the president of the United States. This resulted in the American Wildlife Conference of 1936, which was conducted under government sponsorship and which established pattern for the later North American Wildlife and Natural Resources Conferences. He received the *Outdoor Life* Award for meritorious service to wildlife conservation in 1934. Died April 27, 1949.

JAMES B. TREFETHEN

Biographical Dictionary of the American Congress. Washington, D. C.: U. S. Government Printing Office, 1961.
Who Was Who in America, 1951–60.
Who's Who in America, 1948–49.

WALFORD, LIONEL ALBERT (1905–   )

Born May 29, 1905 in San Francisco. Stanford University, A.B. 1929; Harvard University, M.A. 1932, Ph.D. (biology) 1935. He was a fishery biologist for the California Department of Fish and Game, 1926–31; assistant in biology at Harvard University, 1934–35; and an instructor in zoology at Santa Barbara State College, 1935–36. He joined the United States Bureau of Fisheries (later named the United States Fish and Wildlife Service) in 1936, and served in biological and research capacities including director of the Atlantic Fishery Oceanographic Laboratory in Washington, D. C., 1958–60, and director of the Sandy Hook Marine Laboratory, New Jersey, since 1960. He has written numerous scientific papers in addition to two books, *Marine Game Fishes of the Pacific Coast*, 1937, and *Living Resources of the Sea*, 1958. He was editor of *Copeia*, the journal of the American Society of Ichthyologists and Herpetologists, 1937–47; was three terms chairman of the Committee on Research and Statistics, International Commission for the Northwest Atlantic Fisheries, 1955–58; and is an honorary member of the Atlantic Estuarine Society. Also, he is a member of the Panel on Marine Productivity of the National Research Council, the Committee on the International Union of Biological Science, and representative of the United States Bureau of Sport Fisheries and Wildlife in the Division of Biology and Agriculture, National Research Council. He has participated in numerous scientific expeditions and has been a delegate, observer, or advisor in many international fishery meetings. He led the United States scientific delegations to the International Commission of Northwest Atlantic Fisheries and the International North Pacific Fisheries Commission, and was instrumental in interjecting modern fishery management procedures into international programs.

DANIEL A. POOLE

American Men of Science (The Physical and Biological Sciences), 11th ed., 1965.

WARD, HENRY BALDWIN   (1865–1945)

Born March 4, 1865 at Troy, New York. Williams College, B.A. 1885, Sc.D. 1921; Harvard University, A.M. and Ph.D. 1892; University of Cincinnati, Sc.D. 1920; University of Oregon, LL.D. 1932; University of Nebraska, LL.D. 1935. He went to the University of Nebraska as associate professor of zoology in 1893 and had become head of the Zoology Department by 1906. In 1909 he was made head of the Department of Zoology at the University of Illinois, a position which he held until his retirement in 1933 at the age of 68. He was associated with a biological survey of the Great Lakes and with Alaska and Pacific salmon investigations. He was a Fellow of the American Association for the Advancement of Science, was vice president in 1905, and was permanent secretary, 1933–37. President of the American Fisheries Society in 1913. He was member of the State Conservation Commission of New York in 1918 and of the State Game and Fish Commission of Oregon in 1925. An active member of the Izaak Walton League of America, he contributed many papers on conservation subjects to its journal *Outdoor America*, and was its national president from 1928 to 1930. Author of many papers on parasites and on a variety of other biological subjects, he was also a former associate editor of the *American Naturalist*. Among his well-known writings were *Freshwater Biology*, 1917, of which he was editor, and *Foundations of Conservation Education*, 1941. He founded the *Journal of Parasitology* in 1914. Died November 30, 1945.

GEORGE W. BENNETT

American Men of Science, 1944.
Who Was Who in America, 1943–50.

WARDER, JOHN ASTON   (1812–83)

Born January 19, 1812 in Philadelphia, Pennsylvania. Jefferson Medical College, M.D. 1836. Then practiced medicine in Cincinnati, Ohio for nearly two decades. Gave up medical practice in 1855 and bought a farm near North Bend, Ohio. From 1850 to 1853, he edited *Western Horticultural Review* and contributed to the *American Journal of Horticulture*. He fostered landscape gardening and park beautification. Chronologically, his writings fall into three major periods. Prior to 1855 he published two medical treatises; from 1855 to the late 1860s his publications were mostly on horticulture; and from 1870 on his works were chiefly on forestry. Many papers written at the request of the Agricultural Division of United States Patent Office were published in the division's annual reports. He was the first person to propose planting a belt of trees on the great western plains. In 1873 he was a United States commissioner to the International Exhibition in Vienna, and wrote the official report on forests and forestry. In 1875 he founded the American Forestry Association and was its first president. In 1882 he was responsible for merging the Association with the American Forestry Congress, of which he had been an organizer. Thus the American Forestry Association continues as the nation's oldest citizens' organization devoted to conservation. Died July 14, 1883.

FRED H. HORNADAY

Dictionary of American Biography, 1936.

WATSON, CLARENCE WILFORD (1894–   )

Born December 28, 1894 in Boston, Massachusetts. Yale University, Ph.B. 1916, M.F. 1920, Ph.D. (forest soils) 1930. After employment by the United States Forest Service beginning in 1917, he was a Fellow of the American Scandinavian Foundation at the Royal Forestry College in Stockholm, Sweden, 1920–21, then assistant professor of forestry at the University of Idaho, 1921–27. He received a National Research Council Fellowship for 1930–32. He was then with the Civilian Conservation Corps and was forestry supervisor of Essex County (New Jersey) Parks, 1933–35. From 1936 to 1941, he was employed by the More Game Birds in America Foundation and by Ducks Unlimited (Canada). From 1942 until his retirement in December 1964, he was southeastern regional supervisor, Branch of Federal Aid, Bureau of Sport Fisheries and Wildlife, United States Department of the Interior. During those 23 years he made outstanding contributions to interstate and federal-state relations in fish and wildlife conservation. An honorary member of the Wildlife Society, he was a founder and the first president of the society's Southeastern Section and chairman of its Forest Game Committee from 1955 to 1964, when numerous cooperative state-federal forest-wildlife research and management programs were developed. Upon retirement he received the United States Department of the Interior's Distinguished Service Award. In his honor the Southeastern Association of Game and Fish Directors, the Southern Division of the American Fisheries Society, and the Southeastern Section of the Wildlife Society created the C. W. Watson Fund and an annual award and medal for the career individual making the greatest contribution to wildlife conservation in the Southeast.

LEONARD E. FOOTE

American Men of Science (The Physical and Biological Sciences), 11th ed., 1967.

WAYBURN, EDGAR (1906–   )

Born September 17, 1906 in Macon, Georgia. University of Georgia, A.B. 1926; Harvard University, M.D. 1930. He began medical practice in 1930, served as a major in the Army Medical Corps during World War II, and for most of his professional career has been in California. Joined the Sierra Club in 1939; has served on the Board of Directors since 1957; was vice president, 1959–61, and 1964–67; and president, 1961–64, and 1967–69. He was chairman of the Eighth Biennial Wilderness Conference of the Sierra Club in 1963, and was chairman of the Club's Conservation Committee, 1954–63. He was the club's volunteer leader in the successful campaign for the Redwood National Park, and since 1968 has been actively involved in the club's efforts to preserve key elements in Alaska's environment. In addition, he has served as president of the Federation of Western Outdoor Clubs, 1953–55, and was president of

Trustees for Conservation, 1958–60. The recipient of awards by the California Conservation Council in 1957, the Marin County Conservation Council in 1965, and the Marin Conservation League in 1969, he was thus honored for his work in behalf of the California State Park system. In 1964 he received an American Motors Conservation Award in national recognition of his efforts. He has contributed many articles on conservation to the Sierra Club *Bulletin* and to *California Medicine*.

LUELLA K. SAWYER

Sierra Club Handbook, 1967.
Who's Who in the West, 11th ed., 1968.

WEAVER, RICHARD LEE (1911–64)

Born April 6, 1911 in Howard, Pennsylvania. Pennsylvania State University, B.S. (biology); Cornell University, Ph.D. (conservation and natural history) 1938. His career in conservation progressed through positions as head of the Science Department at Maumee Valley Country Day School in Ohio, 1933–36; naturalist at Dartmouth College, 1938–42; extension specialist in conservation at the University of New Hampshire, 1942–43; director of the Connecticut Audubon Nature Center, 1943–47; program director of the North Carolina Resource-use Education Commission, 1947–52; and professor of conservation at the University of Michigan, 1952–64. He was a Fulbright lecturer in Pakistan, 1960–61. He was a key figure and office holder in state, regional, and national professional organizations; served as president of the National Association of Biology Teachers in 1950 and as president of the American Nature Study Society in 1957. In 1956 he received the Nash Motors Award for outstanding contributions to conservation education. He was author of numerous books and articles; was best known for his writing, research, and leadership in the development of conservation education, philosophy, teaching techniques, and action programs. As a highly effective teacher he had a strong influence on his students, many of whom became leaders in conservation and conservation education. Died 1964.

BERNARD L. CLAUSEN

American Men of Science, 10th ed.,

WELCH, PAUL SMITH (1882–1959)

Born January 28, 1882 in Oconee, Illinois. James Millikin College, A.B. 1910; University of Illinois, A.M. 1911; University of Michigan, Ph.D. (zoology) 1913. He began his teaching career in entomology at Kansas State College, and in 1918 became assistant professor of zoology at the University of Michigan, where after 34 years of service he was appointed emeritus professor in 1952. His teaching of invertebrate zoology and limnology on the main campus of the university at Ann Arbor and at the University Biological Station at Cheybogan profoundly influenced the ecological philosophy of two generations of aquatic resources researchers, managers, and administrators. His scientific papers and textbooks on limnology continue to contribute to the training of aquatic ecologists and fishery scientists. He was acting director of the Michigan Biological Station in 1924 and 1925, and assistant director in 1929 and 1930; was assistant curator of the William Barnes Lepidoptera Collection from 1906 to 1910; and was on the staff of the Lake Laboratory of the Ohio State University in 1917. A prominent member of several scientific societies, he was secretary-editor and president of the Microscopy Society; a fellow of the Entomological Society of America, and second vice president in 1925; vice president of the Ecological Society of America in 1934; and was secretary-treasurer of the Limnological Society from 1935 to 1945 and president in 1946. He is the author of the textbook, *Limnology,* 1935, revised 1952; and of *Limnological Methods,* 1948. Died October 1, 1959.

P. A. DOUGLAS

American Men of Science, 9th ed., 1956.

WESTWOOD, RICHARD WILBUR (1896–1961)

Born July 8, 1896 in Newton, Massachusetts. Columbia University School of Journalism, A.B. 1918. He served in the United States Army in France during World War I, was wounded at Verdun, and was awarded the *Croix de Guerre*. Beginning in 1919, he worked on newspapers in New England; from 1921 to 1923, he was a reporter for the *Christian Science Monitor*, writing frequently on conservation topics. His writings attracted attention, and he was invited to join the editorial staff of *Nature Magazine*, published by the American Nature Association in Washington, D. C. From assistant editor in 1923, he advanced to managing editor in 1927, and in 1937 he became editor, serving as such until 1960 when the magazine was merged with *Natural History*. He was also secretary of the American Nature Association from 1927 to 1946, and was president thereafter until his death. Organized in 1922 to promote public interest in nature and the out-of-doors, the Association and its magazine led a militant campaign for the conservation of the environment, particularly for protection and improvement of rural roadsides and the elimination of unsightly roadside billboard advertising. Beginning in 1957, he was secretary of the National Roadside Commission, and as its representative before legislative committees he was a leader in the fight for preserving the natural beauty of the countryside. Prominent in the movement for the conservation of all resources, he was notably energetic in advocating the establishment of parks and recreational areas. A life member of the National Parks Association, he was active in the International Union for the Conservation of Nature, the American Nature Study Society, and other bodies dedicated to natural resources. He was especially effective in conservation education of students as *Nature Magazine* went regularly to many schools. Died February 13, 1961.

HENRY CLEPPER

Washington, D. C. *Evening Star*. Obituary, February 14, 1961.
Who Was Who in America, 1961–68.

WHARTON, WILLIAM P. (1880–)

Born August 12, 1880 in Beverly, Massachusetts. Harvard College, A.B. 1903; Harvard Law School. He became an extensive tree planter on his lands in Massachusetts, and was manager of the Groton (Massachusetts) Town Forest which he was instrumental in establishing. He was president of the Massachusetts Forest and Park Asociation, was active in the Society for the Protection of New Hampshire Forests, and obtained endowments for promoting research in forest production. He was one of the organizers of the Committee for the Suppression of Pine Blister Rust in North America and was active in organizing the National Conference on the Dutch Elm Disease. To increase his knowledge of forestry, in 1913 he traveled throughout the scientifically managed forests of western Europe. In recognition of his contributions to forestry the Society of American Foresters elected him to associate membership in 1924. He was a director of the American Forestry Association from 1923 to 1950. In addition to his forestry activities, early in this century he served as secretary of the American Bison Society, the organization principally responsible for saving this species. After a trip to western national parks in 1912, he became an influential advocate of park development and protection, and was an early proponent of the creation of Everglades National Park and of Olympic National Park. He helped found the National Parks Association and was its president. He was an early supporter of the National Association of Audubon Societies, the Northeastern Bird Banding Association, and numerous other conservation bodies. His interests and activities covered all phases of natural resources conservation, and for a half-century he occupied positions of leadership with leading organizations in this field.

FRED E. HORNADAY

WHIPPLE, GEORGE CHANDLER (1866–1924)

Born March 2, 1866 in New Boston, New Hampshire. Massachusetts Institute of Technology, S.B. (sanitary engineering) 1899. He worked as a biologist in the Boston Water Works, later becoming director of the Mount Prospect Laboratory of the New York City Department of Water Supply, Gas, and Electricity. He then became a partner in the sanitary engineering consulting firm of Hazen and Whipple, New York. During 1911, he was professor of sanitary engineering at Harvard University, and was professor of sanitary engineering at the Massachusetts Institute of Technology from 1914 to 1916. Between the years 1914 and 1923, he was a council member of the Massachusetts State Department of Health. In 1917 he was commissioned a major and made a member of the Red Cross Mission to Russia. In 1919 he became senior sanitary engineer for the United States Public Health Association, and chief of the Department of Sanitation for the League of Red Cross Societies. He was a Fellow of the American Academy of Arts and Science. One of America's pioneers in limnology, he wrote many technical books on water, among them the classic *Microscopy of Drinking Water*, 1889; and was co-author of one of the first textbooks on limnology, *Fresh-Water Biology*, 1918. Died November 27, 1924.

P. A. DOUGLAS

Who Was Who in America, 1897–1942.

WHITE, GILBERT FOWLER (1911–   )

Born November 26, 1911 in Chicago. University of Chicago, B.S. 1932, S.M. 1934, Ph.D. (geography) 1942; Hamilton College, LL.D. 1954; Swarthmore College, LL.D. 1956; Haverford College, D.Sc. 1956; Earlham College, LL.D. 1958. Joined the staff of the Mississippi Valley Committee and Natural Resources Board in 1934. He was then secretary of the Committees on Land and Waters Resources for the Natural Resources Planning Board, 1936–40; and was with the Bureau of the Budget, 1941–42. During World War II, he was on overseas duty with the American Friends Service Committee. In 1946 he became president of Haverford College and left in 1956 to become professor of geography at the University of Chicago. In 1970 he moved to the University of Colorado as director of the Institute of Behavioral Science. Among his numerous public service assignments dealing with natural resources have been the following: He was a member of the task force on natural resources of the Hoover Commission on Reorganization of the Federal Government in 1948, and was vice chairman of the President's Water Resources Policy Commission, 1950–51. During 1954–55, he was United States member on the Advisory Committee on Arid Land Research of the United Nations Educational, Scientific and Cultural Organization, and during 1967–70 of its Committee on Natural Resources Research. He was chairman of a Special Committee on Natural Resources Problems for the National Research Council, 1955–56, and a member of the United Nations Panel on Integrated River Basin Development, 1956–57. He has been a consultant to the United Nations Development Program and the Lower Mekong Coordinating Committee. In 1960 he was consultant to the Senate Select Committee on Water Resources. During 1961–62, he served as president of the Association of American Geographers. He was chairman of a task force on Federal Flood Control Policy which drafted a new national policy on flood loss reduction, and also was on the Special Commission on Weather Modification of the National Science Foundation, both during 1965–66. In 1964 he became chairman of the Committee on Water for the National Academy of Sciences. Among his books are *Human Adjustment to Floods*, 1942; *Science and the Future of Arid Lands*, 1960; *Social and Economic Aspects of Natural Resources*, 1962; *Choice of Adjustment to Floods*, 1964; and *Strategies of American Water Management*, 1969. He is editor of *Water, Health and Society* (the writings of Abel Wolman), 1969.

HENRY CLEPPER

American Men of Science (The Social and Behavioral Sciences), 11th ed., 1968.
Who's Who in America, 1968–69.

WILLIAMS, DONALD ALFRED (1905–   )

Born July 14, 1905, at Clark, South Dakota. South Dakota State University, B.S. (civil engineering) 1928, Doctor of Agriculture (honorary) 1956. After five years in private and state engineering work, he entered the United States Department of Agriculture's newly created Soil Conservation Service in 1935 as a Civilian Conservation Corps camp superintendent. From 1935 to 1947 he held field and regional jobs as conservation engineer; then became assistant regional director in the Pacific Coast Region, 1947–50; flood control survey officer, office of the Secretary of Agriculture, 1950–51; assistant chief of the Soil Conservation Service, 1951–53, and administrator in November 1953. He retired in December 1968. During his administration, Soil Conservation Service responsibilities expanded from virtually a single program of technical assistance to soil conservation districts to an agency with major responsibilities in 15 programs. In 1953 the Soil Conservation Service was assigned responsibility for the Department of Agriculture flood prevention and river basin investigation activities, and in 1954 for the small watershed program, which carried out soil and water conservation methods in an entire watershed area. Under his leadership the resource conservation and development projects, first authorized in 1962, provided better economic opportunities for rural people through planned, integrated development of the area's natural resources. He originated and directed a National Inventory of Conservation Needs, carried out between 1957 and 1962, which gave the nation its first authoritative survey of land conditions, conservation needs, watershed potentials, and land-use trends on the nonfederal lands of the country. He was also largely responsible for the development of the Great Plains Conservation Program, enacted in 1956, to provide assistance for farmers and ranchers in a major area with severe land-use problems. He received the Distinguished Service Award of the National Association of Soil and Water Conservation Districts in 1957, the United States Department of Agriculture's Distinguished Service Award in 1958, and the Rockefeller Public Service Award in Administration in 1967. Internationally, he is a soil and water conservation consultant to the Ford Foundation on its program to help India increase food production. He is a Fellow of the Soil Conservation Society of

America and the American Association of the Advancement of Science.

F. GLENNON LOYD

Who's Who in America, 1968–69.
Who's Who in Engineering, 8th ed., 1964.

WIRTH, CONRAD LOUIS (1899–)

Born December 1, 1899 in Hartford, Connecticut. University of Massachusetts, B.S., Doctor of Landscape Architecture (honorary); New England College, Doctor of Civil Law 1955; University of North Carolina, L.H.D. (honorary) 1958. In 1928 he began work with the National Capital Park and Planning Commission, and in 1931 transferred to the National Park Service as assistant director in charge of land planning. In 1933 he was also given supervisory responsibility for all state and county park activities of the Civilian Conservation Corps; in 1935 this supervisory responsibility was extended to all the bureaus of the Department of the Interior. Author of the Park, Parkway and Recreational Area Study Act of 1936, he directed the state-by-state studies; this act was used in 1962 to establish the new Bureau of Outdoor Recreation pending its basic legislation. In 1951 he became director of the National Park Service and served in that capacity until his retirement in 1964. During this period, he initiated "Mission 66," the service's protection, improvement, and extension program. Awards received for his accomplishments in conservation, planning and park management include the Distinguished Service Award of the Department of the Interior; the Conservation Award of the American Forestry Association; the Rockefeller Public Service Award; the Pugsley Gold Medal and the Horace Marden Albright Scenic Preservation Award of the American Scenic and Historic Preservation Society; the Theodore Roosevelt Medal for Conservation of Natural Resources of the Theodore Roosevelt Association. Following retirement from government, he has served as executive director of the Hudson River Valley Commission, 1965–66; a commissioner of the

Palisades Interstate Park Commission since 1964; member of the National Capital Planning Commission since 1966; chairman of the New York State Historic Trust since 1966; and consultant on conservation and park matters to Laurance S. Rockefeller and the Rockefeller Brothers Fund. He is life director of the National Conference on State Parks, life trustee of the National Geographic Society, and honorary life member of the Sierra Club. He is a Fellow of the American Society of Landscape Architects and of the American Institute of Park Executives, and a director of the American Shore and Beach Preservation Association.

HOLT BODINSON

Who's Who in America, 1968–69.

WOODWARD, HUGH BEISTLE (1885–1968)

Born April 29, 1885 in Clearfield, Pennsylvania. Dickenson College, Ph.B. 1908, M.A. 1910, LL.B. 1910, LL.D. (honorary) 1959. He was admitted to the Pennsylvania bar in 1911, the Colorado bar in 1914, the New Mexico bar in 1915, and was licensed to practice before the Supreme Court in 1923. During a long legal career in New Mexico, he promoted conservation as a personal crusade. He was active in the New Mexico Wildlife and Conservation Association, the National Audubon Society, the Izaak Walton League of America, the Wilderness Society and the American Forestry Association. He served both as lieutenant governor and district attorney for the Eighth Judicial District of New Mexico, and as United States Attorney for New Mexico in addition to activities associated with his private law practice and work with finance and construction firms in the southwest. He made several contributions of a national nature which led to receipt of the Nash Conservation Award in 1953. He was active in fighting demands by livestock interests to gain control of Federal grazing lands. He was a member of the National Advisory Committee on Multiple Use of National Forests. He joined others in drafting early versions of the Wilderness Act. For ten years, he served as regional director of the National Wildlife Federation and as a member of the Board of Trustees of National Wildlife Federation Endowment. During his tenure, he was instrumental in the location of the national headquarters of the National Wildlife Federation in a "permanent home" in Washington, D. C. Died August 18, 1968.

NATIONAL WILDLIFE FEDERATION

WRIGHT, MABEL OSGOOD (1859–1934)

Born January 26, 1859 in New York City. She promoted the organization in 1898 of the Audubon Society, State of Connecticut, and served as its president continuously until 1925. She was a director of the National Association of Audubon Societies, now the National Audubon Society, from its organization in 1905 until 1928, and also served as contributing editor of *Bird Lore*, which became *Audubon* magazine. She was elected an associate member of the American Ornithologists' Union in 1895 and a member in 1901. Birdcraft Sanctuary, near her home in Fairfield, Connecticut, was a forerunner of modern outdoor educational centers; there she gathered a group of children whom she called her "bird class" to teach them about nature. Author of *Birdcraft*, 1895, one of the earliest successful field guides to birds, she wrote numerous other books and pamphlets that bridged the gap between professional ornithologists and the lay public. Among these books were *The Friendship of Nature*, 1894; *Citizen Bird*, 1897; *Four-Footed Americans and Their Kin*, 1898; *The Flowers and Ferns In Their Haunts*, 1901; and *The Garden of a Commuter's Wife*, 1902. The drawings of Louis Agassiz Fuertes, noted illustrator of birds, first appeared in her books. Died July 16, 1934.

CHARLES H. CALLISON

The Auk. Obituary, 51:564–65.
Bird Lore. Obituary, July–August 1934, p. 280.
National Cyclopaedia of American Biography, 1904.
Who Was Who in America, 1897–1942.

YARD, ROBERT STERLING (1861–1945)

Born February 1, 1861 in Haverstraw, New York. Princeton University, A.B. 1883. His career in journalism began in 1887, first with the *New York Sun*, then with the *New York Herald* in 1891 where he was editor until 1900. With Charles Scribner's Sons as book advertising manager, 1901–5, he was then editor for other companies until he became editor-in-chief of *The Century Magazine*, 1913–14, and later Sunday editor for the *New York Herald*. From 1915 to 1919, he helped to establish the National Park Service and was chief of its Educational Division. When the National Parks Association was founded in 1919 he became its executive secretary, continuing until 1934. One of the eight organizers of the Wilderness Society in 1935, he was its secretary-treasurer until 1937, and was president and permanent secretary until 1945; in addition, he was first editor of *The Living Wilderness*, the Society's quarterly journal, from 1935 to 1945. Among his published works were *The National Parks Portfolio*, 1916; *Glimpses of Our National Parks*, 1916; *The Top of the Continent*, 1917; *The Book of the National Parks*, 1919; *Our Federal Lands, A Romance of American Development*, 1928. Died May 17, 1945.

MICHAEL NADEL

The Living Wilderness, July 1945, vol. 10, no. 13; and December 1945, vol. 10, nos. 14 and 15.
Who Was Who in America, 1943–50.

YOUNG, STANLEY PAUL (1889–1969)

Born October 30, 1889, in Astoria, Oregon. University of Oregon, B.S. 1911; graduate work at University of Michigan where he served as assistant in geology, 1914–15. Much of his early professional life was spent in the West and Southwest where he entered the Forest Service, United States Department of Agriculture, in Arizona in 1917, then transferred to the Bureau of Biological Survey as a government hunter. His work on the control and biology of the larger mammalian predators occupied much of his long career, first in ground control work in 1919 and coyote control in New Mexico in 1920. He was leader of predator control in Colorado and Kansas, 1921–27; and later, in Washington, D. C., in administration and research in the Bureau of Biological Survey and its successor agency, the Fish and Wildlife Service as assistant head, Division of Economic Investigations, 1927–28; principal biologist in charge, Division Predatory Animal and Rodent Control, 1928–34; chief, Division of Game Management, 1934–38; biologist, Division of Predator and Rodent Control, 1938–39; member of the staff dealing with zoology, wildlife research, and North American fauna publications, 1939–57; and director of Bird and Mammal Laboratories, 1957–59. Upon his retirement in 1959, he became collaborator of the Bureau of Sport Fisheries and Wildlife. One of wildlife conservation's most colorful figures, he was a member of wildlife expeditions to Louisiana and Mexico in 1934 and 1937. He was an honorary member of the Wildlife Society and a member of the American Society of Mammalogists. He received the Distinguished Service Medal of the United States Department of the Interior in 1957. A prolific writer, his best known books include *The Wolves of North America* (with Edward A. Goldman), 1944; *The Puma-Mysterious American Cat* (with Edward A. Goldman), 1946; *The Clever Coyote* (with H. H. T. Jackson), 1951; and *The Bobcat of North America*, 1958, all published by the Wildlife Management Institute. He was still publishing articles dealing with America's larger predatory animals when he was close to 80 years old. Died May 15, 1969.

DANIEL L. LEEDY

American Men of Science (The Physical and Biological Sciences), 11th ed., 1967.
Journal of Wildlife Management. Obituary, 33(4):1056–57, October 1969.

ZAHNISER, HOWARD CLINTON (1906–64)

Born February 25, 1906 in Franklin, Pennsylvania. Greenville College (Illinois), B.A. 1928, Litt. D. 1957. After graduation he taught high school for a year in Greenville, then entered the Department of Commerce in 1930. From 1931 to 1942 he served the Bureau of Biological Survey and its successor agency the United States Fish and Wildlife Service as editor, writer, and broadcaster on wildlife research, administration, and conservation, in charge of the agency's Section of Current and Visual Information. From 1935 to 1959 he was an essayist and book editor of *Nature Magazine*; from 1940 on he was an annual contributor to the *Encyclopedia Britannica* on "Wildlife Conservation" and on "Wilderness Preservation." From 1942 to 1945, he was principal research writer of the Bureau of Plant Industry, Soils, and Agricultural Engineering in the United States Department of Agriculture's Research Administration. As head of that bureau's Division of Information he directed its publication and research-reporting program. He was also chairman of the United States Department of Agriculture's Special Committee on Improvement of Publications. He joined the staff of the Wilderness Society in 1945 as executive secretary (later executive director) and as editor of its quarterly magazine, *The Living Wilderness*, where he remained until his death. He was one of the organizers in 1946 (chairman 1948–49) of the Natural Resources Council of America; president of the Thoreau Society in 1957; a member of the Advisory Committee on Conservation to the Secretary of the Interior, 1951–54; vice chairman of the Citizens' Committee on Natural Resources in 1955; and was honorary vice president of the Sierra Club. A free lance writer of articles and verse, his book contributions include the chapters "Parks and Wilderness" in *America's Natural Resources*, 1957, and "Wilderness Forever" in *Wilderness: America's Living Heritage*, 1961. He was the father of the Wilderness Act of 1964, which he was largely instrumental in writing and seeing through to enactment. Died May 5, 1964.

MICHAEL NADEL

The Living Wilderness, No. 85 Winter–Spring 1964.
Who Was Who in America, 1961–68.

ZIMMERMAN, GORDON KARL (1910–)

Born November 4, 1910 in Spokane, Washington. University of
Maryland, A.B. (business administration) 1932. After working as
a reporter for the *Washington* (D. C.) *Daily News*, 1932–35, he
joined the Department of Agriculture's newly created Soil Conservation Service in 1935, advancing through various professional
public information positions to chief of the Division of Information,
a position held from 1942 to 1951. Long a close associate of H. H.
Bennett, first chief of the Soil Conservation Service, he served as
Bennett's principal public relations adviser and writer. Manager of
the public relations department of Harry Ferguson, Inc., in Detroit,
1952–55, he was then research director for the National Grange in
Washington, D. C., 1955–58. Since 1958 he has been executive
secretary of the National Association of Soil and Water Conservation Districts which represents more than 3,000 local conservation
districts in the 50 states, Puerto Rico, and the Virgin Islands. He
has served on the National Livestock and Meat Board, with the
American Dairy Association, and as a member of the Agriculture
Committee of the National Planning Association. He is vice chairman of the Natural Resources Council of America, and is serving
his seventh term as chairman of the Steering Committee of the
National Watershed Congress. He is a member of the Citizens'
Advisory Committee on Environmental Quality and of the National
Conservation Committee of the Boy Scouts of America.

NATIONAL ASSOCIATION OF SOIL AND WATER
CONSERVATION DISTRICTS

ZINN, DONALD JOSEPH (1911–)

Born April 19, 1911 in New York City. Harvard University, B.S.
1933; University of Rhode Island, M.S. 1937; Yale University, Ph.D.
(marine biology) 1942. Following service from 1942 to 1945 as
aviation physiologist with United States Air Force, he was a
naturalist at the Marine Biological Laboratory, Wood Hole, Massachusetts, 1945–46. He joined the faculty of the University of Rhode

Island in 1946, and rose to professor in 1961 and chairman of the
Department of Zoology in 1962. He was director of the Agassiz
Memorial Expedition to Penikese Island; research associate of the
Narragansett Marine Laboratory; and delegate to the Fifteenth
International Congress of Zoology. Member of 11 professional scientific societies; Fellow of the American Association for the Advancement of Science, and a Fellow of the Academy of Zoology. He has
been a member of the board of directors of the Rhode Island Wildlife Federation since 1947 and served as secretary, president, and
delegate to annual meetings of the National Wildlife Federation. In
1960 he was elected to the Board of Directors of the National
Wildlife Federation; was elected president in 1967, 1968, and 1969.
The author of more than 60 research papers and articles on various
aspects of animal life, he is recognized as one of the nation's leading marine ecologists and has served on the International Task
Force for the Conservation of Aquatic Ecosystems.

WILLARD T. JOHNS

American Men of Science (The Physical and Biological Sciences), 11th ed.,

ZIVNUSKA, JOHN ARTHUR (1916–   )

Born July 10, 1916 in San Diego, California. University of Cali-
fornia, B.S. 1938, M.S. 1940; University of Minnesota, Ph.D.
(agricultural economics) 1957. United States Navy, 1942–45;
Lieutenant Commander. Starting as instructor in forestry at the
University of Minnesota in 1946, he went to the University of
California School of Forestry in 1948, was advanced to professor
in 1959, was acting dean, 1961–62, and has been dean since 1965.
He was a consultant in forest economics to Stanford Research
Institute, 1953–54, and in 1963; to the Forest Industries Council,
1955–56; to the United Nations Economics Commission for Asia
and the Far East in 1957; to the Navajo Tribal Council in 1958; to
the Weyerhaeuser Timber Company in 1959; to the Michigan-
California Lumber Company, 1960–62; and Forest Industries Committee on Timber Valuation and Taxation in 1963. He is a member

of the Forestry Research Advisory Committee, United States Department of Agriculture. Was visiting (Fulbright) lecturer in forestry to the Agricultural College of Norway, 1954–55; and organizer of the Section of Forestry for the Tenth Pacific Science Congress (Hawaii) in 1961. He is the author of 50 articles and publications in forest economics. A member of the Society of American Foresters since 1938, he was elected Fellow in 1963; served on the Council, 1962–63; was chairman, Division of Economics and Policy in 1959; was a member of Committee on Civil Service, 1956–61; was a member of the Advisory Board for *Forest Science*, 1957–63; and was Visiting Scientists' Program lecturer, 1961–63. Author of *U. S. Timber Resources in a World Economy*, 1967.

SOCIETY OF AMERICAN FORESTERS

American Men of Science (The Social and Behavioral Sciences), 11th ed., *Journal of Forestry*. Forestry News, 63:146, 1965.

ZON, RAPHAEL (1874–1956)

Born December 1, 1874 in Simbirsk, Russia. Immigrated to the United States in 1898; became a citizen in 1903. Had previously received bachelor of arts and bachelor of science degrees in Russia; Cornell University, F.E. (forest engineer) 1901. Entered the United States Forest Service in 1901 and was assigned to forest investigations; six years later he was made chief of the Office of Silvics and in 1920 was put in charge of special investigations in forest economics. In 1923 he became director of the Lake States Forest Experiment Station at St. Paul, Minnesota and remained there until his retirement in 1944. In 1904 he became a member of the Society of American Foresters and in 1918 was elected a Fellow. He served on the editorial board of *Forestry Quarterly* from 1905 until it was merged with *Proceedings of the Society of American Foresters* in 1916 to become the *Journal of Forestry*; was editor of the Society's *Proceedings* during most of this time; then was managing editor of the *Journal of Forestry* from 1917 to 1923 and editor-in-chief from 1923 to 1928. In 1952 the Society awarded him the Gifford Pinchot

Medal. The book, *The Forest Resources of the World,* compiled in collaboration with William N. Sparhawk, published in 1923, was the first attempt to make a systematic and accurate inventory of the earth's forests. A pioneer in the study of the relation of forests, streamflow, and flood control, he set forth his findings in 1927 in a bulletin, *Forests and Water in the Light of Scientific Investigation,* which attracted widespread attention. He has published 200 contributions to forestry literature. An enthusiast about shelterbelt planting, he helped plan the Prairie States Forestry Project which started in 1934. Died October 28, 1956.

SOCIETY OF AMERICAN FORESTERS

American Men of Science, 8th ed., 1949.
Journal of Forestry. Obituary, 54:850, 1956.

Contributors

CONTRIBUTORS